We Overcame

The Story of Civil Rights for Disabled People

By Richard Bryant Treanor

Published in the United States of America

First Edition, Regal Direct Publishing,
Falls Church, Virginia

We Overcame

The Story of Civil Rights for Disabled People

By Richard Bryant Treanor

Published by: Regal Direct Publishing
Post Office Box 8225
Falls Church, Virginia 22041
United States of America

First Printing: 1993

Library of Congress Number: 92-083770

ISBN Number: 0-9631345-2-3 $14.95 Softcover

DEDICATION

To King Richard III

"But I, that am not shaped for sportive tricks, Nor made to court an amorous looking-glass; I, that am rudely stamped, and want love's majesty. To strut before a wanton ambling nymph, I, that am curtailed of this fair proportion, Cheated of feature by dissembling nature, Deformed, unfinished, sent before my time Into this breathing world, scarce half made up, And that so lamely and unfashionable That dogs bark at me as I halt by them; Why, I, in this weak piping time of peace, Have no delight to pass away the time, Unless to spy my shadow in the sun And descant on my own deformity."

SHAKESPEARE

King Richard III, Act I, Scene I

ACKNOWLEDGMENTS

Many people contributed to this book, either by providing needed information concerning historical events, or giving suggestions and leads.

First, thanks must be given to Frank Bowe, a leader in this great movement. Frank is deaf, and provided valuable information, especially concerning the 1977 take over of the HEW buildings. Frank also edited this manuscript.

Also, thanks to: Mary Jane Owen, Eunice Fiorito, Harold Snider, Hugh Gallagher, Richard Heddinger, Judy Heumann, Fred Fay, Justin Dart, Evan Kemp, James L. Cherry, Mike Auberger, Mark Johnson, Eric Griffin, Mark Conly, Robert Lenham, John Wodatch, Beverly Silverberg, Dennis Smurs, Dennis Cannon, Dale Brown, the late Tim Cook, Phillip Savage, Paul Marchand, Michael Frisenger, Phil Calkins, John Nelson, Salvatore Parlato, Vivian Berzinski, Marilyn Golden, John Johnson, Daniel Webster Herlong, Sunie Barr Clark, Marilyn Recinto, Bob O'Regan, Ted Munter, Stephen Diaz, Dianne Webb, Pat Fairchild.

Also, Margot Lovell, John Bryant, Jim Bryant, Mello Cottone, Tony Dene, Jane Dene, the late Frank Conroy, the late James Cooke, Dick Westbrook, Eileen Carver, Congressman Charles Bennett, Paul Cullen, Joe Califano. Last but not least, my office helper, Michael Thomas.

TABLE OF CONTENTS

INTRODUCTION

It was May 1987. I had just retired from a government career and was launching into an exciting new job with a law firm on K Street in downtown Washington, D.C. Also.....I had a brand new wheelchair.

Contracting polio in 1945 had left me with leg braces, and until that May, I had always used crutches. So being on the street in a wheelchair was a challenging experience! At lunch time, I would roll out on the sidewalk to explore. The K Street corridor was filled with elegant shops and smartly dressed pedestrians. Here and there stood stalls filled with colorful flowers; sidewalk vendors sold wallets, neckties, jewelry, hats, pictures, and whatever. All the sidewalks had curb cuts, so you could travel in a wheelchair for blocks. Most of the stores were at sidewalk level, and therefore, completely accessible. There were two subway stops nearby; you could take the elevator down and travel anywhere in the city on the Metro. At International Square, you could get lunch at a dozen fast food places and then sit beside a fountain in the huge atrium to enjoy it. You could go on the roof to lunch there and savor the magnificent view of downtown Washington. After years of struggling with the great difficulty of going everywhere on crutches, being in a wheel chair was – well – exhilarating.

One warm spring noon, I sat in my chair on the sidewalk at 18th and K and asked myself, How did all this accessibility happen? Were the curb cuts in the sidewalks put there just for me? It appeared to me that I was the personal beneficiary of a lot of planning, designed to make life a lot easier. After years of battling every inch of the way, it seemed almost too good to be true. How did it all happen? Was this just a pleasant dream, only to disappear as spring flowers do?

At that point I knew nothing of the history of civil rights for disabled people. I didn't realize that disabled people even have civil rights.

When I first came to Washington almost thirty years ago, there were no curb cuts in sidewalks nor handicapped parking spaces; many stores were unapproachable, transportation was totally inaccessible, and there were few jobs considered possible for disabled people. If you were disabled, it was just tough luck. You were expected to behave, as best you could, as a non-disabled person. If you failed at this, it was unfortunate. You couldn't expect all of society to adapt to your personal, individual needs, now, could you? You couldn't complain and you dared not demand. You didn't want to make yourself anyone's "pain in the neck."

Until then, I had never regarded myself as a disabled person. My job was to adapt, to conform. At the time, I didn't know many other disabled people; I didn't belong to any disability organizations, and I didn't have the "support group" which psychologists consider so essential. Like Frank Sinatra, I was doing it my way, but "my way" wasn't necessarily the right way, or was it?

I decided that I should do some research and write a book about civil rights for disabled people. I was motivated partly by curiosity. I sensed that a great revolution had taken place, and I was totally ignorant of its causes. And I was moved by gratitude. I was thankful that I lived in this city, in this place, and at this time. (Later, I learned that there were many more obstacles to be overcome). I was also motivated by guilt. I had done nothing to advance this great cause. I was more than happy to enjoy the benefits of the movement, but I realized that I had offered little to bring it about--except I had tried to "mainstream" as much as possible, to make myself as independent as achievable and to benefit from what others had accomplished.

I debated whether to call the book *We Overcame* or *They Overcame*. Calling it *We* Overcame sounded slightly egotistical, since I had not, until then, actively participated in the "movement." I hadn't overcome anything unless you count learning how to use the Shift key on a word processor. On the other hand, *They* Overcame didn't sound quite right. I had a suspicion, later proven correct, that the disability movement had gathered strength from the black civil rights movement, when the song, *We Shall Overcome,* became a battle cry. When thousands of blacks assembled at the Washington Monument grounds for the March on Washington in August 1963, they didn't sing *They Shall Overcome*.

When I began work on this book, I had never heard of the Americans With Disabilities Act (ADA). This Act was introduced as a bill in Congress in 1988 and was reintroduced in 1989. It was finally enacted into law, when President Bush signed it, on July 26, 1990.

In the months that followed my decision to write a book, I learned a great deal. Though life seemed good for me, I discovered that I had been naive. I found out that the curb cuts, the store entrances, and the subway elevators which made Washington, D.C. so accessible didn't necessarily exist in other parts of the country. I learned that two out of three disabled people were totally without employment, and disabled people applying for jobs were more often than not faced with prejudice and discrimination. I learned that although there was some "mainstreaming" of disabled students in public and private schools, there was a large drop-out rate and the percentage of disabled students actually getting a high school diploma was much lower than it should be. I learned that those few disabled students who went on to a college or university, and actually graduated, were often faced with a cruel hoax: they had become fully prepared BUT the jobs weren't there. I learned that the income level of disabled people was by far the lowest of any minority group, and that many, many disabled people seldom left home (assuming they were fortunate enough to live at home rather than in an institution), seldom went to the movies, a concert, or a football or baseball game. I learned that many disabled people were in institutions not because they couldn't live independently but because they did not have the financial resources to hire personal care attendants. I realized that society's attitude toward disabled people was, in many places, based on prejudice and that, although there had been progress in making air carriers and trains accessible, most city and private buses were hopelessly unapproachable.

In short, I learned that although great progress had been made, the situation for many, many disabled people was nothing short of a national disgrace. I came to these conclusions, not because I wanted to, but because I was led to them through studies of government agencies, opinion polls, surveys, reports of Congressional committees, as well as the professional opinions of numerous experts in the fields of health care, education, sociology, and civil rights. Very real problems had brought about pressure from the disabled community for change.

This pressure, which in the sixties, seventies, and eighties had led to federal civil rights legislation for the disabled, in 1990 led to the crowning achievement of the disability civil rights movement: the Americans With Disabilities Act.

The civil rights movement for people with disabilities has been a remarkable, historical evolution and a largely untold story. It has become as significant to disabled people as the black civil rights movement is to blacks and the feminist movement to women. In many respects it has been a silent revolution, making the story all the more difficult to tell. While the struggle benefited vast numbers of disabled people, the movement, itself, was brought about by a relatively small group of individuals, disability organizations, and legislators.

The theme of this book is an account of the Americans With Disabilities Act, the civil rights legislation preceeding it, the effect that legislation has had and will continue to have on the lives of disabled people, and a developing awareness that the Americans With Disabilities Act (described more fully in Chapter Six) is to the disability community what the Civil Rights Act of 1964 was to the black community and to other minorities. It prohibits discrimination against disabled people in employment, in transportation, in communications, and in privately owned public places such as stores and theaters. I discovered that from the beginning, with the terrible racial conflicts of the fifties and sixties, the disability community had been pushing for civil rights no less than those given to racial minorities and women. Blacks were upset because they had to sit in the back of a bus--disabled people, in most cases, couldn't even get on the bus.

The Americans With Disabilities Act didn't just fall out of the sky. Its enactment in 1990 was the culmination of a long, fascinating, and tortured struggle for equality for disabled people. Their needs were many, yet simple. They wanted a level playing field: jobs, housing, accessible transportation, access to stores, restaurants, theaters, sports arenas. In 1990, ADA promised all this, on paper at least. It wasn't until 1990, that the first stage of the ongoing struggle was over. The disability community got almost everything it wanted.

The story involves leaders, with disabilities covering a wide range from deafness and blindness to many other physical impairments. It involves disability organizations and legislators, many of whom have disabled relatives or were themselves disabled. It involved legal battles in the courts, lobbying by disabled groups for their rights versus the lobbying by business interests against them. There were, unlike the black civil rights movement, no mass lynchings, fire bombings, or assassinations, and few melodramatic events that journalists enjoy writing about and readers find so fascinating. Although there were many arrests (of wheelchair users demanding accessible transportation, for example), this civil rights movement reached its success through the democratic process and through the courts. Unlike the black civil rights movement, there was no single leader, such as Martin Luther King. There was, rather, a group of determined, effective, and courageous leaders.

The Americans With Disabilities Act was in one sense a paradigm of the validity of ideas. The many provisions of the Act were hammered out, word by word and paragraph by paragraph. The spotlight of reason and argumentation was placed on the wording of the statute. If the idea presented was a valid one, it stuck, but if not, more likely than not it was dropped. Compromises, requested by the business community concerning their fears for costs and operating difficulties, were inserted and eventually agreed upon. The final version of the Act was a finely tuned accommodation to most, if not all, concerns.

However, its passage involved more Congressional hearings, more lobbying, more intensive legal maneuvering, than almost any other piece of federal legislation in recent times. You could complain about the delay in passing the Act. (Why was civil rights for minorities given in 1964, but it was to take *twenty-six years* for similar guarantees to be provided for disabled people?) You could speculate whether the act would really change anything and wonder how it would play out in the future, how lives of disabled people would change.

You could and should ask questions, but no one would deny that the Americans With Disabilities Act was enormously significant civil rights legislation. If any disabled person is the victim of discrimination in employment, transportation, telecommunications, or in a public place, he or she does not have to fold up helplessly and go home. Now, there are legal rights to be enforced when necessary.

The disability community had struggled for and won their own Emancipation Proclamation – the Americans With Disabilities Act. In 1990, when the act became law, they had achieved a federal mandate that applied to every nook and cranny in the United States, to restaurants in small towns everywhere, to bus companies, to all employers except those with only a few employees. The nationwide telephone systems were to become totally accessible, through relay operators, to all hearing impaired people. The goal sought for decades by disabled people had finally been won.

Finally, the Americans With Disabilities Act is a model for other nations, most of whom (especially those advanced nations claiming to be the repository of civilization) have very primitive laws relating to people with disabilities. I remember being carried up the outside steps of the Louvre in Paris because those preciously historic, marble steps didn't have railings. I remember vacationing in St. Martin in the Carribbean and finding not one sidewalk accessible to a wheelchair, except for the one where the curb had deteriorated due to lack of repairs. I can remember being in Barcelona when a protest rally was staged by a group of frustrated disabled people.

When President Bush signed the Americans With Disabilities Act on July 26, 1990 on the White House grounds, it was a glorious day for the approximately 2000 disabled people who witnessed the event. Though realizing there were battles still to be fought, disabled people everywhere were exultant. They had fought and had won. They overcame.

And it all began so many years ago.

CHAPTER I

THE BEGINNINGS

There was a steep, pine-needled path, winding through towering pines, down to the lake. The other fifteen year old campers at Camp Tuscarora were already on the dock stripping and being handed cakes of yellow soap, to wash with since the camp had no showers. After a week of camp, their bare bodies were already completely tanned; swim suits were not permitted in the morning, in the afternoon they were optional. They jumped, naked, into the sunlit lake, yelling, shouting, pushing, and lathering up.

The crippled boy hadn't had a bath in a week, and the counselors decided firm action was necessary.[1] *Two counselors carried him, fireman style, down the steep path, being careful to avoid slipping on the pine-needles. The boy protested, but the counselors placed him on the dock and began to undress him. His wasted legs looked pitifully like match sticks. The counselors lowered him into the choppy, sunlit water; one counselor began washing his back and hair. The boy felt embarrassed and fearful among all the other healthy, naked boys; sobs came uncontrollably. "I can't do this," he thought. After several minutes of total misery, the counselors decided to call it off. They lifted the boy out of the water, toweled and dressed him, and carried him back up the hill. So ended this primitive effort at mainstreaming. It wasn't very successful, but it wasn't a complete failure, either, though that wasn't obvious at the moment.*

On August 9, 1921, Franklin Roosevelt, age 39, was having a glorious sail on the Bay of Fundy, just off his summer home in New Brunswick, Maine. Suddenly, the wind picked up, catching the sail and tipping the sailboat. Franklin fell overboard, but quickly climbed back aboard. The party had had enough, and returned home. For an hour afterward, Franklin sat on the lawn in his wet bathing suit while he read his mail. The next day a high fever gripped him and he took to bed. Soon after, he was diagnosed as having infantile paralysis (later it was called poliomyelitis). He became paralyzed from the waist down. His arms were quite weak, and at first, he could not sit up. His wife, Eleanor, patiently nursed him day and night, and slept in a camp cot in his room. Eleanor followed the advice of the doctor and gave him gentle and soothing massages. Soon Franklin assumed a more active role in his own convalescence and tried various remedies: exercise, warm and cold baths, ultraviolet lights, electric current, and walking in leg braces with the aid of parallel bars. He liked to have his family around, and carried on animated conversations while doing his therapy. But it soon became apparent that the regimen was of little avail, and he would remain permanently paralyzed from the waist down.

How did the man who, was later to become president of the United States, cope with his disability, personally, with other disabled Americans, and later in his political career?

While Franklin was recuperating, the question of his political future loomed. Franklin and, especially, Eleanor decided that his political career should continue in spite of formidable obstacles. He and his family regarded it as extremely important that publicity concerning his disability be kept to a minimum. This objective was successfully achieved during the rest of his life.

Early in his convalescence, Franklin began to deal with his afflicition in a realistic way. He visited Warm Springs, Georgia, which had natural hot springs. There, he partook of therapy which included swimming treatments. Then in 1926, with his law partner Basil O'Connor, he bought the place and added improvements – ramps, an elevator, and an accessible swimming pool. Hydrotherapy, as a treatment, was developed with the help of Leroy Hubbard, a New York orthopedic surgeon. Many people, with paralysis from the highly feared polio of those days, came to visit, and Franklin developed a friendly rapport with them. Among them were countless young people who mingled, shared in parties, games and entertainment. Franklin hired "push boys," local high school youths, to help the girls; and young maidens to be assistant physical therapists. If romance blossomed, why that was just "splendid, splendid." It was relaxing and it was fun.[2]

Some of the non-disabled guests, who were "taking the cure" didn't like the new goings on, but Franklin sent them packing. After Franklin bought the place, he established the Warm Springs Foundation, for the treatment of polio. The center had a shop which improved and expanded orthopedic devices; it was here that researchers developed hand controls for automobiles. When Franklin became president, he built a six room, white frame, Little White House adjacent to the foundation grounds.

In 1937 Roosevelt helped organize the Fund for Infantile Paralysis, which later became the March of Dimes. The first Board of Trustees was formed out of immense wealth and prominence: Basil O'Connor as president with Jeremiah Milbank, Edsel Ford, Marshal Field, Averell Harriman, Edward Stettinius, James Forrestal and Thomas Watson.

Hugh Gallagher (who also contracted polio), in his book, *FDR's Splendid Deception,* details the extraordinary effort Franklin and his family made to conceal FDR's disability from the public. Of 35,000 photos of Franklin in the Presidential Library, only two show him in a wheel chair. No news reels ever showed him in a wheel chair, and not one cartoon. The media, unlike modern times when LBJ's abdominal scars appeared in livid color on the front pages of newspapers, as did Reagan's skin cancers, acquiesced in the conspiracy. If you could deny that the emperor had no clothes, it was easy to deny a disability. As Gallagher maintained, *"In the 1920s, to be handicapped, in some visible way, carried with it social opprobrium. The handicapped were kept at home, out of sight, in back bedrooms, by families who felt a mixture of embarrassment and shame concerning their presence ."*

Irving Zola, professor of sociology at Brandeis University, in reviewing Gallagher's book, said:

> *"By never going public with his disability, FDR indeed did all of us a disservice. We lost a great role model in some ways precisely because of the way he dealt with parts of his disability. He correctly saw that much of disability lay in the public's eye and in the social and physical environment. And so he changed it. In order to gain access to the world he needed, he had ramps built, elevators installed, railings raised. In short, he altered his environment. Symbolically, however, the altering was but temporary. Upon his death, every ramp, railing, and raised entrance was dismantled. The message of this is twofold: he recognized that to function in mainstream America it is necessary and possible to change the environment; on the other hand, by defining this as an individual solution to an individual problem he made its social and political impact invisible. "* [3]

When Franklin decided to run for governor of New York, it was not surprising that his health became an issue. The opposition whispered that he was unfit for the job. Franklin reacted by campaigning vigorously, but always concealing the disability as much as possible.

He had a steel bar installed in his car so that he could stand up for speeches; the audience had little inkling of any disability. He tried setting up campaign stops in convenient places, but on one occasion he was scheduled to speak in an auditorium on an upper floor. Not to be out done, he dragged himself all the way up the fire escape on his fanny. When he became governor, he altered the Governor's Mansion in Albany with ramps, an elevator, and a swimming pool.

In 1929, in his first annual message to the New York legislature, he advocated rehabilitative programs for disabled people, but his proposals met with little success.

Franklin, during his campaigns, used whatever mode of mobility was least conspicuous. Sometimes he used a wheel chair, sometimes two canes, and at times he walked with an assistant on one arm and carried a cane. He was lifted in and out of cars behind a portable plywood screen to block out viewers. Once in 1932 while attempting to give a speech, both speaker and podium crashed to the floor, and thereafter the advance men always ensured that the podium was bolted to the floor. Photographers were present at that incident, but not one picture was taken, because of the unspoken code. In June 1939, at a rally attended by 100,000 people at Franklin Field in Philadelphia, his leg brace unlocked while he was attempting to shake hands and he fell on the podium scattering the papers for his speech. He was immediately surrounded by aides, and few in the audience realized what had happened.

After he became President, the Secret Service constructed ramps at the Capitol, the Executive Office, and St. John's Church, but these were removed after his death.

Paul K. Longmore, who specializes in disability issues, remains severely disabled by polio and is a professor at Stanford University's history department. In a paper entitled *Uncovering the Hidden History of People With Disabilities, (Reviews in American History, September, 1987),* he presents some interesting insights on President Roosevelt and disability issues. Though FDR's era was a turning point in society's perception of disabled people, there was the negative aspect of too much stress on "overcoming" personal limitations with not enough thought given to the benefits of civil rights.

> *"[The 'overcoming'] image became and has remained the preferred, even required, mode of self-presentation for people with physical and sensory (not mental) disabilities. It involved an implicit bargain in which the nonhandicapped majority extended provisional and partial tolerance of the public presence of handicapped individuals so long as they demonstrated continued cheerful striving toward normalization. This arrangement defined disability as a private physical and emotional tragedy to be managed by psychological adjustment, rather than a stigmatized social condition, and it disallowed collective protest against prejudice and discrimination, permitting at most efforts to educate away 'attitudinal barriers.'"*

FDR tried to visit his Little White House twice a year, often at Thanksgiving, to have dinner with the Foundation's small patients. He reveled in driving his 1938 Ford, custom equipped with hand controls. Franklin died of a massive brain hemorrhage at Warm Springs, on April 12, 1945, an event that saddened the entire world.

For a time after Franklin's death, his town became somewhat of a ghost town, but it has since become revitalized. It is now operated by the state of Georgia as the Roosevelt/Warm Springs Institute for Rehabilitation with a budget of $18 million annually. It is comfortably situated on 900 acres with more than fifty buildings. The braceshop, excitingly innovative with orthopedic devices, has 400 skilled employees. Mary Thrash, a state ranger at the Little White House, pointed out how Roosevelt, who had labeled them the "Foundation Gang," was an inspiration to all of them. *"It was not in spite of polio that he had become president but probably because of it," she said.*

President Roosevelt had been concerned with handicapped issues, which he regarded as only one of a larger fabric of programs that became known as the "New Deal." He created a Committee on Economic Security which proposed what later became the Social Security Act of 1935. The director of the Committee was Edwin Witte, whose key assistant was Wilbur J. Cohen. Cohen helped draft the Social Security Act and was awarded the first Social Security card and continued on as technical adviser to the Board. President Kennedy named him Assistant Secretary of Health, Education and Welfare (HEW), and Johnson appointed him Secretary in March 1968. Cohen made enormous contributions in the areas of welfare, education, consumer protection, rights of children and the elderly, civil rights, and issues affecting disabled people. In 1965 he helped bring about Medicare. Today one of the main headquarters of HEW's successor, the Department of Health and Human Services, is named the Wilbur J. Cohen building.

The 1935 Social Security Act provided old age and survivors insurance, unemployment compensation, and it funded state grants for vocational rehabilitation of disabled people. Title X of the Social Security Act provided, separately, for blind persons, at the urging of the American Foundation for the Blind. The legislation, however, did little to promote independence and access for disabled people; it did nothing for disabled people unless they were also elderly. The legislation was motivated by the social policy of supporting those who needed support (provided they were elderly), and not by the concept of independence and the removal of barriers. The vocational rehabilitation program was merely a funds transfer to state vocational rehabilitation departments, with the federal government assuming no active role.

It was not until 1956 that legislation was passed which provided for income maintenance for the disabled who were not elderly, but only for age 50 and over, or dependent, disabled children, aged 18 or over who had became disabled prior to age18.[4]

After the Social Security Act of 1935, Congress – urged by FDR – passed the Randolph-Sheppard Act of 1936, which authorized vending facilities for blind persons in public buildings. In 1938 the Wagner-O'Day Act s required the federal government to purchase products from workshops for the blind.

Vocational rehabilitation was very much a part of the New Deal, but the idea originated after World War I. It took fifty years for people to realize that it did little good to spend funds for training if no jobs were available at the end of the training period and it was impossible to travel to a job even if one happened to be obtainable. In 1917 the Smith-Hughs Act established the Federal Board for Vocational Education which involved the government in rehabilitation in a significant way. Congress, in 1918, passed the Smith-Sears Vocational Rehabilitation Act to provide vocational training to veterans of World War I, but the program ran into problems caused by underestimating the numbers of veterans who needed training and by bureaucratic confusion.[5]

In 1918 Massachusetts became the first state to adopt a program of vocational rehabilitation. This was followed by an important program adopted in New Jersey. Both the First and Second World Wars created labor shortages which provided an impetus to programs for rehabilitating disabled persons to become productive members of the labor force. In 1920 Congress extended vocational rehabilitation to civilians. The federal government, under this Act, provided matching funds to states participating in the program. There was a tendency for states to use federal money for the less severely disabled, which resulted in blind persons being limited to support payments. Ohio, in 1921, became a leader in providing programs for the care, education, and rehabilitation of physically disabled children.

Roosevelt's New Deal legislation had approached disability issues in terms of providing federal money for the support of the elderly disabled and for continuing the traditional vocational rehabiliation program. Although vocational rehabilitation was theoretically available to all disabled people regardless of age, the programs were not very successful. The concept of removing architectural barriers simply didn't exist in the thirties and forties. The problems of disabled citizens were thought of primarily as a problem of providing welfare, and the idea that disabled people had any civil rights had not yet arrived. Roosevelt seemed to regard disability issues as requiring charity; hence the March of Dimes. If unemployed, able bodied, skilled workers had to stand in bread lines during the Depression, the issue of providing jobs for disabled people was too formidable to even consider. Though Roosevelt had, at his command, carpenters to make ramps, Secret Service people to advance a trip, and, as President, as much employment as anyone could possibly want, it probably seemed out of the question to provide for others the advantages he held, however sympathetic he might have been to the lot of disabled people.

A particularly poignant moment in FDR's life occurred near the end, in February 1945. World War II was winding down, and Roosevelt had just returned to Washington after an exhausting trip abroad, which included talks with Stalin and Churchill at Yalta. He had aged terribly, and death was to occur two months later. Addressing a joint session of Congress in the House of Representatives to report on his trip, he began with a remarkable and uncharacteristic comment:

> *"I hope that you will pardon me for an unusual posture of sitting down during the presentation of what I want to say but I know that you will realize that it makes it a lot easier for me in not having to carry about ten pounds of steel around the bottom of my legs; and also because I have just completed a fourteen-thousand-mile trip. First of all, I want to say, it is good to be home."* [6]

One could raise the question whether the national interest was harmed in any way by Franklin's *Splendid Deception.* It seems fair to say that his disability, affecting only his mobility and not his intellectual or leadership capacity, was in truth not a very relevant factor. In no small part, this was due to his undeniable "overcoming" of his disability. In fact it has been suggested that his disability was a motivating factor which contributed to an iron will for power and for leadership. *"He had the special type of courage of the cripple who will not admit that he is crippled; this was a kind of defense mechanism since, at all costs, he had to protect himself from the invasion of any doubt or underconfidence."* [7]

Perhaps the nature of his disability, indeed, did not affect his qualifications, but no doubt, disabilities should be made known to the public; there is a need and a right to know. Another point about FDR's disability is that he came from an affluent family, he contracted polio when he was an adult and had the support of a wife and children. He had the tireless support of Eleanor and influential friends. These resources often are not available to disabled people, especially if they are disabled at birth or as children.

In the present day, when privacy, especially that of public leaders, has become obsolete, one could debate the wisdom of Roosevelt's concealing his disability and marvel at the uncharacteristic restraint of the press in surpressing significant, and to some, morbidly interesting, details. For a political figure to parade a disability could very well jeopardize a career, although one could make the point that Franklin, at least, did not attempt to obtain votes by soliciting sympathy from voters. No doubt, many public figures may be torn between the desire to conceal and the desire to exploit. During the era in which Roosevelt lived, to be disabled was often regarded as a shameful thing.

R.C. Elmslie, a leading medical authority of the day, issued a cruel threat: *"A failure in the moral training of a cripple means the evolution of an individual detestable in character, a menace and burden to the community, who is only too apt to graduate into the mendicant and criminal classes."* [8]

Gallagher wrote:

"There was no such thing as mainstreaming for the severely and visibly handicapped in the 1920s. Often they were not allowed to use public transportation or to attend theaters and movies. Their clumsy gait and movement were still the object of fun and ridicule: vaudeville entertainers could always raise a laugh with a limp, palsy, or a speech impediment. In fact, for the handicapped to appear in public was considered by many to be in dubious taste. They, along with pregnant women, were expected to keep out of sight. The idea that the severely disabled could participate in elective politics was quite simply unheard of."[9]

The noted authority on disability policy, Edward D. Berkowitz, says that in 1925, a Detroit auto maker required any employee with an amputation to wear an artificial limb. This was not to improve the capability of the employee, but to help the morale of other employees, who might feel uncomfortable with the sight of a limbless co-worker.[10]

Prejudice and ignorance about disabled people were wide spread and some injustice continues still. An article in the prestigious *Yale Law Journal*[11] suggests that prejudice against disabled people is responsible for society's unsatisfactory response, both social and legal, to the problems of disabled people. The author notes that in the past, disabled people have been prevented from holding public office,[12] serving on juries,[13] marrying,[14] working in certain occupations,[15] bearing children'[16] attending school,[17] and even being seen on the street.[18]

Indeed, in the twenties, and the forty years following, many disabled people could not attend church or college, could not visit most restaurants, theaters and movies houses, could not ride buses, trains or planes, could not participate in sports or the arts, because there were no curb cuts in sidewalks, no ramps to buildings, no elevators in many buildings, no accessible buses, trains or planes. Disabled people stayed home or remained in an institution, because there was no place to go. There were few if any handicapped groups to promote common interests and miniscule leadership.

An articulate description of the lives of disabled people is found in *Law Reform in Disability Rights, Volume 1,* published by the Disability Rights Education and Defense Fund, November 1981:

"The evolution of disability policy in the United States can be described as the increasing humanization of disabled people: humanization is described as a recognition that disabled people have human needs and characteristics and public policy should be designed to reflect and further this human potential."

"People who are disabled have historically been treated as objects of pity and fear—as individuals who are incapable, neither expected nor willing to participate in or contribute to organized society. Thus, a societal attitude developed that this class of persons, viewed as unhealthy, defective, and deviant required special institutions, services, care, and attention in order to survive. This social construct [was] supported by national welfare policies to care for the deserving poor; charitable programs to help the unfortunate; continued application of the medical/health model to disability; rehabilitation services provided in a manner that undermines self-initiative, self-respect and perpetuates stereotypical education and employment avenues, has resulted in discriminatory programs, policies, and laws designed to deny disabled people's participation in organized society. These discriminatory policies and practices affect all classes of disabled people in virtually every aspect of their lives."

These are harsh words, and extremely generalized, but there is enough truth in them to make the conditions alarming, not only in the twenties and thirties, but continuing today. The authors are advocates, seeking to persuade courts to adopt positions to improve the lives of the plaintiffs they represent. "Society" could be accused of either neglecting disabled people, or, on the other extreme, coddling, patronizing, and encouraging dependency.

To a person in a wheel chair, attempting to mount a curbstone in a sidewalk without curb cuts, it matters little whether the lack of access was due to a conscious desire by society to isolate, stigmatize, and discriminate, or whether the barrier exists because of lack of attention or planning. Disabled people, themselves, are players in the game, and they can choose isolation and dependency, and contribute to a self-fulfilling prophecy.

As time passed, more and more disabled people saw that there had been choices and they needed to make their wishes known. A third alternative, between the extremes of neglect and dependent care, gradually occurred: the movement toward access, independence, mainstreaming, and self-fulfillment. Disabled people began to achieve spectacular successes in legislation, in government administration, and in court litigation, which transformed, and are still transforming the American landscape.

In 1919 an Elyria, Ohio, businessman, Edgar Allen, began the National Society for Crippled Children to help children with disabilities. The Society much later changed its name to National Easter Seals Society. It was not until 1934 that the Easter Seal motif was begun, when the well known cartoonist, J. H. Donahey, designed the first Easter Seal. Initially, the Society had a slow start; the public knew little of the problems of disabled people. The 1934 Easter Seals campaign featured pathetic little children, and photographs became the catalyst for very large financial contributions from an emotional public. From rather wimpy beginnings, the Society has evolved into an extremely responsible and effective organization. Today, some 190 affiliates operate 400 service centers throughout the country. Easter Seals Societies today serve more than one million people, the majority of whom are orthopedically disabled. A 1990 telethon with 125 participating stations generated more than 42 million dollars. Contrary to myth, the Society serves people of all ages, not just children. Its programs include physical, occupational, and speech/language therapy, vocational evaluation and training, camping and recreation, psychological counseling and prevention. It has a strong legislative advocacy program and has been instrumental in developing standards for architectural access for people in wheelchairs.

In 1920 the Disabled American Veterans (DAV) organization was formed by disabled veterans returning from World War I. More than three hundred thousand veterans had disabling injuries, battle scars, or gas seared lungs from that terrible war. When the ticker tape parades were over, many veterans felt themselves forgotten, and in anger, joined groups which eventually led to the establishment of the DAV, which Congress formally chartered in 1932. In the early days, the DAV processed so many claims for benefits for veterans that a separate government agency, the Veterans Administration, was formed to handle them. When veterans returned from World War II, the DAV began a training program for DAV National Service Officers who helped other disabled veterans with counseling, filing claims, and similar activities. The DAV today has a professional legislative affairs staff, which lobbies Congress, not so much in the area of civil rights as in the area of veterans' benefits. The DAV also has an employment program that attempts to remedy the appallingly low employment rate of disabled veterans. It has publicized the need for special license plates for disabled drivers, and it serves as a "watch dog" over the Department of Veterans' Affairs and Veterans' Hospitals.[19] Membership in DAV is available to any honorably discharged veteran with a disability incurred in wartime military service or under conditions similar to war. Today, DAV claims more than a million members, one third of whom consist of Vietnam war veterans. A recent commander, Billy E. Kirby, was wounded in World War II. The present commander is Joseph C. Zengerle. In 1993 President Clinton appointed Jesse Brown to be Secretary of the Department of Veterans Affairs. Brown is a black veteran of the Vietnam conflict; his right arm was wounded in combat. Prior to this appointment, he had been Executive Director of the DAV National Service and Legislative Headquarters, located in Southwest Washington, D.C.

A significant milestone in the history of programs relating to blind persons was the creation of the American Foundation for the Blind in 1921. This was a merger of the American Association of Workers for the Blind and the American Association of Instructors of the Blind. A leader of the American Foundation of the Blind was Robert B. Irwin, blinded at the age of five. He earned degrees at the University of Washington and Harvard and earned money by operating a vendor's stand in an office building in Seattle. He was a leader in opposing mere handouts for blind people and advocated self-help and mobility.

The twenties was a time when the progressive, socialistic, mood of pre-World War I gave way to a feeling of prosperity and self-reliance; anyone, including disabled people, could succeed if they tried hard enough. This viewpoint was shattered by the Depression, and Roosevelt reflected the changing mood when he advocated programs specifically directed at disabled people. The Social Security Act of 1935 was not original in providing for vocational rehabilitation but it made permanent what had previously been haphazard. The monumental upheaval caused by the Depression affected social thinking: misfortune was more often than not due to the "system" or the "economy" and under the New Deal, help was given where help was needed.

The 1930s saw the beginnings of organized protest by disability groups whose viewpoint was that equal access and equal opportunity for disabled people was a matter of civil rights. In New York a group of disabled young adults formed the League of the Physically Handicapped to protest job discrimination, especially in WPA projects.

The thirties were difficult times, but a few notable, disabled people, in addition to FDR, became successful: Al Kapp, the cartoonist who created Lil Abner (Kapp lost his left leg at the age of nine); Alec Templeton, a blind comic musician who entertained in night clubs and concert halls; James Thurber, the writer and social satirist, who eventually became blind; Glen Cunningham, "the world's fastest man" who ran the mile in 4 minutes and 4.4 seconds, participating in the 1932 and 1936 Olympics, though, as a youth, he had been severely disabled in a gasoline explosion.

If disabled Americans were largely neglected during these times, they could be considered fortunate compared to what was going on in Germany!

While the decade of the thirties was living through the rise of Nazi Germany and the following devastation of World War II, the issue of civil rights for disabled people was very much a part of all of this terrible history. Long before the rise of Hitler and Naziism, members of the German medical profession espoused sterilization and euthanasia for certain disabled people in Germany. Between July 14, 1933 and the beginning of the war on September 1, 1939, the Nazis reported the sterilization of 375,000 persons in the following categories: congenital feeble mindedness, schizophrenia, epilepsy, acute alcoholism, manic depressive insanity, hereditary deafness, severe hereditary physical deformity, hereditary blindness, and St. Vitus dance.

Some time in September 1939, Adolf Hitler signed a secret order, dated back to September 1, 1939, the first day of World War II when Germany invaded Poland. The order was not publicized through usual channels because Hitler did not want to alarm or provoke protest from the German public. The order stated, "Reichsleiter Philip Bouhler and Karl Brandt, M.D., are charged with responsibility of enlarging the authority of certain physicians to be designated by name in such a manner that persons who, according to human judgment, are incurable can, upon a most careful diagnosis of their condition of sickness, be accorded a mercy death." This "euthanasia" program became known as Aktion T-4. Pursuant to the program, 200,000 disabled people, including thousands of children, were taken by bus from institutions and gathered to be killed, often by poison gas in a shower room, or a gunshot to the back of the neck, or by other means. The euthanasia program was intended to be administered by physicians, but not all German physicians participated in the program; some did resist it.

The philosophical underpinnings of the euthanasia program relied on Social Darwinism, in which the fittest were expected to survive, to the advantage of everyone. Erudite articles in professional journals were published long before the Nazis came to power, advocating euthanasia in certain cases. Certain German doctors heartily endorsed and participated in the killing program, which became more and more intense as the war continued.

If euthanasia could be justified, so too, could the elimination of others regarded as undesirable. The "justification" for the euthanasia program created both a historical and a philosophical precedent to the genocide of the Jews, which came later. Dr. Andrew Ivy, who worked with the prosecution at the war crimes trial at Nuremburg, said, "*Had the [medical] profession taken a strong stand against the mass killing of sick Germans before the war, it is conceivable that the entire idea and technique of death factories for genocide would not have materialized.*" Just as many disabled citizens were regarded as "useless eaters," unworthy of life, so also, millions of Jews were put to death with a similar rationale. The attitude of the Nazis toward both disabled people and Jews, as well as the methods of extermination, were too similar to be merely coincidental. The murdering of the severely disabled and of Jews had to be motivated by the same rationale: to rid German society of the inferior, the weak, the impure, and the undesirable.

Still, there was one difference between the genocide of the Jews and the killing of disabled people. When the euthanasia program leaked out, there were protests, and the euthanasia program, unlike the Jewish program, was terminated. It was too easy for town folks to see the buses full of disabled people travelling regularly to the killing institutions and to smell the smoke coming from the crematoria. Newspaper accounts commonly falsified the cause of death, but suspicions arose when so many deaths at the killing institutions occurred on the same day. Many Germans had disabled relatives, sons, daughters, parents, and they were naturally concerned with what was happening to them. The program of euthanasia was not at all popular with the German populace, as Hitler shrewdly anticipated when he made his order secret. Letters were written by concerned relatives to the government, but these were never truthfully answered, and the degree of social unrest became a matter of acute concern to Nazis at the highest level.

Popular resistance to the euthanasia program became so strong that eventually the Nazis were forced to terminate it. No other program was ever terminated by the Nazis because of the people's resistance – and most regrettably the killing of the Jews continued.

One of the leaders of this resistance deserves a place in the history of civil rights for disabled people. Clemens August Graf von Galen, the Catholic bishop of Munster, was from an old and distinguished aristocratic family. He was loved and respected by people in his diocese. He was tall and handsome, with a powerful speaking voice. He gave three sermons at his cathedral which earned him the nickname, "Lion of Munster." When he heard that the Gestapo was ready to arrest him, Bishop von Galen sent word that if they wanted him, they would find him standing at the door of the cathedral, in full bishop's regalia, including miter and crook. He was never arrested. The three sermons criticized the Nazis, particularly with respect to the Nazis harrassment of church property and people. The last sermon dealt with euthanasia. The Gestapo came and confiscated copies of the sermons, but other copies had been surreptitiously made. The sermons were printed and widely circulated. The last sermon, on euthanasia, was delivered August 3, 1941. Bishop von Galen told the congregation about the secret killing program. Not long after this speech, Hitler, on August 24, 1941, ordered the killing program to be stopped. Bishop Galen in his sermon said:

> *"On orders from Berlin. mentally sick patients, who long have been under treatment and who may seem incurable, are being forcibly removed from psychiatric clinics. Shortly afterwards, as a regular practice, the family receives a notification stating that the patient is dead, that the body has been cremated and that the ashes may be collected. Broadly speaking, there is near certainty that none of the unexpected deaths of these mental cases have been due to natural causes, but were artificially induced, in accordance with the doctrine that authorizes the elimination of what are called 'unworthy lives' and, consequently, the killing of innocent people, if their existence is no longer held to be productive for the nation or for the state. It is a frightful concept that seeks to justify the murder of innocents and allows the killing of invalids incapable of work, of the infirm, or incurable, and of old men and women afflicted by senility. Confronted with this doctrine the German bishops declare: No man has the right to kill an innocent person, no matter what the reason, except in case of war or in self defense."* [20]

If disabled people have a patron saint, it must surely be Bishop von Galen.

There is a postscript to the Nazi euthanasia program. In January 1993 German physician Hans-Joachim Sewering resigned as president-elect of the World Medical Association, as a result of a controversy in which it was alleged that

Sewering, a member of the Nazi party and Nazi SS in World War II, ordered a 14 year old epileptic girl to the Haar-Eglfing "healing clinic." The "healing clinics" were, in fact, death camps and the young girl was indeed executed. Although Sewering denied that he knew the girl would be killed, four nuns and a hospital director dismissed his claim. The hospital staffers said that the killings continued until 1944, and more than 900 of their patients were sent to these "healing clinics."

The euthanasia program of the Nazis, and subsequent euthanasia discussions in Germany and America, have made disability groups extremely sensitive to the issue, and rightly so. It is not difficult for a disabled person to oppose a program if the program advocates his or her own premature demise, whatever the social justification may be. Many disability groups see the issue as not open to debate and not open to exceptions. For example, they oppose life termination in even the most extreme cases. Lengthy prolongation of life by artificial means was not much of an issue in the thirties and forties because the technology did not exist. Today it does, and questions of continuing indefinitely the life of comatose persons confront us today. While some may advocate terminating the lives, whether actively or passively, of severely comatose persons, the advocates of such a position must necessarily grapple with the difficult problem of drawing lines. There may be some who would see the line where the Nazis and the German doctors drew it.

When World War II ended, the killing stopped, but disability issues did not disappear. Thousands of injured and disabled veterans returned from the war. American disabled veterans became, gradually, a strong force toward civil rights for disabled people. The lot of the returning disabled war veteran was not enviable. Many spent their lives in Veterans hospitals, never to be seen again by the outside world. Many were unable to get jobs. After the war, the Disabled American Veterans organization gained muscle power and a huge increase in membership. Veterans benefits were then increased.

The tiny Paralyzed Veterans of America was born and developed into a powerful advocate for disabled people. Many veterans were incensed at the poor treatment they were receiving. It was not to be expected that those who fought bravely during the war were ready to sit back and accept whatever intolerable conditions were thrown at them. If every cloud has a silver lining, perhaps the silver lining of World War II was that the thousands of returning disabled veterans provided, in their own discontent and the actions of political leaders, the seeds from which eventually came great progress for disabled people.

Assistance to disabled people, both veterans and non-veterans alike, came during and after World War II. In 1943, in the Barden-LaFollette Act the federal government became even more involved in rehabilitation services and vocational training. A new federal unit replaced the rehabilitation function previously provided by the Office of Education. The new unit, called the Office of Vocational Rehabilitation, later in 1953, evolved into the Department of Health, Education, and Welfare. President Roosevelt had attempted to unify vocational rehabilitation programs for veterans and civilians, but the lobby for returning war veterans was too strong, and the two programs continued to remain separate.[21]

During the Second World War, one young man who left pre-medical studies at the University of Kansas to enlist in the Army, soon became a platoon leader in the legendary Tenth Mountain Division in Italy. In 1945 he was seriously wounded on the battlefield and was later awarded the Bronze Star with an Oak leaf Cluster and two Purple Hearts. At the age of 26, after the war, he was elected to the Kansas House of Representatives. From there his career took him to the United States Congress, where he enjoyed a distinguished reputation, and on November 28, 1988, he was elected for the third time by his colleagues to be the Senate Minority Leader. This nationally known figure, who has been at the fore front of disability rights legislation, is Robert Dole.

In 1946 the Kennedy family founded the Joseph P. Kennedy Jr. Foundation in memory of their eldest son, who was killed in World War II. The Foundation has two main objectives: to attempt to prevent mental retardation and to improve the means by which society deals with its mentally retarded citizens. Each year, an agenda is developed, which includes grants for medical research, demonstration and training projects, and development of model services. The Foundation, which has developed programs relating to teen pregnancy, bioethics, and public policy for the mentally retarded, has been directed for many years by Eunice Kennedy Shriver, sister of President Kennedy.

On October 10, 1935, George Gershwin's hit musical, *Porgy and Bess,* opened at the Alvin Theatre in New York. It was about a good natured, black, crippled man named Porgy and his wife Bess. Porgy got about on a skate board, and he would have laughed had you told him he was disabled and not crippled. Before the show opened, there was some thought that it would open in an opera house. The decision was made not to, on the grounds that the show was not sufficiently "cultured." (Evidently Rigoletto, the handicapped harlequin, was okay for opera audiences, but not Porgy.) The show became a great success (though not during Gershwin's lifetime) in part because of Gershwin's hauntingly beautiful music. Was it offensive? Did it perpetuate stereotypes about blacks and disabled people? Could it be produced today? It was a product of its times. The public found Porgy amusing and his disability only subliminally relevant. His role was almost that of a poignant caricature. The show was great entertainment, but it was not about civil rights. Porgy sang: " *I've got plenty of nuttin, and nuttin's plenty for me.*" It was sad that Porgy had nothing, and even worse that he was willing to put up with nothing. At least the show blended art with truth and made the public aware that disabled people are, after all, human, possibly too comfortably human. About the same time, the film *Snow White and the Seven Dwarfs* hit the theaters. The question whether the show was about disabled people never even came up. If the film were produced today, would it have to be called *Snow White and the Seven Persons of Short Stature* because many find the term "dwarf" offensive? Are civil rights bad for art? Porgy and Bess, in a way, summed up society's attitude toward disabled people during these times: we know there are problems out there but what do you expect us to do about it? The answer was: plenty of nothing.

It was not until fifty years later that a modern version of Porgy and Bess appeared, in 1990, in the film, *My Left Foot*.. Like Porgy, Christy Brown was disabled (with cerebral palsy). Like Porgy, he loved and lost. The film was an honest portrayal of a person with a severe disability. It achieved artistry because it was truthful. The public applauded it, and did not need the sugar coating of the music hall to make it palatable. Daniel Day-Lewis won the academy award for Best Actor. We've come a long way, indeed.

CHAPTER II

FIFTIES and SIXTIES

A first year student at Harvard Law School, who had contracted polio at age 13, had no use of his legs, but with leg braces and crutches he was able to walk a bit. It was a snowy day in January 1954, when he emerged from the dining room at Harkness Commons. The sidewalks had been partly cleared, but here and there icy patches still glistened. Slowly and gingerly he proceeded to the foot of Langdell Hall, where his Torts class was held. He carried a small notebook which he brought to all classes, because he could not handle the heavy case books. He waited a bit at the foot of the steps, which had no railings. Two friendly students noticed his quandary and carried him up the steep incline; caked ice on the steps would have made it impossible for him without help. Just inside the building, Dean Griswold, whose wife used a wheel chair due to polio, happened by and said, "Well, bravo, old chap, but why didn't you go to Stanford instead of here? It's usually warm and sunny there." The student mumbled something incoherent and proceeded into the large, amphitheatre type classroom. The bespectacled Torts professor asked the class to turn to page 63 of the text. The student didn't have the Torts book, and seats on either side were empty, so he couldn't peek at his neighbor's book. The classroom discussion of page 63 went on for twenty minutes, but it was so much gobbledygook to the student. Finally class was over and the student went to the top of the icy outside steps and waited five minutes; finally, a friendly student came and helped him down. It never occurred to the student to ask that railings be put on the massive marble steps. This was due, in part, to his immaturity, but more to the fact that he didn't want to ask for special favors. In the fifties, you just didn't do things like that. The classrooms were sometimes filled with discussions about "civil rights," "equity," and "social policy," but no one ever mentioned railings on steps. And the idea never occurred to Dean Griswold either, though he was a nationally known legal scholar, widely regarded for his brilliance and insight.

When World War II finally ended in 1945, an estimated 2500 veterans were left with spinal cord injuries and a life expectancy of one to five years. Most of them were patients at the Birmingham Hospital in Van Nuys, California.

Toward the end of the war, in Bushnell Hospital in Utah, a small group of bilateral amputee veterans formed into a group called BLACA, for Bilateral Leg Amputee Club of America. They went around the country selling savings bonds and generally creating drunken brawls.

From the model of BLACA emerged a new, upbeat group which became the precursor of the Paralyzed Veterans of America, located in Birmingham Hospital. Fred Smead, Randall Updyke, and later Ted Anderson were leaders.[1] On February 7, 1947, the Paralyzed Veterans of America was called to order, in a formative meeting, by Acting Chairman Harold A. Scharper of the Veterans Administration Hospital in Hines, Illinois. There were delegates from various Veterans Hospitals from all over the country.

All of the members of PVA were World War II veterans and almost all were paralyzed with spinal cord injuries. PVA later was to play the role of David against the Goliath of governmental inaction regarding accessibility for the handicapped. Many important court cases were won through the efforts of PVA, a tiny organization in comparison with others, such as the Disabled American Veterans. After eleven years as executive director, Jack Powell resigned in 1990. During those years the PVA grew from having 25 employees to 270, and its budget expanded from $7 million to $45 million a year. PVA in the nineties endowed a chairmanship for spinal cord injury medicine at Stanford University and also has begun the endowment of a research center at Yale.

In 1950 Mary Switzer was appointed head of vocational rehabilitation in the Office of Vocational Rehabilitation, which a few years later became part of the Department of Health, Education, and Welfare. She was a leading figure among those interested in assisting disabled people toward independence. She developed programs to train professionals in dealing with the special problems of disabled people.

Vocational rehabilitation had originated after the first World War, partly to remedy defects in workmen compensation laws, the first of which were enacted by New Jersey and Wisconsin in 1911. Vocational rehabilitation has been supported by the federal government ever since World War I, but programs were administered by the states. Large amounts of federal funds were available, peaking in the seventies, but between 1974 and 1982, the real value of federal funding spent on vocational rehabilitation declined by 31 percent.[2]

In 1951 the Korean War raged and over 600,000 young men and women were inducted into the armed services. A shortage of labor for defense industries occurred, and Mary Switzer helped form, with Dr. Howard Rusk, a "Task Force on the Handicapped" to help disabled people get jobs. "Operation Knoxville" was organized in Tennessee to locate disabled people who could be trained for jobs in the defense industry. The program became a community affair and a model for rehabilitation for the country.

When Eisenhower was elected President in 1952, he appointed Oveta Culp Hobby to be the first Secretary of the new agency, called the Department of Health, Education and Welfare, in 1953. Switzer, having grown up in Democratic administrations, was told by Hobby that she would be replaced, but because of Switzer's tremendous support from the disability community and her invaluable efforts in rehabilitation (along with some judicious lobbying by Dr. Howard Rusk with presidential assistant Sherman Adams) she was allowed to keep her job.[3]

Mary Switzer undoubtedly advanced the cause of civil rights for disabled people. As she often said, *"It is not what you have lost that matters, but what you have left."* Today, one of the headquarters buildings of the Department of Health and Human Services in Washington, D.C. is called the Switzer building.

Although Mary Switzer's efforts did much to help disabled people toward independence, conflicts arose between the concepts of vocational rehabilitation and the concept of independent living. For one thing, vocational rehabilitation got into the hands of professional health care people, who often had college and even graduate degrees, and who excluded others from participation. Volumes of academic articles by professionals were written, and the attitude was that neither disabled people nor any one else had the expertise necessary to steer disabled people toward jobs. Much of the vocational rehabilitation program involved grants for technical, including college, training, which perhaps explains why vocational rehabilitation later became the responsibility of the Department of Education, rather than the Department of Labor.[4]

Vocational rehabilitation at least had the goal of making disabled people independent, rather than the objective of merely supporting them. But the failure rate was high, and only a small percentage of those receiving vocational rehabilitation assistance actually got jobs. Another problem was that the professionals, seeking to improve their batting averages, often selected mildly disabled persons for rehabilitation, neglecting the more severely disabled. This problem was not remedied until the seventies. Another problem with vocational rehabilitation was that it cost money, and there were other programs and other agencies competing for funds. The idea of independent living, for example (see Chapter Twelve) was a concept in which people wanted to be free of the control and management of the professionals. The program of independent living was later funded by Congress, but was managed by the same people who administered the vocational rehabilitation program.

President Harry Truman was interested in helping disabled people, especially disabled veterans, who, returning from the war, were having difficulty finding jobs. Truman helped create the President's Committee on Employment of the Handicapped, in 1947. (Later, the name was changed to the President's Committee on Employment of Persons With Disabilities.) Originally it began as a voluntary, private organization, under government auspices (the Department of Labor), but later became a federal agency. It perhaps began with Paul Strachan, who founded, in the forties, the American Federation of the Physically Handicapped to promote civil rights for disabled people. He began the National Employ the Handicapped Week, an effort which was regarded by many as "out of step."[5] But Strachan's effort led to the President's Committee on National Employ the Handicapped Week, which eventually evolved into the President's Committee.

On May 23, 1957, the President's Committee was to give its annual award to the "Handicapped American of the Year," at the Departmental Auditorium on Constitution Avenue in Washington. The recipient was Hugo Deffner of Oklahoma City, who was cited for his work on behalf of people using wheel chairs. Unfortunately, he couldn't get up the steps of the building, until two Marines came and lifted him up. This event was a catalyst, because it got Harold Russell, Chairman of the President's Committee and a disabled veteran, and others to start thinking about architectural barriers.[6]

The Advisory Council of the President's Committee in May 1959 asked the American National Standards Institute (ANSI) for assistance in creating standards for architectural access, such as ramp design, door width, restrooms and the like. ANSI is a non-profit entity with many technical organizations, public interest groups, and private companies as members. Its function is to create standards for building design and other uniform standards. In 1961 ANSI approved standards, with help from the Easter Seals Society, PVA, DAV, the American Institute of Architects, the AFL-CIO, the National Association of the Physically Handicapped, the Associated General Contractors, and the National Rehabilitation Association. The standards are known as ANSI A 117.1 (1961).[7] Later, the standards developed by ANSI were to acquire the force of law, pursuant to various federal statutes.

The President's Committee was extremely influential in the beginning, because in the fifties there were few disability support groups; the Committee's ideas were the seeds from which other programs later developed. The Committee has no compliance authority, unlike other agencies, but can only advise and coordinate. Its former Chairman, Harold Russell, who lost both hands in World

War II, has been a giant in causes for disabled people, being affiliated with the President's Committee for decades; for 25 years he had been Chairman. In 1989 he retired, and was replaced by Justin Dart Jr.

Justin Dart was to become another great leader in the history of civil rights for disabled people, as recounted in other chapters. But in the early fifties, he became involved in civil rights activities that deserve mention. Justin incurred polio in 1948 and has used a wheel chair ever since. Brought up in Illinois, he attended the University of Houston in Texas. In 1952, as a student there, he and four others started an association the purpose of which was to promote racial integration at the university. At that time, the university had only white students; the movement for civil rights for blacks was in its infancy. Of the fifteen thousand white students there, only Justin and his group of five were at all interested in racial integration at the university. One other member of this small group was in a wheel chair, and one was a double amputee. It was remarkable that this small group of white students, three of whom were disabled, were interested in promoting civil rights for blacks. It was ironic that their agenda did not at all include the goal of civil rights and access for disabled students. In the early fifties, civil rights for disabled people was an unheard of notion, an idea that had not yet come.

Another event of major significance that occurred in the fifties was the passage, for the first time, of social security benefits for disabled people who were not elderly. This was an idea that had been brewing for years but objections were raised that income maintenance payments for disabled people would be prohibitively costly. In 1955 Democrats in Congress became interested once more in the issue of social security for disabled people. That year, Jere Cooper, Democrat from Kentucky, became Chairman of the House Ways and Means Committee and pushed legislation providing social security support payments for disabled people, regardless of age.

In the Senate, conservatives opposed the idea on the ground of cost, and pushed the idea of vocational rehabilitation instead. Wilbur Cohen, a giant in the field of programs for disabled people, and later Secretary of HEW under Johnson, supported broad social security coverage for disabled people. Finally, with backing from the AFL-CIO, on August 1, 1956, President Eisenhower signed into law a provision giving social security benefits to disabled people, but they had to be over 50 years of age. It was not until 1960 that this age limitation was lifted. A spokesman for the American Medical Association exclaimed, "This is the end of the medical profession."

The new federal legislation at least had the advantage of providing uniform federal rules for determining who was disabled, unlike state workmen's compensation laws, which were a patch work quilt. Social Security maintenance payments became, in later years, enormously costly, a fact which triggered a movement for less costly rehabilitation and independent living programs. A defect with the social security maintenance programs was that they were seen as encouraging disabled people to remain out of the work place and into perpetual dependence; yet, there were many disabled people who were unemployable and had no other means of support. Edward Berkowitz objected not so much to the concept of maintenance payments but to the failure by government to blend in a sophisticated way the idea of appropriate income maintenance and appropriate rehabilitation.[8]

The fifties were a time when the egalitarian climate of World War II continued. World War II made everyone equal, at least in theory. There had been a tremendous effort by every one to contribute to the war effort. Rationing of food, gasoline and fuel fell on everyone equally, at least it was supposed to. Shirkers, the disadvantaged, and the off beat were out of favor. Disabled men were classified 4-F, and were exempt from the draft, a fact which sometimes provoked unfair criticism from society. Still, labor was in short supply during World War II, and disabled workers filled essential jobs in factories and elsewhere, and contributed to the war effort. When the war was over, many disabled workers were discharged and remained unemployed, their jobs taken over by returning veterans. Society had an image of itself, reflected in movies and magazines of the day, in which all the right people were the same: dedicated, patriotic, and squeaky clean. The sexually liberated or merely adventuresome were in many places looked on as social outcasts. Conservative religious values influenced people; some would say smothered them. It was not a good time for nonconformists or the slightly different. It was a time when left handed students were told to put their left hands behind their back, in writing class. It was a time when Henry Ford said that he would paint his cars any color you wanted as long as it was black. It was particularly not a good time for intellectuals, disabled people, or Negroes, as blacks were then called.

In the fall and winter of 1953-1954, Senator Joseph McCarthy began a crusade to root out those who did not measure up to his idea of the patriotic American. Hearings were held to investigate alleged Communist infiltration into Hollywood and the arts, and into government agencies, particularly the State Department and the military services. People were black listed and condemned, often losing their jobs and suffering life long misfortune. The McCarthy crusade was anti-intellectual, anti-minority, anti-civil rights. The United States Constitution was trampelled on. Finally, a courageous Harvard Law School graduate, Joseph Welch, artfully posing as "just a poor country lawyer" succeeded in exposing McCarthy's malice, and subsequently McCarthy was censured by the Senate. It was a divisive time in America; hatred and hostility were running rampant, and it was not the same country after this terrible episode that it had been before.

On the surface, the McCarthy "era" seemed to have little to do with civil rights for disabled people, but indirectly there was definitely an influence on subsequent events. McCarthyism was basically an effort by government, in the form of Senator McCarthy, and the Senate and House Committees, to shred the constitutional rights of individuals, in the name of patriotism. The due process clause, the equal protection clause, and the Fifth Amendment were all made a mockery. The FBI kept files on thousands of "suspects."

A concrete example of the impact of McCathyism on civil rights, especially with respect to disabled people, is the story of a courageous lady, who was both blind and black, Beatrice Murphy Campbell. On November 22, 1954, Mrs. Campbell was suspended from her job as a procurement clerk at the Veterans Administration. She was told that the reason was because in 1940 or 1941 she joined a group called the Washington Bookshop Association, which was on the list of subversive organizations of the United States Attorney General. Mrs. Campbell hired an attorney and after a well publicized hearing in which she proved she never joined the orgnaization but only attended two meetings, she was reinstated in her job. In the 1960s she organized volunteer counseling service for the blind and served on advisory committees of the American Foundation for the Blind as well as the Columbia Lighthouse for the Blind. In 1967 she became legally blind. She published three volumes of her own poetry and organized the Negro Bibliographic Center. In January 1992, she was honored at the District of Columbia Public Library's Annual Martin Luther King, Jr. Leadership Awards Gala. She died at age 84 in May 1992.

With the censure and death of McCarthy, there was a sense of relief, a rediscovery of old values, a healing, and a resurgence of liberalism. In 1954, during this divisive era, the Supreme Court decided Brown versus Board of Education, and ruled that separate but equal schools for black children were not permitted by the Constitution. In 1953, President Eisenhower appointed Earl Warren as Chief Justice of the Supreme Court. Warren had been the liberal governor of California, and his influence on the Court led it to a series of "liberal" rulings, many of them related to the McCarthy hearings and their aftermath. William Brennan's appointment to the court in 1956 also promoted the cause of civil liberties.

The Warren Court struck down Pennsylvania's sedition law on the ground that federal laws pre-empted. The court upheld the defense of self-incrimination and reversed the firing of a Brooklyn College professor who had taken the Fifth Amendment before a Senate Subcommittee. In 1957 the Warren Court ruled that bar associations could not reject applicants for admission solely for refusing to answer political questions. The Warren Court ruled that Clinton Jencks, who had been convicted of perjury in signing the Taft-Hartley Act's non-communist oath, could see the FBI file which contained reports of accusing witnesses. In Sweezy versus New Hampshire, the Warren court struck down a contempt verdict against a Marxist professor who refused to answer questions of New Hampshire Attorney General Louis Wyman. When Eisenhower saw what his appointee was doing on the court, he called it the worst mistake he had ever made, in slightly more colorful language.

The public was tired of McCarthyism and reacted against it. In 1956 liberal Frank Church, who much later toured the United States Capitol in a wheelchair to see if it was accessible, defeated McCarthy's ally, Herman Welker for the Idaho Senate seat. In 1960 Kennedy and Nixon debated on television during the presidential campaign. Though Nixon had a reputation for being anti-communist, he stayed away from the issue, as did Kennedy. The Kennedy family had once been friends with McCarthy, and both candidates sensed that there was little to be gained and possibly much to lose if that explosive issue were brought up again.

Segments of the population that had been hounded and harassed by McCarthy resisted or became "rehabilitated" after his demise. In 1960, at a House UnAmerican Activities Committee hearing in San Francisco, students protested; they were beaten by police and dragged down the steps. The HUAC's hearings on Women Strike for Peace drew ridicule when women brought bouquets to the hearing. HUAC expired in 1975 and the Senate Internal Security Subcommittee terminated in 1977.

Many artists and actors had been blacklisted, but in 1971 Ring Lardner Jr., though once blacklisted, won an Oscar for MASH, and Charlie Chaplin, who left America in 1952 because of accusations, received an Oscar in 1973.

The Communist Party of America had been founded in 1929. One of its platforms was social insurance. The Communist Party and anyone remotely connected with it were, of course, targets of McCarthy and the Congressional security committees. The idea of compulsory health insurance and support payments for disabled people and other social programs, was still regarded by many as socialistic if not communistic or subversive, even though Social Security had been passed in 1935. With the end of McCarthyism, these social ideas gained more acceptance. The Civil Rights Act of 1964 passed, and liberal Democrats were in power in the White House and in Congress. Hubert Humphrey wanted to amend the Civil Rights Act to include disabled people. As late as 1967, Wilbur Cohen was attacked for his social security and other social programs, on the ground that they were socialist and even communist inspired.[9]

Although McCarthy's witch hunt turned on the question of people's political beliefs, the atmosphere was one of shredding the rights of individuals, particularly minorities. The reaction against this terrible inquisition led to reform and to advances in the cause of individual civil rights, in the courts, in the political make-up of Congress and in the views of many of the citizenry. If the forces of McCarthyism had prevailed instead of the voice of reason, can anyone predict what would have happened to the civil rights of disabled people?

Shortly after the end of World War II, an event occurred that was historically significant in terms of the disability civil rights movement. Four veterans, who had been war-injured and used wheelchairs were enrolled as students at the University of Illinois. The University planned to transfer to the Champaign-Urbana campus, which was architecturally inaccessible to the veterans. Angrily, they took to demonstrating, at the state capitol and elsewhere, and with public attention focused on the problem, they were able to persuade the University to make the new campus accessible. Ever since, the University of Illinois has been sensitive to the needs of disabled students, and today there are over 200 disabled students enrolled.

In 1950, at the beginning of the black civil rights movement, the Leadership Conference on Civil Rights was formed by black activists A. Philip Randolph, Roy Wilkins (who was one of the leaders of the NAACP), and a Jewish liberal, Arnold Aronson. This historic event was prior to the Supreme Court decision in Brown v. Board of Education, requiring desegregated public schools, and prior to the bus boycotts and lunch counter sit-ins of the late fifties and early sixties. The Leadership Conference at that time was eclipsed in importance by a related entity, the Southern Christian Leadership Conference, with which Martin Luther King and other black leaders were affiliated. But as the decades passed, The Leadership Conference has become much more broad based, and today has members consisting of organizations representing every conceivable minority, including the NAACP, the Southern Christian Leadership Conference, labor unions, disability groups of all sorts, fraternities and sororities, the American Civil Liberties Union, the Newspaper Guild and scores of other organizations. Its Executive Director is Ralph G. Neas and its chairperson, Benjamin Hooks, the noted black civil rights leader. Counsel was the liberal attorney, Joseph L. Rauh Jr., until his death in 1992. Clarence Mitchell, a black NAACP activist, though deceased, is an honorary chairperson. The Leadership Conference, according to its literature, is "*committed to an integrated, democratic, plural society in which every individual is accorded equal rights, equal opportunities and equal justice without regard to race, sex, religion, ethnic origin, handicap or age; and in which every group is accorded an equal opportunity to enter fully into the general life of society with mutual acceptance and regard for difference.*" The Leadership Conference lobbied successfully for all the Civil Rights Acts, the Voting Rights Acts, the Fair Housing Act and the Americans With Disabilities Act. It was instrumental in obtaining the defeat of the nominations to the Supreme Court of Clement Haynsworth, G. Harrold Carswell, and Robert Bork. Although the relationship was not to develop until many years after its organization in 1950, the Leadership Conference, today, provides a link between the goals for equal justice and civil rights of the disabled community and similar goals of other minorities.

On March 2, 1955, a fully occupied bus drove up Dexter Avenue in Montgomery, Alabama, past the Dexter Baptist Church where Martin Luther King was later to become a preacher. The front of the bus was filled with whites, the back was filled with Negroes, and the no-man's land in the middle was filled with Negroes. When the bus stopped and a few whites attempted to board, the bus driver turned around, pointed at the middle section, and said "*Give me those seats*" to the four Negro women seated there. Two got up to stand in the aisle, but two stared straight ahead. The bus driver left the bus to hail a policeman, who arrived in a squad car with two other policemen. A Negro man relinquished a seat, but the last holdout was a high school student named Claudette Colvin. She was arrested, handcuffed, and dragged screaming from the bus.[10]

It was the beginning of a long and bloody drama, lasting for some fifteen years, which saw in Montgomery, in Birmingham, in Atlanta and throughout the south, violent demonstrations, lynchings, assassinations and firebombings. Committed to Ghandi's principles of non-violence, the Negro leadership struggled for civil rights for Mississippi sharecroppers and Alabama farmers and Georgia train workers. Blacks, time after time, were the victims and not the perpetrators of this violence.

Later, disabled people complained that blacks were at least allowed on the back of the bus, while many of them in wheel chairs couldn't get on a bus at all.

SIXTIES

It was July, 1964, and there had been lunch counter sit-ins by Negroes all over the south; Jacksonville, Florida was no exception. On that sultry day, a group of mostly teenaged negro youths decided to "integrate" the swimming pool of a local motel. Among them was a young white man, Harold Snider, who was blind. The group changed into swimming trunks and began diving in. The manager of the motel came out and shouted to "you niggers" to leave. They refused, whereupon the manager called the police. The group was arrested and brought to the police station in three squad cars. Included was Harold Snider, who, when they arrived at the police station, was handcuffed to a desk. After an hour or so, the desk sergeant said to him, "Ain't no way I'm going to detain a blind white boy. Get out, and get out fast! " The negro youths spent the night in jail. Harold's father, a state legislator, was shocked; he came and drove Harold home.

Harold Snider later went on to be an activist in the disability civil rights movement. Among other things he participated in the 1977 sit-in at HEW and has lobbied for the Americans With Disabilities Act. He has been a director of several non-profit and civil rights organizations, and recently was named Deputy Director of the National Council on Disability.

The sixties brought the great Civil Rights March on Washington in August 1963, when Martin Luther King, at the Lincoln Memorial on the Mall, dazzled the huge throng with his "I Have a Dream" speech. The sixties brought the assassination of President Kennedy, the assassination of Martin Luther King, the assassination of Robert Kennedy, and the beginning of the Vietnam War. It was a decade of ferment and protest, a decade which was to lead to great advances in the cause of civil rights. It was a decade when the blunders of government exposed a raw nerve in the public psyche. Unfortunately, those blunders were to continue in the seventies with the fiasco of Nixon's Watergate caper, the continuation of the Vietnam War, and Nixon's resignation. The ferment of the sixties was still in the public memory in the eighties when George Bush, running for president in 1988, pleaded for a "kinder, gentler" nation. The sixties brought the Civil Rights Act of 1964. You could say that more than any other decade, the sixties sowed the seeds which made possible President Bush's signing of the Americans With Disabilities Act on July 26, 1990.

The disabled community during the sixties was still a miscellaneous collection of individuals, without cohesive unity and without strong support groups, but as the decade wore on, they became more unified. Later, in the seventies, they were to coalesce and to unify, and to borrow, at least by way of example, from the black civil rights movement. But in the sixties, they were in transition.

Leaders among the disability organizations included veterans groups, such as the Disabled American Veterans (DAV) and the Paralyzed Veterans of America (PVA) (both described earlier).

After World War II, the DAV membership swelled to six figures. Unlike PVA, which is open to veterans with non-service connected disabilities, the DAV has a requirement that members have a disability incurred in wartime military service or under conditions similar to war. It was instrumental in securing benefits for disabled veterans, including special auto licenses for handicapped parking. To a lesser extent, it was involved in advocacy on civil rights issues. After World War II, a formal program to train DAV National Service Officers was started at American University. There, disabled veterans learned skills needed to help other veterans, such as counseling on veterans' benefits, filing claims, writing briefs and appearing before government agencies.

Groups of disabled persons began to take more militant positions, and many wanted to follow the black civil rights role model of demonstrations and civil disobedience. A prominent organization was the Center for Independent Living in Berkeley, California, founded by Ed Roberts, who is severely disabled due to polio, and who had pressured his way into admission as a student at the reluctant University of California at Berkeley, in 1962. When Roberts had applied for admission as a student, he was accepted, but the University did not know he was disabled. When they found out, there was a problem of how he would manage and where he would live. Eventually the University housed him and other disabled students in the top floor of the university hospital building.

Another organization was Disabled In Action (DIA), which began in New York City in 1971, founded by Judy Heumann. Judy uses a wheelchair, because of polio. After graduating from college, she brought suit against New York City in order to get a teaching certificate. By 1972, DIA had 1500 members, and several Chapters in several cities. Judy became a national leader in the disability civil rights movement. In 1977, she participated in the protest at HEW, both in San Francisco and Washington; the protest led to the signing of the section 504 regulations by HEW Secretary Joseph Califano (See Chapter Three). Judy cofounded along with Ed Roberts, the World Institute on Disability in Oakland, California. She is an activist in the cause of personal assistance services. In 1991, she won a $50,000 prize as the first recipient of the Henry B. Betts award, which recognized her for "*significantly improving the quality of life for people with physi-*

cal disabilities" The Award was established by the Prince Charitable Trusts and is named for Dr. Henry B. Betts, medical director of the Rehabilitation Institute of Chicago.

Also developing during the sixties were public interest legal centers that assisted disabled persons on civil rights issues. One of the first was the National Center for Law and the Handicapped, in South Bend, Indiana. It was sponsored by Notre Dame Law School, the American Bar Association, and the National Association of Retarded Citizens, and received financial aid from HEW. Other legal centers included PILCOP (Public Interest Law Center of Philadelphia), CDF (Children's Defense Fund) and INSPIRE (Institute for Public Interest Representation) based at Georgetown University.[11]

The Easter Seals Society, described in Chapter One, continued its advocacy program in the sixties; it has had great influence in areas of civil rights programs and the elimination of architectural barriers. In 1945 the American Institute of Architects consulted Easter Seals with an eye toward developing architectural access standards, the first access standard being adopted in 1961, with Easter Seals help, by the American National Standards Institute ((ANSI). In 1960, Easter Seals awarded a research grant to the University of Illinois for development of design criteria for accessibility.

The 1961 ANSI architectural access standards just described, known as Standard A117.1, became widely used and with a lot of twists and turns, led to other standards that in the eighties and nineties were adopted by government agencies and had the force of law, rather than just voluntary guidelines. The ANSI standards related to such details as the minimum requirements for structures such as walkways, parking spaces, ramps, stairs, waterfountains, public telephones, and warning signals. When the Architectural Barriers Act was passed by Congress in 1968, the various federal agencies charged with enforcing (or complying with) the act adopted versions of the ANSI standards. Under the Rehabilitation Act of 1973, and regulations under section 504 of that Act, federal facilities were required to conform to minimum architectural access guidelines. The regulations said that conformity with the ANSI standards would suffice, but other methods would be allowed if they provided equivalent access.[12]

About half the states actually adopted the ANSI standards or a 1971 modified version. But the ANSI standards had drawbacks and were being administered by different federal agencies in different and inconsistent ways. In 1974, the Department of Health, Education and Welfare, with assistance from the President's Committee and Easter Seals, awarded a contract to Syracuse University's School of Architecture to revise the 1961 ANSI standards. A revised version of the ANSI standard was promulgated in 1980, though some federal agencies voted against them. Adding to the confusion was that in 1978, Congress required the Architectural and Transportation Barriers Compliance Board to proceed with "Minimum Guidelines and Requirements." Four days before President Reagan took office, the board published the minimum guidelines, which were then characterized by Reagan's Regulatory Review Task Force as overzealous and an example of unnecessary government regulation. The Office of Management and Budget even threatened to abolish the board itself, an event that never took place. After stormy sessions within the board, which consisted of 11 members (nine of whom were disabled) representing the public and 11 members representing various federal agencies, the 1981 standards were revised and compromise standards were published in August 1982, which were similar to but not identical to the ANSI standards.

Under the Americans With Disabilities Act (see Chapter Six) the board issued Minimum Guidelines on July 26, 1991, one year after passage of ADA. On the same day, the Justice Department issued identical access guidelines. The board's guidelines specifically adopted some but not all of the ANSI guidelines. The board's 1991 regulations, adopted pursuant to ADA, basically relate to the private sector. As for federal agencies, the Architectural Barriers Act of 1968 (ABA) mandated that federal agencies have architectural access standards. Although the agencies used the ANSI standards as a point of departure, the guide lines were not consistent. Finally in 1984, federal agencies issued the "federal" standard, known as the Uniform Federal Accessibility Standard (UFAS), which apply to federal buildings.UFAS in turn was based on the board's Minimum Guidelines. In the meantime, the Department of Housing and Urban Development, pursuant to the Fair Housing Amendments Act of 1988, published access guidelines relating to new housing that is covered by the act.

The reader may be confused about this bubbling stew, consisting of the ingredients of ANSI standards, Minimum Guidelines, USAF, and Housing Guidelines. The prospective builder ought to inform himself as to which of these many different sets of rules will apply. Although the many different guidelines provide employment for lawyers and bureaucrats, the actual application of access guidelines is of vital importance to disabled people. Sometimes a variation of just one half inch in the width of a door opening can exclude or include a person in a wheelchair. In fact, in the spring of 1990, a militant disability organization, ADAPT, protested in front of the HUD building because of the prospect of HUD issuing guidelines that were not strict enough. To disabled people, the issue is not which guidelines applies, but can they get into the building, use the toilet, drink from a fountain, or make a telephone call!

Thus it can be seen that the ANSI standards, first published in 1961, had a vast influence on subsequent efforts at architectural access, although two decades were to pass before real progress was made.

Back in the sixties, although organizations such as PVA and the Easter Seals Society were beginning to have an impact, they, at first, had little influence in proposing or securing federal legislation aiding disabled people. The federal government seemed detached from the point of view of the disabled community; the government seemed to regard its role as that of providing service and support, and lots of money. This was in part due to the historical role of the federal government in vocational rehabilitation: various vocational rehabilitation acts since World War I resulted in the federal government pumping money to the states, which administered generally unsuccessful vocational rehabilitation programs. The concepts of access and independence were only embryonic in the sixties.

A factor that led to the development of disability groups and modest successes in employment and prosperity for disabled people was the fact that America was changing from an industrialized society to an intelligence, service, and computer society. The industrial era had a tendency to rigidity and conformity: in the early days, only a limited number of models of typewriters, for example, were available. Jobs in factories also were uniform and lacked variety; they were not easily adaptable to people with disabilities. But as the decade wore on, there were greater varieties of cars, home appliances and just about everything manufactured. Jobs became more varied and oriented more toward mental than physical skills. In the eighties this trend accelerated, with the advent of computers that many disabled people adapted to and which allowed them to earn a comfortable living. These advances in computer technology also enabled many disabled people with mobility problems to earn a living while working at home.

The early sixties saw a continuation of the black civil rights struggle begun in the fifties. During the presidential campaign of 1960, John F. Kennedy somewhat nervously danced around this civil rights issue. He chose Lyndon Johnson, a southerner, with the obvious attempt of securing southern votes. It was thought that too strong an embracing of the civil rights goals might cause a backlash among southern voters; nothing short of the presidency was at stake. A meeting with Martin Luther King was not warmly regarded by Kennedy, but eventually such a meeting was held. After being elected President, Kennedy became more and more drawn in to the civil rights issues. Voter registration drives were begun in the south with the organization of Kennedy's agents, Burke Marshall, John Doar, and John Seigenthaler, not to mention his Attorney General brother, Robert. United States marshals had been sent by President Eisenhower to Little Rock, Arkansas in an effort to enforce desegregation requirements ordained by the Supreme Court. President Kennedy had little choice in 1962 but to take steps to assure the admission of James Meredith to the University of Mississippi against the will of Mississippi Governor Ross Barnett.

The Ol' Miss episode was a turning point in the civil rights saga; 160 United States Marshals were injured in the riots that accompanied James Meredith's admission, and eventually 23,000 United States troops, Marines, Air Force and Army personnel, surrounded Ol' Miss.[13]

The show-down at Ol' Miss had an indirect bearing on civil rights for disabled people. After all, James Meredith was trying to get an education, and a million disabled youngsters were also not in school. In 1973, the Rehabilitation Act was passed. Section 504 in effect required admission to schools, including most colleges and universities. It required changes in architecture to make the schools accessible. It no doubt would have been a surprise to Governor Barnett if he had known that, years later, the federal government would require ramps and railings and lowered drinking fountains and telephones on college campuses. The Sheriff's Department might have been surprised to learn that federal law was to mandate that deaf people have telephone access to the police and that county jails, by federal law, must be accessible to inmates in wheelchairs. In retrospect, it's easy to say that the federal government would prevail over the forces of states rights. But in the early sixties, the defeat of Governor Barnett was by no means inevitable. There were many, many throughout the country who regarded individual liberties as a matter for state and not federal law. While it was all very well for the federal government to have a national armed forces, national postal system, and, even, if we must, a national social security system, matters of education, discrimination in employment, and even voting registration were regarded by many as matters for the states and not the federal government. The Civil Rights Act of 1964 had not yet passed, and federal social welfare programs of the Johnson Administration had not yet taken place. Some states passed laws requiring access in public buildings to disabled people, and if the states rights mood had prevailed, there could very well not have been any federal civil rights legislation for disabled people. The Ol' Miss episode led to greater involvement by the federal government in issues of individual civil rights. The Ol' Miss episode was one of the historical factors which led to the eventual success of the disability civil rights movement.

Because of his involvement in black civil rights issues, President Kennedy became committed to civil rights, at least of the racial kind, as did his successor, Lyndon Johnson. It was only natural that a liberal Democrat such as Kennedy came to embrace the liberals' idea of equality; liberalism was not to become a "dirty word" until much later. Kennedy's brother Robert was to participate in voter registrations and other civil rights issues in the south, and he made trips to South Africa. Robert became something of a cult figure to many blacks.

Still, President Kennedy had a somewhat old school, paternalistic attitude toward disabled people, and he did not view disabled people as having civil rights in the same sense that blacks were regarded as having civil rights. Kennedy's family was no stranger to disability problems. His sister Rosemary was mentally retarded, and with great family sorrow, was placed in an institution. The family patriarch, Joseph P. Kennedy, suffered a stroke in later life and was severely disabled. Various members of the Kennedy family have made enormous contributions to disability issues as we shall see, but in terms of national legislative policy, there was little innovation under Kennedy; the old approaches of spending massive amounts of money for vocational rehabilitation and other programs that could be called welfare, continued. Kennedy liked to be photographed with cute disabled kids; it was great theater and great politics.

On February 9, 1961, he recommended an increase in federal matching funds for the traditional vocational rehabilitation programs. He said, *"This administration intends to see that the rehabilitation of disabled Americans and their return to active and useful lives is expanded as rapidly as possible."*

On August 21, 1961, he held a concert on the White House lawn for disabled children from the Washington area. There was a symphony orchestra conducted by Dr. James Pfohl and the Brevard Music Camp of Transylvania County, North Carolina. On August 14, 1962, he honored, in his oval office, Edward Friskie, as "Mr. Rehabilitation of 1962." Friskie had been injured in an auto accident and became a teacher. Said Kennedy, *"We are saluting the fact that, for the first time in the history of this country, we have reached the target of 100,000 disabled people who are annually rehabilitated."* He also recognized Dr. Mary Switzer, head of the Vocational Rehabilitation unit of HEW, and Secretary Anthony Celebrezze of HEW. On September 7, 1962, he signed H.R.10743 to increase disabled veterans' disability benefits, the first increase in five years. He said, *"Our first concern in a veterans' program is to provide adequate benefits for those who have become incapacitated or handicapped as a result of their service in our armed forces"* On May 9, 1963, President Kennedy appeared at the Departmental Auditorium. He said he had hired a young handicapped man to work on the White House grounds. David Hall, who was injured in an auto accident, was named Handicapped American of the Year by the President's Committee. On November 7,1963, Kennedy gave a reception in the Flower Garden of the White House for State Governors Committees on Employment of the Handicapped.

But none of Kennedy's State of the Union messages ever mentioned the issue of civil rights for disabled people, except that in his third message, on January 14, 1963, he mentioned the mentally retarded, a subject in which he often showed a special interest. He said, *"Finally, and of deep concern, I believe that the abandonment of the mentally ill and the mentally retarded to the grim mercy of custodial institutions too often inflicts on them and their families a needless cruelty which this nation should not endure."*

Kennedy again mentioned mentally retarded people in a message to Congress on February 5, 1963, and a memo to Heads of Executive Departments and Agencies on September 13, 1963 urged employment of mentally retarded people in federal agencies.

Kennedy was a great believer in the ability of individual people to make a difference. *"Ask not what your country can do for you,"* he said, *"Ask what you can do for your country."* Probably, Kennedy would have agreed if someone suggested that independence and equal access for disabled people should be a national goal, but it was not an idea that was sufficiently developed, either by disabled people themselves, or anyone else, to get very far. It seems fair to say that, if Kennedy had been present when Congress passed the Americans With Disabilities Act in 1990, he would have enthusiastically supported it.

Under Kennedy's successor, Lyndon Johnson, liberalism ran slightly amok. It almost seemed that every imaginable social ill could be cured with massive amounts of federal money, and God help any Congressman who voted for fiscal restraint. The War on Poverty, the Great Society, Appalachia, Head Start, Aid to Education, Aid to Minority Businesses, the list of spending programs went on and on. All these programs were needed; there was much poverty and lack of development in America, but excesses and poor administration occurred. The Civil Rights Act of 1964 was passed, omitting disabled people. If ever there was a time when disabled people could have been covered by civil rights legislation, it was during the Johnson Administration. But civil rights for disabled people came to mean, in the eighties and nineties, independence, equal access, the right to work, the right to be free of dependent care provided by massive government subsidies (a reduction rather than an increase in government spending). Such an idea was foreign to the spending liberals of the sixties, and curiously, was an idea that became embraced by conservative Republicans in the late eighties.

But the Johnson Administration did advance the cause of individual civil rights, though not specifically for disabled people. Johnson's commitment to civil rights for racial minorities was at times sincere, at times transparently political. Robert A. Caro published a second critical biography of Johnson – *The Years of Lyndon Johnson, Means of Ascent* (Knopf, 1990–) in which he recognized Johnson's contribution to the civil rights movement, whatever the political motivation behind such a position:

> *"Many of the ends of Lyndon Johnson's life-civil rights in particular- but others too-were noble: heroic advances in the cause of social justice...those ends are a part of that life: many liberal dreams might not be reality even today were it not for Lyndon Johnson."*

The Civil Rights Act of 1964 prohibited discrimination on the basis of race, religion, and national origin, but not on the basis of handicap. It was not until years later that disabled people were regarded as requiring federal legislation guaranteeing civil rights. (The Rehabilitation Act of 1973 and the Americans with Disabilities Act of 1990, described in later chapters, provided civil rights protection to disabled people.) It is curious that the Civil Rights Act of 1964 had this glaring omission. Possibly it can be explained on the ground that racial unrest drew the public's attention; firebombings, assassinations, and other blatant acts of discrimination were almost daily front page news. Hundreds of thousands of blacks converged on Washington in protest marches and demonstrations. The disabled community was silent, practically invisible. And possibly the black community did not want a civil rights bill to be "watered down" to include too many groups.

In 1965 Lyndon Johnson reached the high water mark in his determination to promote civil rights for racial minorities. Until then, his commitment to civil rights were regarded by many as insincere. Protests were continually being held by blacks and later by the peace movement which opposed the war in Vietnam. In March 1965, hundreds gathered at the White House, singing *"We Shall Overcome."* Johnson was driven to the Capitol, where he addressed a joint session of Congress. In his speech he said he would submit a new civil rights bill to supplement the act passed the previous year. As Johnson spoke of the Negroes who marched at Selma, Alabama and rallied continually for their civil rights, he said, *"Their cause must be our cause, too. Because it is not just Negroes, but all of us, who must overcome the crippling legacy of bigotry and injustice."* As Caro said, *"The next four words fell like sledge hammers: 'And we shall overcome.'"* After a moment of stunned silence, applause swept the chamber. In Selma, Martin Luther King, with others, watched the speech, on television, and he did something no one ever saw him do before, he started to cry.

Caro in his book traces the origin of the song *We Shall Overcome*. In Negro churches a century earlier a hymn was sung which contained the line "I do not yield." In October 1945, black women tobacco workers in South Carolina on strike added new lines to the hymn and sang, on the picket line, *"We will win our rights" and "We will overcome."* The theme *"We Shall Overcome"* was adopted by a "folk school" in Tennessee (attended by two of the picketers) that was founded to train labor and civil rights organizers and in the fifties and sixties the song swelled to a crescendo. And as we shall see later, scores of demonstrations and protests took place by disability groups. Invariably, among other songs of protest, they sang *"We Shall Overcome."*

In the humid weeks of July 1966, the Senate held hearings in Washington relating to federal programs for disabled people. The proceedings were chaired by Robert Kennedy. The hearings were not a shining moment for Robert Kennedy, but the Kennedy family, including Robert, otherwise have made and continue to make enormous contributions in the cause of disabled people: the Joseph P. Kennedy, Jr., Foundation, Special Olympics, Very Special Arts, and other programs by Senator Ted Kennedy, Ted Kennedy Junior, Eunice and Sargent Shriver, Jean Kennedy Smith and others, described in other chapters. Almost all the witnesses at the hearings were government employees, mostly from HEW, with the exception of Harold Russell, who was Chairman of the President's Committee on Employment of the Handicapped.

The emphasis of the entire Senate proceedings was exclusively on financial assistance and support programs and on the question of whether the diverse federal programs were properly coordinated and cost effective. The viewpoint was that of a prior age: that the disabled needed "support services" and it was up to the government, be it federal, state or local, to provide those services. There was not a word in the hearings about attempting to secure access and independence for the disabled. They were a protected minority and it was up to government to protect them. Even Harold Russell, a disabled veteran, avoided the question of legislation, and somewhat naively thought that the interests of the disabled in securing employment would be furthered by voluntary cooperation from the private sector, stimulated by publicity campaigns. Robert Kennedy was obsessed by statistics, of the financial sort, and peevishly questioned witnesses about the accuracy of numbers of disabled, amount of dollars spent,etc., etc. There was testimony that there were 846,000 disabled persons on public assistance and it was costing close to one billion dollars a year in support payments. Dr. Winston of HEW tried to explain one of the HEW training programs and the number of people it dealt with in the program.

A prominent witness at the 1966 hearings was Wilbur J. Cohen, Undersecretary of HEW (later to become Secretary), for whom the old HEW building was later named. Although a giant in the field of federal social welfare programs, especially social security programs and programs for the elderly, again, the emphasis in his testimony was on "help" and "support" and not at all on independence and access. There was testimony that in 1967, some 9.1 billion dollars would be spent on 80 different programs, or 12.5 percent of total domestic federal cash outlay. The five programs administered by HEW outlined by Wilbur Cohen were: (1) income maintenance, including veterans benefits and social security; (2) bringing health services to the disabled; (3)training (of health professionals, not of disabled people themselves); (4) medical research; and (5) "research, demonstration, and dissemination of information."

Only Dr. Howard Rusk, director of the world renowned Institute of Rehabilitative Medicine, which cared for many para-and quadriplegics, seemed concerned about a lack of government goals. He testified that spinal cord injured were living longer lives and have a "*better production rate, a lower absentee rate, and from five to nine times less turnover than so-called normal working side by side with them.*"[14]

The nineteenth century attitude toward rehabilitation displayed in the 1966 Senate hearing was to change dramatically, beginning in the late sixties and culminating in the seventies. The change that was monumentally significant to the disabled population was essentially a change from the idea that disability was a governmental and institutional problem and responsibility to the idea that disability issues were fundamentally civil rights issues. The disability community began to feel that the goals to be achieved were independence for disabled people; that disabled people and not government were responsible for their own lives, that disabled people were entitled to be free from discrimination in all areas of life, in employment, in transportation, in community access, in housing. If laws were needed to enforce these rights, it was only because the Constitution guaranteed to disabled people the same equal opportunities that others enjoyed. Government participation, and government funds, were needed, not, as in earlier times, because the government paternalistically knew what was best for disabled people and controlled their fate, but because some government assistance, in the form of federal civil rights laws, courts to interpret them, and seed money for independent living and rehabilitation programs, were needed.

The late sixties was the beginning of this dramatic shift. The black civil rights movement, begun in the fifties, provided a model and method for this new emphasis on civil rights. But civil rights issues were not limited to blacks. The women's movement gained strength. Suits for sexual harassment were common place, and women were concerned that jobs performed by women didn't command the same pay as work done by men. In New York, after years of harassment by police, gays at a gay bar rebelled with two days of rioting after being further harassed. American Indians agitated for equality of opportunity and for a withdrawal of control by the federal government over their lives. Hispanic Americans formed leagues and protested against terrible agricultural conditions.

Protest was the vogue. Parades, placards, buttons, speeches and signs became a familiar sight. There were in communities across America "single issue" protests such as protests against taxes or utility rates. The environment became a concern. People were shocked by the terrible damage being done to rivers, lakes, the atmosphere and land-fills by large corporations, and people became aware of the fact that this pollution was not only unsightly but also could be damaging to health. In practically all of these protests, it was a question of "people" versus " institutions."

Later in the sixties, the peace movement took hold. College campuses were awash with protest demonstrations against the Vietnam war. Daily television news broadcasts showed combat action in Vietnam in vivid color, and the phrase "body count" referring to the number of Americans killed, became a news item. College students in general were opposed to the war, no doubt on the ground in part that they themselves were likely to get killed or wounded. On May 4, 1968, students protested the war at Kent State and met gunfire from the National Guard. Four students were killed and one was paralyzed for life.

The Vietnam War produced thousands of disabled veterans, but the protest movement, though waving the flag of civil rights, was not very much concerned with rehabilitation of disabled veterans. The protesters were concerned with stopping the war. To them, disability was something to be prevented, not cured. As the winless war trudged on, thousands of GI's returned home with missing limbs and countless other disabilities. Ron Kovic, who started the war as a gung-ho Marine, was spinal cord injured and became a nationally known civil rights advocate. The movie about his life, *Born on the Fourth of July,* starred Tom Cruise, and its Director, Oliver Stone, won the Academy Award for Best Director in 1990. The Vietnam War, tragic and shamefully costly though it was, at least provided a strong impetus to the disability civil rights movement.

The protest movements involving Vietnam, the feminist movement, gays, Indians, Hispanics, and the environment gathered strength during the late sixties, but the civil rights movement of disabled people, with few exceptions, lagged behind and was not to reach a culmination until ten years later. Perhaps this was because these movements were a matter of "people" versus " institutions." There were plenty of institutions concerned with disabled people, such as health care providers, the March of Dimes, American Red Cross, and countless others, but you could say that disabled people as "people" were invisible. Disabled people had always been isolated, segregated and shut out. In the sixties, there were few disabled people who took up the banner of civil rights in the same way that women and other minorities did. But the enormously wide-spread civil rights movement of the sixties almost inevitably was to produce the cosmic change in attitudes regarding disabled people and led to the spectacular accomplishments in civil rights for disabled people that were to occur in the seventies, eighties, and early nineties.

When the Americans With Disabilities Act was signed by President Bush on July 26, 1990, it was a great victory for civil rights for disabled people, but there were many who said it came twenty-five years too late. The sixties, at least, saw the beginnings of civil rights for disabled people. In 1968 two events occurred that, in retrospect, were the precursors of dramatic events that were to take place in the seventies.

First. a small group of dissatisfied disabled persons complained about lack of access to government buildings and monuments. To publicize their concerns, they demonstrated at the Lincoln Memorial. It seemed to them that the Lincoln Memorial symbolized the equality of all Americans – all but disabled people, who couldn't even get into the building. Harold Snider, blind, was an organizer.

An LBJ intern, he was a liberal activist in the cause of minority civil rights, including rights for blacks as well as for disabled people. About 300 disabled persons attended the protest. Robert Kennedy sent a message; it was but a month before he was assassinated. The fruit of this protest, many years later, was the installation of an elevator at the Lincoln Memorial, handicapped parking, and similar facilities at the Washington Monument and the Jefferson Memorial!

The second important event that occurred in 1968 was the enactment of the Architectural Barriers Act. This legislation, sometimes known as the Bartlett Act, after Democratic Senator E.L. Bartlett of Alaska, was given birth through the efforts of three persons: Senator Bartlett, Congressman Charles E. Bennett of Florida, and Hugh Gallagher, a legislative aide to Senator Bartlett. Gallagher, due to polio, uses a wheelchair. When he requested that the National Gallery of Art install a ramp, they refused, saying it would ruin the architecture.[15] The board of directors of the Gallery reversed their position after an appeal by Senator Bartlett. The Library of Congress agreed to install a ramp after requests by Bartlett, who, interestingly, reviewed library appropriations. Gallagher later worked for the Bureau of the Budget in the inaccessible Executive Office Building and had to be carried up stairs by Secret Service officers!

Gallagher and Bartlett went to the Senate Committee on Labor and Public Welfare to propose the idea of legislation removing architectural barriers in federal buildings and federally financed buildings. Although there was some opposition due to the fact that the National Commission on Architectural Barriers was studying the problem but had not finished its report, a bill was introduced requiring new federally financed buildings to be accessible, but did not require changes in existing buildings. The bill had no enforcement mechanism. Bartlett commented:

> *"[The bill] contains no seeds of controversy, carries with it no appropriation, and will cost the taxpayers of this country only a nominal amount. Its advantages for one segment of our country's citizens are not counter balanced to any extent by disadvantages for another, nor does it have any accompanying appropriation – or the prospect of appreciable costs in the future – over which we, as Members of Congress, must agonize ."*[16]

Bartlett was right about it costing little, precisely because it had no enforcement mechanism, but he was dead wrong about it being noncontroversial, for the same reason.

On the House side, an identical bill was introduced by Congressman Charles E. Bennett, Democrat from Florida. Congressman Bennett had contracted polio in 1945, and uses canes. After forty years, he is still in Congress. His Congressional office in Jacksonville Florida, in the federal building, could be reached only through the back door, because the front of the building had numerous steps.[17] Fed up with lack of building access, Bennett heartily agreed with Bartlett. Testimony was received at the hearings form the President's Committee, the Easter Seals Society, the National Rehabilitation Association, the Vocational Rehabilitation Administration, and from HEW, HUD and GSA. Some, mostly agency heads, opposed the bill because of the pending study by the Architectural Commission. Some thought that responsibility should be given, not to GSA but to the Vocational Rehabilitation Administration of HEW, headed by Mary Switzer. With little floor debate, the measure sailed through the House and Senate, and was signed into law on August 12, 1968.

The Architectural Barriers Act did not apply at all to existing buildings. It required access standards for certain new federal buildings, the standards to be applied by GSA, HEW, HUD, Defense, and the Postal Service. Waivers could be given on application by an agency. The act itself was very weak, but it served as a prologue to the Rehabilitation Act of 1973, which created the Architectural and Transportation Barriers Compliance Board. The latter act put teeth into the mandated access to federal buildings.

Another event that occurred in the late sixties was the development of the internationally recognized logo for wheel chair access, now seen almost everywhere in the United States, and in many foreign countries. The President's Committee claims credit for originating the idea, in the mid-sixties. It forwarded a suggestion that a logo be developed to Rehabilitation International. In 1968, Rehabilitation International (then known as International Society for Rehabilitation of Disabled), referred the idea to its Committee on Technical Aids, Housing and Transportation, chaired by Karl Montan at the ITCA Information Center, Bromma, Sweden. Suggestions for a logo were turned over to a jury consisting of representatives from Switzerland, Sweden, France, Poland, England, the United States and Austria. The jury met at the World Congress of Rehabilitation International in 1969 in Dublin, Ireland. They recommended and the Assembly accepted the version created by a Danish design student. The 65 countries present voted to accept it and ever since it has been used as a symbol of access to buildings, restrooms, parking and the like. The logo is a stripped down picture of a wheelchair, usually blue with a white background, or vice versa. The logo was promoted by each country, and in The United States primarily by Easter Seal and the President's Committee. Some efforts were made by commercial companies to adopt and exploit the symbol, but these efforts were rejected. The danger of commercial exploitation led to proposals in Congress for Congressional adoption and legal protection, but this was rejected on the ground that the symbol, unlike the Red Cross and Smokey the Bear, was too generic for legal protection.[18] Some deaf and blind groups object to the logo on the ground that it refers only to the mobility impaired and not to deaf and blind people.

In 1968, two psychiatrists, Dr. William H. Grier and Dr.Price M. Cobbs, published a small book entitled *Black Rage*[19] that tried to explain the anger and frustration of blacks that had led to the riots in Watts, Detroit, Washington, D.C. and elsewhere. Using actual case histories, the authors described the historical and cultural background that led to so many feelings of alienation among blacks in America. The book became enormously popular, and was influential in focusing attention on minorities of all kinds, including disabled people. Leaders of the disability civil rights movement, such as Mary Jane Owen, regard the book as one of the most significant civil rights books ever written.

The sixties ended with a feeling of euphoria about what could be done in the field of civil rights. In 1969 man landed on the moon, and the next year the first Earth Day celebration was held. People began to think that if you could get to the moon, you could do anything. There was a feeling that anything was possible, and a feeling that the "people" could prevail against the "big institution" be it big government, big business, or big charity. All you needed were a few placards and some like minded protesters and you were in business.

CHAPTER III

THE REHABILITATION ACT of 1973 and THE PROTEST of 1977

It was New Year's Eve, 1969. Charles and his wife, Lucille, had made plans to go out. Charles was a Vietnam veteran who had taken a well aimed bullet in his lower back and it had left him with a severely injured spinal cord. He had gotten a job at the mammoth federal agency, HEW, in Southwest Washington, D.C. and lived in an apartment nearby on Fourth Street. He commuted to work via wheelchair, but was forced to use the street since the sidewalks had no curb cuts. He enjoyed the setup, except on rainy and snowy days. Charles and Lucille had made New Year's Eve reservations at Harrigan's, a neighborhood joint close by, but too far to go by wheelchair. Formerly a warehouse, the restaurant sat in the middle of an unpaved, dark parking lot near the murky, and as yet undeveloped, waterfront. Charles and Lucille went out on Fourth Street to look for a taxi. Two empty taxis slowed but didn't stop. A third stopped, and the driver and Lucille helped Charles and his wheelchair into the cab. Harrigan's was a fun place with colorful oil paintings on the wall and a three piece jazz band. A black waiter helped Charles up the one step, and they sat at a large table occupied by three other couples, whom they didn't know. Pitchers of beer were brought and funny hats were donned. As the evening wore on the couples got real friendly and the other couples were thrilled to hear Charles' Vietnam War stories. They told ethnic jokes, dirty jokes, and LBJ jokes. They traded names and addresses and talked about meeting again, monthly. Charles announced that he was mighty glad the sixties were coming to an end in a few minutes. After all, it was the decade when JFK, Robert Kennedy, and Martin Luther King were all assassinated, the Vietnam War began, and Charles was injured. Then it was midnight, the horns and whistles came out, and they all made a hell of a racket. Then Charles decided he needed to take a leak, but the rest room was inaccessible. Charles decided to pay the bill, but in searching his pockets he discovered that he had lost his wallet. They looked outside, thinking he had lost it when he paid the taxi fare, but it was nowhere to be found. Charles needed to take a leak real bad after all that beer, so he wheeled to the rear of the building, which was dark and occupied only by a scurrying rat. He unzipped his fly and aimed a steady stream between his shoes and the footrests of the wheelchair. Suddenly a flashlight lit up the involuntary deposition and a policeman approached. "Just what do you think you're doing?" "Well, Ossifer," said Charles, who was feeling no pain, "When you got to go you got to go." The officer booked Charles for disorderly conduct and indecent exposure, and with the help of another officer put him, the wheelchair, and Lucille into a squad car and took them down to the station. "What the fuck do you assholes think you're doing?" asked Charles. "I'm a goddamned war hero and I had to take a leak. This town was built by able bodied people without kidneys!" The desk sergeant, who was up for promotion, bawled out the officers and released Charles. "No way I'm goin' to book a Vietnam War hero," he said. Realizing that Charles had really lost his wallet, the officers drove the two of them home, where they arrived at 3 A.M. "Well, Happy New Year, Honey," Charles said to Lucille as he kissed her. "You win some and lose some."

On September 26, 1973, a reluctant President Nixon (having twice vetoed earlier versions) signed the bill that became known as the Rehabilitation Act of 1973. This extraordinary piece of legislation, enacted with little debate, put in place forces that, several years later, were to be responsible for enormous advances for disabled people – in all areas of life in which the federal government was involved, directly or indirectly. Transportation, housing, education, and employment, were all required to be accessible to disabled people. (In 1990 the Americans With Disabilities Act was passed, which among other things, extended these provisions to the private sector. See Chapter Six.)

Coverage under the Rehabilitation Act of 1973 was broad, because all organizations, programs, and activities that received federal assistance were required to comply. The Rehabilitation Act of 1973 was Public Law 93-112[1] and had a variety of provisions and purposes. It really had two parts, vocational rehabilitation, which was an embellishment of vocational rehabilitation laws that had been on the books for decades, and a completely novel access or anti-discrimination part. Because of the new access and anti-discrimination portion, which had no statutory precedent, the word "vocational" was dropped from the title of the original bill, and the act became known as the Rehabilitation Act of 1973.

The first part of the act related primarily to vocational rehabilitation, and was an expanded version of earlier vocational rehabilitation acts. The Senate Report gave a bit of history: the first vocational rehabilitation act was in 1917 and related to disabled veterans' programs. In 1920, President Wilson signed the Smith-Fess Act (P.L. 66-236) providing for vocational rehabilitation for both the military and civilian disabled. There were later acts in 1943, 1954, 1965, 1967, and 1968. The 1943 act added the mentally ill and retarded as beneficiaries. In 1954 there were added provisions for research, demonstration and training activities. In 1965 requisites for workshops and rehabilitation centers were added. In 1967, the Vocational Rehabilitation Administration in HEW was renamed the Rehabilitation ServicesRSA

Administration (RSA). Later, the RSA was transferred to the Department of Education.

The Senate Report to the Rehabilitation Act of 1973 has a lengthy description of the issues that led to the vocational rehabilitation portion of the act. There were complaints that the program was not working well and was not reaching the targeted groups, that the severely disabled were not being rehabilitated at all, not only for job placement, but also for independent living. There were complaints about failures in the Rehabilitation Services Administration. This portion of the act related to expanded programs of vocational rehabilitation, funding, and coordination of programs among many agencies of the federal government, and with states, who were the primary administrators of the programs. Any participant in a vocational rehabilitation program became a participant in an "individualized written rehabilitation program," drawn up jointly with the administrator. Special emphasis (rather than priority, as originally provided) had to be given to the severely disabled. A National Institute of Handicapped Research was set up, as well as the National Council on the Handicapped, at least five members of which had to be disabled or the parent or guardian of a disabled person. The portions of the legislation just described did not relate to access and independence so much as to traditional types of vocational rehabilitation; this portion of the legislation, was not nearly as controversial as the access and anti-discrimination stipulations

As a result of objections that vocational rehabilitation was not reaching the most severely disabled, one article of that segment of the bill provided for a program for "independent living." This program was probably part of President Nixon's objections, leading to his veto, discussed later in this chapter. The 1973 act was somewhat of a compromise between Congress and the White House. The independent living program was deleted (and added subsequently) but there was to be, beforehand, a study of the concept. See Chapter Twelve.

The access and anti-discrimination provisions were – unlike the vocational rehabilitation requirements – novel, unprecedented, controversial (later, though not initially), and extremely broad in scope and results. Paradoxically, the legislative history of this portion is the scantiest. For some strange reason, the sections were placed in Title V, under the heading "Miscellaneous."

Section 501 of this portion of the act provided for an Interagency Committee on Handicapped Employees, consisting of members of various, too-numerous-to-mention federal agencies. As is the way in Washington, everyone sticks fingers into the pie, requiring one large Sticky Finger to do the coordinating. The Committee was charged with seeing that each agency had an affirmative action plan for the hiring, placement, and advancement of handicapped individuals in that department. It seemed to be an attempt by the federal government to get its own house in order.

Section 502 of the act created the Architectural and Transportation Barriers Compliance Board (ATBCB) as a federal agency. It was, and still is, charged with implementing access provisions of the act and of the Architectural Barriers Act of 1968, which had no enforcement mechanism. There were to be studies concerning access in transportation and housing. This board was also an attempt to put the federal government's house in order. Since the act required compliance not only by the federal government itself, but by any program or activity financed by the federal government, including schools and colleges, the board's powers are quite broad. Unlike the President's Committee on Employment of Persons with Disabilities, which is advisory only, the board has compliance authority.

Section 503 requires that any federal contractor with a contract in excess of $2500 must have an affirmative action program to employ and advance in employment qualified, handicapped individuals.

Section 504 of the act is the guts of the civil rights access-anti discrimination portion. Though based on the Civil Rights Act of 1964, which did not cover disabled persons, it was novel, significant and controversial. It has engendered scores of court cases, several finding their way to the United States Supreme Court. It had no specific provision requiring regulations; regulations were later drafted by HEW and , because of years of delay in finalizing them, the Protest of 1977 occurred at HEW, as described at the end of this Chapter.

Section 504 provides that *"no otherwise qualified handicapped individual in the United States...shall solely by reason of his handicap, be excluded from participation in, be denied the benefits of, or be subjected to discrimination under any program or activities receiving Federal financial assistance."*

In a nutshell, this single sentence required modifications in the area of buildings, housing, transportation, employment, and education access. It applied to the "federal sector" meaning not just the federal government and federal agencies, but any program or activity by anyone receiving federal financial assistance. Examples of the scope of the section are: federal buildings and federal contractor buildings had to provide ramps or wheelchair access. Since many if not most schools and colleges receive federal assistance, they had to be made accessible, and they could not deny admission to a qualified handicapped individual who applied for enrollment. Where feasible, disabled students had to be "mainstreamed" with regular students, although the word "mainstream" is found nowhere in the act or in the legislative history. Qualified disabled persons could not be excluded from employment by the federal government or the federal sector. Public transportation companies receiving federal assistance had to provide accessible transportation, i.e., buses, trains and airplanes. An important provision of section 504 of the act redefined the term "handicapped." Previously, the term had been defined in terms of employability, but there were many of the severely disabled who could not be employed through existing programs. The term "handicapped" was broadened to include those with major life-activity disabilities, those who had been previously disabled (such as those who've recovered from heart disease), and those who were regarded as disabled (persons with epilepsy or recurring diseases).

Section 504 of the act was only one sentence and it needed to be fleshed out; subsequently, regulations were set in motion which contained provisions for delayed implementation with respect to new construction, definition of handicapped, type of compliance needed, and so forth.

What led to section 504, which, though a seemingly obscure part of the Rehabilitation Act of 1973, was the corner stone of the disabled civil rights movement and was to have truly revolutionary consequences?

In the sixties, as we have seen in the previous chapter, civil rights organizations became more and more effective. Not only the black civil rights movement was continuing, but agitation concerning the Vietnam war became stronger and stronger. Liberalism in the cause of social reform was thriving and not yet suspect. The Architectural Barriers Act, enacted in 1968, demonstrated good intentions, but compliance with the requirement for accessible federal buildings was weak.

In 1970, Congress enacted the Urban Mass Transportation Assistance Act. Selection 16 provided that *"elderly and handicapped persons have the same right as other persons to utilize mass transportation facilities and services, that special efforts shall be made in the planning and design of mass transportation so that the availability to handicapped persons of mass transportation which they can effectively utilize will be assured."*

Mass transportation, for some obscure reason, was the province of the Senate Committee on Banking and Currency. This committee's Subcommittee on Housing and Urban Affairs, held hearings in early 1970 to consider appropriations for improving the nation's mass transportation systems. It is reported that not one disabled person testified at the hearings.[2] Disabled riders were mostly overlooked; however, Secretary of Transportation John Volpe did say in passing that *"there is the need to provide an adequate transportation system for the young, the old, the handicapped and the poor. ..."* [3] But disabled people were not mentioned in the bill that was introduced to the Senate.

A freshman Democratic Congressman from the Bronx, Mario Biaggi, came to the rescue and introduced a floor amendment, though he was not a member of any transportation committee. Somewhat naively, he said that it would entail very little additional costs. The Biaggi Amendment, as it has been called, became section 16 of the Urban Mass Transportation Assistance Act, quoted above. The provision uses the word "rights" but also the phrase "special efforts." These two concepts were later to evolve into raging controversies that even today are not fully resolved. The emphasis on "rights" is described as full mobility or equal access, meaning that all transportation facilities, such as buses and trains, must be accessible, for example, by providing wheelchair lifts on all buses. The "special efforts" phrase has been described as intending "effective mobility" which means that alternative modes of transportation, (called paratransit) such as taxis or special vans, may be used, and waivers and exemptions may apply.[4]

There is little doubt that Congressman Biaggi, the author of the amendment, thought the amendment would provide equal civil rights or full mobility. He said:

> *"Congress has authorized expenditures to remove barriers for the elderly and handicapped in other areas...[My] amendment would extend this existing policy to mass transportation systems that are federally supported so that such barriers to travel can be removed at the program's inception with very little if any additional costs...We are simply talking about granting equal rights to a large segment of our population to use public facilities with the same ease as everyone else. Other proposals have been offered that would set up special transportation facilities for the elderly and handicapped. Others would provide subsidies so that these people could use more expensive services such as taxi cabs or limousines. However, besides the factor of costs for these programs, they would further serve to segregate the elderly and the handicapped from our society."*

Needless to say, the disabled community favored the equal rights approach, while the transit associations favored effective mobility, which would provide "paratransit" facilities for disabled people, such as vans and taxis. This conflict was to erupt many times over the years to come. Local governments favored effective mobility because, even though it involved the complexity of alternative systems, it was regarded as less costly.

Another unexpected and somewhat fortuitous provision relating to the transportation needs of disabled people occurred in 1973, when Congress passed the Federal-Aid Highway Act. Once again disabled people did not participate in hearings, there was little debate, and the amendments were mostly riders to a financing bill. There were several features relating to disabled people. An amendment introduced by Representative Bella Abzug, D-N.Y., authorized loans and grants to non-profit organizations to provide alternative transportation such as mini-buses and dial-a-ride services, where regular facilities were unavailable, insufficient, or inappropriate. Another provision was funding for the D.C. subway systems to provide elevators for disabled people.

Previously, Richard Heddinger had successfully sued the D.C. Metro Authority; the court required elevators to be installed at all subway stops, but there were no appropriations. The price tag for the elevators under this amendment was 65 million dollars.[6]

The amendment was added to the Highway Act, despite opposition from DOT, but with the active support of Kenneth Gray, Chairman of the House Subcommittee on Public Buildings and Grounds. Gray said that the transit industry, as a whole, resisted the idea of transit for wheelchair users but that Congress had specifically mandated that the D.C. Metro be accessible to all disabled people, not just to some of them.[7]

The third addition to the Highway Act was a provision prohibiting the DOT Secretary from approving any capital assistance project for construction or acquisition of new urban mass transit facilities unless he determined the project provided "reasonable access" to elderly and handicapped persons or unless he found that "alternative actions" had been taken to ensure access, again an effective mobility approach rather than a rights approach. This provision sailed through with no debate and without the involvement of handicapped groups.

In 1975 the same Congressman Biaggi, concerned that DOT was weakening his 1970 amendment by opposing a San Francisco Bay Area Rapid Transit (BART) plan for accessible buses, succeeded in tacking a rider to the DOT appropriations measure which prohibited the use of funds for the purchase of trains or buses unless they were *"designed to meet the transportation needs of the elderly and handicapped."* The provision was also backed by Congressmen John McFall, D-Calif., and Silvio Conte, R-Mass. Congressman Biaggi explained unambiguously the need for what became section 105 of the Federal-Aid Highway Act. Referring to the failure to implement section 16 of the Urban Mass Transit Act, he said:

> *"When this policy was first enunciated in my amendment to the 1970 Urban Mass Transportation Assistance Act, it [was] hailed as the emancipation proclamation for the handicapped. ... The vast majority of the handicapped and elderly people – including those in wheelchairs – could be served through the general transportation system for little or no added cost. Why then does the Department [of Transportation] continue to subsidize buses and mass transit systems that cannot be used by the handicapped? ... What is happening here is out and out discrimination. If the Department of Transportation is allowed to continue on its present route, the elderly and the handicapped will be denied access to mass transit for many years to come."*[8]

During this period of the early seventies, the provisions just described occurred as tangents to other bills, were little debated, and arose outside committees with more direct jurisdiction over disabled affairs. There was little debate, discussion, or even input from disabled groups. In part all of this may have been due, at least in the House, to jurisdictional disputes between two House committees, the Committee on Banking and Currency and the Public Works Committee. The former's Urban Mass Transit Subcommittee, while claiming primary jurisdiction over mass transit, still exercised a myopic view of the needs of disabled people. The Subcommittee proposed half fare tickets for the elderly and disabled during off-peak hours, their only contribution to the cause. The Public Works Committee claimed to be in the forefront for disability causes; they had sponsored the Architectural Barriers Act of 1968 and in 1974 they proposed that all mass transit systems be accessible to the elderly and disabled.[9]

The Public Works Committee was generally in favor of a "rights" approach, with the exception of Republican Congressman James Cleveland of New Hampshire (a state which had little in the way of urban mass transit). The two committees could not resolve their jurisdictional dispute and would not even meet together; ultimately the views of the Urban Mass Transit Subcommittee prevailed, at least temporarily, and the half fare provision was enacted.[10]

But in January 1975, the Public Works Committee was given primary jurisdiction over mass transit and was renamed the Committee on Public Works and Transportation. Although it provided a focal point for disability groups, it also was receptive to the views of the transit industry.

The transportation provisions just described were mere skirmishes and initially had little effect because compliance was uncertain and embryonic. But they contributed to the concepts that ultimately prevailed in the enormously more significant Rehabilitation Act of 1973, which, as described above, required access in areas of architecture, employment, housing and transportation in all programs and activities in which the federal government provided financial assistance.

The precursor of the civil rights portion of the Rehabilitation Act originated in identical proposals by Congressman Charles Vanik, D-Ohio, and Senator Hubert Humphrey, D-Minn.[11]

Vanik introduced his bill on December 9, 1971. He said that his bill would provide equal employment and education opportunities for the handicapped. He declared that *"masses of the handicapped live and struggle among us, often shunted aside, hidden, and ignored."* They were at times kept in "*snake pit mental institutions,*" and *"one million children are kept from schools....employers fear to hire the handicapped."* The *"treatment and regard for the rights of the handicapped citizens in our country is one of America's shameful oversights."*[12]

Senators Humphrey and Percy on January 20, 1972, introduced a bill to amend the Civil Rights Act of 1964 in order to prohibit discrimination on the basis of physical or mental handicap in federally assisted programs. The bill would have added "physical or mental handicap" to race, color, and national origin as illegal grounds for discrimination. This bill was the precursor of the Rehabilitation Act of 1973, although the latter act did not explicitly amend the Civil Rights Act. Senator Humphrey was eloquent in his oratory:

"The time has come when we can no longer tolerate the invisibility of the handicapped in America...I am insisting that the civil rights of 40 million Americans now be affirmed and effectively guaranteed by Congress-our several million disabled war veterans, the 22 million people with a severe physically disabling condition, the one in every ten Americans who has a mental condition requiring psychiatric treatment, the six million persons who are mentally retarded, the hundreds of thousands crippled by accidents and the destructive forces of poverty, and the 100,000 babies born with defects each year.

"These people have the right to live, to work to the best of their ability to know the dignity to which every human being is entitled. But too often we keep children, who we regard as 'different' or a 'disturbing influence' out of our schools and community activities altogether, rather than help them develop their abilities in special classes and programs. Millions of young persons and adults, who want to learn a trade, work like other people, and establish their self-worth through a pay-check are barred from our vocational training programs and from countless jobs they could perform well. And yet we have sufficient statistics clearly demonstrating the benefits to the national economy and the investment return of income tax revenues resulting from vocational rehabilitation and job placement for these citizens. Where is the cost effectiveness in consigning them to public assistance or (terminal) care in an institution?

"These are people who can and must be helped to help themselves. That this is their constitutional right is clearly affirmed in a number of recent decisions in various judicial jurisdictions. Every child–gifted, normal, and handicapped–has a fundamental right to educational opportunities and the right to health."

Richard Scotch in his book, *From Good Will to Civil Rights*, says that the Humphrey and Vanik amendments were not debated and no hearings were held. He suggests that opposition came from blacks, who feared weakening of the Civil Rights Act.

"In earlier Congresses, southern Democrats and the conservatives had attempted to weaken existing civil rights legislation by expanding coverage beyond the capacity for enforcement, and civil rights advocates were concerned that any significant broadening of the scope of the Civil Rights Act

would necessarily distract from and thus diminish enforcement of the existing provisions. Whatever the motivation, the amendments were not seriously considered."[13]

Whether this speculation is true or not, the provision which followed these amendments, the Rehabilitation Act, adopted similar requirements without, however, amending the Civil Rights Act. There is little doubt, though, that civil rights legislation for disabled people was modeled after similar legislation for racial minorities, and the disabled civil rights activists in many ways borrowed from the black civil rights movement. The black civil rights movement, early during the Roosevelt administration, targeted the Defense Department as the focus of efforts to secure equal employment opportunities.[14]

Like the black civil rights movement, the disability movement initially targeted the federal government because it was regarded as both a unified, single target, an extremely broad one, and one possibly more responsive than states and the private sector to demands for equal rights.

The Civil Rights Act of 1964 and later Civil Rights Acts prevented discrimination in general against racial and religious minorities, and later, against women, but not against disabled people. The acts generally applied both to the federal and the private sector, i.e. to everyone. It is difficult to explain why the Rehabilitation Act of 1973 only prevents discrimination in the federal sector, as previously explained. It was not until 1988 and 1989 that an effort was made to extend the principles from the federal to the private sector. (See Chapter Six). The limitation to the federal sector in 1973 may have been due to opposition by blacks, as just explained, or to the fact that some Congressmen who were instrumental in passing the 1973 legislation had their own motivations. (Congressman Bennett, who had contracted polio, had difficulty getting access to the building where his Congressional Office was located). Then too, section 504 required costly renovations such as ramps, elevators, curb cuts in sidewalks, and the like, and the Congressional wisdom may have decided to "remove just one step at a time," so to speak. In addition, unlike the black and women's movement, the disability civil rights movement was only just beginning. It may be that Congress was totally embarrassed that their own Capitol building, the Lincoln Memorial, the Washington Monument, and other federal buildings were totally and unreasonably inaccessible to many disabled persons.

The failure of the Humphrey and Vanik amendments was only temporary. In 1972, the vocational rehabilitation appropriation law was expiring and needed to be continued. This was an opportunity for the liberals in Congress to promote social causes, including civil rights provisions for disabled people. This was a time when the liberalism of the sixties was continuing, mostly in the costume of the Senate Labor and Public Welfare Committee and the House Committee on Education and Labor. However, liberalism was beginning to run into opposition from conservatives, mostly Republican, and from the budget consciousness of the Nixon years. It was a time when big-spending, sometimes irresponsible liberalism, for social causes was beginning to face opposition from hard-headed Republican conservative frugality. The Watergate scandal was brewing, and it was a time when a Democratic Congress was to continually confront a hostile Republican presidency.[15]

The Vocational Rehabilitation law, up for appropriations renewal, provided the perfect opportunity for liberal expansion. This time, hearings were held and disability groups participated. Senator Humphrey, defeated in his effort to have the anti-discrimination amendment as part of an amended Civil Rights Act, succeeded in having the civil rights amendment incorporated in the Rehabilitation Act proposal that had been proposed by Senator Jennings Randolph, D-W.Va., chairman of the Senate Subcommittee on the Handicapped under the Committee of Labor and Public Welfare.[16]

Congress, with input from the National Rehabilitation Association, the House Committee on Labor and Education, the Senate Labor and Public Welfare Committee, and the GAO adopted the Rehabilitation Act amendments, including the civil rights anti-discrimination provision that later became section 504, and sent it to the Nixon White House. Several liberal amendments were included, in addition to continuing appropriations for vocational rehabilitation. More severely disabled persons were brought into the vocational rehabilitation program and, in fact, the word "vocational" was dropped because there was a shift in emphasis away from employment as an exclusive goal and more toward life adaptation. An Office of the Handicapped was proposed, to be created within HEW, and an Architectural Barriers Compliance Board was to be established to enforce the ineffectual Architectural Barriers Act of 1968. The amendments, at first, did not contain what later became section 504. These were added by staff members late in the legislative process. Richard Scotch in his book, *From Good Will to Civil Rights,* pp 49-50, gives credit to Jack Duncan, staff member to the House committee, and a former assistant to Commissioner Mary Switzer of HEW. Scotch says that the idea for including an anti-discrimination provision in the Rehabilitation Act of 1972 came up in late August at a meeting of staff members to discuss the marked up bill. Staff members were concerned that, when disabled persons completed vocational training, they would meet opposition from prospective employers reluctant to hire them. And of course, the idea of an anti-discrimination provision had also evolved from the Humphrey and Vanik unsuccessful amendments.

The Rehabilitation Act of 1972 sailed through both houses of Congress, with little debate, and almost no attention given to the anti-discrimination section, 504.

The bill landed on Nixon's desk, who in a fit of fiscal conservatism, (the price tag was $17 billion) refused to sign it, thereby pocket-vetoing it. His veto message of October 27,1972, complained of costs, new programs and administrative confusion, and intrusion on the prerogatives of the executive branch.[17]

The Washington Post for October 28, 1972, noted that Nixon had vetoed the bill, along with nine bills affecting the District of Columbia. On the same day he announced the sale of 300,000 tons of corn to China; the FBI halted file-keeping on members of Congress, Watergate data was being subpoenaed, and Vietnam peace plans were being drafted.

After the 1972 election, which Nixon won by a landslide, an almost identical vocational rehabilitation bill was introduced. Hearings were held. John Nagle, director of the Washington office of the National Federation of the Blind, testified:

> *"The provision...prohibiting discrimination against the physically and mentally impaired in any Federally assisted program is of major consequence to all disabled people as they strive to surmount the difficulties and disadvantages of their disabilities and endeavor to attain a normal, productive and fulfilling life. This civil rights for the handicapped provision brings the disabled within the law when they have been so long outside the law. It establishes that because a man is blind or deaf or without legs, he is not less a citizen, that his rights of citizenship are not revoked or diminished because he is disabled. But most important of all, the civil rights for the handicapped provision...creates a legal remedy when a disabled man is denied his rightful citizenship rights because of his disability. It gives him a legal basis for recourse to the courts that he may seek to remove needless barriers, unnecessary obstacles and unjustified barricades that impede or prevent him from functioning fully and in full equality with others."*[18]

After the hearings, both House and Senate again passed the Rehabilitation Act, now called "of 1973" instead of 1972, on March 15, 1973. House manager John Brademas, D-Ind., said not many Congressmen would "*want to vote against the crippled more than once in a session*." But Senate Minority leader Hugh Scott, R-Pa., said it was a *"budget buster"* and predicted Nixon would veto it. OMB Director Roy Ash said it was *"incapable of being administered."* Once more Nixon vetoed it on March 27, 1973. He lambasted the *"big spenders"* and said it could result in a 115 percent increase in income tax, and that it would *"cruelly raise the hopes of the handicapped"* because it was unadministrable. Further, he felt that it was not limited to vocational rehabilitation, but got into medical research and welfare programs, best handled by other programs. Majority leader Mike Mansfield, D-Mont., said there was a reasonably good chance Congress would override. Caspar Weinberger, Secretary of HEW, wrote an article in the Washington Post, April 3, 1973, supporting Nixon's veto. He claimed that Congress was *"playing political football with the hopes and aspirations of less fortunate Americans."*

An editorial in *The Washington Post* the same day urged Congress to overturn the veto. It was a *"meritorious bill which has become a pawn in the bitter struggle between an obstinate Congress and an equally stubborn President."* But the move to override failed by four Senate votes, even though about thirty disability groups assembled in the Senate chambers on the day of the vote. Republicans, initially 35 to 2 for the override, switched to 311-10 against. On the same day, John Dean invoked executive privilege in an attempt to block inspection of documents relating to the Watergate affair. President Nixon called the failure to override *"a resounding victory for the American taxpayer."*

After the two Nixon vetoes and the failure to override, the disabled community was outraged. A demonstration was organized in May 1973, by disabled people attending the annual meeting of the President's Committee on Employment of the Handicapped. The PCEH, as it was known, provided a focal point for diverse groups including the deaf, the blind, and the mobility impaired.

The annual banquet of the President's Committee seemed to be the logical time for a protest. In May 1972, more than 100 disabled persons, many in wheelchairs, marched down Connecticut Avenue, from the Washington Hilton, where the banquet was held, to the Capitol. In one rousing voice, they sang, *We shall Overcome.*

Organizer Judy Heumann outlined five complaints:

(1) Equal education opportunities;
(2) Job opportunities;
(3) Public transportation;
(4) Housing;
(5) High curbs, inaccessible bathrooms and lack of building access.

Some demonstrators had to be carried up the steps of the Capitol. Senator Harrison Williams, D-N.J., was the main speaker; a letter was read from Senator Humphrey who suggested the Civil Rights Acts be amended to include disabled people.

Eunice Fiorito, who is blind, and who later became president of the American Coalition of Citizens with Disabilities and a leader in the 1977 protests at HEW, described a demonstration after one of the President's Committee banquets:

> *"... We planned a demonstration at the Lincoln Monument. We all came out of the President's Committee the night of the big banquet, all of the kids had this march and demonstration and then had this all night vigil, over at the Lincoln Monument. I went to the banquet in my very formal outfit and then (demomstrated) in the rain for about six hours."* [19]

On May 23, 1973, the bill was reintroduced, for the third time, but this time with substantially less funding and fewer new programs.[20]

After both the House and Senate passed the bill, it landed on Nixon's desk. On September 26, 1973, Nixon finally signed the historic Rehabilitation Act of 1973, Public Law 93-112. In The Washington Post, the next day, there was a photo of Nixon (who had twice vetoed earlier versions) standing at his desk after signing, hands down, palms outstretched, with a look of utter disgust as though to say, "What monstrosity have I created?"

Thus was born the first federal law providing full civil rights in all areas of life (though limited to the "federal sector," a large universe) explicitly for disabled people. The single sentence in section 504, had been adopted, not because of a coordinated and universally agreed upon goal, but rather because of the vision of a few far-sighted Congressmen, Senators, and some disabled civil rights organizations. It was adopted with little debate and little understanding of its significance, as much by chance as by anything else. Yet it was to prove to be the Magna Charta, the Declaration of Independence, the Bill of Rights, and the gateway to equality for all disabled Americans. And it was to be the historical preceden t that brought about the Americans With Disabilities Act which, finally in 1990 (see Chapter Six), brought civil rights to theprivate sector.

Section 504 of the Rehabilitation Act of 1973 (now contained in section 794 of Title 29) is both majestic and maddening in its simplicity. The substance of the section says it all in just one sentence:

"No otherwise qualified handicapped individual in the United States...shall, solely by reason of his handicap, be excluded from the participation in, be denied the benefits of, or be subject to discrimination under any program or activity receiving Federal financial assistance or under any program or activity conducted by an Executive agency or by the United States Postal Service."

This single sentence sounded like declaring that "motherhood" and the "flag" are symbols of reverence, a conclusion against which hardly anyone can argue. It was a platitude, right up there with other world class platitudes such as "Honor thy father and mother" and "Have a nice day." Who would deliberately exclude disabled people from any reasonable activity? As a pronouncement of social policy it was beyond dispute, but it was a law—and a law which begged to be clarified, delineated, administered, and enforced. Indeed, the very simplicity of the section, no doubt, was responsible for its speedy and little debated advancement through Congress. The American public was almost totally unaware of its existence, as were many members of the disabled community, at whom it was directed. Yet in a few years this single sentence was to transform the American landscape as few one sentence pieces of legislation have ever done. As we will discover, the law required accessible facilities and programs for all federal projects and/or federally financed projects. Since most public schools and colleges receive federal financial assistance, this meant that the law was directed at most schools and colleges. The law required accessible buildings, accessible public transportation, non-discrimination in federal and federally financed employment; it meant ramps to buildings, railings, elevators in some cases, sidewalk curb cuts, and equal access to employment, education and housing.

While most of the world seemed indifferent to this important legislation (at least at the time it was passed), some members of the disabled community were not. Scattered throughout the country were various organizations in one way or another determined to push forward on disabled legislation. The black civil rights movement of the fifties and sixties served as a model for protest and politics. Some of the individuals and groups that had been involved in efforts for the handicapped in the sixties and early seventies began to get together to form a more cohesive lobbying effort. The Paralyzed Veterans of America (PVA), the Disabled American Veterans (DAV), the Easter Seals Society, the American Federation of the Blind, and many others were each in their own way beginning to coalesce into a somewhat coherent lobbying group.

In 1974 the American Coalition of Citizens with Disabilities (ACCD) was formed, in part, because of the impetus given by the Rehabilitation Act of 1973.

A leading organizer of ACCD was Dr. Frank Bowe, who became executive director. Almost totally deaf as a result of contracting measles while a child, Frank had long been a respected leader in the disability movement. Tall, boyish looking, and well liked, he had written several books regarding disability issues which became classics. He coordinated the various elements of ACCD and developed a plan of action. His ways were the ways of Washington: lobbying of the traditional sort. At times he disagreed with, and at times was overruled by, more militant elements of the coalition. To finance the protests, he utilized income from the books he wrote. He was able to get grant money from HEW, which ironically was used later to protest at HEW (something like biting the hand that feeds you?). Frank speaks quite well, and "listens" through lip-reading or sign.

He subsequently became Regional Commissioner in New York for Rehabilitation Services within the Department of Education. He is unquestionably a leader in the handicapped civil rights movement, and his several books on the subject are well written, well researched, and authoritative. He received an honorary doctorate in law from Gallaudet College and that year was the commencement speaker. He headed a United Nations delegation related to 1981 as the International Year of the Disabled. Today, Frank is a professor at Hofstra University in New York. In 1992 he received the Distinguished Servive Award of the President of the United States in recognition of more than fifteen years of contributions to disability issues.

Other organizers of ACCD were Eunice Fiorito, who is blind, Fred Fay, spinal cord injured, Al Pimentel, who is deaf (the first President of ACCD), Roger Peterson, who is blind, Deborah Kaplan, T.J. O'Rourke, who is deaf. In San Francisco, Mary Jane Owen and Judy Heumann (both use wheelchairs) were leaders.

Those just mentioned, along with Frank Bowe, were unquestionably the leaders of the disability civil rights movement during those heady days. All were severely disabled and all were motivated by the desire to obtain greater civil rights for disabled people. They were disgusted with discrimination in all areas of life. They knew that government financial hand-outs were not the answer. They wanted a level playing field and equality of opportunity which had been consistently and cruelly denied. Many are continuing their efforts today in other phases of the great cause. In 1990 most of the same leaders worked actively and successfully for the Americans With Disabilities Act. The entire disabled community is forever indebted to these faithful and fearless leaders.

If Bowe was urbane and conservative, Eunice Fiorito was the opposite. Growing up in Chicago, she was blinded by disease while in high school. In the fifties she worked at a sheltered workshop for ten cents an hour. She graduated from Loyola University in Chicago and subsequently moved to New York City, where she had a job with the Democratic administration of Mayor Beame, working on handicapped issues. She campaigned for Carter both before and after his nomination in New York City during the summer of 1976. Working in the Americana Hotel, she helped set up some of Carter's campaign stops, including one of the first after the nomination, in Warm Springs, Georgia. Warm Springs was a center for people with paralysis, and the disabled community thought it a hopeful sign that Carter would begin his campaign there.[21] Later, she became an official at the Rehabilitation Service Administration of the Department of Education.

Fred Fay suffered an injured spinal cord at age 16, as a result of a fall fro m a back yard gym. Later, he obtained a Ph.D. at the University of Illinois. His mother, Janet Fay, like Fred, has long been active in civil rights issues for the disabled. At the time ACCD was organized, Fred Fay proposed a national demonstration with techniques borrowed from the black civil rights movement. Fred was a cofounder of the Boston Center for Independent Living, which is one of over 200 centers throughout the country. The Center has promoted advocacy, attendant care, and training skills for apartment living. Some centers run housing complexes for disabled people.

Judy Heumann had contracted polio at an early age; as a child in New York City, she was told by teachers that her wheelchair was a fire hazard. She received a BA in speech pathology from Long Island University in Brooklyn and an MPH in administration and planning from the University of California, Berkeley School of Public Health. After graduating from college, she was denied a teacher's certificate and was told that she was not suitable for the occupation of teaching. She turned to the courts and a law suit! Later she helped found the World Institute on Disability, headquartered in Berkeley, and she travels extensively to speak in foreign countries on issues relating to access. In 1989 and 1990, she appeared before Congressional Committees debating the Americans With Disabilities Act and her lobbying efforts helped enact that historic legislation. She is the recipient of the Disability Rights Education and Defense Fund Edward M. Kennedy Life Achievement Award. She is a member of the Executive Committee of the National Council on Independent Living. In 1990 she was the recipient of the Henry B. Betts Award. The prize of $50,000, established by the Prince Charitable Trusts, was presented to her at the Library of Congress.

Mary Jane Owen also was, and still is, a leader. Due to a form of meningitis, she has several disabilities and uses a wheelchair. In 1977 she was in San Francisco as a leader in the San Francisco takeover at HEW. She has become a nationally recognized writer and speaker on disability issues. She directs Disability Focus in Washington, D.C., which is concerned with disability issues, especially civil rights. Like so many others, she lobbied strenuously for the passage of the Americans With Disabilities Act in 1989 and 1990.

Another leader of ACCD was Terrence James ("T.J.") O'Rourke, who was profoundly deaf. T.J. attended the California School for the Deaf, Gallaudet University, the University of Maryland, and Catholic University. He taught at Gallaudet and at residential schools for the deaf in North Dakota. Subsequently he joined ACCD, first as vice-president and then as president. As time wore on that winter and it became evident that there was going to be a protest, those in ACCD who were government employees became apprehensive for their jobs. Eunice Fiorito, though nominally president, was represented in discussions with government officials by T.J., who subsequently became president of ACCD. T.J. went on to found a successful publishing company located in Silver Spring, Maryland. The company publishes literature relating to the hearing impaired, including a text book on American Sign Language. T.J. has been a leader in promoting American Sign Language rather than Signed English. (Although Signed English is used by a majority of the hearing impaired, it is a derivative of English. American Sign Language, on the other hand is more independent of English and thus is really a second language, usable by other groups such as Hispanics.) He was coauthor of *A Basic Course in American Sign Language*. Regrettably, T.J. died in January 1992.

Al Pimentel is deaf and is presently an instructor at a school for the deaf in Connecticut. Back in the seventies, he helped draft the articles of incorporation and by-laws for ACCD. Roger Peterson is blind and is a scientist in Palo Alto, California. He was on the board of directors of ACCD and was also the office manager. Deborah Kaplan uses a wheelchair. An attorney, she presently works for the World Institute on Disability in California. In the seventies, she was on the board of directors of ACCD.

ACCD was a loose coalition of various disability groups, which however, did not contribute financially in a sustaining way, and that led eventually to its demise in 1983. Ironically, the ACCD received a sizable grant, about $50,000 from HEW, for the purpose of research, but some of the financial support went toward promoting the 1977 protest at HEW. Even after the sit-in, HEW continued funding ACCD. It was only after the Reagan Administration cut off funds that the organization went out of existence.

The ACCD claimed to represent 84 national, state and local organizations of and for virtually every category of handicap. It was governed by an annual delegate assssembly and a board of directors elected by the assembly. The member organizations represented over seven million of the nation's thirty-six million disabled persons. Some organizations that it represented included the American Council of the Blind, Coalition for Barrier Free Living, Disabled in Action from various states, including New Jersey, New York, and Pennsylvania, the National Association of the Deaf, National Association of Physically Handicapped, National Paraplegia Foundation, Association for Children with Learning Disabilities, National Association for Retarded Citizens, Goodwill Industries, Easter Seals Society, Children's Defense Fund, and many others.[22]

ACCD was very concerned that section 504 of the Rehabilitation Act of 1973 was not being implemented by HEW. The Rehabilitation Act had been passed in 1973, but regulations still had not been issued at the beginning of 1977. Regulations were of crucial importance, because without them, the one sentence platitude, that was section 504, was but an empty shell. In addition, section 504 did not mention that regulations were to be issued, and some government attorneys felt there was no need and no authority to issue them.

President Ford, before leaving office in 1977, decided that the responsibility for implementing section 504 fell on HEW. The newly appointed Secretary of HEW, Caspar Weinberger, had his agency write to the Senate Labor and Public Welfare Committee asking how to administer the section, a difficult question in view of the absence of legislative history. Members of the Senate Subcommittee on the Handicapped responded that there was a statutory mandate to administer the Rehabilitation Act; in effect, though the act contained no provision for regulations, regulations were to be issued. The task of preparing the regulations was delegated to a division within HEW, the Office for Civil Rights (OCR). A young attorney, John Wodatch, was given the task of drafting proposed regulations, along with a staff which included Ann Beckman.[23]

Others, who helped, included Raymond (Bud) Keith, himself blind, and Ed Lynch, an attorney who had worked for the President's Committee on Mental Retardation. Caspar Weinberger's successor as Secretary of HEW, David Mathews (also a Republican) worried about drafts of regulations being prepared in his agency. But even as drafts of regulations were being prepared, there continued to be doubt as to whether section 504 gave any authority to HEW to issue regulations.

In the summer of 1968, not too long after the riots in Washington, D.C. following the assassination of Martin Luther King, a severely disabled young man using leg braces and canes, entered Howard University Law School, which was situated not far from the riot devastated downtown area. The student body, overwhelmingly black, was preoccupied with civil rights for racial minorities. James L. Cherry, the disabled young man, was one of a few white students. Cherry had a difficult time climbing the hill to the law school, getting up the steps and into class. He asked the dean for a handicapped parking space and a key to the elevator, since some of his classes were on the second floor. His requests were denied. Cherry had to continue to struggle up the stairs, and in class he listened to discussions of civil rights issues – which did not include elevators for handicapped students. As previously pointed out, the black civil rights movement served as a precedent and a model for the disability effort, but specific examples documenting it are hard to find. For Cherry, at least, the analogy between civil rights for blacks and civil rights for disabled people was all too painfully obvious, though the point was seemingly lost on the law school administration.

At Howard University Law School, Cherry's feelings crystallized and he subsequently became an advocate for civil rights legislation. He lobbied the state legislatures in Georgia and in Kentucky and was influential in bringing about state access laws long before the federal government began considering similar legislation.

In the seventies Cherry had to use a wheelchair to get about. Fed up with the delay in issuing section 504 regulations, James L. Cherry took it upon himself to begin litigation, which in retrospect was of great historical significance. Cherry is a disabled veteran whose disability, a rare muscular disease, required him to be discharged from the navy in 1965; he later spent 19 months, mostly in bed, at Bethesda National Institute of Health. While confined to bed, he became more and more interested in disability issues and in the fact that, while section 504 had been passed in 1973, HEW Secretary Mathews was still fiddling with drafts of regulations in 1976. He first brought an administrative proceeding against HEW under the Administrative Procedure Act to get HEW to issue regulations. Cherry then wrote for Congressional materials relating to section 504, and while a patient at NIH organized his lawsuit against Secretary Mathews. A lawyer by training, he single-handedly developed briefs and a litigation strategy while confined to his hospital bed. Although he attempted to rally the support of some of the disability groups, his pleas fell on deaf ears, and he basically had to act alone.[24]

Later he was joined by the Georgetown Law Center Public Interest Law Institute, called INSPIRE, and together, they brought suit against Secretary Mathews, demanding that regulations be issued under section 504. The trial was handled by Victor Kramer, who ironically had been a legal colleague of the next HEW Secretary, Joseph Califano.

On July 19, 1976, Judge John L. Smith of the United States District Court for the District of Columbia ruled in favor of the plaintiffs, James L. Cherry and the Action League for Physically Handicapped Adults, and against the HEW Secretary, David Mathews. Judge Smith held that section 504 was not self executing, and Congress contemplated "swift action" which required HEW to issue regulations promptly. HEW initially denied there was any authority to issue regulations, but all the while its attorneys were working on drafts of regulations. Further, Judge Smith ruled that there was too much delay and regulations were to be issued *"with no further unreasonable delays."*

Spurred on by the decision in Cherry v. Mathews, work on the regulations continued. By the end of the summer of 1976 the regulations still had not emerged, though drafts were being circulated. Jimmy Carter was campaigning for president, and in November 1976 was elected. The disability movement had ties to the Democrats and to Carter; his election sent a signal that some progress would be made. All during this time the HEW attorneys were drafting and redrafting; the secretaries were typing and retyping, coffee breaks in the halls of HEW and conferences with "policy makers" were going on continuously. During that summer and fall of 1976, the HEW staff consulted with various groups, not only the disabled community, but also the National League of Cities, the National Governors Association, and the U.S. Conference of Mayors. Also consulted were the American Hospital Association, the National Association of State Directors for Special Education, the Council for Exceptional Children, the National Association of College and University Business Officers, and the College and University Personnel Association.

In the meantime, the disabled community was fretting. By the fall of 1976, three years had gone by since the passage of the Rehabilitation Act, and still there were no signs of final regulations under section 504.

To be sure, drafts of proposed regulations were circulated. Secretary Mathews was concerned about several provisions. By January of 1977, revisions had been made to reflect his concerns. The requirement, in the proposed regulations, that they cover certain alcoholics and drug addicts was retained over his objections. State agencies were to be required to supervise and control local agencies in their administration of section 504. Federally financed entities were required to pay a "fair" wage to disabled workers, but not necessarily a minimum wage.

On January 10, 1977, Martin Gerry, Director of HEW's Office of Civil Rights, submitted the final proposed regulations to Secretary Mathews for his approval and publication in the Federal Register. But on January 18, two days before he left office and a few days before Jimmy Carter's inauguration, Secretary Mathews decided that the proposed regulations were too controversial, and the intent of Congress too ambiguous, for him to sign. Accordingly, he sent the draft regulations to the Senate Committee on Labor and Public Welfare, asking for their comments or approval. In a letter to Committee Chairman Harrison Williams, Mathews stated that the language of section 504 was unclear. Many, including the disability groups and some staff members of OCR, thought it was a stall.

In fact, about two weeks earlier, members of the disabled community discovered that Mathews intended to send the regulations back to Congress. Dr. Frank Bowe, Dan Yohalem, Miriam Edelman, and a half dozen others gathered outside Secretary Mathews' office to protest. Secretary Mathews said section 504 was only one sentence while the regulations were fifty pages long; he said he couldn't predict the intentions of Congress. Infuriated, Frank Bowe and others began to yell and scream at Mathews. After three years of delay and innumerable hearings all over the country, sending the regulations back to Congress was an absolutely outrageous and unusual move. An executive agency charged with administering and interpreting a law was choosing not to do so and was turning to Congress to ask "how" to do it. If every agency thus returned every issue to Congress with a request for an advisory opinion, Congress would have no time to do anything else! Yet, given the Rehabilitation Act's ambiguity and lack of legislative history, Congress got what they deserved from Mathews. Also, the strategy cleverly, albeit temporarily, removed HEW's responsibility for adopting regulations that would require far reaching changes in buildings, schools, employment, and other programs.

The disabled community, however, saw nothing clever about the move; they thought it was a cop-out and they were enraged. In the meantime, pressure by the disabled groups in the courts continued. The July 1976 decision in Cherry v. Mathews, requiring Mathews to issue regulations, was reopened and in January 1977, on the same day that Mathews sent the regulations to Congress, the federal district court issued a restraining order directing the Secretary to cease further delay and to issue regulations. On January 19, the order was stayed by the U.S. Court of Appeals in order to give a full hearing. Secretary Mathews' involvement in the suit became moot with his resignation, but the court order, in theory, continued to apply to his successor, Joseph Califano.

The Cherry case is significant because it was one of the first successful lawsuits brought by an individual, acting for himself, against a federal agency with the purpose of improving civil rights for disabled people. As a result, the section 504 regulations were ordered by federal court to be issued by a federal agency. It was also significant that James Cherry's efforts were not supported by disability organizations; civil rights for disabled people, at this time, rested in the hands of a few individuals, with institutions and organizations lagging behind. To put Cherry's accomplishment in perspective, a year after his successful suit in 1977, he was on the board of directors of the Action League for Handicapped Adults, in Louisville, Kentucky, which received county funding. When word spread of his successful lawsuit, he was removed from the board, because his civil rights involvement was regarded as too extreme. Civil rights was not a popular pastime in many areas in the mid-seventies, particularly in the South. The Cherry case was basically the result of one disabled man being fed up with the status quo, and he had the determination, courage, and ability to do something about it.

Jimmy Carter was duly sworn in as president in January of 1977, and one of his first acts was to appoint Joseph A. Califano Jr. Secretary of HEW and heir to the 504 controversy.

Califano had been a bright student at a college founded by the Jesuits, Holy Cross in Worcester, Massachusetts. He graduated in 1952, a year ahead of the author. He became an even more notable student at Harvard Law School, graduating magna cum laude in 1955, again a year ahead of the author. His law degree, along with excellent review credentials, earned him a job in New York with the blue stocking firm of Dewey, Ballantine. Hours of drudgery doing corporate law resulted in boredom, which prompted him to seek a political career in Washington. He became a deputy to Secretary of the Army, Cyrus Vance, under the LBJ administration. He became known in Washington for his smarts and political savvy. He was extremely competent and extremely affable, but with an explosive temper. When Carter became president, he became a star in the cabinet galaxy, as Secretary of HEW. He was regarded as an excellent choice.

But Califano, urged to sign the proposed regulations immediately, instead, delegated them to a task force.

With the new administration, the ACCD decided it was time for action. Dr. Frank Bowe became executive director of the ACCD, and Eunice Fiorito, who is blind, became president. As time wore on and there were still no signs of final section 504 regulations, the ACCD, and Bowe, Heumann, Fay, O'Rourke, Fiorito, and the others became more and more concerned. Mathews' decision to table the regulations, and the installation of the new administration, meant that it was time to move. The ACCD assembled a coalition of diverse groups representing a substantial number of the nation's 36 million disabled persons. Other concerned individuals and groups included Deborah Kaplan, director of the Disability Rights Center, a Nader-founded organization, Kitty Cone, Roger Peterson, Reese Robrahn of the American Council of the Blind, and Daniel Yohalem from the Children's Defense Fund. These individuals and groups had been meeting continually with HEW. They agreed to have Daniel Yohalem represent ACCD. He wrote to Califano:

> *"The Department's failure to issue regulations has meant that hundreds of thousands of intended beneficiaries of HEW programs throughout the country who are handicapped continue to be subjected to discrimination in employment, health, social services, education, and access to programs."*

Frank Bowe and Eunice Fiorito thought it was becoming clear that the new administration was stalling and there was fear that the drafts of regulations would be weakened. The ACCD Board decided that action was necessary.

What exactly were the concerns of the disabled community? What did they want from section 504 and what did they want from Califano? First, it should be pointed out that the focus at this time was entirely on the federal government, because 504 only related to federal programs and federally funded programs. Concentrating on the federal government had a precedent. Very early in the black civil rights movement, leaders attempted to make an issue of racial discrimination in the Defense Department. While the federal government was broad, it was not the entire universe. But within the umbrella of federal jurisdiction, there were significant issues. If the federal government could be persuaded to accommodate their needs, perhaps the private sector would follow.

And what were the needs? Disabled people had been excluded from admission to many schools and colleges, and even if admitted, were treated rather badly because of barriers, architectural and otherwise. Today a curb cut in a sidewalk allowing access to a wheelchair seems a simple, almost universally accepted concept. (There are, these days, curb cuts in such unlikely cities as Tijuana, Mexico.) The simplicity of the idea seems, in retrospect, almost comparable to such outstanding examples as the invention of the wheel and sliced bread. Curb cuts, like many other things, became obvious realities in retrospect, but unknown and possibly unimagined before the miracle of their invention.

In 1976 and 1977, curb cuts were largely unknown. And what difference did it make? The answer is, a great deal. Disabled people were isolated from the mainstream of society. They were isolated from the good things of life because good things cost money and money meant you have to have a decently paying job. A decent job means you have to have the skills to do the job which, in turn, means that you have to have an education and training. Disabled people felt that colleges and universities were closed to them because of their inaccessibility. This meant that jobs were not available, and even if jobs were available in many cases, you couldn't even get from your home to your place of employment because you couldn't get on a bus. Even if you managed to get to a job location you often couldn't even get into the building where the job was. All because of a scarcity of curb cuts.

But, of course, curb cuts were not the entire story. There was the problem of no elevators and no ramps. There was the problem of inaccessible facilities on buses, trains, and planes. There was the problem of housing because, in many cases, you couldn't even get into the building, but if you could, you couldn't get into an apartment, but if you could, then you couldn't get into the bathroom!

And diverse disabled groups had their own different concerns. The problems of blind people were different from the problems of deaf people, which were different from the problems of the mobility impaired. But they all wanted one thing which could be summed up in a word: *access.*

The ACCD installed themselves in a tiny 10 foot by 15 foot corner storage area at the end of a hallway in a Connecticut Avenue brick building owned by the International Association of Machinists. Joseph Califano was seen as *"the one person whose signature could transform the lives of tens of millions of disabled Americans."* [25]

In another link with the black community, Frank Bowe arranged with Clarence Mitchell, head of the Washington branch of the NAACP, to meet with Califano, who insisted he had never heard of 504 until a few days earlier. The ACCD decided they should go to the White House. They did, in fact, meet with Stuart Eizenstat, Carter's domestic adviser. Eizenstat told them Carter was committed to cabinet government, but *"don't worry, Joseph Califano is a reasonable man."* [26]

Peter Libassi, General Counsel of HEW, invited Bowe to HEW. Libassi believed the regulations were long overdue. As reported by the Washington Post on March 30, 1977, Libassi spoke out:

"The Secretary did not want to sign the regulations and put his name on a document when he was not sure of what the consequences of the new regulation would be. The feelings of the disabled community were not unjustified. These people have suffered injustices for a long time. They finally get a bill past Congress. And now the Secretary won't sign."

With the disappointing start of the new administration, the disabled community was in a frenzy. ACCD received letters, phone calls, and telegrams from all over the country.

"Organizational membership [in ACCD] doubled, then tripled, as people with deafness, blindness, cerebral palsy, paraplegia, quadriplegia, mental retardation, and epilepsy, together with their families, counselors, teachers and friends sensed in ACCD a vehicle for the long awaited breakthrough that would transform their lives."[27]

As Frank Bowe said almost ten years later, *"We had a tremendous effort of sending thousands upon thousands of letters, telegrams, phone calls to every organization of or for disabled people. We also printed up thousands of buttons that said, SIGN 504. People sent us money. The phone never stopped ringing! Never! It was unbelievable! The response was overwhelming! We put people in touch with their local demonstration leaders. People threw themselves into this. Nobody could have anticipated that kind of outpouring.!"*[28]

Dozens of lawyers offered help, including lawyers from the Children's Defense Fund and the Georgetown University Institute for Public Interest Representation (INSPIRE). Others involved were Judy Heumann, Mary Jane Owen, Kitty Kone, Harold Snider, Ed Roberts, Tom Gilhool, Frank Laski, Fred Fay, Andrea Schein, Fred Schreiber, and Terrence O'Rourke.

Les Whitten, of Jack Anderson's column, said to Bowe: "This isn't a legal battle, Frank. It's a political one. What you need now is pressure. And more pressure." Bowe personally flew around the country, talking up support.

Eunice Fiorito thought the time for talk was over and it was now time to act. Eunice and Frank didn't always agree. The anecdotists told of Eunice, blind, shouting in the general direction of Frank, who of course, being deaf, didn't hear a word.

In any event, the ACCD determined that it was time to act. The decision was made to concentrate on Califano, and it was agreed that there should be a takeover.

On March 18, 1977, Frank Bowe of the ACCD sent a letter to President Carter, with a copy to Califano. A deadline was set. If the regulations weren't signed by April 4, there would be a massive sit-in and takeover at HEW offices in Washington as well as in ten other cities – Boston, Seattle, New York, Atlanta, Kansas City, Philadelphia, Chicago, Dallas, San Francisco, and Denver.

The HEW reaction was a freeze. No one at HEW was permitted to talk to Bowe.

ACCD lobbied Congress. Rep. John Brademas, D-Ind., a strong advocate for disability civil rights, promised his support. Democrats and Republicans on Capitol Hill urged Califano to sign the regulations. Mayor Beame of New York City, whose father was blind, supported the movement. In a newspaper interview, Frank Bowe said:

"This is not a sudden effort. This is an action we are taking only after 3 1/2 years of quiet and patient work with people in the government to urge them to implement the law. We have failed, and I believe the disabled people of this country understand what they must do. We are demonstrating Tuesday because the secretary has refused to sign the regulations."

March went by and still no action.

In a column in *The Washington Post on March 26, 1977, Jack Anderson wrote:*

"The disabled are furious over what they see as a retreat by President Carter on his promises to help the nation's 28 million handicapped. The handicapped, in what would be their most forceful protest in history, are also considering blocking traffic with wheelchairs and vans. They attracted national attention in 1973 when they ringed the Nixon White House with wheelchairs. Some time after April 4, unless Carter acts on their demands, on March 18, 1977, blind mothers, palsied children and medal wearing paraplegics from the Vietnam war plan to swarm into the HEW offices. Already, placards are being designed, chants written, and a network of recruiters set up...The anger among handicapped people stems in part from Carter's dramatic campaign promise to make the disabled active partners in our attempts to achieve...full civil rights. Carter blasted the Ford administration for refusing to enforce equal rights laws for handicapped job seekers. The disabled took Carter at his word and supported him by large majorities. After Califano took over the HEW, one of his first actions was to stall even further by appointing a task force to study the equal rights legislation. Handicapped people felt they had been betrayed once again."

Frank Bowe wrote in his letter to Carter: *"Vast numbers of us endorsed your candidacy and worked vigorously for your election...We are dismayed by this apparent breach of faith..."* He warned that if there continued to be no action, by April 4 the handicapped would be forced to *"implement nationwide political activities."*

On March 31 Peter Libassi revealed some of the proposed changes that Califano wanted to make. Some were trivial, but others, according to Frank Bowe, were major and would have had a devastating effect on the disabled community (*Handicapping America*, Harper & Row, 1978, p. 209).

April 1 arrived and with it the first spring daffodils, jonquils, and magnolias. The cherry blossom buds at the Tidal Basin were gently swelling, in preparation for their annual explosion.

Yet another explosion was brewing. Joseph Califano got wind of the storm clouds and became nervous. He was somewhat paranoid about leaks from HEW's secretarial staff. He made John Wodatch, one of the draftsmen of proposed regulations, swear that his secretary was reliable and leak-proof. Out of fear of disclosure, Califano transferred Wodatch's office from the old HEW building to the new one, closer to Califano's supervision.[29]

On Sunday, April 3, Eunice Fiorito, the blind president of ACCD, was in New York, where she lived. She had been commuting to Washington practically all during the winter and spring for various ACCD conferences. That Sunday, she knew that the next day was the deadline for the signing of the regulations, and if they weren't signed, the demonstrations would certainly begin on Tuesday. Yet, she didn't want to go to Washington. She worked for Democratic Mayor Beame, and she somewhat feared for her job. At least, she was concerned about embarrassing a Democratic administration. Her ex-husband visited her apartment and told her, *"Eunice, you're president of ACCD; there's no way you can't go."*

Monday arrived and a meeting was arranged to include Secretary Califano, Peter Libassi and his task force, and representatives of the disability groups. Califano began the meeting at 1:30 in the afternoon, by explaining that delay was needed in order to become familiar with the new rules in the proposed regulations. He praised the sit-ins planned for the next day and compared them to Martin Luther King's tactics.[30]

But disabled leaders felt that more delay was unreasonable. They abruptly walked—wheeled themselves out—of the meeting with TV cameras rolling. Califano was upset and hurt. But the deadline set by the protesters for Califano to sign the regulations would not be met that day. Tomorrow the demonstrations would begin.

The next day, Tuesday, Eunice Fiorito in New York City, put on her rust colored suit, guided herself along the well traveled path to the kitchen where she made coffee and a small breakfast, then took a taxi to LaGuardia Airport. Heavy rain delayed departure for several hours. Finally, around two in the afternoon, she arrived at Washington National Airport, and a taxi quickly took her to the HEW Hubert Humphrey building on Independence Avenue, Southwest.[31]

Already, on that Tuesday morning, April 5, the demonstrations had begun. In the morning, scores of disabled persons, led by Frank Bowe, visited the Capitol to talk to Congressmen and hold a press conference. *"The Secretary has failed to fulfill the promise of equal rights,"* he said. He felt that Califano wanted time to put in *"loopholes, waivers, and exemptions."* Despite the appeal of hundreds of lame, blind, and deaf citizens, there was opposition. *"You have to remember,"* one said, *"that these [proposed] regulations were written by the same folks who banned boys' choirs and father-son dinners in public schools."* Some complained that the Rehabilitation Act, section 504, was passed with little debate and no hearings.

Bowe and others then marched down Independence Avenue to the HEW building at the foot of Capitol Hill. Three hundred disabled people flocked into the building, many in wheelchairs. Some carried signs saying, *"We Want 504."* Joseph Califano had given orders to allow free access to the HEW building, a tactic which upset Frank Bowe and his two lawyers as they marched down Capitol Hill. Califano invited Bowe with some others into his sixth floor office on this fateful Tuesday morning.

Frank Bowe declared Joe Califano to be wily as a fox.[32] Waiting until the last day of the deadline (Monday, April 4), he had summoned Bowe and others to his office and invited the press and TV cameras. He announced that he *"endorsed"* the demonstration. He said, *"I have asked all HEW personnel to cooperate fully with the protesters in their exercise of constitutionally protected free speech."*

The protesters continued to fill the HEW corridors. They then went to Califano's reception room on the sixth floor where those in wheelchairs, deaf and blind people, and many others congregated. Harold Snider, who is blind, tells the story of blind people helping wheelchairs up the curbs because curb cuts on sidewalks were unheard of in Washington, and that was part of what the protest was about. At the time, Harold Snider worked in the National Air and Space Museum located diagonally across the street. The Museum had accessible restrooms, unlike HEW; Snider, a federal employee, risked his job by inviting disabled people to use the rest rooms at the Museum. Ironically, the Hubert Humphrey building, where the demonstration took place, was accessible, and the old HEW building had access for wheelchairs at the rear of the building on C Street. But the protesters weren't satisfied with that, any more than the blacks in the south were satisfied with being told to sit in the back of the bus. The protesters wanted more accessible federal buildings, more accessible federally funded colleges and universities (which is just about all of them), and more accessible anything funded with federal funds, including housing and places of employment. The protesters were tired of being excluded from the social mainstream and they were very weary of promises. The federal government became the focus because of the power and breadth of the government and because it could not be expected that without federal action, society would suddenly become benevolent and do what was only right and fair.

Once inside the building, negotiations began with Bowe and others on one side and Peter Libassi, the HEW General Counsel, and Ben Heineman on the other. Heineman was a well known Ivy Leaguer with an impressive resume. Bespectacled and pipe smoking, he informed Bowe that after a while, no other protesters would be allowed in (but anyone could leave!), and no other supporters bringing food would be allowed in. Libassi recalled that on the day before:

> *"I had the Secretary meet with the group of handicapped representatives and they walked out on him. Joe Califano did not take kindly to that. He had put himself out, had been willing to meet with them; they asked him two questions and then got up and walked out, and they had the TV cameras there taking pictures of them walking out. OK, guerrilla warfare was a little passe at that point. It was 1977, and that was not going to move people on policy."*[33]

As Tuesday morning wore on, the protesters assembled outside Califano's office. He came out of the inner office and stood on a coffee table. *"Small beads of sweat were forming on my forehead and upper lip,"* he said in his book, *Governing America.*[34]

Although he was receptive to the protesters he was not about to sign the regulations then and there, but promised they would be signed "soon." He said the previous administration had two and a half years to look at regulations and he was entitled to two and a half months. But he was shouted down. Frank Bowe got up and said:

> *"Mr. Secretary, with all due respect, that statement is not what we came here for. We've heard 'soon' too many times for the word to have any more meaning. And if you are serious about ending the injustice we are protesting, WE ASK THAT YOU ISSUE RULES, AND DO IT NOW."*

The room erupted. Califano, speaking above the shouts of the crowd, said that regulations presented difficult questions such as whether a drug addict or alcoholic should be considered "handicapped." *"I will do my best to be as fair as I can and to act on your just and legitimate needs."* Outside HEW, about 200 protesters marched in a circle, carrying placards and singing, "*We Want 504*" and civil rights songs of the sixties. One of the protesters, George Reed, who was 65, black, and blind, said, *"I marched for my civil rights as a black man in the sixties. I never thought I would see this day come when handicapped people would rise up and demand their rights. We've been begging for a long time. Now we're demanding our rights."* [35]

Califano's concern about drug and alcohol addicts possibly being protected by regulations was not a whim, but was part of the Califano psyche. Califano had been a four pack a day cigarette smoker until he quit in 1975. He began a crusade against substance abuse; in 1992 he began the Center on Addiction and Substance Abuse.

In the meantime Eunice Fiorito, having shuttled from New York City to Washington, D.C., was being helped by several deaf Gallaudet college students to get out of a taxi in front of the building, She arrived in Califano's office in the middle of the speeches. A cheer went up as she was recognized. When she approached Califano, she towered over the short and stocky man.[36]

Finally Califano left. The group started singing *We Shall Overcome* and *We Shall Not Be Moved*, songs borrowed from the black civil rights movement, and *We Want 504.* HEW officials informed the group that HEW would not be responsible for problems resulting from lack of medications if anyone should need medication. All present realized there were many who did, including some with heart conditions.

As the day wore on, many of the protesters left the building, but a small group of them, from fifty to seventy-five, decided to spend the night. They settled on rugs in the large, plush, outer office or in chairs, but there was little sleep. They were not allowed to bring in food. The protesters then insisted that they would not negotiate unless food was brought. The answer was that HEW was NOT a hotel. Peter Libassi, HEW General Counsel left, but returned at 2 A.M. The group decided they would keep him up all night. Defying instructions, someone found a bag of apples, which was confiscated when discovered.[37]

Joseph Califano was livid over the all night sit-in. *"They stayed in the HEW building. . .overnight, and Joe was really upset about that, because he did not want to sort of say this was a reawakening of the sixties. (His attitude was) 'we're not going through this crap anymore. It's bad politics. It's bad for the country. It's bad for the causes to think that sit-in demonstrations were the way the government was going to make basic policy.'"* [38]

The GSA guards said the protesters had to be evicted, if not arrested, but Libassi said, no way:

> *"With the seeing eye dogs too? What are you going to do with the electric wheelchairs? Can you get them in the paddy wagon? You guys must be kidding. All I need is that. And dropping somebody. So they finally abandoned all notions of that, and they agreed that the negotiated solution was the way."* [39]

The next morning, Wednesday, a delayed decision was made by Califano himself to give each person one cup of coffee and one doughnut; previously, he had prohibited food from being provided.

Califano in his book, *Governing America*, said he issued a statement:

> *"They seek redress for discrimination they have suffered...The lawful actions of handicapped men, women and children...are in the great tradition of the nation." He asked HEW personnel to be "especially sensitive to these demonstrators and to respect their sincere exercise of fundamental First Amendment rights."* [40]

That Wednesday morning, after spending the night in the HEW building, some wanted to leave, but Frank Bowe and others feared a dribble exodus that would weaken the protest; they finally voted to leave the HEW building en masse, after about 28 hours inside. For this, they were later criticized by the San Francisco protesters, who were to spend weeks inside the San Francisco HEW building.

The day before, protests had begun simultaneously in ten other cities in which HEW had regional offices, including San Francisco and Denver. The Denver protesters were disappointed that they were not arrested; one reason was that the Denver jails were inaccessible to disabled people. The protest in San Francisco was the lengthiest; the sit-in took several weeks. The protesters there were more experienced and more militant, and they were sustained during the long weeks by Safeway Stores and the Black Panthers, who brought in food and supplies. Mary Jane Owen, who is visually impaired and uses a wheelchair due to multiple impairments, was one of the leaders of the San Francisco protest, along with Judy Heumann. Owen described the plans that were laid that spring:

> *"The bone-chilling cold of the vast expanse of the converted car dealership forced us to huddle around a small electric heater. We had come after hours to plan a West Coast response to the Washington D.C. based American Coalition of Citizens with Disabilities (ACCD) [which requested] that we plan some sort of rally or event to focus attention on the slowness of the Carter*

administration's campaign promise to move to formalize the civil rights protections for disabled citizens. Our passion ran high and I remember assuring Judy Heumann that, if we planned to sit in, I would be there as long as anyone. The others agreed. We would plan to stay ourselves and suggest to others that they come prepared for such an event, but not to make a point of confrontation. We were not yet sure others would care to follow our example." [41]

The San Francisco protest was well organized. The press and city officials were briefed. Many of the protesters had friends in government. The agenda was set. Mayor George Moscone and Congressman Phillip Burton were sympathetic. The protesters entered the HEW building and spent the first night on the hard floor. The next day, mattresses were brought from the State Health Department. Food arrived from McDonald's and from Safeway. The Mayor himself brought in shower attachments to be used in the rest rooms.

The protesters at one point got out of their wheelchairs, assisted by their blind, deaf, and mentally retarded cohorts, and sat on the floor in the long corridors. They formed a human chain, all facing the same direction, and each massaged the shoulders and neck of the person in front. Each received and passed along the touch. As Mary Jane Owen recalled years later, "*After those evenings of connection, the floor seemed not quite so hard as we located spots around and under the desks. Love and kindness grew with each day. We were a family--a close community of shared concern.*" Mary Jane Owen and others began a hunger strike, taking only fruit juice for days. After days, then weeks, bodily needs had been cared for, including at least one instance of copulation in front of Mary Jane Owen, who didn't notice, however, being visually impaired. At one point, for those who didn't join the hunger strike, Black Panthers were prohibited from bringing food in, a situation that ended when Congressman Burton appeared. As Mary Jane Owen said later:

"There were so many - Steve, who lay, day after day and night upon night, taping events around him on a tape recorder because he knew that what was happening was important enough to risk his health; Jeff, who brought his guitar and proved to be a master cheer leader with chants on the bull horn. He wrote new words for old civil rights songs with which we loudly greeted federal employees in the morning; the members of the Butterfly Brigade, a gay street patrol that loaned us their walkie talkies when officials turned off our telephones; the deaf woman who entered the building to teach a class in sign language and stayed; the mentally retarded woman who always injected a note of realism into our too-abstract deliberations late at night when we talked of possible arrest or forcible removal." [42]

Guitar playing Jeff, mentioned by Mary Jane Owen, is Jeff Moyer, who is blind. In addition to his musical interests, he is director of technology at the Cleveland Sight Center.

Kitty Cone, who uses a wheelchair, was another leader of the San Francisco protest. Years later she reminisced:

> *"Everybody was involved in a committee. There was the food committee, for instance. They were involved in soliciting food. There was a fund raising committee. There was a Sunday morning religious service committee. And one of the things I remember the most was the amount of singing we did. It was very reminiscent of the black civil rights movement. We sang all the time. We sang 'We Shall Overcome.' We sang civil rights songs."* [43]

Judy Heumann, who uses a wheelchair due to polio, and who is co-director of the World Institute on Disability, was another leader of the San Francisco sit-in at HEW. As she recalled:

> *"We really had no opposition. We were sleeping on mattresses provided for us by our state Department of Health. And there were also demonstrations that took place down south in California, near Pasadena."* [44]

The San Francisco sit-in began on April 5 and ended on April 28. Fifty of the 120 people who burst in on April 5 remained until the end. They left only when it was official that Califano had signed the regulations. The 25-day occupation of HEW offices in San Francisco became the longest occupation of a federal office by protestors in United States history.

The Washington protesters, unlike those in San Francisco, were, on the whole, naive. Little thought was given to whether they would disobey laws, or to whether they would be arrested (in fact, none were), or what they would do if arrested. Many forgot to bring medication. And almost nobody had prepared to spend the night.

In retrospect, the Washington protest, along with the cumulative effect of protests in other cities, was remarkable in that it was entirely peaceful, it was short-lived, but its consequences were extraordinarily far reaching. It was almost a model of a successful effort to put pressure on a reluctant government – pressure that was immediately felt, almost to a point of panic, which eventually led to receiving most of what was asked for. And the disabled community owes a large debt to the black civil rights movement – as debt almost entirely due to the advantage of precedents and techniques set by the black civil rights movement, rather than from explicit support, although the Black Panthers in San Francisco were of great help. Frank Bowe, director of ACCD, had been in contact with Clarence Mitchell, head of the Washington office of the NAACP. Though blacks endured so many lynchings, assassinations, and fire bombings, the disability movement, thus far at least, has neither initiated nor been the recipient of violence.

In looking at the relationship between those in the civil rights movements of the sixties and the disabled community itself, perhaps a potent point could be made for the fact that the disabled community, unlike the blacks, had no visible enemy—precisely because they, themselves, at that time were mostly invisible. Certainly, all of the disabled are indeed indebted to all of those who protested during those fateful days.

Another factor contributing to the success of the handicapped movement was the legacy of the FDR New Deal, Kennedy liberalism, and LBJ's "Great Society." It was a time when "liberal" was not yet an unmentionable word. Many liberal politicians rose to national prominence on issues relating to the disadvantaged and the poor. The general consensus was that you would shoot yourself in the foot if you opposed such policy. Only a few hard-headed Republican conservatives would dare. Although Nixon and Ford did not share those liberal ideas, many in Congress were liberal Democrats who favored legislation for disabled people. It was a time when the federal budget deficit was much smaller and not an issue.

Paradoxically, although the federal legislation up until 1977, relating to disabled people, was almost entirely due to Democrats in Congress, the heat of the 1977 protests was directed at a Democratic president, a Democratic secretary of HEW, and a Democratic-controlled Congress. This was mostly due to timing; there was a long repressed and pent up demand for action, as well as disappointment that the promises of the Carter administration on behalf of disabled people had not been immediately fulfilled.

The Washington protesters left the HEW building on Wednesday afternoon, April 6, feeling they had really accomplished something, but they were not entirely sure when, if ever, the 504 regulations would be signed. In the meantime in San Francisco, the demonstration continued, and it continued for several weeks. The San Francisco protesters, being residents of Protest City, were more experienced and more militant. The sit-in continued for more than two weeks. Finally, the San Francisco protesters voted to leave the building and go to Washington, D.C. to continue the squeeze. Mary Jane Owen, however, stayed in San Francisco in order to maintain pressure there.

Judy Heumann, a leader of the San Francisco group, was also vice president and a board member of ACCD. Frank Bowe had mixed feelings about their coming to Washington; Frank's approach was traditional lobbying; he was used to Washington ways and he saw some, in the San Francisco group, as radicals. Nevertheless, the San Francisco group flew to Dulles airport, and took a van to a friendly District of Columbia church, where they were invited by the pastor to spend the night. Instead of sleeping, they began a strategy session around midnight. The participants were mostly in wheelchairs; some were blind or deaf.

Everyone was considered equal. All listened as each, around the table, shared life histories and ideas of what should be done. At 3:30 in the morning, they voted to chain themselves to the Soviet Embassy the next day, but Frank Bowe, appalled, talked them out of it. The theory was that they thought they could get better treatment in the Soviet Union than in America, but then, Frank asked them how many had ever been to the Soviet Union. Finally, the whole idea was dismissed as being ridiculous.

At this point it was about five in the morning, and the decision was made to go to Califano's home. Bowe objected to this, for he did not see it as the Washington way and thought it an intrusion on the privacy and family of a public figure. He was outvoted and early that morning a van unloaded outside Califano's home in Northwest Washington. (Califano in his book, *Governing America,* mistakenly says that there were demonstrations outside his home on Sunday, April 3, two days before the HEW demonstrations began. This did not actually take place until later in April, as witnessed by Bowe and Fiorito.)

The protesters brought candles, and assembled outside Califano's home. They sang songs from the sixties using slightly different words:

"Tell Jimmy Carter, we will not be moved. Tell Califano we will not be moved like a tree that stands by the water. We will not be moved."

Califano's golden retriever went out to investigate, but Califano quickly brought him back in, fearing an unpleasant headline if a wheelchair protester was bitten. Finally Califano went out his back door and was driven to HEW. The San Francisco group went to the White House for an all day protest, and a small group led by Judy Heumann had a meeting with Stuart Eizenstat. Califano's home was guarded by security people and police. On Friday, two dozen of the group tried to speak to Califano at HEW but were turned away by armed security guards.[45]

The San Francisco group followed President Carter to his church – again, against the wishes of Frank Bowe. A few days later, the group left for home.

The *Washington Post*, in an editorial on April 7, grumpily said:

"Mr. Califano was absolutely right to refuse to sign these regulations...They are terrible regulations, confusing, prolix, complicated, fuzzy and bound to do far less for the disabled seeking fair play than for the lawyer, seeking a guaranteed annual income."

The editorial was concerned that under the regulations, employers might be required to hire drug addicts. A footnote to history is that Califano, in earlier years, had been legal counsel to *The Washington Post*.

Letters to the editor by Frank Bowe and Marilyn G. Rose, co-chairperson, Health Task Force, Leadership Conference on Civil Rights, complained about the editorial, pointing out that HEW had already held 22 hearings on the regulations while Califano continued to rehash matters previously considered.

At seven in the morning of April 28, in her apartment in New York City, Eunice Fiorito received a call from Peter Libassi who said that Califano was going to sign the regulations that day.

Indeed, Secretary Califano finally signed the Section 504 regulations on April 28, 1977. The next day The Washington Post quoted him as saying that the acceptance of 504 regulations would "*work fundamental changes in many facets of American life and opens a new era of civil rights in America.*" HEW estimated that the cost of implementing them would be 2.4 billion dollars, primarily for education. The Washington Post, in an editorial on May 1, gave grudging approval. The revised regulations, according to the editorial, were better, but they predicted a "*welter of lawsuits and quarrels. ... Hopefully, the positive values involved in the drive to end discrimination against the disabled are what will prevail.*" George Will, in a column on May 5, said that "*To be fully effective, the new HEW regulations really require a degree of social consciousness that if it existed, would make the regulations unnecessary...now the handicapped are moving toward full citizenship. This has been a long time in coming because the handicapped are a varied and invisible minority.*"

Historians could debate whether the protest had any effect on Califano's decision to sign the regulations. Califano himself, told the author that the regulations would have been signed anyway.[46]

Others believe that the regulations would have been signed later but they would have been weakened; therefore, the protest was extremely effective. Califano said the delay in signing was, in part, due to his desire to study a difficult subject, to make possible changes, and also to provide media attention to inform the public, otherwise unaware of the significance of the issues.[47]

There is no doubt that Califano was put off by, and felt threatened by, the protesters. And, there was more than a slight chance that the regulations would have been weakened by exemptions, exclusions and waivers. John Wodatch, a leader in drafting the regulations at HEW, said the protest served to put the regulations at the top of Califano's agenda and persuaded him that the issue was really a civil rights issue.[48]

Another point was that President Carter was going to hold a White House Conference on the Disabled the next month, which was planned to attract disabled people from all over the country. If the regulations had not been signed, few in the disabled community would have come, a result the White House would have found intolerable.

Kitty Cone, a leader of the San Francisco sit-in, said later:

"I think [the protest] was really a turning point in the disability rights movement. It helped us to be seen as an oppressed group with a legitimate struggle for civil rights. I think there are many things today that we take for granted. Bathrooms are accessible. Curb cuts. Access in so many different ways is either directly or indirectly a result of those regulations." [49]

Judy Heumann said,

"...there's not a doubt in my mind that those regulations would not have come out the way they did had we not been working in a national coalition ...There was a real sense of victory and power which was not an illusion....people believed at that point that they could make a difference. I think we really felt that we had nothing to lose...We were willing to do anything to get what we believed in. There's not a doubt in my mind that it was worth it. It was another stage in the movement and that's what's important, to give a historical perspective to the movement...We should remember that the movement has been going on for hundreds of years, and we continue to play an important role. We need to work in broad based coalition, not just cross-disability, but cross-movements. Every individual has the ability to make a difference and abrogating that responsibility is an individual failure." [50]

Dr. Frank Bowe said later,

"Was it worth it? Without any question. There was a Louis Harris poll that was just released...This was the first national poll ever to ask people with disabilities about their lives. The overwhelming majority said their lives had improved greatly in the last decade, probably because of 504. But here's my point: those of us who did it, and there were many of us, I don't think we ever had a chance to have such a massive impact on the lives of tens of millions of people. That was a very unprecedented event. And that's why I don't think any of us ever experienced anything quite so great." [51]

The disabled community could rightly claim success. They had marched for something extraordinarily important and had achieved it. They had overcome!

CHAPTER IV

THE 504 REGULATIONS

Five years ago, Greg Solas, now 39, lay pinned under a twenty ton bridge girder that had slipped when a crew tried to lift it onto the Route 25 overpass for Cape Cod's Bourne Bridge. Solas, who now uses a wheelchair as a result of that accident, invoked section 504 in a blizzard of cases. So far, violations have been found in 37 schools, mostly in Rhode Island. If Rhode Island doesn't comply, the state could lose 27 million dollars in federal funds. Critical of Solas' enthusiasm is John F. Sharkey, director of special services for the Warwick School District. Said Sharkey: "We will do what we have to do, but taking our resources and diverting them to re-cutting doors that may never be used is a terrible mistake – an absolute disgrace." But in April 1991, Sharkey signed a compliance agreement with the U.S. Department of Education consenting to correct 57 violations in six schools, costing about $250,000 to make changes ranging from providing raised lettering signs for blind students to installing accessible bathrooms.

The telephone rang unexpectedly in Eunice Fiorito's New York City apartment early on the morning of April 28, 1977. It was Peter Libassi, the HEW General Counsel, who said that Califano was to sign the 504 regulations that morning. Later in the morning, Califano called a press conference and said that he had signed the regulations at 7:30 that morning. The 504 regulations were published in the Federal Register on May 4, 1977.

Under these historic regulations, qualified disabled individuals could not be denied enrollment in schools and colleges, could not be denied employment in the federal sector, could not be denied accessible public transportation. Although the regulations did not apply to the private sector, the federal sector was very broad and included schools and colleges receiving federal aid (practically all of them), most airlines, and urban transportation. The complex and lengthy new regulations required that all new facilities built with the assistance of federal funds must be designed to be fully accessible. All existing facilities had to be made accessible within two months, with substantial structural changes such as ramps or elevators having a three year grace period.

As Frank Bowe in "Changing the Rules" said, the regulations

"changed the entire fabric of American society, from day care for preschoolers to public education, from vocational-technical trade schools to Harvard and Stanford Universities, from the subways in New York City to the airport in Seattle, from the libraries in Portland, Maine, to the senior centers in San Jose, California." [1]

The news of the signing of the regulations was front page, lead story news in The Washington Post, April 29, 1977. The article quoted Califano: *"The regulations would work fundamental changes in many facets of American life and opens a new era of civil rights in America."* An accompanying photo showed sit-in protesters, Karen Emerson and Chris Brewer, in wheelchairs, embracing when they heard the news. HEW estimated that the cost would be 2.4 billion dollars, mostly for education.

Denning Gearhart, who uses a motorized wheelchair, said of the regulations:

"Hopefully, the era of Tiny Tim is gone forever. We've been too used to sitting on Bob Cratchit's shoulder, saying, 'God Bless Us Every One,' instead of saying: Dammit, I'm as qualified as the next person."

The 504 regulations took at least three years to finally adopt. Some minor revisions were made in first drafts, but on the whole, the regulations appeared to give the disabled community what they wanted. The April 1977 protests, no doubt, speeded up the signing process and added pressure on an already beleaguered Joseph Califano. Peter Libassi, the HEW General Counsel under Califano, said that Califano was initially skeptical about the draft regulations. He *"saw the regulations as a reflection of the demands of the disabled groups without appreciation of the political and financial implications."*[2]

An important point about the 504 regulations is that they served as a model for regulations under the Americans With Disabilities Act of 1990, described in Chapter Six. Section 504, as we discussed, only applied to the federal sector, including entities that received federal subsidies. This led to anomalies. For example, airlines that received federal subsidies were subject to 504, but airlines that did not, were not. Some private schools that received no federal subsidies were not subject to section 504. Section 504 was progress, but it left holes. The holes were filled later, in 1990, when the Americans With Disabilities Act did for the private sector and the sector of state and local government what section 504 had done in the federal milieu.

The 504 regulations thus far have been of tremendous benefit to the disabled community, although there have been some court cases interpreting them that have been discouraging. Also, an offshoot of the HEW 504 regulations, the Department of Transportation regulations, has had a stormy, and still not entirely resolved, history. See Chapter Fifteen. (Various federal agencies, including DOT, HUD, and the Postal Service were charged with the task of "borrowing" from the HEW regulations and the principles contained therein, and publishing their own regulations relating to their own jurisdictional role, i.e., buses, trains, and airplanes, in the case of DOT.)

To understand the present impact and meaning of the section 504 regulations, some history may be appropriate.

Section 504 of the Rehabilitation Act of 1973 did not, as such, require implementing regulations. Nor did it say which federal agency would do the implementing, if it were required. After inquiries from HEW staff to the Senate Labor and Public Welfare Committee and its Subcommittee on the Handicapped, the committees responded that HEW, in the person of Secretary Caspar Weinberger, was indeed, the logical entity to implement the new statute. Within HEW, the Office of Civil Rights (OCR) was assigned the task. The Rehabilitative Services Administration, within HEW, declined the responsibility. This was probably due to the fact that the Rehabilitation Act of 1973 gave RSA responsibility over the vocational rehabilitation portions of the act, but not over the civil rights portion.

The OCR staff quickly established itself as pro-equal rights and affirmative action in their approach to writing regulations. They believed that factors such as cost or inconvenience were irrelevant when a target entity was required to comply. OCR director, Peter Holmes, delegated responsibility for the regulations to his deputy, Martin Gerry, who had participated in the important case of Lau v. Nichols, relating to bilingual education in public schools. Gerry was assisted by John Wodatch, a young attorney who also had a rights orientation. Other staff members included Ann Beckman, attorney Raymond (Bud) Keith, and Ed Lynch, also an attorney.

One problem that the OCR staff immediately encountered was that the definition of "handicapped" in the Rehabilitation Act was too restrictive; it evolved from the vocational rehabilitation objectives of previous legislation. It defined "handicapped" as any individual who (A) has a physical or mental disability which would constitute a substantial handicap to employment and (B) can reasonably be expected to benefit in terms of employability from vocational rehabilitation services.

The difficulty with this definition was that it confined the term "handicapped" to the employable and, within that group, a class that would benefit from vocational training. It excluded many others, such as the unemployable, severely disabled, the elderly, children, and the like. Further, it rested on an erroneous premise because the Rehabilitation Act was not directed solely at employment but covered a wide range of life activities, including housing, transportation, and education. The OCR staff met with the Subcommittee on the Handicapped and as a result a broader definition of handicapped became the law in lieu of the earlier definition. Under the Rehabilitation Act amendments of 1974, the term "handicapped" was defined as

> *Any person who (A) has a physical or mental impairment which substantially limits one or more of such person's major life activities, (B) has a record of such impairment, or (C) is regarded as having such impairment.*

Category (B) was intended to cover such cases as individuals who had had heart illness , and recovered, but were still discriminated against. Category (C) was intended to cover persons such as people with severe facial burns who may not have had a handicapping illness at all but who were regarded as having a disability and therefore were discriminated against.

The conference committee that approved this language also gave some legislative history, not only for the 1974 amendments, but also retroactively, when they injected legislative history that was missing when the 1973 act was adopted. The Committee indicated that 504 was indeed patterned after the anti-discrimination language of Section 601 of the Civil Rights Act of 1964 and section 901 of the Education Amendments of 1972:

> *[504] therefore constitutes the establishment of a broad government policy that programs receiving federal financial assistance shall be operated without discrimination on the basis of handicap. It does not specifically require the issuance of regulations or expressly provide for enforcement procedures, but it is clearly mandatory in form, and such regulations and enforcement are intended.*[3]

The conference report also specifically delegated to HEW the primary enforcement authority. The committee somewhat naively predicted that regulations would be issued by the end of 1974.

The Senate adopted the conference committee's proposed amendments, and the House followed suit, with a vote of 334-0. But President Ford vetoed the measure, objecting to costs and administrative complexity of the overall bill. The House then overrode the veto, 398-7, as did the Senate, (See the 90-1 Congressional Record, November 20, 1974, pp. 36621-22.) Then, because of difficulties with Ford's pocket veto, the same measure was passed again and sent to the White House, where President Ford signed it, in early December 1974, realizing that another veto would have been futile.

Even with the 1974 amendment redefining "handicapped," the OCR staff had to further spell out the term "handicapped;" at the same time they began the arduous task of drafting regulations, which, eventually, were to fill many pages. One problem with the term "handicapped" was finding a uniform definition suitable for various federal agencies with varying purposes. Another problem was relating the poor, the elderly, homosexuals, and both drug and alcohol addicts; were they all "handicapped?" John Wodatch believed that the poor, the elderly, and homosexuals should not be regarded as handicapped, but that addicts should, since addicts could be regarded as afflicted with a debilitating disease. This was to prove a controversial issue. Ultimately, drug and alcohol addicts were, in general, regarded as handicapped, but only under certain conditions. For example, there was no employment requirement for an addict who was disruptive or unable to do the job. This same controversy continued when the Americans With Disability Act was being debated.

Another problem faced by the OCR staff was whether to make existing buildings totally accessible, a costly proposition since many schools which were recipients of federal funds had old buildings that would be expensive to renovate. Yet, if waivers were applied everywhere, there would be little progress, except for new construction. Wodatch reached a compromise, in which "program accessibility" was substituted for "building accessibility," meaning that not every building had to be accessible if every program were in some way accessible. A stricter standard was offered for new construction, since pre-planning could result in lower costs. Wodatch recommended that new construction be required to conform to the barrier-free standards developed by the American National Standards Institute (ANSI), a clearinghouse and coordinating body for standards, including architectural standards – whose members include trade associations, professional groups, consumer groups, technical societies, and private companies.

After months stretching into years of drafting and redrafting regulations, the proposed regulation finally landed on Secretary Mathews desk. As Martin Gerry said:

> *"His basic inclination was to just let the whole thing go away; he didn't want to put out regulations ... He really just didn't get the idea that these were rights and that you really weren't talking about nice things to do for Easter Seal children. Then when we got to alcoholics and drug addicts, he really flipped out. These were obviously derelicts, and they were so far from Easter Seal children, things had truly run amok."* [4]

Although Republican Secretary Mathews didn't ask for specific changes in the draft regulation, he was able to table the regulations by seizing on a technicality. Executive Order 11821 required that any proposal by a federal agency requiring expenditures of over 100 million dollars had to include an assessment of its impact on inflation. It was obvious that 504 would cost at least that; Mathews asked for such an inflation analysis. Dissatisfied with the OCR inflation report, Mathews commissioned Dave O'Neill from a private consulting firm, the Public Interest Institute, who did a study and concluded:

> *"The benefits forthcoming (psychic as well as pecuniary) provide a substantial offset to the costs that will be incurred. The cost involved will not be as great as is widely thought and the compelling situation of some of the handicapped persons involved tips the balance in favor of proceeding with immediate implementation of the regulation."*[5]

After the inflation report was received, Martin Gerry again, on March 11, 1976, resubmitted the draft regulations to Secretary Mathews. Disability groups began having meetings with the OCR staff, but the regulations were stuck on Mathews' desk. Congress, in the form of Senators Williams and Randolph, put on pressure. Disabled leaders protested the delay in David Mathews' office in the spring of 1976. Finally, draft regulations were issued to the public on May 17, 1976. Interestingly, Mathews' doubts were so strong that the regulations were not even "proposed" regulations, unlike the usual situation where regulations are first proposed, and then after public comment, finalized. That is, instead of a Notice of Proposed Regulations, there was only a Notice of Intent to propose regulations. In other words, the regulations were sort of a draft of a draft. A thirty-day period was allowed for comments; hundreds were received. OCR staff held hearings in ten cities. Disability groups favored the draft; opposition came from recipients of federal funds who objected to cost. A new draft was published on July 16, 1976. Some drug addicts and alcoholics continued to be regarded as "handicapped," despite protests. The draft did not exclude Medicaid providers from the requirements. A sixty-day comment period was provided.

Disability groups which continued advocating for regulations included the American Council for the Blind, represented by Durwood McDaniel, and Frank Bowe and Eunice Fiorito from the American Coalition of Citizens with Disabilities, along with many others. OCR staff began to hold "town meetings" at twenty-two cities throughout the country where local involvement and dialogue were sought.

As publicity became more widespread, more interest developed and the comment period was extended to October 14, 1976. Over 850 written comments were received. Major issues were referred by the OCR staff to Secretary Mathews. These included the drug addict and alcoholic issue; Mathews retained the provisions defining these persons as "handicapped." State agencies were to be required to inform local agencies of their responsibilities. Federally financed institutions were to be required to pay a"fair stipend" to disabled workers, but it did not have to be the minimum wage.

On January 18, 1977, two days before he left office as a result of Jimmy Carter's victory over President Ford, Secretary Mathews sent the final package of regulations, all 185 pages, to the Senate Committee on Labor and Public Welfare, in effect asking them to explain what Congressional intention was when the Rehabilitation Act of 1973 was enacted.

The move surprised everyone. It was the final stalling tactic. When Joseph Califano took office a few days later as Mathews' successor, he was to meet a storm of controversy from disability groups. That story is told in Chapter Three; the story ended (with only minor changes made by Califano) with astounding victory for the disabled community, when Eunice Fiorito's telephone rang early that morning of April 28, 1977.

A postscript to the signing of the 504 regulations is that a few weeks later, in late May 1977, the first annual White House Conference on Handicapped Individuals was held at the Sheraton Park Hotel, attended by over 3000. It was a celebration of the new historic regulations. There were many speakers—Califano and heads of other federal agencies, including DOT, Labor, and HUD. Evelyne Villines, who had had polio, was now the head of Iowa's office of civil rights. She stated that what was needed to give full legal protection to disabled people was an amendment to the Civil Rights Act of 1964. The crowd was generally exultant and demanding. Harold Snider, who is blind, tells the story of his meeting a man of short stature, who stood up on Harold's table and told him what was going on, a true symbiotic relationship.

President Jimmy Carter was the featured speaker and gave a sincere and moving speech, a model of the art of rhetoric, to the triumphant crowd. He praised the leaders of the disabled community for their long and sometimes discouraging struggle. He said he was going to enforce the newly signed section 504 regulations. *"And Joe Califano assures me and assures you that these regulations are going to be enforced."* He praised Max Cleland, the disabled veteran who became head of the Veterans Administration. He praised his teacher, Julia Coleman, who was a principal in a tiny country school he attended when he was a country boy. Though severely handicapped, she taught him how to write and to enjoy music, how to debate, and how to appreciate works of art. He said:

> *"For too long, handicapped people have been deprived of a right to an education. For too long, handicapped people have been excluded from the possibility of jobs and employment where they could support themselves. For too long, handicapped people have been kept off the streets and sidewalks, have been excluded from private and public transportation, and have been deprived of a simple right in many instances just to communicate with one another. ...*
>
> *"Your conference is important. You're intelligent, courageous leaders. But because you have experienced suffering and because you have overcome it, I think the recommendations that will be coming from you that will affect the*

lives of many millions of people now and in the future will have the same extra dimension. Our country needs you, and I know that you will never disappoint those who look to you for leadership. Thank you very much."

The historic section 504 regulations were in place. They have proven to be enormously effective in requiring access to schools and colleges for disabled students, in requiring accessible airplanes, trains, buses, and federal buildings. Incredibly, during the early eighties, the Reagan Administration, crusading against "unnecessary" regulations, tried to abolish them, but Vice President Bush, after protests from the disabled community, came to the rescue and the section 504 regulations were not changed!

CHAPTER V

THE DISTRICT of COLUMBIA SUBWAY

Imagine, if you will, a spaceship from earth landing on a distant planet, known to be civilized but as yet unexplored. The doors open, and out jump two astronauts, wearing heavy shoes to counteract a weak gravitational force. Something in the planet's magnetic system results in the metal shoes being immovable, and the astronauts are unable to proceed farther to explore the new civilization's version of restaurants, doctors, dentists, girls, bars, movie theaters, clothing stores, and an intergalactic McDonald's.

Though an exaggeration, this was something of the predicament of people with disabilities, up until the mid-seventies. Though mobility was possible through expensive taxis or uncertain friends, otherwise disabled people had extreme difficulty in traveling to any destination in any modern city. Buses and subways were totally inaccessible to wheelchairs, and there were no sidewalk curb cuts, or ramps in buildings.

Disabled people have been and continue to be, by far, the least employed, the least mobile, the most isolated, and the most impoverished of any minority. They are the *Untouchables, the Pariahs, the Disenfranchised*. They have been trying to improve their lot, and in some cases succeeding. Public transportation that is accessible has been a sore point. Getting from Point A to Point B is a challenge and a frustration. How can you have a job if you can't get to the work place?

The District of Columbia in 1960, like most large cities, was almost totally inaccessible to disabled people, particularly wheelchair users. There were no curb cuts in sidewalks, no accessible buses, few buildings had ramps, and there were practically no accessible restrooms or telephones. Handicapped parking spaces were non-existent, as were handicapped license plates. Taxis might or might not stop for a wheelchair user.

The National Federation of the Blind (NFB) can rightly claim credit for helping bring about federal legislation that provided for equal access for disabled people in the District. The legislation set in motion forces that were to transform the District from a city that was almost totally inaccessible to one that, today, is quite adequately accessible.

In 1970, with the urging of the NFB, the old District of Columbia City Council passed a non-binding resolution that deserves to go down in history as one of the more enlightened pieces of work of any City Council. Call it, if you will, a Magna Charta of civil rights for disabled people. The reason it was non-binding was that at that time the District still could not make a move without the approval of the House and Senate District of Columbia Committees. There was no home rule; there was a commissioner form of government with commissioners appointed by the president. One prominent commissioner, who functioned somewhat as a mayor, was Walter E. Washington. One of the council members, Dr. Henry S. Robinson Jr., presented the following resolution, which deserves to be quoted in full:

NOW THEREFORE BE IT RESOLVED by the District of Columbia Council that:

Section 1. It is the policy of this city to encourage and enable the blind, the visually handicapped, and the otherwise physically disabled to participate fully in the social and economic life of the city and to engage in remunerative employment.

Section 2. The blind, the visually handicapped, and those otherwise physically disabled have the same right as the able-bodied to the full and free use of the streets, highways, sidewalks, walkways, public buildings, public facilities, and other public places.

Section 3. It is the policy of this city that every totally or partially blind person should have the right to be accompanied by a guide dog, especially trained for the purpose, without being required to pay an extra charge for the guide dog.

Section 4. Private businesses, owners and operators, are hereby called upon to assure blind and physically handicapped persons the same treatment as is afforded other persons.

Section 5. It is the policy of this city that the blind, the visually handicapped, and those otherwise physically disabled shall be employed in the District of Columbia government, and in all other employment supported in whole or in part by public funds on the same terms and conditions as the able-bodied, unless it is shown that the particular disability prevents the performance of the work involved."

This somewhat rudimentary resolution was the first civil rights statute in the District for people with disabilities. Two years later in 1972, somewhat improved and enlarged, its successor, Public Law 92-515, was passed by Congress and became incorporated into the D.C. Code as Section 6-1701 et seq. The fact that Congress had to pass a federal law that related only to the District was a relic of the historical notion that the District was incapable of governing itself, a notion which in spite of Home Rule and an elected mayor and city council, still has vestiges left today. But the fact that the House and Senate District Committees considered the law and Congress passed it, produced what might be described as an unexpected favorable turn of events for disabled people.

Because of the District of Columbia's unique status as a federal-city enclave, the legislation was federal legislation. But many states passed their own access and civil rights legislation, many of which predated federal law. In 1980, Georgia became one of the first states to pass a voting access law, requiring polling places to be accessible to disabled people, and to provide auxiliary assistance such as TDD transmitted information. Following the lead of the states, in 1984 the federal government passed Public Law 98-435, the Voter Accessibility for the Elderly and Handicapped Act, requiring cities and towns holding federal elections to make the polling places accessible.

The District of Columbia equal access law was a federal law giving, for the first time, civil rights to disabled people within the District, but it only applied within the District of Columbia. The very next year however, Congress passed, and President Nixon signed, the Rehabilitation Act of 1973 – which was the first significant federal law of national scope that gave civil rights to people with disabilities. Section 504 of that act applied in every city and town in the country, not just in the District. It applied to any federal program or activity. (See preceding chapters). Perhaps the District of Columbia Committees in Congress started the ball rolling by first endorsing the civil rights legislation applicable to the District, Public Law 92-515, in 1972. Civil rights for disabled people was clearly an idea whose time had come.

Public Law 92-515 elaborated on the 1970 City Council Resolution quoted above. Title 6-1701 repeats Section One of the Resolution. Section 1702 provides for equal access to "common carriers, airplanes, motor vehicles, trains, buses, streetcars, boats, or any other conveyances or transportation, hotels, lodging, public accommodations, public amusements or resorts." Section 1703 provides for architectural barrier free design requirements. The prohibition against discrimination in employment was expanded to cover employment with any employer, public or private, doing business in the District; disabled people were not limited to the dubious fate of working only for the city government.

Both the House Report (H.R. 92-1005) and the Senate Report, (S.R. 92-1238) to Public Law 92-515 give credit to the National Federation of the Blind for introducing the elements of the bill. Senator Tunney introduced the bill for the Senate District Columbia Committee and Congressman John L. McMillan introduced it for the House District Committee. Senator Tunney said the bill is to "*serve as a bill of rights for those residents of the District of Columbia who are blind or otherwise physically disabled.*" Public hearings were held by the Senate Committee on August 9, 1972; there was no testimony in opposition. A letter from Assistant D.C. Commissioner Graham W. Watt, on behalf of Commissioner Walter E. Washington, to Senator Eagleton, supported the bill. President Nixon signed it on October 21, 1972.

Public Law 92-515 (which for lack of a better description, can be called the "D.C. Equal Access Law") was of great historical importance, not only because it was the forerunner of federal legislation, enacted in 1973, that applied throughout the country, but also because it provided the basis for much needed improvement in access within the District. It became the District law that ALL sidewalks within the District had to have curb cuts at crossways for wheelchairs; today there's, at least, ninety percent compliance with that requirement. Charles Williams – Acting Chief, Construction Division, D.C. Department of Public-Works – recalls that there may have been isolated instances of curb cut installations in the District as early as 1973.[1]

In any event, on September 11, 1973, Director Wallace of the Public Works Department, through Deputy Assistant J. H. Brindle, Jr., issued a memo requiring that all new construction and repair projects at crosswalks in the District should be built with wheelchair curb cuts, according to specifications devised by the department. Although it may be impossible to pinpoint where and when the first curb cut was constructed, the event was of great historical significance to disabled people. The location deserves a plaque; to disabled people the event was as significant as Plymouth Rock, on which the pilgrims first landed in 1620.

Curb cuts in District of Columbia sidewalks have an interesting side effect. The District of Columbia is both a municipality in its own right and a location for federal buildings and federal jurisdiction. For example, there are city police and there are National Park Service (federal) police. The federal government has prescribed curb cuts for certain federal areas, near some federal buildings and federal agencies. For example, the Pennsylvania Avenue Development Agency is a federal agency which developed down town Pennsylvania Avenue. Here, the curb cuts conform to the federal design and they are wider and more gently sloped. Further out on Pennsylvania Avenue, the city design for curb cuts prevails. If the lawyers ever get stumped concerning the boundary between federal and District jurisdiction, they could ask some one in a wheelchair who rolls around on the streets and sidewalks of downtown Washington!

On May 15, 1973, the D.C. City Council approved a program of special parking for handicapped drivers. In August, 1973, Mrs. Erwin Griswold, who used a wheelchair due to polio, and who was the wife of Dean Erwin Griswold of Harvard Law School, became the first person in Washington to apply for and receive a handicapped parking permit. This program was sponsored by City Councilman Tedson Meyers, at the urging of Mrs. Griswold.

Subsequently, handicapped parking places were designated in cities and towns throughout the country. The disabled driver finds reserved handicapped parking spaces more than mere luxury; they are a necessity. One complaint is that there are not enough of them, and too many times the space is occupied by a nondisabled driver. Cities have become more aware of the problem, and in 1989 the District drastically increased the penalty for illegally using a handicapped parking space. In 1990 the City of Marlborough, Massachusetts, became possibly the first city to adopt, pursuant to state legislation, a program whereby fines and penalties for unauthorized parking would go into a fund to be used for the benefit of disabled people. Chapter 123 of the acts of 1990 was signed by Governor Dukakis on July 18, 1990, and much of the credit goes to Mary Dalpe, Director of Human Services in Marlborough, for her persistent lobbying effort.

With more and more states passing laws providing for licensing of handicapped drivers, and with handicapped drivers traveling more often in more than one state, a move was begun for uniform state laws providing for handicapped parking and licensing, so that the traveling driver could know what to expect. In 1983 Congress passed Public Law 98-78, which notes that since state laws vary, it is the sense of Congress that coordination among states, through the National Governors Conference, should work out problems. In 1987, in Public Law 100-17, section 161, Congress provided for a study of parking and driving problems for disabled travelers, with a view toward possible uniform state laws, the project to be coordinated by the Department of Transportation. Many states require special license plates with the wheelchair logo on it; others require either special plates or a card displayed in the windshield. A difficulty of the latter is that it is too easily abused.

The D.C. Equal Access law described above was also instrumental in bringing about a D.C. subway system that was accessible to people with disabilities. When the District of Columbia started planning a subway in the early sixties, some consideration was given to access to disabled riders, but it was to prove a long struggle, in which court litigation, protests, legislation and the involvement of several federal and local agencies, took place. Although the battle is far from over, today the District of Columbia has a modern, prize winning, usually well functioning subway system, with an adequate degree of accessibility for disabled people, as well it should. It is generally regarded as one of the best in the nation.

In the mid-sixties, the Washington Metropolitan Area Transit Authority (WMATA, or Metro, as it was known), planned a modern, 4.6 billion dollar subway and rail system, to have 87 stations and 97 miles of rail extending into Virginia and Maryland. All during the seventies, and even into the eighties, Washington streets were blocked off or restricted as jack hammers and pile drivers did their work, night and day. Even today the system is not completed, and construction continues.

The disabled community felt that it was absolutely necessary that the system be accessible. This meant either vertical elevators or inclined elevators, know as inclinators. Persons in wheelchairs and many on crutches are unable to use escalators. Without either elevators or inclinators, the entire system would be inaccessible. In 1964 representatives of the Washington Architectural Barrier Project met with officials of the National Capital Transportation Agency, the predecessor of Metro, to advise them of the needs of disabled people. The Senate Committee which approved legislation for the basic Metro system in 1965 directed that the system be made *"readily accessible to disabled, elderly, and all other handicapped persons."* The Architectural Barriers Act of 1968, which required access in any new construction funded with federal money, seemed to provide a legal requirement that the new subway system be accessible, as did the D.C. Equal Access law.

By 1967 Metro had vetoed the idea of a vertical elevator and suggested the inclined elevator. Although further study was needed for this proposal, Metro claimed that no funds were available for a study project.[2] Later, Mr. E.H.Noakes, a well known architect who had been involved in the problems of disabled people, undertook an extensive study of the inclined elevator idea under the aegis of the President's Committee on Employment of the Handicapped. The study, "Barrier Free Rapid Transit" presented by Noakes in 1969, was ignored by Metro,[3] not withstanding the Architectural Barriers Act of 1968 which required that all new buildings and facilities constructed with federal financial assistance had to be accessible. In 1970, a local television station aired the issue and noted the reluctance of Metro to do anything on the accessibility issue.[4] As a result of publicity, the Metro staff at a Board meeting on August 27, 1970, recommended that Metro apply for a grant from DOT to study the feasibility of an inclined elevator. At the meeting, a motion picture was shown showing Metro's General Manager sitting in a wheelchair while riding on an escalator, which served to demonstrate Metro's lack of real interest since use of a wheelchair on an escalator is usually impractical, not to say dangerous. DOT turned down the request for funds for a study project. There was evidence that it would cost $44 million to install inclinators at all Metro subway stops, and $60 million for vertical elevators. But the technology for the inclinator existed; it was in use in Stockholm, Sweden, and the Otis Elevator Company could build them.[5]

After being turned down by DOT, Metro then reversed itself and decided that a vertical elevator was most feasible. As footdragging by Metro continued, the GSA and the Washington Metropolitan Area Council of Governments urged the accessibility issue on Metro.

In 1971 members of the disabled community discussed mass protest, but it was decided instead to pursue the matter in court. Because of Metro's inaction, the law firm of Arnold and Porter and the Institute for Public Interest Representation, affiliated with Georgetown Law Center, were engaged. Suit was filed on April 19, 1972, by the Washington Urban League, Paralyzed Veterans of America, National Paraplegia Foundation, and Richard W. Heddinger, in the United States District Court for the District of Columbia. The involvement of the Urban League, which was black oriented, shows once more the connection between the black civil rights movement and the disabled movement. However, later, when the Gallery Place subway stop was closed by court order because of lack of access, and merchants in the area of Gallery Place protested that they were losing business, the Urban League, which had ties with the business community, dropped out of the litigation.[6]

At about the same time the suit was filed, Secretary of Transportation Volpe announced a $3.1 million grant to study the D.C. subway blueprints. The grant was made to the Metropolitan W ashington Council of Governments (COG).

A month later, on May 5, 1972, about 100 disabled people, mostly in wheelchairs, marched from the Washington Hilton (site of the annual meeting of the President's Committee on Employment of the Handicapped) to the Capitol, singing *We Shall Overcome.* A leader was Judy Heumann; the group complained about lack of equal job opportunities, accessible architecture, public transportation, and housing. Senator Harrison Williams, D-New Jersey, spoke to the group. A letter was read from Senator Humphrey who suggested that the Civil Rights Act of 1964 be amended to prohibit discrimination against disabled people.

The only individual plaintiff in the Metro suit to install elevators was Richard Heddinger, who uses a wheelchair, as a result of contracting polio in September, 1954, while he was a teenager. He spent a month in an iron lung, followed by almost two years in hospitals, in Delaware County Memorial Hospital and Sacred Heart Hospital in Norristown, Pennsylvania, and later in a rehabilitation center. In 1956 he began looking for a job, unsuccessfully, so he attended college at the University of Pennsylvania. He married in April, 1963; his wife also had contracted polio; they have raised two daughters. When Heddinger's wife first became pregnant, the obstetrician was "very distraught" about her having a baby and disclaimed any responsibility if anything went wrong. They found another obstetrician with a better attitude. Since they live in Bowie, Maryland, a Washington suburb, Richard got a job as a statistician for the Labor Department in Washington, but commuting presented a definite problem. This factor motivated his decision to join in the lawsuit.[7]

In the beginning, the plaintiffs sought only a temporary injunction which would prevent construction of Metro in such a way as to interfere with the eventual installation of elevators. Metro countered that such an injunction would bring all construction to a halt, including tunneling and construction of station stops, a far-fetched argument, since the suit related only to construction in the vicinity of the public access points. At a hearing before the House Public Works Committee, regarding the issue of access, Metro stated that it wanted to make the stops accessible but did not have the $65 million it would take for elevators, though the federal government had recently guaranteed some $800 million in WMATA bonds for Metro construction. Metro said that the bond money could not be used for elevators. At a court hearing on the injunction suit filed in April, 1972, Metro argued that because Metro was formed under an interstate compact it was not subject to federal law requiring access, another far-fetched argument. It was also argued that it could not spend federal money on elevators because elevators were not in the original Metro plans.

In June, 1972, Judge William B. Jones issued a declaratory judgment that the law required Metro to be accessible to disabled riders and that elevators must be provided, regardless of whether additional funds had been provided. The judge issued a bench order that did not interfere with construction immediately, but he warned that stops might not be opened if elevators were not provided. Judge Jones denied the request for an injunction because, although Metro was required by law to make the subway stops accessible, Congress at that point had not provided funds for the purpose. He gave Metro time to obtain funds for the elevators. At the end of June 1972, Congressman Kenneth J. Gray, D-Illinois, and chairman of the House Public Works Committee, angrily accused Metro officials of ignoring the law requiring elevators and "*flouting the direct will of Congress.*"

In July 1972 Metro officials were still stalling, not withstanding Judge Jones' threat. General Manager Jackson Graham and Deputy Manager Warren Quenstedt said there was a bill in Congress sponsored by Congressman Biaggi that would provide funds to study the problem; the officials thought the GSA should look into the matter. Ex-Congressman Carlton Sickles of Prince George's County, Maryland, opposed the elevators because he feared that funding elevators would leave Metro short of funds to extend the system into Maryland.

In October 1972, the House Public Works Committee added to the Highway funding bill $65 million for Metro elevators, saying that the refusal of Metro on this issue was "*intolerable.*" Chairman Gray said that if elevators were planned and installed during construction of the system, rather than after construction was completed, it would only cost $35 million.

In June 1973 Judge Jones, in an oral opinion, said that Metro will be forbidden to open any stations at all without elevators, and it was up to Metro to find the money. Finally, in August 1973 with Metro under construction but far from finished, the $65 million was provided in the Federal Aid to Highways Act. Federal funds would pay for 80 percent of the cost, but it was up to the local governments and COG to find the other 20 percent.

In early October 1973, Judge Jones issued the previously threatened injunction, because Metro had not firmly committed to constructing elevators before the stops were open to the public. The injunction prohibited opening stops unless they had elevators. Judge Jones said there was not enough progress and if Metro did not comply with the injunction they would be in criminal contempt. Metro officials agreed to comply. But it was not until the middle of 1974, four years after Metro construction began, that work was started on an elevator shaft at the first station.[8] In November 1973, the Metro Board officially voted to install elevators in the first five stops. But although Congress had voted funding for the elevators, the money had not actually been appropriated; Metro said it would borrow the money.

With Metro, the courts, and Congress finally committed to providing elevators, the first phase of the lawsuit was finished. But there was a sequel. The disabled community, studying the Metro plans, felt that at some stops, only one elevator was not enough and in some cases, the planned elevator was too far away to provide "ready access." So phase two of the litigation began.

In 1975 Metro came back to court asking that they be allowed to open three stations without elevators: Gallery Place, Union Station, and Farragut North. The disabled community agreed to exclude Farragut North because land for the elevator site had not been acquired. They also conceded Union Station, because of a contractor's strike. But they drew the line at Gallery Place. Gallery Place was an intersection between two lines. For people with disabilities, one elevator would not serve both lines. Also, the distance between the sidewalk, where the elevator was to be, and the train platform was too great. The injunction had said elevators had to be provided at each station, and Gallery Place, according to the plaintiffs, was two stations. Metro had agreed to provide an elevator, but only one elevator, and only when the "second" stop at Gallery Place was opened. Metro wanted to open Gallery Place without waiting for this elevator. Metro turned the argument around and said there was only one station at Gallery Place and only one elevator would be provided. The disabled community felt that one elevator was insufficient. Judge Jones upheld the plaintiffs and said that Gallery Place could not open without an elevator. As a result of Judge Jones' order, Gallery Place remained closed. Metro otherwise began to open, but trains had to speed by Gallery Place, not stopping, to the outrage of merchants such as Downtown Progress. With the merchants and the press adding pressure, finally GSA provided a waiver for Gallery Place, Judge Jones' order was avoided, and Gallery Place opened without an elevator, which was then being constructed. The GSA decision was given without input from the disabled community, who were caught off guard. With the station opened, but an elevator to be provided in the future, the disabled community felt it would be useless to attempt to overturn the GSA decision. They waited six months for the elevator to be completed.

Members of the disabled community were still pressing the issue of "ready access," and with the illness of Judge Jones, the case passed to Judge Oberdorfer. The plaintiffs wanted two elevators in some places, such as L'Enfant Plaza, Gallery Place, and Metro Center, and ramps in some surface stops. Judge Oberdorfer in an attempt to settle, advised a study group of the parties.[9] Compromises have been worked out. For example, if an additional entrance is ever provided at L'Enfant Plaza, it was agreed that a second elevator would be provided. (To reach some lines at L'Enfant Plaza, the wheelchair traveler today must use three elevators at three different levels.)

The issue of maintenance continues to be a problem, because the elevators do break down. The elevators often smell of urine, because Washington, D.C. is a city designed for people without kidneys. An article in the Washington Post, September 6, 1985, describes an elevator break-down at L'Enfant Plaza, causing a 2 1/2 hour delay for two passengers in wheelchairs, Lex Frieden and Ken Ogden. Habitual subway riders include Dennis Cannon, a quadriplegic staff member of the Architectural Barriers Board. Dennis Smur, of PVA, was also a subway commuter before his regrettable death in 1989. Both Dennises have been brilliant advocates in the cause of civil rights for disabled people. On the whole, except for second elevators at some stops, the subway system became reasonably accessible, and a great benefit to the disabled community. Officials within Metro began to be more willing to work with the disabled community to improve the system.

Metro puts out a guide called Metro System Guide for Senior Citizens and People with Disabilities. Reduced fares are provided for seniors and disabled riders. For visually impaired riders, there is a fourteen inch smooth granite strip at the edge of the platform. When a train approaches, lights along the platform edge blink to alert hearing impaired riders. At some subway stations, TDD's have been installed at public telephone booths for hearing impaired riders. Parking spaces have been designated for handicapped drivers at some Metro parking lots. The bus system is partially but not completely accessible to wheelchair users. Certain fixed routes have regularly scheduled lift equipped buses. Alternatively, a disabled rider may call in advance (sometimes 24 hours in ahead) to request a lift equipped bus at a certain stop.

Richard Heddinger, in his article "The Twelve Year Battle for A Barrier Free Metro" published in June 1976, in American Rehabilitation (before the first Metro stop opened), gave his opinion concerning the causes of the initial delay in providing elevators:

> *"I am convinced that the reasons [for the delay] deal with a lack of concern and ignorance of the desires, needs, and abilities of elderly and physically handicapped persons. There also exist among some a strong desire to keep the handicapped closeted. The view "out of sight out of mind" unfortunately still remains in some sectors of society. Far too few in society, be they METRO officials, designers, members of the public, or even rehabilitation experts, are able to admit maturely and realistically the possibility that they themselves, or their loved ones, may at some time in the future have a need to use the so-called "facilities for the handicapped" within METRO stations. The truth is that no one is immune. Full recognition of this most obvious fact will do more than anything else to assure that, in the future, there will be a barrier free, man-made environment for all."*

There are few forces as powerful as a successful idea. A Metro spokesperson[10] informed the author that originally, Metro opposed the elevators on grounds of cost, and on grounds of lack of utility by many disabled even if the elevators were constructed. But as time wore on, more and more began to use the elevators, including the elderly and mothers with baby strollers and the like. Metro turned full circle and now heartily supports the concept, though maintenance problems continue. Ironically, when the Forest Glen station in Silver Spring opened in Septembers 1990, the tracks were 120 feet below street level, and a high speed elevator was installed for all riders, whether disabled or not. The Wheaton station has the longest escalator in the world, outside of the Soviet Union.

The District of Columbia subway is a model for accessible subways in other cities, not only in America but throughout the world. Many cities have totally inaccessible subways; some have partially accessible subways. Mexico City recently built a magnificent multimillion dollar subway system, totally inaccessible. The Americans With Disabilities Act of 1990 has provisions that will require subways to be more accessible. Great care is taken in this legislation to deal with the cost factor. New York City, for example, would have to spend billions of dollars if every subway stop was required to have an elevator. A compromise was reached under which only certain "keystations" must be accessible, and there is a generous, extended time period for complying with the 1990 Act.

The success of the District of Columbia Metro has been due to community support for the concept of access, to lawyers who brought the litigation to a successful conclusion, to judges like Judge Jones who had the vision and courage to rule with fairness and compassion and to do what needed to be done, and, most of all, to determined individuals like Richard Heddinger, who desperately needed accessible transportation, and who was not about to take "No" for an answer!

CHAPTER VI

THE AMERICANS with DISABILITIES ACT – HOW it HAPPENED

At the age of 25, I was told to leave a plane on my return trip to my job here in the United States Senate because I was flying without an attendant. In 1981, an attempt was made to forcibly remove me, with a disabled friend, from an auction house because we were "disgusting to look at." In 1983, a manager at a movie theater attempted to keep my disabled friend and myself out of his theater because we could not transfer out of our wheelchairs.[1]

The Rehabilitation Act of 1973 and the section 504 regulations, adopted in 1977 after the protests by the disabled community, did much to improve the lives of disabled people, but only in the federal sector. Outside the federal sector there is a large universe, consisting of privately owned businesses, transportation companies, private employers, and state and local governments. Disabled people looked around and saw advancement for blacks and other racial minorities, for women, and gays, but in the world outside the federally protected area, there was little real progress for them. A Harris survey in 1986 showed social and economic conditions for disabled people to be appalling – far worse than that of any other minority. Two out of three of employment age were completely out of work. They were fed up with isolation, poverty, unemployment, lack of access, lack of the ability to travel and earn money at productive jobs. Perhaps this unconscionable lack of progress was in part due to the fact that the disability community was fragmented into hundreds of groups and thousands of individuals with varying disabilities – including mobility impairment, blindness, deafness, and many other limitations. Those with mental retardation were really without a political voice except to the extent expressed by support organizations, such as the Association of Retarded Citizens. If an individual were out of sight because of being institutionalized, were without purchasing power because he or she couldn't find work, then political power, even multiplied by huge numbers, could not be worth much. Still, the need was there and the amazing historical fact is that from isolation and powerlessness came spectacular success in the political arena.

The Americans With Disabilities Act (ADA) was signed by President Bush on July 26, 1990.[2]

This tremendously significant legislation fills a vacuum left by the Rehabilitation Act of 1973, which was limited to the federal sector and to entities receiving federal funds. Under ADA, discrimination against disabled persons is now prohibited by private employers. All "public" places (even though privately owned) constructed after an effective date subsequent to date of passage, must be made accessible. For example, a restaurant constructed after the effective date must be accessible. Existing places of public accommodation must be made accessible if "readily achievable." Extensive new rules require that public and privately owned transportation, such as buses and trains but excluding air carriers, must be accessible. A new system of TDD telephone relays for hearing impaired persons will be implemented. The ADA is called the *Emancipation Proclamation*, the *Magna Charta* and the *Declaration of Independence* for disabled people.

The story of how this legislation wended its way through Congress, through Committee hearings, floor amendments, floor votes, and intensive lobbying by disability groups and business interests is fascinating. It, most certainly, is a story of democracy in action.

The Americans With Disabilities Act is historic, far reaching legislation that will reduce or eliminate discrimination against disabled people in all areas of life and will provide access to transportation, jobs, telecommunication and places of public accommodation such as shops, restaurants, and theaters. It is truly an instrument of emancipation for disabled people.

How did this historic legislation come into being? Who were the people and what were the influences that made it happen? It certainly didn't drop out of the sky. The story involved hundreds and thousands of disabled people and disability groups. It included scores of United States Senators and members of the House of Representatives, numerous hearings, voluminous testimony, and heated debates. The story implicates opponents of the bill, in the form of business interests and transportation companies. ADA is probably one of the most debated, lobbied for and against, committee-considered bill in recent memory. The act is a triumph and a tribute to the democratic process. It achieved nearly everything the disabled community wanted and at the same time was artfully designed to accommodate the cost-fears of those required to comply with its provisions.

Though sweat from hard labor and head toil poured out over this bill, it is worth noting that no actual blood was shed by those who were demanding what was rightfully theirs but had been cruelly denied for too long. This peaceful revolution contrasts remarkably with the fire bombings, assassinations, and riots of the fifties and sixties, when blacks were demanding their civil rights. It seems that terrible bloodshed, in some subtle way, made it possible for the disabled community to achieve their goals through a peaceful, democratic process.

In 1984 an original proposal for a federal civil rights law for disabled people was made by the National Council on the Handicapped (subsequently called the National Council on Disability, since the word "handicapped" is becoming obsolete). Bob Burgdof, among others, worked on drafts of language, some of which found their way into the final act. The National Council was a federal agency staffed by Reagan appointees. In 1986 The National Council issued a report called "Toward Independence." It recommended federal legislation to improve the lot of disabled people in many areas. The inside joke was that since the council was located near Independence Avenue in Southwest Washington, the title of the report was merely a guide for staff people to find a bus stop! The council, after coming up with a draft of possible legislation, delivered it, in February 1987, to Congressman Coelho and Senator Weicker.

Playing an instrumental role at the National Council was, among others, Paul G. Hearne who helped organize a system of networking for people from business, government, and the disabled community. Mr. Hearne, himself disabled, was awarded a Reginald Heber Smith Community Lawyer Fellowship to practice poverty law in Brooklyn. He founded and directed the Handicapped Persons Legal Support Unit and authored one of the first books on the legal rights of people with disabilities. In 1989 he was made president of the Dole Foundation.

In 1988 Senator Weicker took the draft, revised it, and introduced it as bill S 2345. Weicker was joined in the effort by Senators Dole, Harkin, Simon, Stafford, Kennedy, Dodd, Matsunaga, Chafee, Kerr, Packwood, Leahy, Inouye, and Cranston. In the House the identical bill, HR 4998, was introduced by Congressman Coelho, with help from many other congressional members.

In May 1988 to facilitate gathering information on the extent and nature of disability discrimination in America, Major R. Owens, Chairman of the Subcommittee on Select Education, established the Task Force on the Rights and Empowerment of Americans with Disabilities. Justin Dart Jr. was appointed chairman, and Elizabeth Boggs, co-founder of the Association for Retarded Citizens, was appointed co-chairperson. Lex Frieden, executive director of the Institute for Rehabilitation Research and former executive director of the National Council on the Handicapped, was appointed coordinator. Frieden had been injured in an automobile accident and uses a wheelchair. He was refused admission as a student to a large Oklahoma university on the grounds that his presence on the campus would violate the school's image. Later, he attended the University of Tulsa and became a leader in the Independent Living Movement.

Mr. Dart chaired 63 Task Force public forums involving people with disabilities, advocates, service providers, and government officials in all 50 states, the District of Columbia and the territories. In all, an estimated 8000 people attended these forums. The Task Force submitted a report to Congress outlining its findings and recommendations.

The list of members of the Task Force reads like a distinguished *Who's Who* of leaders in the disability community; many of these leaders are mentioned throughout this book because of their great contribution to the cause of civil rights for disabled people. They include Elmer Bartels, Massachusetts Rehabilitation Commission; Wade Blank, Atlantis Community; David Bodenstein, National Association of People with AIDS; Frank Bowe, Hofstra University; Marca Bristo Kettlewell, National Council on Independent Living; Dale Brown, President's Committee on Employment of People with Disabilities; Philip Calkins, of the same committee; David Capozzi, Project ACTION; Julie Clay, University of Montana; Susan Daniels, President's Committee; James DeJong, Illinois Coalition of Citizens with Disabilities; Eliot Dober, Office of Protection and Advocacy for Handicapped and Developmentally Disabled Persons; Don Galloway, Keith Gann, P.W. Alive, James Havel, National Alliance of the Mentally ill; King Jordan, Gallaudet University; Paul Marchand, Association for Retarded Citizens; Connie Martinez, California State Council on Developmental Disabilities;, Celane McWhorter, the Association for Persons With Severe Handicaps; Oral Miller, American Council of the Blind; Gary Olsen, National Association of the Deaf; Mary Jane Owen, Disability Focus; Sandra Parrino, National Council on Disability; Ed Roberts, World Institute on Disability; Joseph Rogers, National Mental Health Consumers Association; Liz Savage, Epilepsy Foundation of America; William A. Spencer, the Institute for Rehabilitation and Research; Marilyn Price Spevack, National Head Injury Foundation; Ann Vinup, Association for Children and Adults With Learning Disabilities; Sylvia Walker, Howard University; Patrisha Wright, Disability Rights Education and Defense Fund; and Tony Young, Fairfax Opportunities Unlimited.

Also participating in the drafting of the proposal was Chai Feldblum. After graduating from Harvard Law School, Chai clerked for Justice Blackmun of the Supreme Court and works for the American Civil Liberties Union. Still another leader of the civil rights movement is Bob Burgdof, who is a professor at the District of Columbia School of Law. Roger Slagle is a staff member of the House Committee on Public Works and Transportation and was closely involved in the legislative process. Karen Strauss is an attorney with the National Center for Law and the Deaf and has been involved with Title IV, relating to telecommunications for the hearing impaired.

Because of pressure from other matters, Congress did not get into ADA in 1988. In 1989 virtually the same bills were reintroduced in the House and Senate. In the House the bill was HR 2273. Section 2 of the bill, (which is contained in the final act) states that Congress finds that some forty three million Americans have disabilities, and the number is increasing as the population gets older. Additional "Findings and Purposes," contain a devastatingly strong snapshot description of the plight of the disabled, even at this late date:

> *Congress finds that: (2) historically, society has tended to isolate and segregate persons with disabilities, and, despite some improvements, such forms of discrimination against persons with disabilities continue to be a serious and pervasive social problem;*
>
> *(3) discrimination against persons with disabilities persists in such critical areas as employment, housing, public accommodations, education, transportation, communication, recreation, institutionalization, health services, voting, and access to public services;*
>
> *(4) unlike individuals who have experienced discrimination on the basis of race, gender, national origin, religion, or age, individuals who have experienced discrimination on the basis of disability have often had no legal recourse to redress such discrimination;*
>
> *(5) individuals with disabilities continually encounter various forms of discrimination, including outright intentional exclusion, the discriminatory effects of architectural, transportation, and communication barriers, overprotective rules and policies, failure to make modifications to existing facilities and practices, exclusionary qualification standards and criteria, segregation, and relegation to lesser services, programs, activities, benefits, jobs, or other opportunities;*
>
> *(6) census data, national polls, and other studies have documented that people with disabilities, as a group, occupy an inferior status in our society, and are severely disadvantaged socially, vocationally, economically, and educationally;*
>
> *(7) persons with disabilities are a discrete and insular minority who have been faced with restrictions and limitations, subjected to a history of purposefully unequal treatment, and relegated to a position of political powerlessness in*

our society, based on characteristics that are beyond the control of such persons and resulting from stereotypic assumptions not truly indicative of the individual ability of such persons to participate in, and contribute to, society;

(8) the Nation's proper goals regarding individuals with disabilities are to assure equality of opportunity, full participation, independent living, and economic self-sufficiency for such citizens; and

(9) the continuing existence of unfair and unnecessary discrimination and prejudice denies people with disabilities the opportunity to compete on an equal basis and to pursue those opportunities for which our free society is justifiably famous, and costs the United States billions of dollars in unnecessary expenses resulting from dependency and non productivity.

On June 22, 1989, the Senate Committee on Labor and Human Resources held the last of four days of testimony concerning the Senate version of the Americans With Disabilities Act. Distinguished senators on the committee included the chairman, Ted Kennedy, as well as Howard Metzenbaum, Paul Simon, Orin Hatch, and Senator Harkin, D-Iowa. Prominent witnesses were Attorney General Thornburgh, whose son is brain impaired as a result of an auto accident, and former Republican senator Lowell Weicker of Connecticut, whose son has Down's syndrome. The audience was packed with many of the leaders of the disabled civil rights movement: Justin Dart, Mary Jane Owen, Evan Kemp, Ralph Neas, Jim Brady, Dennis Smurr, Richard Heddinger, Pat Wright, and many others. Although there was apparent unanimity as to the goals of the proposed legislation, Attorney General Thornburgh stated that some items should be given further study: whether to include punitive damages as a remedy, and whether there should be exceptions to the requirement for accessible buses in cities with inclement weather. Also, he questioned the meaning of the phrase "readily achievable" which requires places of accommodation to be accessible to the extent that goal is readily achievable. He was concerned about costs and burdens on business, especially small businesses. Senator Simon said that 54 percent of the disabled who have completed schooling or college are still without jobs a year after graduating. Former Senator Weicker gave a ringing and eloquent endorsement of ADA in a speech which had many in the audience in tears; he was heartily applauded.

In late July 1989, tensions started rising between the disability community and the White House in conjunction with Republicans in Congress. The Administration wanted the bill to have no provision for compensatory or punitive damages in private suits; it was feared that such remedies would impact too severely on large and small businesses. On the morning of July 27, in Senator Robert Dole's office, a pow-wow began. Senator Kennedy was there, as was John Sununu from the White House, Attorney General Dick Thornburgh, Transportation Secretary Sam Skinner, and Senators Hatch and Harkin. Although President Bush promised to sign an ADA bill, Sununu wanted limitations. Bobby Silverstein of the subcommittee staff was explaining to Sununu the purposes of the bill. Sununu lost his temper and started shouting at Silverstein. Suddenly, Ted Kennedy slammed down his hand on the table and in a loud voice told Sununu that an attack on Senate staff was an attack on the Senate itself."If you want to yell at me go ahead, but that is not the way we do things here. If this is the way you want to continue, we are walking out of here right now." A cloud of silence descended and then negotiations began in earnest. The Republicans agreed to wider coverage, and the disability community gave up the damages provision; a compromise was reached. Though the disability community gave up the provision for compensatory damages, in return there was an expansion of the definition of "places of public accommodation." Although the Civil Rights Act of 1964 narrowly defined places of public accommodation – mostly in terms of restaurants, lunch counters, and the like (as a result of the lunch counter sit-ins of the sixties) – the ADA bill expanded the definition to list just about every privately operated place to which the general public had access, including doctors' offices, pharmacies, and the like.

On August 2, 1989, pursuant to the compromise, Senate leaders and the White House endorsed the ADA, as revised. The bill was endorsed 16-0 by the Senate Labor and Human Resources Committee.

"This bill is going to change this country forever," said Senate sponsor Tom Harkin, D-Iowa. *"This bill is to the disabled community what the Civil Rights Act of 1964 was to the black community. That important."* For its part, the White House said that President Bush is *"committed to a bill that can be signed this year."*

However, the business community expressed reservations. "It's still a bad bill," said Fred Krebs, manager of business and government policy for the U.S. Chamber of Commerce. Krebs said that language such as "reasonable accommodation" creates uncertainty for businesses. The American Bus Association, through spokesperson Susan Perry said the bill was a "death sentence" for private bus companies because it would increase costs. A compromise in the bill is to initially exempt businesses with 25 or fewer employees and later businesses with 15 or less. Commercial buildings constructed in the future would be required to provide complete access, but owners of existing facilities could ask for an exemption on the ground of undue hardship. All newly purchased public buses must provide wheelchair lifts, but private systems would get up to six years before new buses must be equipped with lifts. Telephone companies would be required to provide special TDD facilities for the hearing impaired. Pat Wright of the Disability Rights and Education Defense Fund called the agreement a "major victory for the disabled community."

The next day, August 3, the House Judiciary Committee held the first day of hearings on the House version, HR 2273. The Chairman was Don Edwards of California, who introduced the first witness, Jim Brady, who had been Press Secretary to President Reagan, and who had been shot in the head at the same time President Reagan was shot. He is currently vice president of the National Organization on Disability. In a simply worded and moving speech, he recounted that civil rights for disabled people had been a conservative Republican objective, from President Eisenhower to George Bush. But he said disability knows no political party, no distinction, it could happen to anyone. He supported the concept of equal access and the goal of reducing dependency costs. With a note of humor, he excused himself and said he had to go see his "physical terrorist." Another witness, Peter Addesso, was shot when he was a Marine in Vietnam, which resulted in his becoming a paraplegic. He recounted how his doctor advised swimming, but he wasn't allowed into the public pool.

On September 6, 1989, an editorial in the *New York Times* discussed the bill and expressed reservations about it, under the heading, "Blank Check for the Disabled?" It said the bill had received "surprisingly narrow public scrutiny," it was "vague" and the costs could be "monumental." Bus companies were "angry." It ended by saying, "*No one wishes to stint on helping the disabled. It requires little legislative effort, however, to write blank checks for worthy causes with other people's money.*"

In spite of that editorial on September 7, 1989, the Senate overwhelmingly (76 to 8) voted for their version of ADA. Working late into the night, the Senate warded off some weakening amendments but agreed to amendments excluding persons with certain sexual and mental disorders, although the bill does cover persons with AIDS. Senator Ted Kennedy said "*This really is the emancipation proclamation for the disabled in this country...a proud day in the history of civil rights.*" For the first time, the Senate agreed that debate on the bill would be communicated through sign language. The Senate voted unanimously to allow courts to consider good faith in compliance when considering suits under the act. The jobs provision will be phased in over four years, ultimately applying to employers employing more than fifteen employees. The transportation provisions have a grace period: privately owned bus systems would have to be made accessible within six years after enactment for large systems and seven years for smaller ones. Subway and other transit stations would have to be accessible within twenty years. Existing restaurants and other public places will have to take steps to improve access under standards that include cost factors. A victim of discrimination could seek relief in court, including injunctions and back pay. For public accommodation discrimination, the Attorney General can seek monetary damages and civil penalties.

After approval by the Senate, various House Committees held hearings on the House version. The House Subcommittee on Surface Transportation held its hearing on September 20, 1989, chaired by Congressman Mineta, D-Calif., who said that ADA was *"first and foremost a civil rights bill."* Republican Congressman Shuster, who said his mother was a double amputee, was concerned with increased costs to bus companies, which might reduce service. Congressman Petri of Wisconsin, saying it was *"deja vu all over again,"* opposed the requirement that all new buses have lifts and favored local flexibility and paratransit. A panel of witnesses from DOT, including Roland Mross, Deputy Administrator, Urban Mass Transportation Administration (UMTA), generally favored the bill, to the satisfaction of the disability community. Under severe questioning by Congressman Shuster, the panel admitted that many of the details would have to be left to DOT regulations. There was testimony that a wheelchair lift would cost about $10,000 to $12,000 per bus, but that was less than the cost of air conditioning, and less than ten percent of the cost of a new bus. There was testimony that in some cities, such as Seattle, wheelchair ridership was only one every other day, but the ridership could be expected to increase with greater accessibility. The federal funds portion, in the form of subsidies by UMTA for public but not private buses, was estimated at 35 million annually. Congressman Shuster felt there were gaps in the bill and said *"Go back and fix it."*

Justin Dart Jr., chairman of the President's Committee, testified eloquently in favor of the bill and felt that the costs of equality were not negotiable. *"Partial equality is not equality."* He said that all governments, federal, state and local, are currently spending $246 billion annually on maintenance payments to disabled people; passage of ADA would automatically reduce that huge financial burden.

On September 26, 1989, the House Surface Transportation Subcommittee held another hearing, this time focused on private bus companies such as Trailways and Greyhound, and independent tour operators. Generally, private bus lines are of two types, the quasi-public kind which service inter-city routes, such as between New York and Philadelphia, and private tour companies which provide leisure time tours, mostly for senior citizens. It quickly became apparent that of all the ADA issues, the question of wheelchair lifts for private bus companies was the most sensitive. Testimony from the disabled community, including Tim Cook, director of the Disability Action Center, and Marilyn Golden of DREDF, indicated that compromises had been made in the bill, such as extending the effective date for compliance for six or seven years, requiring a study, and no requirement for retrofitting. Under the extended grace period, bus companies could continue purchasing inaccessible buses for seven years, meaning that the disability community would have to wait until the year 2010 for fully accessible systems. They questioned low ridership figures on the grounds that many disabled would-be riders don't bother to complain or request service because it would be a "futile gesture." They testified that ADA doesn't necessarily require wheelchair lifts on all new buses but only "accessibility" which could be ramps or external lifts or elevated platforms.

Representatives of private bus lines objected strongly to the ADA provisions requiring that all new buses be accessible. They said that many bus companies operate at marginal profits, that bus tickets are "price sensitive" and compliance with ADA would require dropping some routes and forcing some companies out of business. They argued that it was inconsistent for ADA to require lifts but not accessible restrooms, which would be prohibitively expensive. They complained about loss of regular seats, which could be as much as 20 percent of total seat capacity, with revenues declining by one third. They complained about low ridership by disabled patrons and extremely high lift capital and maintenance costs. Fred Currey, Chairman of Greyhound Bus Lines, said that ADA was a "*bullet to the heart*" but offered a five point alternative; (1) permit disabled persons to travel alone; (2) an 800 number staffed by disabled persons to handle phone queries from disabled people; (3) design of a new exterior lift to be used in 200 key stations; (4) a $100,000 contribution to study technical improvements; (5) further studies in the area of frequency of use. He favored pools of accessible buses that could be transferred when requested, but disabled advocates objected that this would require advance notice, sometimes 48 hours in advance. Mr. Currey objected to the provision mandating accessible buses and then mandating a study on the issue; he argued that the study should come first.

On September 28 the Subcommittee on Transportation and Hazardous Materials held hearings. Several representatives of public transit authorities were concerned about costs and ambiguities. Carol H. Lavoritano, director of the Program and Policy Analysis Department of the Southeastern Pennsylvania Transportation Authority, was concerned about many issues: the question of retrofitting existing rail vehicles, the problem of access to single-car trolley cars, the problem of paratransit. On the latter issue she was particularly concerned that operators would be required to remove architectural barriers such as putting in curb cuts, and she was concerned that many disabled people able to use public transportation might nevertheless request paratransit. As a result of this and other testimony from transit authority officials, compromises were made in the bill so that extensive retrofitting would not be required, accessible single-car trolleys would not be required, and requisites on paratransit services would be limited.

On October 11, 1989, the House Subcommittee on Civil and Constitutional Rights of the Judiciary Committee held hearings. Chairman Don Edwards and Congressman Sensenbrenner sharply questioned witnesses representing small businesses which expressed concerns about ambiguities and excessive costs. John Motley testified for the National Federation of Independent Businesses and was concerned about the public accommodations portion as it affected small businesses. He argued that there was an exemption in the employment section for small employers but no similar exemption in the public accommodation section. (Later, Attorney General Thornburgh rebutted this argument by replying that whereas only 20 percent of employers are exempt under the small employer exemption, 90 to 100 percent of small entrepreneurs would be exempt if a small business exemption were incorporated into the public accommodation provision, because so many places of public accommodation are operated by very small businesses.) Motley feared there would be requirements to lower shelves and widen aisles in retail stores which could be prohibitively expensive. He suggested a dollar cap based on a percentage of net profits and feared that Congress was not aware of the "real world." Congressman Sensenbrenner of Wisconsin in a heated exchange said that his wife was a paraplegic and the witness showed an unawareness of the "real world" of disabled people. He said that he had received a "Guardian of Small Businesses" award from the witness's association and said he didn't care if he never got another award. On the other hand James A. DiLuigi representing Marriott Corporation and the American Hotel and Motel Association said that Marriott generally favored the legislation and there had been meetings with the Paralyzed Veterans Association to work out solutions to problems. He suggested there could be tax credits for certain costs relating to accessibility.

Laura Cooper, who uses a wheelchair due to multiple sclerosis and who represented the American Bar Association's Committee on Disabled Lawyers, testified in support of ADA. She recounted personal experiences of discrimination, including being rejected hundreds of times for employment as a lawyer, after graduating from law school. She had lived in a nursing home for lack of accessible facilities and once spent a week in a van while touring California because of inaccessible places of public accommodation. She termed the Americans With Disabilities Act the *Emancipation Proclamation* for disabled people. Congressman Edwards assured her that he knew what she was talking about because his son, a lawyer, had spinabifida:

(Congressman Edwards) *"Well, in my family we have the same kind of an experience with discrimination in employment. One of my sons has a disability because of spinabifida. He can walk, but with great difficulty, and he has lost a lot of his height, and so forth. He is a good lawyer, a graduate of Stanford and of Santa Clara Law School. He cannot get a job."*

Ms. Cooper murmured, "*Sounds something like me.*" Congressman Edwards continued, " *So he has to open his own law office with his wife as his secretary and get cases from the judges when a public defender is disqualified.*"

At the October 11 hearing there was testimony that the Act does not include homosexuals as "disabled" but does include people with HIV infections as disabled. Another provision defines disabled as including persons who are "regarded as" disabled. The question was raised whether a homosexual who does not have HIV infection is given protection under the act on the grounds that he might be "regarded as" having the HIV infection. There was no clear answer to this question.

On October 12 the hearing concluded with testimony from the Associated General Contractors of America. While supporting the goals of ADA, they were concerned with two issues: drugs on the work site and potential injuries on the job site. They declared that in some areas, 30 to 50 percent of job applicants could not pass pre-employment drugs tests. And they were concerned that construction workers with various ailments such as back injuries might be encouraged to apply for jobs and incur serious injuries. Later, Yolanda Suarez de Balcazar, Barbara Bradford, and Stephen B. Fawcett, introduced a survey of disabled people entitled "Common Concerns of Disabled Americans: Issues and Options." In general, the survey showed great dissatisfaction with almost every category, such as housing, public access, and employment.

Paul A. Roth of Roth Theaters in Maryland, presented lengthy testimony which requested clarification of where wheelchair patrons should sit in theaters; he preferred seating near exits. Once again, the argument of fire hazard, burdensome cost, and low patronage was raised. Robert L. Burgdorf Jr., Associate Professor of Law, District of Columbia School of Law, and one of the drafters of the original ADA bill, also testified and presented a thoughtful paper outlining areas of discrimination and support of ADA.

Another witness was James W. Ellis, president of American Association of Mental Retardation and professor of law at the University of New Mexico. In his testimony he presented shocking examples of discrimination against disabled people. Such discrimination has been called "grotesque" by members of the Supreme Court in the city of Cleburne [Cleburne Living Center, 473 US 432, 454, 461 (1985)]. He cited State ex rel. Beattie v. Board of Education, 169 Wis. 231, 172 NW153,154 (1919) in which the Supreme Court of Wisconsin approved the exclusion of a boy with cerebral palsy from public school because he *"produces a depressing and nauseating effect upon the teachers and school children."* He quoted Bard & Fletcher, *The Right to Die*, in The Atlantic Monthly, 59, 64 (April, 1968):*"(there is) no reason to feel guilty about putting a Down's Syndrome baby away, whether it's 'put away' in the sense of hidden in a sanitarium or in a more responsible lethal sense...True guilt arises only from an offense against a person, and a Down's is not a person."* Said Ellis: "*The tone of these attempts to justify discrimination against citizens with disabilities is more offensive than anything encountered by any group in American society since the days of slavery.*"

The U.S. Chamber of Commerce in a prepared statement opposed the House ADA bill, H.R. 2273 for a variety of reasons, mostly having to do with ambiguities and the fear of burdensome costs.

In the late fall of 1989, Congress, preoccupied with other matters, adjourned until January. One of Washington, D.C.'s coldest Decembers set in. A letter writing campaign on behalf of ADA was begun by a consortium of disability groups.

Paul Marchand, of the Association For Retarded Citizens, has been active in pushing civil rights for the disabled. For many years he has been chairman of the Consortium for Citizens With Disabilities, which is a national organization made up of scores of disability organizations, formed for the purpose of lobbying. It has thirteen Task Forces in areas such as civil rights, education, housing, long term care, health and employment. In the fall of 1989 the Consortium began a post card campaign to members of Congress, asking support for the Americans With Disabilities Act.

The business community, however, was not idle. An editorial in *The Nation's Business* criticized ADA as being vague and confusing, but offered no constructive alternative. A January thaw set in. Mayor Marion Barry was arrested on cocaine charges at the Vista Hotel, and it seemed that all eastern Europe was becoming democratic and independent of Moscow. A symbolic architectural barrier, the Berlin Wall, came tumbling down, but walls separating the disabled from society were all too prevalent. President Bush in his State of the Union speech in January 1990 said he supported mainstreaming disabled people into American life, but the transportation companies were still trying to get weakening amendments into ADA.

On February 22, 1990, the House Committee on Small Business held a hearing on ADA. Business organizations objected to many provisions. One business representative said, *"a lot of other people...like myself...do not want to go and be around a lot of other people in wheelchairs or other handicapped."* Directing Attorney Arlene Mayerson of the Disability Rights Education Defense Fund (DREDF) said, *"what you just stated [are] the most compelling arguments I have heard in a long time for ADA."* She said that years of experience with section 504, passed in 1973, had not given rise to the litigation nightmare that many feared. She drew the historical analogy to the black civil rights movement. *"This idea of customer preference was thrown away in the civil rights movement. Every single white shop keeper in the south said, 'I am not going to have other customers in here if I have to hire a black person.' We have in this room now articulated the strongest reason why there has to be a civil rights law."*

During the first week of March the House Surface Transportation Subcommittee of the Public Works Committee held what was to be the last of the hearings on ADA. Chairman Mineta of California did a commendable job in supporting the basic provisions of ADA. That day, the disability community, who packed the crowded hearing room, came off with a win, a loss, and a draw. Early in the hearing, a compromise amendment was reached which would defer implementing the private bus requirements until a three year study was completed.

The bill had required all new private buses to be accessible, after a grace period. The compromise left the entire issue up in the air for another three years. Next an amendment was introduced which would require only one car per commuter rail-train to be accessible instead of every car. This amendment narrowly squeaked through, by a vote of 20 to 18. But this setback was offset by a resounding victory for the disabled community. An amendment had been introduced which would provide procedures for granting a waiver from the bus requirements for communities of less than 200,000 people, a weakening amendment which could exempt practically the whole state of Vermont! After a lively debate the proposal was roundly defeated by a vote of 24 to 14.

Though ADA seemed headed toward passage in the early spring of 1990, some diffusion in support was occurring. The militant edge of the disability movement, ADAPT (Americans Disabled for Accessible Public Transportation), got wind that some weakening regulations, relating to access standards for new housing construction, were being proposed under the Fair Housing Amendments Act. Worse, some of the disability groups were said to favor them, notably the Paralyzed Veterans Association. PVA, which in the past had scored great victories in court and in Congress on behalf of the disabled, was beginning to lose its steam, as some leaders, such as Dennis Smurr, died, and others, such as Gordon Mansfield and David Capozzi, left. Another issue that threatened to divide support for ADA was the fact that Senator Kennedy and others had introduced a bill called the Civil Rights Act of 1990. This bill would reverse the result in several employment discrimination cases decided by the Supreme Court, such as Patterson and Wade Packing (see Chapter Fourteen), which severely restricted aggrieved employees' rights in discrimination suits. A provision of the bill would provide for damages in private suits against employers, a remedy that Kennedy felt was essential. In the summer of 1989, a similar punitive damages provision had been objected to, and the disability groups agreed to a compromise which removed it. President Bush's Chief of Staff, John Sununu, was said to have been concerned that the Civil Rights Bill would reincorporate punitive damages into ADA.[3]

A rumor, which proved to be false, swept around that President Bush had withdrawn his support from ADA. But the existence of the Civil Rights Bill tended to muddy the already murky waters. Congressman Steny Hoyer, at least, felt that whatever damages provision was inserted into the Civil Rights Bill should also be incorporated into ADA, since disabled people should not be treated worse than any other minority.[4]

With the House hearings finished, the disability community became engaged in a dramatic demonstration and lobbying effort in the week of March 12, 1990 in Washington D.C. Termed "Wheels of Justice" and primarily organized by ADAPT, the aggressive edge of the civil rights movement (though many other organizations participated), disabled people came in from all over the country for a week of protests. The Comfort Inn, not far from the U.S. Capitol, was the headquarters. In the parking lot there were dust covered, wheelchair-equipped vans from all over the country. They came from Colorado, Texas, Georgia, Tennessee, Massachusetts, and New York. The leaders of ADAPT, on Sunday, March 11, discussed the week's events over coffee and Danish. They included Wade Blank, a minister and civil rights activist, Mike Auberger, a leader and spokesman from Denver ,who with long braids, looked like a Sioux Indian chief on the warpath, Bob Kafka an affable, full-fuzzy bearded coordinator from Austin, Texas, and clean shaven, eager, and articulate Mark Johnson, from Atlanta. Stephanie Thomas, Dianne Coleman, Ben Freeman, and Bernard Baker, were there as leaders, planners, and coordinators. Auberger, Kafka and Johnson use wheelchairs as a result of spinal cord injuries. That afternoon Washington held its annual St. Patrick's Day parade, a happy, family affair, on Constitution Avenue, but few of the disabled visitors were present, unless you count some marchers with walking sticks and shillelaghs.

The next day, Monday, March 12, saw the heat turned up in more ways than one. Washington was in for record-shattering heat; the mercury reached 89 that day and continued hot all week. The cherry blossoms astounded everyone by blooming three weeks early. The disability groups assembled in front of the White House at noon – with the ADAPT members, but other groups as well, including blind and deaf people. Small children in wheelchairs joined the group. Almost 1000 strong, they began the long march down Pennsylvania Avenue, stopping traffic, carrying signs such as *"Civil Rights for Disabled People."* They chanted, *"What do we want? ADA!! When do we want it? NOW!"* An attempt was made to keep the marchers in single file, but by the time they got the seventeen blocks to the U.S. Capitol, there were so many that they were three and four abreast. They climbed up the west front of the Capitol and assembled in the warm sunshine of the plaza to listen to speeches.

Justin Dart Jr., chairman of the President's Committee, said:

"You are the pioneer patriarchs of the twentieth century. We are here today representing forty three million disabled Americans, forced by massive discrimination, to be this nation's most impoverished, most isolated, unemployed, and welfare dependent minority. President Bush has estimated that the cost of keeping disabled persons in a dependent state is 300 billion dollars a year. We are here to tell the Congress that three centuries of discrimination is long enough. We are here today to urge the House of Representatives to pass the Americans with Disabilities Act and to pass it without weakening amendments and without delay. Partial equality is no more acceptable in America than it is in South Africa. ADA will be a landmark civil rights law, like the Declaration of Independence; ADA will pave the way for independence for hundreds of millions throughout the world...Disabled people all over the world will become taxpayers, producers, consumers, and participants in their cultures...let us go forward, in the spirit of Ghandi and Martin Luther King, with love, with reasoned truth, with unyielding insistence on respect for the sacred value of each human life. Let us speak with one thundering voice.

We are Americans. We will be united for however long it takes to achieve the same rights that other Americans have. We are Americans. We have a right to work. We are Americans. We have a right to use public places, public transportation, and telephones. We are American citizens and we will be part of the American dream. Equality NOW! ADA NOW!"

Congresswoman Pat Schroeder spoke on behalf of ADA, and said the march was reminiscent of the March on Selma in the sixties. It is unbelievable that this nation can send people to the moon but can't provide access for disabled people. Congressman Major Owens also spoke. He reminded the crowd of 1966 when Robert Kennedy spoke in South Africa urging equality and an end to discrimination. The greatest and most powerful opposition to ADA came from Greyhound. Delay is the real enemy. We will pass this bill with an overwhelming majority. King Jordan, first deaf president of Gallaudet University spoke in support of ADA and said if we don't get what we want, perhaps we will come back and simply stay. *"We will come back again and again. We've had enough delays. We demand the same rights that other Americans have."* Evan Kemp, Chairman of the Equal Employment Opportunity Commission also spoke on behalf of ADA, as did Jim Brady, President Reagan's press secretary.

The final speaker was Mike Auberger of ADAPT, one of the leaders of the march. In a stirring speech, he said:

"Twenty years ago, I walked up these steps without assistance. Today I sit before them, with you, as second class citizens, legally discriminated against, daily. Women gained the right to vote in the twenties. African Americans gained their civil rights in 1964. Today, disabled people are still legally denied the right to employment, to transportation, to telephones. We are here today to demand that ADA be passed immediately, without weakening, without delay, without compromise. We represent those who came before us and those who will become disabled in the future. We represent those who are here in spirit, those in institutions. Some of us have had children taken away solely because we are disabled. Many of us have not lived to see our dreams fulfilled. The steps we sit before are a symbol of discrimination against the disabled. We have been denied housing, jobs. These indignities and injustices must not go on. We will not permit these steps to continue to be a barrier to our rights to equality. We will not let any barrier prevent us from the equality that is rightfully ours. The preamble to the United States Constitution does not say, 'We the Able Bodied People,' but 'We the People.' We are the people. The Pledge of Allegiance does not say with liberty and justice for all except disabled people; it says with liberty and justice for all. We are here to demand our civil rights now. We are here to demand passage of the ADA NOW."

After the speeches, many abandoned their wheelchairs and climbed on their fannies up the 83 steps on the outside of the Capitol as a symbolic gesture to dramatize the architectural and other barriers faced by the disabled today. Pictures of this event appeared in Time magazine and other magazines, as well as television, but The Washington Post, preoccupied with the antics of the Poindexter trial and the troubles of Mayor Barry, ignored the entire day's historic events.

The next day, Tuesday, March 13, dozens of ADAPT members filled the huge rotunda at the Capitol and heard speeches by Speaker Foley, Congressmen Michel, and Steny Hoyer. Speaker Foley himself had asked for the meeting with ADAPT, though he had preferred that it be held outdoors.[5]

Speaker Foley said he couldn't promise ADA would be voted on in two days, more like two months. The crowd was unhappy with this and started chanting "ADA NOW!" Foley and Michel, somewhat disconcerted, left, but Congressman Steny Hoyer stayed, then left with a thumbs up signal. The police told the chanters to leave. Most refused; 104 were arrested and were packed off in police vans to headquarters. Some police used rubber gloves and wire cutters to cut chains binding wheelchairs together. The protesters were given bologna sandwiches and juice, then paper processing began. After that they were taken to Superior Court for more paper work; most didn't get back to the hotel till midnight.

The next day, Wednesday, more ADAPT members assembled in Congressman Shuster's office in the Rayburn Building. Shuster had supported weakening amendments to ADA. After staying several hours in his office, around sixty of the protesters were arrested and taken to the parking garage in the basement. Again the group didn't get home until the wee hours of the morning. Some jammed the office of Representative Hamilton Fish, who supported ADA, and others crowded into the hearing room of the Judiciary Committee. On the same day, some attended a markup session of the House Energy and Commerce Committee. Congressmen Dingell and Lent pushed through a substitute amendment relating to the transportation provisions of ADA. The substitute would require that within five years Amtrak must have at least one accessible car per train, but, with certain exceptions, all new cars must be fully accessible. After ten years, Amtrak must have available a number of spaces on coaches to park and secure wheelchairs. Equivalent food service must be provided in the most integrated setting practicable. Within five years all commuter trains must have at least one accessible car per train. All new cars purchased by commuter systems must be accessible. No restrooms need be provided for the disabled unless restrooms are provided for other passengers. All new stations used by Amtrak or commuter rails must be accessible. Amtrak, within 20 years, must make existing stations accessible. Commuter systems, within three years, must make key stations accessible, but a waiver of up to twenty years may be granted by DOT for certain extraordinarily expensive structural changes. The Energy and Commerce Committee defeated proposals by Congressman Dannemeyer to exclude AIDS sufferers from the benefits of ADA. After hearing arguments, the Energy and Commerce Committee approved ADA with a vote of 40-3.

The next day, Thursday, a small group of wheelchair users (their numbers diminished because so many were in court) assembled at Housing and Urban Development headquarters in Southwest Washington. They demanded to see Secretary Jack Kemp, but were told he was out of town. They were concerned about proposed amendments that would weaken the access standards under the Fair Housing Amendments Act. One of Jack Kemp's assistants, Gordon Mansfield, who uses a wheelchair and who had recently been with PVA, came down to the lobby. The police told the group they were blocking the entrance and to go outside. They refused, and chanted "DelliBovi, DelliBovi!" Alfred DelliBovi was the Housing Under Secretary. Finally Alfred DelliBovi came down, no one was arrested and there was a constructive talk. On Friday, another demonstration occurred at the Greyhound terminal. and then the group started heading home. The difficulties in planning the march, coming to Washington, protesting, getting arrested, and then driving the long way home had been enormous.

Ernest Taylor, from Denver, black, using a wheelchair as a result of being shot in the back, thought it had all been worthwhile. He had been arrested many times before in many other protests. The question of whether to be arrested was a matter of individual conscience; many chose not to be. The fines in many cases were ten dollars, although Mike Auberger suffered a $500 fine, a twenty day suspended sentence, and one years probation. The charges were unlawful entry and unlawful parading in a federal building. Many of the ADAPT members were put on probation, but filed a discrimination suit when they learned that the Probation Office on E street is inaccessible to wheelchairs. Ginger Lane, who uses a wheelchair, drove from Chicago; she thought ADA was needed to prevent discrimination against disabled people. To her, Washington, D.C. seemed quite accessible when compared to Chicago. "Plucky" Puckett, of Atlanta, was concerned about housing and transportation access. The group left Washington with hope of victory and feelings of accomplishment.

The press generally gave good coverage to the dramatic events of the week. Articles appeared in the *New York Times, Time Magazine, the Washington Times*, and many other newspapers and magazines, but *The Washington Post* was sparse in its coverage. The Post's ombudsman, Richard Harwood, wrote a column decrying the demand of pressure groups for publicity and called ADAPT's historic march a "pathetic event." *USA TODAY*, aware of what went on all week, published an editorial supporting ADA on March 17 but an opposing article on the same page by Bruce Fein was headed, "Disabled don't deserve gold-plated justice." *The New York Times* on March 13, 1990 said that if passed in its present form, ADA would be "the most sweeping civil rights law since the landmark 1964 act." On March 18, Steven A. Holmes wrote an article in the *New York Times* which analyzed the growth of the disabled civil rights movement:

"In many ways, it is a by-product of the technological revolution. Breakthroughs in medicine, the development of computers that allow the hearing and speech impaired to use telephones, and advancements in motorized wheelchairs have meant that more people with severe handicaps can live longer, can do more for themselves and have the potential for enjoying fuller lives."

The article asserted that Dr. Frank Bowe's book, "Handicapping America," published in 1978, is to the disability rights movement what Betty Friedan's *The Feminist Mystique* was to the woman's movement. Dr. Bowe believes that as more of the handicapped live longer lives and can utilize technological advances, they will begin to realize they have civil rights which must be enforced in order to fulfill their capabilities.

After Congress returned from the Easter vacation, things started heating up again by the middle of May 1990. Independence movements continued in Lithuania, Latvia, and Estonia. The Soviet Union was putting the pressure on these republics to stay inside the fold; the Bush administration, occupied with the imminence of the summit conference with Gorbachev, was tiptoeing around the issue. Another can of worms that month was a showdown between the White House and Congress, between Republicans and Democrats, over the crucial domestic budget deficit problem. Although increased taxes were on everyone's minds, they were not on anyone's lips, for Candidate Bush had pledged no tax increases; "read my lips." The pundits mused that Bush merely promised *"no increase in old taxes,"* but didn't promise *"no new taxes."* Again, it seemed that all Washington danced around the dreaded *"T"* word, meaning taxes.

On May 15, word spread that the House of Representatives would finally vote on the Americans With Disabilities Act the very next day. The author dutifully drove to Capitol Hill to attend the historic event, and after a half hour search finally found extremely restricted parking, blocks away from the Capitol. Ironically, the Capitol area has very few handicapped parking spaces available, although arrangements can be made if one only knows the right buttons to push. Regrettably, the trip turned out to be mostly futile, because the House Rules Committee had bottled up the ADA bill, and it was rescheduled for House vote on May 17, the next day. Notwithstanding the postponement, there was some debate on the House floor, in the form of a moving speech by Congressman Charles Bennett of Florida, who uses two canes as a result of a 1945 bout with polio and who has long been an advocate of civil rights for disabled people.

The Rules Committee struggled with the question of what, if any, floor amendments would be allowed. It was rumored that 46 mostly weakening floor amendments had been prepared for consideration by the Rules Committee. It was said that the Rules Committee was going to allow eight amendments. Congressman Steny Hoyer's office, which was coordinating ADA, was deluged with telephone calls from people asking what was going on. Most of the proposed amendments were weakening amendments, opposed by the disability groups and advocated by business interests. Some were slightly hysterical. There was the *Cross-eyed Deputy Sheriff* amendment, which allows police departments to "prescreen" persons applying for jobs that require carrying deadly weapons. There was the *Holier Than Thou* amendment giving churches "*the same exemptions from the employment provisions of the bill as is given to private membership clubs.*" There was the *Perverted Baby-sitter* amendment, relating to certain disabled persons employed by child care employers. There was the *Diseased Waiter* amendment, allowing restaurants to refuse to employ waiters and other food handlers with certain infectious diseases. There was the *Dizzy Ferris Wheel Rider*, allowing amusement parks to refuse rides to certain disabled people. There was the *Say That Again* amendment which defines the essential functions of a job as "*those functions that have been demonstrated by current employees as essential.*" And there was the *Gratuitous Insult* amendment, which says that "*nothing in the bill creates, either directly or indirectly, any right for any person on the basis of the sexual preference of such person.*" Finally, Congressman Shuster stubbornly reintroduced an amendment, roundly defeated in hearings, to provide for waivers from lift purchase requirements for buses in urbanized areas with a population of 200,000 or less. A voice of sanity in all this confusion was a young man named Tom Blatnik, who is a permanent member of the House Doorkeeper's staff, and who works in the House Gallery. Tom has a learning disability (severe dyslexia) and is keenly interested in and aware of what was happening on Capitol Hill on ADA, at a time when others were in the dark.

Thursday, May 17 was the day that ADA finally came to the floor of the House of Representatives. The author, sitting in the House Gallery, was reprimanded twice by staff for taking notes while the proceedings were going on; evidently the rule is that one can see and hear but not write!

For two years the disability community had worked tirelessly for this day. Members of Congress had become deeply involved in the issue, spending hundreds of hours on the bill, the hearings, the speeches, the press releases, and so forth. The bus companies, the trains, small business, medium size business, and big business had all had their say. Congressman Steny Hoyer of Maryland, who coordinated the bill, said that no other bill that session of Congress had had so much consideration. The moment of truth had come.

The first order of business was for the full House to vote on the Rules Committee decision to limit the number of possible floor amendments to eight. Speeches were given on the floor of the House both pro and con. The electronic voting board on the wall behind the speaker's platform lit up with the names of every Congressman. Electronic voting began, with a green dot for *Yes* and a red dot for *No*. Little by little Congressmen filtered onto the House floor to vote and the electronic board began to twinkle. When it was over the vote was 237 to 172 in favor of adhering to the Rules Committee decision to limit the number of floor amendments to eight. The *Yesses* were primarily on the Democratic side and the *Nos* were mostly on the Republican side.

Then the debate on the bill began in earnest. Television was set up in the Hall of Statues where members of the disability community watched entranced, beneath the statues of Alexander Hamilton, Henry Clay, Davey Crockett, Robert E. Lee, and the others. On the House Floor, Coordinator Steny Hoyer began the proceedings with a ringing endorsement of ADA. Others who spoke in support were Representatives Mineta and Edwards of California, Silvio Conte and Ed Markey of Massachusetts, Major Owens of New York, Gunderson of Wisconsin, Jack Brooks of Texas, Murphy of Pennsylvania, Fish and Weiss of New York, and many others. Steny Hoyer said that the monthly disability check that many disabled people receive was the nation's price for inflicting discrimination and isolation on the disabled. He invoked the name of President Johnson, who twenty five years earlier had signed the Civil Rights Act of 1964 and the name of former Congressman Tony Coelho, an epileptic who was one of the cosponsors of the original bill and to whom the disability community was greatly indebted. Former Congressman Coelho later appeared on the House floor to listen to the debate. Congressman Ed Markey of Massachusetts spoke of meeting, in the Subcommittee on Telecommunications, with members of the deaf community regarding the telephone relay provision in Title IV of ADA. Congressman Charles Bennett of Florida, who had had polio in 1945 and now uses two canes, and who had served in Congress for more than two decades, spoke eloquently about ADA. He mentioned that he had sponsored legislation in the sixties (the Architectural Barriers Act) and spoke of the inaccessibility of the federal building in Jacksonville, Florida. He said that ADA would continue the antidiscrimination and access laws now confined to the federal sector. The bill was heralded as being "bipartisan," with Steny Hoyer the coordinator on the Democratic side and Congressman Steve Bartlett of Texas on the Republican side.

Congressman Fred Upton of Michigan said he favored a tax credit for business construction costs relating to access and Congressman Rostenkowski said the idea of a tax credit had "*a great deal of merit*."

Although the various speeches of the Representatives, in general, were supportive of ADA and members congratulated each other for an *"historic"* bill, there were a few down notes. Congressman Tom DeLay, Republican of Texas, bitterly denounced the disability community for showing "no compassion, no compromise" to anyone, namely the bus companies and business interests, and said it was "very sad" that the bill was not better when there was an opportunity to make it better. He concluded by saying that ADA was a *"horrible piece of legislation."*

Congressman Sensenbrenner of Wisconsin continued his effort to water down the remedies section by offering an amendment that would uncouple ADA from the remedies provisions of the Civil Rights Act of 1964. This was a sore point with many of the Republican members: the Civil Rights Act of 1964 did not provide, in general, for compensatory or punitive damages, an omission which Senator Kennedy and others tried to rectify by introducing the Civil Rights Bill of 1990, which was still pending. There were those who thought that the disabled should be treated the same as any other minority, so that if the 1990 Civil Rights Act adopted compensatory damages or punitive damages, the remedies would also apply to violations of ADA. But Congressman Sensenbrenner wanted to keep ADA separate with no damages remedy, no matter what happened to the Civil Rights Bill. According to Congressman Sensenbrenner, if a disabled person were denied access to a restaurant, the only remedy would be a court injunction requiring the restaurant to feed the disabled person, a somewhat unsatisfactory remedy for a hungry diner. In employment discrimination cases, the remedy would be limited to back pay and reinstatement, but not compensatory or punitive damages. Adding to the complexity was the fact that, in the summer of 1989, the disability community, key members of Congress, and the Administration reached a compromise in which the disability community conceded that ADA would have no compensatory or punitive damages. Congressman Sensenbrenner said he was merely trying to carry out that consensus. But Congressman Hoyer said that the amendment was *"the wrong issue at the wrong time in the wrong bill."* The debate reached Alice-in-Wonderland semantics. Both sides were arguing about what MIGHT be enacted in the Civil Rights Act of 1990. And of course, President Bush had threatened to veto any civil rights bill calling for punitive or compensatory damages. He had said in the Rose Garden the week before that he was opposed to any bill that would only generate litigation and fees for lawyers. Thus the debate concerning the damage provisions of ADA was a preliminary skirmish in what was to be a major battle later when the Civil Rights bill was finally debated. In the end, Congressman Sensenbrenner's amendment was defeated by a vote of 227 to 192. Thus, ADA would incorporate any damages provision in the existing Civil Rights Act of 1964, (there are few) but would contain enlarged damages provisions that might be enacted by a future Civil Rights bill. (Finally, in November 1991, President Bush signed a revised Civil Rights Act which provides for limited compensatory damages in some cases of employment discrimination.)

The "bete noir" of ADA, in the eyes of the disability community, Congressman Bud Shuster of Pennsylvania, continued his crusade to water down the bus and rail provisions of ADA, all the while invoking the name of "my dear mother who was a double amputee." Though defeated in Committee, Shuster revived his proposed amendment to allow annual waivers of the bus lift requirements in cities and towns with a population of 200,000 or less.

Later that day, Congressman Jim Chapman, D-Texas, pushed through, by a vote of 199 to 187, an amendment that would permit food service industry employers to transfer workers with AIDS out of jobs that involve food handling. This came about despite statements from the American Medical Association and the Center for Disease Control that AIDS cannot be transmitted through food. Rep. John R. Lewis, D-Ga., a veteran of the civil rights movement, opposed the amendment on the grounds that it was based on fear. He said, *"Discrimination was wrong in 1964, discrimination was wrong in 1965, discrimination was wrong in1968, and discrimination is wrong now."* Congressman Lewis and Congressman Major Owens, both black, were demonstrating once more the link between the black civil rights movement and the disability civil rights movement.

When the session ended that historic day, five amendments had been voted on with the following results. Congressmen LaFalce of New York and Campbell of California introduced an amendment that no civil action could be brought during the first six months after the effective date, against businesses that employ 25 or fewer employees and have gross receipts of one million dollars or less, and during the first year after the effective date against businesses that employ 10 or fewer employees and have gross receipts of $500,000 or less. This proposed amendment passed by a vote of 401 to 0. Congressman Olin of Virginia offered an amendment that would presume an undue hardship to an employer if the cost of making a job accessible came to more than ten percent of the disabled employee's salary. This amendment was defeated by a vote of 213 to 187. Congressman Hansen of Utah offered an amendment to the effect that no individual who desired to enter a wilderness area could be discriminated against because of a disability, including disabilities requiring a wheelchair. The amendment was thought necessary because of possible problems in the interpretation of the Wilderness Act. It was agreed to. Congressman Chapman's amendment to allow employers to not hire persons with AIDS for jobs involving food handling passed narrowly, by a vote of 199 to 187. Congressman McCollum of Florida offered an amendment to the effect that if an employer had prepared a written description before advertising or interviewing applicants for a job, this description shall be considered evidence of the essential functions of the job. This amendment, also, passed by agreement.

After a weekend recess, the House resumed on Tuesday, May 22. Three more amendments were offered. All of them were weakening amendments and all were roundly defeated. The Lipinski amendment to require railroads to have only one accessible car per train was roundly defeated by a vote of 290 to 110. Congressman Sensenbrenner's amendment to uncouple the remedies provisions from the Civil Rights Act was defeated. Congressman Washington of Texas, who is black, had eloquently opposed that amendment. Congressman Shuster's amendment, to provide annual waivers from the accessible bus requirement for cities and towns with a population of less than 200,000, if agreed to by the disability community, was also defeated.

With all eight amendments having been voted on, the final House debate on the bill, as a whole, began. This didn't take long. The various committees had already spent hours on the bill, and two full days of debate had taken place the previous week. All parties had had their say; the moment of truth had come. The disability community, about one hundred strong, assembled in Statuary Hall, and watched the proceedings on closed circuit television. As electronic voting began, the screen recorded the vote.

As the "*YEA*" votes passed the majority mark, assuring passage, pandemonium broke loose in Statuary Hall as the exultant crowd realized they had won. The vote continued, and when it was all over, the Americans With Disabilities Act had passed by a resounding vote of 403 to 20. The cheers of the crowd continued, and several of the leading Congressmen came down to say a few words and receive the congratulations of the crowd.

Congressman Steny Hoyer, who had done a magnificent job of working tirelessly to coordinate the bill, spoke. He was clearly the hero of the hour. Chairman of the House Democratic Caucus, he was the fourth ranking member of his party. ADA was his first major role; when Tony Coelho resigned, he was asked to take over the reins in steering ADA through the House. Hoyer and Coelho were friends, and Hoyer tells the story of the time the two Congressmen, with some others, went to Rome and had an audience with the Pope. Coelho confided that, when he was young, he had entered a seminary, but when it was discovered he had epilepsy, he was told to leave. (Later, the Catholic Church changed its policy to allow for priests with epilepsy.)

Hoyer's negotiating skills were crucial in guiding the bill through the House, sometimes but not always, placating the strongly opposed business interests. Republican Bartlett, coordinating the bill on the Republican side, called Hoyer, "*the most formidable adversary and most reliable ally I've ever encountered.*" Congressman Major Owens came and said, "*Together we shall all overcome.*"

Congressmen Mineta, Anderson, and Edwards of California were there at the Hall of Statues that historic day. Steve Bartlett of Texas and Congressman Ed Markey of Massachusetts said a few words. Senator Harkin, a cosponsor on the Senate side, came by. The crowd applauded them and also Justin Dart Jr., who was the author of much of the language of the bill.

Mary Jane Owen of Disability Focus, spoke eloquently:

"The morning damply cool; a helpful push up the hill; the friendly guard; exchanging greetings with young Joshua as his mother pushed his small wheelchair through the security gate; the empty National Statuary Hall lined with chairs for the expected overflow crowd soon to be watching the floor debate on the chattering TV monitors; the hugs of allies in the struggle; Pfc. Thomas J. Wessenmann of the Capitol police, searching out a battery for my hearing device; movement into the "handicapped" portion of the gallery; the intimacy of those lucky few who could fit into its narrow space; the smiles and hushed greetings; the rotation of young kids in wheelchairs into a spot by the door so they could tell their kids they'd really been here on this historic day; an interpreter down below us signing the debate to the deaf advocates sitting with I. King Jordan; the joy and surreptitious applause as each amendment is voted down; the loud cheers upon passage of the bill itself; a storm of tears and kisses; the smiles of the guards, who seemed pleased, too, not demanding limits to the celebration; moving through the marble halls past statues of other victors and finding the heroes of today's battle: Liz, Pat, Paul, Ralph, Mimi, Heather, Jeanne, John, Randy, Judy, Janet, Moe, Elizabeth, Mike, Bob, Jay, and so many more; the miracle of bumping into Gerald Bastista, a blind colleague from years before and the gracious apology of Bruce, running the Capitol's own subway to the Senate side of the Hill: 'I'm afraid it's not really accessible-but we're going to change that, aren't we;' moving toward Union Station with others not known before but now close friends in our common victory; the snowballing crowd of jubilant advocates gathering around hastily shoved together tables; the red checked table cloths and patient waiters; the cold beer and chilled wine raised in toast after toast to ADA and members of Congress; the red rose presented by Justin Dart; the tears of joy and laughter with a year's worth of warm hugs and sincere acknowledgments, coloring this day, May 22, 1990, with bold flashes of mutual love and respect." [6]

The next day, *The Washington Post* gave the big story page one priority, and on May 24 an editorial in The Post called *"Enabling The Disabled"* praised the House vote and said *"The legislation will greatly increase the opportunities of a group that has too often and destructively been denied them."* Columnist Mary McGrory, wrote an article entitled "A New Day for the Disabled." She described the excitement in Statuary Hall when the bill passed. She mentioned Duane French, from Alaska, who has been paralyzed from the neck down since the age of 14, Kate Wolters, a 3 and 1/2 foot tall executive director of a foundation, legally blind Pat Wright of the Disability Rights Education Defense Fund, Bob Williams of the Cerebral Palsy Foundation, Joshua Chartienitz, age five, who has cerebral palsy, and Ralph Neas of the Leadership Conference on Civil Rights. And of course, there were many other leaders in the disability civil rights movement, too numerous to mention.

After passage by the House of Representatives, things quieted down as minor differences between the Senate and the House bills and the floor amendments had to be reconciled in the Conference Committee before the bill could be sent to the White House for presidential signature. The biggest sticking point for the Conference Committee was the Chapman amendment, which allowed the food industry to place persons with certain infectious diseases (ostensibly including AIDS) in jobs other than food handling jobs. After stormy committee sessions, the Chapman amendment was defeated on June 25, 1990. The conferees killed the amendment even though it had been approved in both the House and Senate bills. It was expected that the conference committee bill would go back to the House and Senate for final approval, so the Chapman amendment could be voted on yet again. Senator Ted Kennedy, who opposed the Chapman amendment, asked the House conferees to drop the amendment, which they did by a vote of 12 to 10 over protests by Rep. Steve Bartlett of Texas. Bartlett stated that such a move could jeopardize passage of the entire bill. *"We would slow down and perhaps kill the bill for this session if we go against a majority of both houses,"* Bartlett said. Proponents of the Chapman amendment insisted that many restaurants would lose customers and could be forced out of business if AIDS carriers could not be prevented from handling food. Opponents such as Senator Tom Harkin said the amendment *"strikes at the heart and soul of the bill by legislating an irrational fear and stereotype."* Senator Kennedy then got the Senate committee to put down the Chapman amendment by a vote of 9 to 1.

If Congressman Bartlett had been getting his back up about the Chapman amendment, so was the disability constituency. The restaurant industry had practically admitted that AIDS cannot be transmitted to diners in restaurants through food handlers, yet the industry feared that the public thought so. It was a matter of "perception," or more accurately, "misperception." The Restaurant Association, back in 1964, had opposed the Civil Rights Act, not because Negroes make poor cooks and waiters, but because the public "perception" was that they would rather dine in an all white establishment. To the disability community, "perception" was what ADA was all about. Disabled people had been denied jobs because of the "perception " that they couldn't do any work, and had been denied accessible transportation because the "perception" was that they were mostly in nursing homes. If Chapman wanted ADA to stand for the proposition that "perception" is important, though the facts contradict the perception, the disability community would have none of it.[7]

Liz Savage, assistant director of governmental affairs for the Epilepsy Foundation and a leading lobbyist for ADA said, *"We feel pretty strongly that this amendment is so antithetical to the whole bill that the disability community couldn't support the bill with the amendment in it."*[8]

Ms. Savage felt that the AIDS amendment cast a dark shadow over the rest of the bill, because it seemed that a disabled person's civil rights could be diminished because of a "perception" by society even though the perception was totally inaccurate.

Thus, in the final week of June 1990, the fate of ADA was very much up in the air. The disability community held its collective breath waiting for optimistic news of the bill's fate.

That final week in June was also a time of extraordinary news events, most of them directly or remotely affecting disability issues. The events brought to mind novelist Flannery O'Connor's phrase: *Everything That Rises Must Converge*. First, the narcotics and perjury trial of Washington's Mayor Marion Barry was in full tilt. The court room displayed the FBI videotape of Barry smoking cocaine at the Vista Hotel on January 18, 1990; later that evening the tape was broadcast on television. It had been reported that in December 1988, Barry failed to show up at a Christmas party for disabled youngsters because he was busy at the Ramada Inn with convicted drug violator Charles Lewis.

Then, the Supreme Court finally decided the Nancy Cruzan case. By a 5 to 4 vote, the Court upheld a Missouri law which prohibited Nancy's parents and health care providers from withdrawing life support systems for Nancy, who had been in a persistent vegetative state as a result of an automobile accident. The court said that although a patient has a constitutional right to request termination of life in certain circumstances, the patient must have made his or her wishes known when mentally competent to do so. The patient has such a fundamental right to life that others such as parents cannot make that decision, unless state law is followed. (Missouri law required "clear and convincing" evidence of the patient's wishes.) The decision received the applause of many, but not all, in the disability community. Many regarded the decision as upholding the civil rights of a disabled person, including persons in a coma, but others saw it as resulting in the needless prolonging of life.

The last week of June was also the week when Nelson Mandela, the formerly jailed South African anti-apartheid hero, came to America for a huge ticker tape parade in New York City, a meeting with President Bush in the White House, and an address before a joint session of Congress. The visit coincided in time with the struggle of the Congress and the White House to deal with the Civil Rights Act of 1990, a measure that pitted liberal Democrats against conservative Republicans. President Bush had stated that he did not approve of the damages provisions and other provisions that smacked of quotas, and he received intense pressure from the Republican right. Still, he wanted to take advantage of Mandela's visit to show his support for American black voters. The fact that the Civil Rights Bill was pending in Congress and was to be voted on was a case of extremely bad timing for the White House; it would be better to have the vote after Mandela's visit. The coincidence in timing between Mandela's visit and the soon-to-be-voted-on Civil Rights Bill, as well as all the other extraordinary events, including the temporary death of the Chapman amendment, conceivably could have wrecked ADA. *The Washington Post*, in an editorial, came down on the side of the White House on the damages provision of the Civil Rights bill and saw nothing wrong with providing damages for racial discrimination but not for other kinds, including discrimination against the disabled.

Other events that occurred that same week and that could have caused ADA to overload, erase, and self-destruct: the Savings and Loan bankruptcy issue was plunging the country ever deeper into debt, and in one of the most remarkable events of that week, if not the year, President Bush said that he would support "increased tax revenues," notwithstanding his widely publicized, *read my lips* campaign pledge that he would not increase taxes. The AIDS conference in San Francisco erupted into loud and disorderly protest, an event not calculated to put the issue of waiters with AIDS on the back page. The public, preoccupied with the drama of the Mandela visit, the titillation of Donald Trump's fall from the pinnacle with possible bankruptcy, the melodrama of the Barry trial, and the patriotic symbolism of an attempt to amend the Constitution to prohibit flag burning, seemed unwilling to grapple with more serious issues of budget, trade deficits, taxes, and civil rights.

The warm windy days of June turned into the humid, unbearably hot days of July. Fireworks lit up the Mall on the Fourth of July, as Congress and much of Washington took a vacation. ADA was stalled in the Conference Committee, as was a lot of moist, humid hot air that overhung Washington. In addition to the issue of the Chapman amendment, involving food handlers with AIDS, the Conference Committee was bogged down in an obscure controversy. ADA, as originally passed by the Senate, provided for private lawsuits in court for individuals claiming employment discrimination by United States Senators. Republican Senators Rudman and Stevens introduced an amendment that would limit employment discrimination complaints against Senators to an arbitration mechanism within the Senate, similar to the bill passed in the House.

Finally on Thursday, July 12, 1990, the Conference Committee finished its work; the Chapman amendment relating to food handlers with AIDS was dropped, and the reconciled bill passed the House by a vote of 377 to 28. The next day, Friday the thirteenth, the same bill passed the Senate by a vote of 91 to 6, and ADA headed for President Bush's desk.

Although Friday the Thirteenth may have been unlucky for some, it was a glorious day for the disability community! The Senate's chief sponsor and architect, Senator Tom Harkin, D-Iowa, said it was his proudest day in the Senate, as he signed a message to his deaf brother, Frank. Harkin, Ted Kennedy, and Orin Hatch told of relatives with disabilities who would benefit from the bill; they struggled visibly with their own emotions. Harkin said ADA *"Sends the world a clear and unequivocal message that people with disabilities are entitled to be judged on the basis of their abilities and not on the basis of ignorance, fear and prejudice." "America will be a better place because of the action we take today,"* said Hatch, who fought back tears as he told of the inspiration he received from a brother-in-law who was stricken by polio and who slept nights in an iron lung, after working every day, until the time of his death. Senator Ted Kennedy spoke of his sister Rosemary, who is mentally retarded, and son, Ted Junior, who lost a leg to cancer.

With action completed by the House and Senate, the bill went to the White House. The air of unreality continued to prevail; all America seemed to be on vacation. Perhaps symptomatically, the Dow Jones, joining the flight from reality that seemed to put the public in a trance, on July 16 approached its all time high mark, 2999.75, but perversely failed to reach the magic number of 3000, by twenty five cents.

On Thursday, July 26, 1990, the Americans with Disabilities Act finally became law, as President George Bush signed it in an elaborate ceremony on the south lawn of the White House. Some 2,000 disabled people were invited to attend. We were asked to assemble at 9 A.M. although the ceremony was to begin at ten. The day dawned cloudlesss and hot. The crowd, in a holiday mood, had put up with the minor annoyance of checking in, complete with frisking, at the southeast gate of the White House. Iced tea was served to the large crowd and the Marine band played. People in wheelchairs, both manual and powered, played *dodge-em* as they assembled on the lawn. With TV cameras in action, President Bush reached the platform. He was introduced by Evan Kemp, Chairman of the Equal Employment Opportunities Commission. Sandy Parrino, head of the National Council on Disability, was on the platform, along with Justin Dart Jr., Vice President Quayle, and Barbara Bush. The audience was one of the largest ever for a bill signing ceremony. Members of Congress who had been instrumental in passing the bill, were in the front row.

President Bush was eloquent in his remarks and the crowd cheered. *"Let the shameful wall of exclusion finally come tumbling down,"* he said, after referring to the demolishing of the Berlin wall as an analogy. Appealing to business, the President said, *"You have in your hands the key to the success of this act for you can unlock a splendid resource of untapped human potential."* A sign language interpreter repeated his speech. Comparing the act with the Declaration of Independence, he said, *"Every man, woman, and child with a disability can now pass through once closed doors into a bright new era of equality, independence, and freedom. Today, America welcomes into the mainstream of life all of our fellow citizens with disabilities. We embrace you for your abilities and for your disabilities, for our similarities and indeed for our differences."* He said that America annually spends almost $200 billion a year to support disabled Americans, and a goal of the act is to reduce those huge expenditures by making disabled folks more independent and productive. He said that ADA was the most important civil rights law in a quarter of a century. He paid special tribute to Evan Kemp, Justin Dart, Sandy Parrino, Senator Dole, and two members of the White House staff, Boyden Gray and Bill Roper. He said that America had become the international leader in civil rights for disabled people, and several foreign countries were considering similar legislation. He mentioned Lisa, from the State of Washington, who has cerebral palsy and who had been excluded from attending a home town movie theater, but was not excluded from the White House that historic day. He mentioned the Little League Challenger Division, in which disabled youngsters play ball with the help of other youngsters. *"Let the shameful wall of exclusion finally come tumbling down,"* he said.

When the applause died down, Bush signed ADA and passed out pens. Reverend Harold Wilke of Clairmont, California, had given the invocation. Armless, he took off a loafer from his left foot and extended the foot to the President, who put one of the pens between his toes. The crowd loved it!

After the ceremony, the crowd was invited to a picnic lunch outside the White House grounds, on the Ellipse. Tents were set up as a rock band played. Members of Congress gave speeches; Ted Kennedy was there, and Steny Hoyer, and many others. The crowd was in an exultant, emotional mood. Many of those present had been leaders, some for many years, in the disability civil rights movement. They had much to be proud of and much to be thankful for.

The Americans With Disabilities Act was the most significant federal legislation relating to civil rights for the disabled since the Rehabilitation Act of 1973. It complemented that act, and provided in the private sector what the 1973 act provided in the federal sector. It affects every private employer, with fifteen or more employees, in the nation . It affects every privately owned place of public accommodation, which means hotels, restaurants, theaters, barbershops, hardware stores, drug stores, lawyers and doctors offices--you might say every listing in the Yellow Pages. It affects all publicly and privately owned bus systems, commuter trains, and interstate trains. The act shows a sensitivity to the needs and costs of the business community and goes out of its way to avoid undue hardship to business.

Although the act was of great interest to bus companies, the restaurant industry and others, it seems fair to say that it was, in truth, a sleeping giant. Although passage was front page news, its development and its impact were never widely publicized. *The Washington Post* pointedly refused to give news coverage to the important March 1990 march on Washington, described earlier in this chapter. Throughout the country, in every town, city, and village there were many large and small businesses which remained totally unaware of the act. No doubt there were many disabled people, in institutions and tucked away in rooms in homes, who were unaware of the act or its significance. Proprietors who constructed new facilities after the effective date of the act and who were unaware of its requirements, probably were shocked. Only time would tell how much litigation would ensue. And, as with the Civil Rights Act of 1964, which provided civil rights to ethnic, religious, and racial minorities, it could not be assumed that wrongs would be righted with the stroke of a pen. It would take time and experience to bring civil rights to fruition and to establish improvement in the quality of life for people with disabilities to whom the act promised so much.

The Americans With Disabilities Act is an important step in assuring equal treatment of disabled persons by all segments of society. It has important enforcement provisions and will mean that people with disabilities will no longer be at the mercy of a sometimes, but not always, benevolent society.

CHAPTER VII

THE AMERICANS with DISABILITIES ACT – WHAT it PROVIDES

A young man, who had endured a spinal cord injury, had a new girl friend and a new wheelchair. He took his date to a bay side restaurant on Maryland's Eastern Shore where they enjoyed a great meal of crab cakes and chilled Reisling wine. After a while, nature called. He went to the rest room, but when he got inside he found the facility was inaccessible. He went to the bar looking for a paper cup but all the bartenders were girls and there were rows of shiny clean glasses under the bar overhead counter, but no paper cups. Discouraged, he went back to the rest room. There was a bunch of fresh daisies in a glass jar on the counter of the sink. He took the daisies out, dumped the water, did his business, washed out the jar, filled it with water, and put the flowers back.

On July 26, 1990 – a hot, sunny day – President Bush signed the Americans With Disabilities Act before about two thousand, mostly disabled people out on the lawn of the White House. This legislation became the crowning achievement in the disability civil rights movement. It was the culmination of decades of effort to achieve the goal of equality in all areas of life – employment, transportation, in places of public accommodation, and in communications. What did this extraordinary legislation provide?

ADA fills the vacuum left by the Rehabilitation Act of 1973, which was limited to the federal sector (or to entities receiving federal funds, such as universities and bus companies). Under ADA, discrimination against disabled persons is prohibited by private employers. All "public" places (even though privately owned) constructed after an effective date, subsequent to the date of passage, must be made accessible. For example, a restaurant constructed after that effective date must be fully accessible. Existing places of public accommodation must be made accessible to the extent of being "readily achievable." Extensive new rules require that public and privately owned means of transportation, such as buses and trains, but excluding air carriers, must be accessible. A new system of TDD telephone relays for hearing impaired persons will be implemented. As previously pointed out, the ADA has been appropriately designated the *Emancipation Proclamation,* the *Magna Charta, AND the Declaration of Independence* for disabled people.

ADA is Public Law 101-336. An effort has been made to summarize the high points; the law itself is quite detailed. During 1989 and 1990, many days of hearings were held in Senate and House Committees. The actual legislative trail takes up hundreds if not thousands of pages, and a researcher can find source material in the Congressional Record and in Committee and Hearing Reports. The House hearings were held by four different committees or subcommittees: the Public Works and Transportation Committee Report No. 101-485, Part I, May 14, 1990; the Committee on Education and Labor Report No. 101-485, Part 2, May 15, 1990; the Committee on the Judiciary Report No. 101-485, Part 3, May 15, 1990; and the Committee on Energy and Commerce Report No. 101-485, Part 4. After varying differences between the Senate bill and the House bill were reconciled, the Conference Committee issued Conference Report No.101-596, July 12, 1990. Each of the four committees had primary jurisdiction over different parts of the bill. The Public Works and Transportation Committee had jurisdiction over transportation and public facilities. The Committee on Education and Labor had jurisdiction over employment provisions. The Judiciary Committee had jurisdiction over various constitutional, coordination, and enforcement provisions. The Committee on Energy and Commerce, through the Subcommittee on Telecommunications and Finance, had jurisdiction over communications provisions of the bill. Another research tool has been hearings before the House Judiciary Committee, Subcommittee on Civil and Constitutional Rights, Serial No. 58, August 3, October 11 and 12, 1989. After ADA was passed and became effective, several federal agencies – including the Justice Department, Equal Employment Opportunity Commission, and the Architectural and Transportation Barriers Compliance Board – published lengthy regulations,

Title I - Employment

The essence of Title I, relating to employment discrimination, is found in Section 102:

> *"No covered entity shall discriminate against a qualified individual with a disability because of the disability of such individual in regard to job application procedures, the hiring, advancement, or discharge of employees, employee compensation, job training, and other terms, conditions, and privileges of employment."*

The anti-discrimination section is directed at all employers with fifteen or more employees engaged in an industry affecting commerce, except that, for two years after the effective date (July 26, 1992), only employers of 25 or more workers are covered. The only exceptions to the definition of employer are the United States (because the United States is subject to other legislation), an Indian tribe, or a bona fide private membership club other than a labor organization. The definition of "industry affecting commerce" is determined under the Civil Rights Act of 1964.

The act prohibits discrimination in hiring, promoting and other areas of employment against a "qualified individual with a disability." Thus, an airline could prohibit a blind person from being a pilot because such an individual is not qualified. "Qualified individual with a disability" is defined as an individual with a disability who, with or without reasonable accommodation, can perform the essential functions of the employment position he or she holds or desires. Consideration shall be given to the employer's judgment as to what functions of a job are essential, and if an employer has prepared a written description before advertising or interviewing applicants for a job, this description shall be considered evidence of the essential functions of the job.

Section 3 of the act defines "disability" as a physical or mental impairment which substantially limits one or more of the major life activities of the individual, a record of such impairment (for example, a cured cancer patient), or being regarded as having such an impairment (for example, a person with severe facial burns). Persons with AIDS are regarded as disabled, but not homosexuals and bisexuals, or those who fit in the classifications of transvestism, transsexualism, pedophilia, exhibitionism, voyeurism, gender identity disorders not resulting from physical impairments, or other sexual behavior disorders, compulsive gambling, kleptomania, pyromania or psychoactive substance-use disorders resulting from current illegal use of drugs.

The question of alcohol and drug abuse was a sensitive one. Many members of Congress were quite concerned about providing civil rights to persons who indulged in illegal drugs on the job. The act resolves this problem by concluding that persons currently using illegal drugs are not "disabled," and thus are not entitled to protection under ADA. However, an individual may be disabled if participating in a supervised drug rehabilitation program (or having successfully completed such a program) and is no longer engaging in the illegal use of drugs. For purposes of determining whether a person is in such a program and is no longer using drugs, the employer may adopt a drug testing program. The term "drug" designates a controlled substance listed under the Controlled Substances Act.

Persons with certain infectious diseases may be "disabled." A controversial issue, discussed in the preceding chapter, was whether employers in the food handling industry could transfer employees with AIDS who were handling food to other jobs. The act provides that the Center for Disease Control shall determine whether AIDS is a contagious disease that can be transmitted through handling food. It was generally understood that the Center would conclude that AIDS cannot be transmitted through food handling.

A considerable issue regarding employment discrimination was the fact that many disabled people could do a job, but only if the work site were adapted in some way. For example, a person in a wheelchair might be a computer whiz, but couldn't get to the job site because of the barrier of steps. The act resolves this by concluding that the employer must make "reasonable accommodation," but not if "undue hardship" to the employer would occur. Congress was extremely sensitive to the fears of the business community that expensive alterations of the job site and other hardships might be imposed. The cost of implementing these adaptations is on the employer, and no federal funding is involved. The act attempts to define in greater detail what is meant by reasonable accommodation and undue hardship in order to provide guidance to the business community, but a great deal of flexibility remains, some of which was resolved in regulations issued by the Equal Employment Opportunity Commission. The business community was somewhat two-faced in demanding flexibility and then claiming the law was so vague as to invite costly lawsuits.

Section 101 (9) of the act provides that the term "reasonable accommodation" MAY (not MUST) include making existing work sites readily accessible, job restructuring, part time or modified work schedules, reassignment to a vacant position, acquisition or modification of equipment or devices, training adjustments, and/or provision of qualified readers or interpreters. The employer need not make an accommodation if he or she could demonstrate that the accommodation would impose an undue hardship on the operation of the business. Undue hardship means an action requiring significant difficulty or expense, determined under certain factors: the nature and cost of the accommodation, the overall financial resources of the facility, the number of persons employed at the facility, the effect on expenses or resources, the overall financial resources of the employer, the size of the business, the number, type and location of facilities, and other factors relating to the operation and administration of the business.

The act describes various forms of discrimination, including failing to hire, promote or integrate disabled workers, testing that unfairly excludes disabled people, and providing qualification standards that screen out disabled people unless the criteria are job related and consistent with business necessity. Medical examinations and pre-employment inquiries may not be made to determine whether an applicant has a disability unless the examination or inquiry is job related or consistent with business requirements. A qualification standard may include a prerequisite that an individual shall not pose a direct threat to the health or safety of other individuals in the work place.

All employers covered by Title I shall post notices in an accessible format to applicants and employees describing the relevant provisions of the act.

What if a disabled person is denied a job and believes there has been a violation of Title I? The question of power and remedies was a controversial one. In employment discrimination cases, possible remedies are: reinstatement with back pay, or compensatory or punitive damages. Back pay is often a very limited remedy, and in aggravated cases, compensatory or punitive damages would seem more appropriate. For example, a discharged employee may suffer emotional and other monetary damages, including medical expenses, that in some cases would far exceed the amount to be received by reinstatement of back pay. The Civil Rights Act of 1964 served as a historical model. It prohibited compensatory damages except in cases of racial discrimination. Because of the limitations in the Civil Rights Act of 1964, Senator Kennedy and others introduced legislation in 1990, called the Civil Rights Act of 1990, that would reverse certain restrictive Supreme Court decisions and expand the damages recoverable in employment discrimination cases. When ADA was signed into law on July 26, 1990, the Civil Rights Bill was still pending in Congress. The White House objected to certain provisions in the bill, especially provisions that were regarded by some as imposing quotas, and the threat of a presidential veto loomed. The ADA provides that in employment discrimination cases, the remedies would be the remedies under the Civil Rights Act of 1964. It was understood that if that Act were amended to provides expanded remedies, those would apply under ADA. When ADA was signed, the Civil Rights Act of 1990 was still pending, and the question of remedies and damages was not resolved. Finally in November 1991, President Bush signed a revised Civil Rights Act, which allows for limited compensatory damages in cases of intentional employment discrimination.

A significant provision in ADA is section 505 which provides that in any action or administrative proceeding under the act, the court or agency, in its discretion, may allow the prevailing party a reasonable attorney's fee, including litigation expenses and costs. This could be a two edged sword, for a plaintiff with a frivolous suit could find him or herself paying the employer's attorney's fees. Section 503 is an anti-retaliation provision which says that no person shall discriminate against any individual because such individual has opposed any act or practice made unlawful or made a charge, testified, assisted, or participated in any investigation, proceeding, or hearing under the act.

A curiosity relating to employment discrimination was treatment and remedies of employees or applicants for employment with Senators and members of Congress. There was some thought that Congress was reluctant to be brought into court in the same way as private employers; so internal Senate and House Rules should provide the procedures and remedies. The outcome of this debate is found in section 509. It seems that with respect to employment by the United States Senate, the provisions of ADA and other acts will apply, although the Select Committee on Ethics will get first crack at any employment complaints. As for the House, the exclusive remedy for employment discrimination is found in House Resolution 15 (January 3, 1989).[1] The employment discrimination provisions of Title I take effect two years after enactment, on July 26, 1992. This grace period was inserted to allow businesses, large and small, time to learn of the act and prepare for whatever adaptations to the work site might become necessary. For two years after July 26,1992, only employers with 25 or more employees are covered.

Title II - Public Services

Title II relates to state and local governments, such as cities, towns and counties, and to AMTRAK and certain commuter authorities. Subtitle A is a general prohibition against discrimination with respect to services, programs, or activities of a public entity. For example, a disabled person could not be excluded from a municipal swimming pool. The term qualified individual with a disability is defined slightly differently from Title I. It means an individual with a disability who, (with or without reasonable modifications to rules, policies or practices, the removal of architectural, communication, or transportation barriers, or the provision of auxiliary aids and services) meets the essential eligibility requirements for the receipt of services or participation in programs or activities provided by a public entity.

Though much of the focus of Title II was on accessible public transportation, found in Subtitle B, Subtitle A is also extremely significant, though less well defined. Within one year after the date of enactment, the attorney general is to publish rules implementing subtitle A. Actually, these rules will be developed by the Architectural and Transportation Barriers Compliance Board. Section 504 requires that not later then nine months after the date of enactment, that Board shall issue minimum guidelines that supplement existing Minimum Guidelines and Requirements for Accessible Design. The Board will develop rules that will require new and newly renovated or altered facilities to be accessible. Thus, the Board will require that if new side walk construction is undertaken, the sidewalks must have curb cuts for wheelchair use. If a new city hall, public school, police station, or jail is built, the building must be accessible. In short, it would appear that the requirements applicable to the federal government under the Rehabilitation Act of 1973, and other acts, will also apply to state and local governments.

The conferees stated the intent to be that emergency 911 telephone calls would be made available to hearing and speech impaired individuals through telecommunications equipment.

By far the most controversial part of Title II is Subtitle B, entitled "Actions Applicable to Public Transportation Provided by Public Entities Considered Discriminatory." This Subtitle relates to transportation services provided by city and state bus and train systems and AMTRAK. The Subtitle is an evolutionary development, the origins of which began in the lengthy and often stormy history of the Department of Transportation regulations issued pursuant to section 504 of the Rehabilitation Act of 1973. (See Chapter Fourteen.) The issue of accessible public transportation was one dear to the heart of the disability community. The aggressive arm of that community, ADAPT (then called Americans Disabled for Accessible Public Transportation) had agitated for several years, in cities throughout the country with protests, sit-ins, and scores of arrests. (The involvement of ADAPT in 1990 on behalf of ADA is discussed in the preceding Chapter.) As far as city and state officials and bus companies were concerned, the issue was one primarily of cost, and to some extent, inconvenience. The issue related to city buses, commuter rails, intercity trains and buses, trolleys, and subways. The disability community, in general, wanted total accessibility, including a provision that all new buses be equipped with wheelchair lifts.

But what was to be done about some of the huge costs that might be involved? Were all the subway stops in New York City, for example, to be provided with elevators, at a cost of billions of dollars? Should paratransit, such as alternative vans, be provided and if so under what conditions? What should be the effective date of any new requirements? Lengthy and sometimes, tense hearings were held by various Congressional Committees, and many weakening amendments were offered to the original bill.

The guts of the Public Transportation provisions are contained in section 222. It shall be considered discrimination for a public entity which operates a fixed route system to purchase or lease a new bus, a new rapid rail vehicle, a new light rail vehicle, or any other new vehicle to be used on such a system, if the solicitation for such purchase or lease is made after the 30th day following the date of enactment, July 26, 1990, unless such new vehicle is readily accessible and usable by individuals with disabilities, including people who use wheelchairs. The Act didn't define what was meant by "accessible" and nowhere is it specifically said that wheelchair lifts must be installed. However, it was generally understood that for new buses, wheelchair lifts would be required. Some subway systems have access directly from a platform level with the passenger car door, in which case lifts would not be necessary. Remanufactured vehicles were required to comply, to the maximum extent feasible.

Section 223 requires a public entity that operates a fixed route system to also provide paratransit that is sufficient to provide a level of service that is (1) comparable to the level of designated public transportation provided to individuals without disabilities, and (2) in the case of response time, comparable to the extent practicable, to regular public transportation services. Within one year after the date of enactment, the Secretary of Transportation is to issue regulations to carry out that section. The statute directs that regulations provide that certain described disabled persons be eligible for paratransit. The service area of paratransit must be comparable to the area served by the fixed route system, except for any portion of the service area in which the public entity solely provides commuter bus service. Regulations are to provide rules to determine the extent to which compliance may be excused because it would impose an undue financial burden on the public entity.

The Public Works and Transportation Committee Report makes it clear that the existence of architectural barriers does not trigger eligibility for paratransit if these barriers are not the responsibility of the fixed route operator. For example, no eligibility for paratransit exists due simply to a lack of curb cuts in the path of travel since, in the short term, such barriers can often be navigated and pressure to eliminate them should be maintained on the local government. Within 18 months of the effective date, the public entity must submit a plan to DOT for implementing paratransit services.

Section 225 provides temporary relief from the requirement that all new buses be accessible where wheelchair lifts are unavailable, with respect to the purchase of new buses, because no manufacturer of lifts could be found.

In some rural areas, there is no fixed route system, but there is a demand response system which depends on requests from the public. In this type of system, the rules are less stringent. The public entity must have new buses accessible, unless the system, when viewed in its entirety, provides a level of service equivalent to the level of service the system provides to persons without disabilities.

Section 226 relates to new facilities, such as bus stations and train stations. All new facilities must be accessible, including accessible to persons using wheelchairs. If alterations are made to existing facilities, the facility must become accessible, to the maximum extent feasible. If alterations are made that affect usability or access to a facility that serves as a primary function, there must be ready access to a path of travel to the altered area, the bathrooms, telephones, and drinking fountains serving the area, if the access changes are not disproportionate to the overall alterations in terms of cost and scope.

Section 227 (b) contains a special rule for rail stations including subway stations. All key stations in rapid rail and light rail systems must be readily accessible by the end of the three year period beginning on the date of enactment. The determination of what is a key station is to be determined under criteria established by the Department of Transportation. Under this section, not all subway stations had to be accessible, only key stations. This was relief directed, for example, at the NewYork City subway system, where the cost of elevators to subway stations would be extraordinarily expensive. The three year period can be extended by DOT up to a thirty year period for key stations where exceptionally expensive structural changes would be needed, except that at the end of twenty years, at least two-thirds of key stations must be accessible. Different rules for stations of commuter rail systems and intercity trains systems are contained in section 242 (e). For intercity rail systems (AMTRAK), all new stations must be accessible. As for existing intercity stations and commuter rail stations, all intercity stations and all existing key commuter rail stations must be accessible, within certain time limits. All intercity existing stations must be made accessible as soon as practicable, but within twenty years of date of enactment. Key stations in commuter rail systems must be made accessible as soon as practicable but in no event later than three years from date of enactment, except the time may be extended by DOT up to twenty years in a case where the raising of the entire passenger platform is the only means available of attaining accessibility or where other extraordinarily expensive structural changes are necessary. Within one year of date of enactment, DOT must issue regulations dealing with accessible transportation, and these regulations must be consistent with minimum guidelines issued by the Architectural and Transportation Barriers Compliance Board.

Although all newly purchased or leased buses or train vehicles must be accessible, there was concern that new vehicles might not be purchased as soon as desirable. Section 228 (b) provides that, whether new vehicles are purchased or not, at least one car per train must be accessible by the end of the five year period, beginning on the date of enactment. This rule does not apply to certain historic trains if alterations would significantly alter the historic character of the train. Within one year of date of enactment, DOT is to issue regulations, consistent with the guidelines of the Architectural and Transportation Barriers Compliance Board. If a transportation facility is planned and a building permit obtained before issuance of final regulations and construction begins within one year of the permit, compliance with the Uniform Federal Accessibility Standards (UFAS) in effect at the time the building permit is issued will suffice to comply with the requirements of the act. UFAS originated in the Architectural Barriers Act of 1968; input from several federal agencies resulted in the UFAS rules.

A special rule applies to single level passenger coaches of intercity trains (AMTRAK). Single level passenger coaches shall be required to be accessible to a person who uses a wheelchair. They must have a space to park and secure the wheelchair, must have a seat to which a passenger in a wheelchair can transfer, and must have a wheelchair accessible rest-room. However, dining cars need not have a rest-room for wheelchair users if no rest-room is provided at all. Bi-level dining cars in any event need not have an accessible rest-room. There was concern that if a great many people in wheelchairs had bought train tickets, there would not be enough spaces to park and store wheelchairs. Limitations were included which depend on the number of single level, rail passenger coaches in the train and in any event, not more than two spaces to park and secure wheelchairs nor more than two spaces to fold and secure wheelchairs shall be located in any one coach or food service car. If a single level dining car is purchased after the date of enactment, table service shall be provided for a passenger who uses a wheelchair, if the car adjacent to the dining car is accessible. Space to park and secure, or fold, the wheelchair must be provided, and appropriate auxiliary aids and services, including a hard surface on which to eat, shall be provided.

In summary, the public transportation provisions are extraordinarily comprehensive and, in time, should provide a fully accessible nationwide public bus and rail transportation system. Great care was taken to insure that the new requirements would be phased in slowly. Although these provisions affect AMTRAK, they do not affect strictly private bus companies, such as Greyhound. Provisions for private bus companies are contained in Title III, discussed below. The United States can justly claim to be a world leader in providing for a fully accessible public transportation system.

Title III - Public Accommodations and Services Operated by Private Entities

Title III is another remarkable, truly historic section.

In essence, it requires private operators of "places of public accommodation" to provide accessible facilities and services. In the fifties and sixties, blacks in many places could not eat in public restaurants or swim in public pools. The Civil Rights Act of 1964 changed that, but did not apply to disabled people. ADA provides, somewhat belatedly, for access by all disabled people to all places of public accommodation, truly revolutionary progress. For example, a newly constructed, altered, or renovated restaurant must be accessible to people with disabilities including wheelchair users and deaf and blind people. Existing places of public accommodation must be made accessible to the extent this objective is readily achievable. "Readily achievable" means easily accomplished and able to be carried out without much difficulty or expense. In determining whether an action is readily achievable, factors to be considered include the nature and cost of the action, the overall financial resources of the facility, the number of persons employed in such a facility, the effect on expenses and resources, the size of the business and the number, type, and location of its facilities, the type of operation including the composition, structure, and functions of the work force, and the geographic separateness, administrative or fiscal relationship of the facility.

The definition of place of public accommodation in section 301 (7) is almost endless: it includes an inn, hotel, motel (unless it contains not more than five rooms and is occupied by the proprietor), a restaurant, bar, motion picture or other theater, concert hall, stadium, auditorium, convention center, lecture hall, bakery, grocery store, clothing store, hardware store, shopping center or other sales or rental establishment, laundromat, dry cleaner, bank, barber shop, beauty shop, travel service, shoe repair service, funeral parlor, gas station, office of an accountant or lawyer, pharmacy, insurance company, health care provider, hospital or other service establishment, bus depot, museum, library, gallery, park, zoo, amusement park, private nursery or school, including postgraduate school, day care center, senior citizen center, hospital, homeless shelter or other social service establishment, gymnasium, health spa, bowling alley, golf course or other place of exercise or recreation. You could say, if it's in the Yellow Pages, it's covered. Regulations to implement this provision were issued by the Justice Department on July 26, 1991; regulations by the Architectural and Transportation Barriers Compliance Board were put out on July 26 and September 6, 1991.

What brought about this extraordinary provision? Congress was very concerned that many disabled people were isolated and shunned, kept at home or in institutions, and were not getting out into the world to participate in every day life as non-disabled people do.[2] The House Committee on Education and Labor said that three major reasons were given by witnesses for the isolation of disabled people. First, people with disabilities often feel that they are not welcome and cannot participate safely in public places because of discriminatory actions that have occurred in the past. The second reason is fear and self-consciousness about their disabilities, also stemming from degrading and discriminatory experiences. The third reason is architectural, communications, and transportation barriers.

The act goes on, in some detail, to provide what has to be done to make a facility accessible. The act makes a clear distinction between existing facilities and newly constructed or altered facilities. The former must be made accessible if doing that is *"readily achievable."* New facilities or newly altered facilities must be *"readily accessible."*

At an early date, there was anxiety in Congress and throughout the business community, that costs required for making facilities accessible might impose a hardship. There was no federal funding to finance these changes. Many questions arose: would ramps, railings, and possibly wheelchair lifts be required? Would elevators be required? What about parking, restrooms, and telephones? Would restaurants be required to have menus in braille? Would waiters be required to use sign language for the hearing impaired? Would every public place be required to have a TDD telephone system? It was decided that existing facilities, in general, need not be altered, unless removal of architectural barriers is readily achievable, but new facilities or renovated facilities would have to be made readily accessible.

It was decided that changes to existing facilities need only be mimimal to become "readily achievable." What can be considered readily achievable depends on a variety of factors, as discussed above.

Although the statute achieved the desired goal of flexibility and restraint, it did so at the expense of clarity and precision. The statute goes on to describe the actions that would be regarded as discriminatory. It shall be discriminatory to deny the opportunity of the disabled person to participate in or benefit from the goods, services, facilities, privileges, advantages, or accommodations of an entity. It shall be discriminatory to afford a disabled individual facilities or benefits that are not equal to those provided for other individuals. It shall be discriminatory to provide a disabled individual a service or benefit that is different or separate from that provided for other individuals. Presumably, this means that a restaurant can not require persons in wheelchairs to sit in a separate room. However, separation may be allowed if necessary to provide the individual with a good, service, or facility that is as effective as that provided others. Presumably, this could mean, for example, that separate sections in sports stadia could be provided for persons in wheelchairs. Goods, services, facilities, and so forth must be afforded *"in the most integrated setting appropriate to the needs of the individual."* It shall be discriminatory to exclude a non-disabled person from benefits because of his or her association with a disabled person. It shall be discriminatory to fail to make *"reasonable modifications"* when such modifications are necessary to afford goods and services and so forth to individuals with disabilities, unless the entity can demonstrate that making such modifications would fundamentally alter the nature of such goods, services, facilities, privileges, advantages, or accommodations. It shall be discriminatory to fail to take such steps as may be necessary to ensure that no individual with a disability is excluded, denied services, segregated, or otherwise treated differently from other individuals because of the absence of auxiliary aids and services, unless the entity can demonstrate that taking such steps would fundamentally alter the nature of the goods, services, and so forth being offered or would result in an *"undue burden." It shall be discriminatory to fail to remove architectural barriers and communication barriers that are structural in nature in existing facilities, where such removal is readily achievable. Even if the removal of a barrier is not readily achievable, the entity must provide readily achievable alternative accommodations.*

As far as new facilities are concerned, an entity need not make certain facilities accessible if it can demonstrate that it is structurally impracticable to meet the requirements, in accordance with issued regulations. Altered primary function facilities must provide a path of travel to bathrooms, telephones, and drinking fountains serving the altered area unless the changes are disproportionate to the overall alterations. It is not necessary to install an elevator for facilities that are less than three stories or have less than 3000 square feet per story unless the building is a shopping center, a shopping mall, or the professional office of a health care provider, or unless the attorney general determines that a particular category of facilities requires the installation of elevators based on usage. The new construction rules take effect for facilities constructed for first occupancy later than thirty months after the date of enactment.

The act applies to both owners and renters of places of accommodation. It has two curious exemptions, one for certain private clubs and one for religious organizations, including places of worship. The latter exemption was put in with the urging of the Latter Day Saints and Senator Hatch of Utah, whose support of ADA was essential; the other religious denominations did not request this exemption. As a practical matter, churches may be subject to state and local building codes, and their facilities would probably have to be accessible if they serve other organizations which are regarded as places of public accommodation that must be accessible. For example, a church basement used by the Boy Scouts might be required to be accessible.

An important issue under the act is the question of enforcement. In general, section 308 provides for certain actions by private individuals in civil suits or actions by the attorney general. The remedies are those provided by the Civil Rights Act of 1964, which are limited in scope, although the Civil Rights Act of 1991 will expand those remedies. Under ADA, a disabled person denied access to a restaurant could only seek in a civil suit an injunction requiring access, or the removal of an architectural barrier, or an injunction to require auxiliary aids or services. No compensatory damages, such as for emotional damages, are allowable in private suits, except that the Civil Rights Act of 1991 will provide for limited compensatory damages in employment cases. Under ADA, the attorney general may bring an action if there is a pattern or practice of discrimination or if there is an issue of general public importance. The court in such an action may grant an injunction or award monetary damages when requested by the attorney general. The Committee on Education and Labor Report No.101-485 says that the term monetary damages does not include punitive damages but includes all forms of compensatory damages including out of pocket expenses and damages for pain and suffering. Also, the court may impose a fine, of up to $50,000 for a first violation or up to $100,000, for subsequent violations. However, no punitive damages may be awarded.

An interesting aspect of the public accommodations provisions is that establishments covered by the act must *"affect commerce"* which is defined as including, for example, commerce among the several states or between a state and a foreign country. This provision might lead the uninformed tiny restaurant in a tiny village to conclude that the act doesn't apply because the establishment doesn't *"affect commerce."* It's not so. This language was put in to put a constitutional peg on which to base a federal statute that will apply in every city, town, village, and hamlet. The *"interstate commerce"* clause of the United States Constitution has been broadly interpreted by the courts as justifying federal legislation that is extremely far reaching. Even the tiny restaurant, just mentioned, is regarded as *"affecting commerce"* in a variety of ways.

One of the most controversial parts of Title III relates to private bus companies such as Greyhound and Trailways. All during the legislative process, Greyhound fought tooth and nail against provisions requiring wheelchair lifts on buses. Greyhound was concerned with the cost of the lifts, space to park the wheelchairs, and the question of whether wheelchair accessible restrooms must be provided. Greyhound, during this period, was faced with a crippling, violent strike, which was pushing the company to the brink of bankruptcy. At the same time, ADAPT, an organization of wheelchair users, was engaging in protests all over the country, often being arrested when they blocked buses on the streets. The result of this intensive lobbying was somewhat of a compromise and a postponement of resolution of the issues. For over the road buses such as Greyhound, the Office of Technology Assessment is to conduct a study to determine the access needs of persons with disabilities and the most cost effective methods of making the buses readily accessible. The act provides that the purchase of new buses shall be made in accordance with regulations to be issued by the Department of Transportation. The final regulations shall be in accordance with the study and shall go into effect in seven years for small providers and six years for the others. The final regulations shall not require the installation of accessible restrooms if such installation would result in a loss of seating capacity. In the interim, DOT will issue temporary regulations which may not require any structural changes to over-the-road buses to provide access. Thus final resolution of this difficult issue was postponed.

Title IV - Telecommunications

One of the largest barriers facing hearing impaired people is the lack of access to usable telecommunications services, such as telephones. While some of the other titles, such as the employment and public accommodations provisions will require changes that assist deaf persons, Title IV relates exclusively to accessible telecommunications. It is remarkable legislation and should prove of incalculable benefit to hearing and speech impaired people.

For years past, hearing impaired persons generally could communicate by telephone only if they had a TDD telephone and were communicating with another person with a TDD telephone. A TDD is basically a telephone with a typewriter keyboard and screen that conveys the written message to the receiver, who must also have a TDD. In general, it was not possible for a TDD to communicate with a normal telephone and vice versa. Title IV allows for nationwide telephone communication through a relay operator who will transmit a TDD message to or from a hearing receiver.

Title IV developed out of lobbying pressure by the deaf community, and it was an extension of legislation already in place in many states. California was the first state to require relay services, in 1987. State laws varied; for example, in New Hampshire relayed calls were limited to five a day, and in Massachusetts the duration of the call was limited to ten minutes for a personal call and twenty minutes for a business call. Problems arose because state laws generally didn't require interstate relay calls. Most state relay systems were underfunded and understaffed.

At the hearings on ADA, Gregory Hlibok, President of the Student Body Government at Gallaudet University, described some of the obstacles to daily living faced by hearing impaired people:

> *"Many of us confront discrimination every day. We have experienced the disappointment of being turned down for a job or promotion because we were told the communication barriers were too great. My own deaf brother was told he had to pay for his own deaf interpreter on his job. We have tried to call the police for help using our telecommunication devices for the deaf, but the police hang up on us, because they have no TDD's. I remember when I was fifteen I left school without money to take the bus home. I had no way to call my parents or the police. I had to walk the three miles home in the snow".*[3]

The Communications Act of 1934 mandated telephone service to all Americans, yet there are at least 26 million hearing or speech impaired persons who cannot use existing telephones. Title IV remedies this defect by amending the Communications Act of 1934 to mandate the operator relay service just described. All common carriers providing interstate or intrastate telephone service must provide to hearing or speech impaired persons telecommunication services that enable them to communicate with hearing individuals. These services must be functionally equivalent to telephone service provided to hearing individuals. The House Reports No. 101-485 further clarify the intent of Congress. It is not the intent to freeze the telecommunication system in existing state-of-the-art relay systems but to allow for advances in technology. The service must be available 24 hours a day and must be provided at rates no greater than normal rates. The FCC is to develop rules to implement the provisions; state relay systems can be certified by the FCC as complying with the Act.

Suppose Johnny, who is hearing impaired, wants to communicate by telephone with Suzie, his girl friend, who is not. Congress was sensitive to the need for privacy. A relay operator may not refuse calls or limit length of calls. Relay operators may not disclose the contents of a relayed message. However, printed records of the calls may be necessary to complete the call, but records are not to be kept after completion of the call. The committees recognized that it may currently be technically impossible to relay recorded messages in their entirety; in that case a communicator should be given the option to have the message summarized. (No one, however, has suggested how to summarize a Shakespearean Sonnet, or an Ode by Shelley!) Relay operators are prohibited from intentionally altering messages.

Some gaps in Title IV include the fact that a deaf person on the street must have access to a TDD in order to initiate a call, either by carrying his or her own TDD or finding one. The act generally does not require ubiquitous public TDD stations. Another unresolved issue is the issue of cost and expense allocation. Relayed calls are more expensive than regular calls and the question of allocating that expense is not fully resolved. Still another issue is whether the relay system must transmit illegal calls. The deaf community fears limitations based on the subject matter of the call. In general, the telephone companies have supported Title IV. For one thing, the provisions are expected to increase telephone company business. However, some telephone companies are concerned about the unresolved issues just mentioned.

The telecommunications provisions of Title IV will provide hearing and speech impaired persons with nationwide telephone accessibility. It will be possible to call for a theater reservation, order a prescription from a drugstore, inquire after a friend or relative, conduct a business, complain to a bureaucrat, ask for a weather report, or call the police. It will be possible to receive telephone calls from anyone for any reason, at any time.

Thus the Americans With Disabilities Act provides for enormous changes and improvements in the lives of all disabled Americans. The promise of ADA is that no longer will so many disabled people be isolated, shunned, and discriminated against, or closeted either in their own homes or in institutions. A new day has dawned! ADA will provide greater access in employment, transportation, telecommunications, public places, and all areas of life for the disabled community

Postscript: In Anderson v. Little League Baseball, Inc., the United States District Court for the District of Arizona decided what is possibly the first case under the Americans With Disabilities Act (794 F. Supp. 342, Ariz. July 8, 1992). In this case, Larry Anderson, who uses a wheelchair due to a spinal cord injury, had coached Little League for several years, usually as a field base coach. The National Little League Organization had adopted a policy of allowing a coach in a wheelchair to coach from the dugout, but he could not be in a coach's box. Anderson argued successfully that such a policy violated the Americans With Disabilities Act. The court, in an excellent opinion, rejected the Little League's argument that Larry posed a "direct threat" to the safety of the youngsters. As the court said:

"The Court gives great weight to the fact that plaintiff has served as a Little League coach at either first base or third base for three years without incident. Moreover, plaintiff's significant contributions of time, energy, enthusiasm, and personal example benefit the numerous children who participate in Little League activities as well as the community-at-large. Plaintiff's work with young people teaches them the importance of focusing on the strengths of others and helping them to rise to overcome their personal challenges."

CHAPTER VIII

THE AIRLINES

A young woman suffered a spinal cord injury when she was hit by a drunken driver. She later received a huge settlement—in the millions. Then, jobless, she took to flying all over the world. It was a serious challenge to her. She always asked for a seat next to the toilet; she also restricted her fluid intake because on long flights she had to drag herself, on the floor, to the accomodations. On one trip she flew Air France to Paris and had a splendid time at the museums, parks, and bistros. Her reservation for the way back was on Northern Airlines, a U.S. carrier. Presenting herself at the gate, she was told that she could not fly without a companion, which would cost another $950 in first class. She not only didn't have the funds, she didn't have the companion! She had to return to her hotel and wait three days to fly back, on her own, on Air France.

While it is generally conceded that the disabled are the most impoverished, most isolated, most immobile, and most unemployed of all minority groups, quite a few individuals have broken out of this ghetto and, while they're not exactly jet-setters, they have taken to the air. There are, in numerical terms if not in percentages of people disabled, many who fly on business or for sports or recreation. Many disabled people have important jobs in industry or government that require traveling constantly from city to city. Many leaders of the disabled community are in demand as lecturers and seminar participants, not only in America but throughout the world. There are quite a few wheelchair sports teams that have schedules throughout the nation and in foreign countries. There are even some disabled people who have some money left over after all their expenses and simply want to take a vacation!

Air travel has become increasingly accessible to disabled travelers, but progress hasn't come easily. It has come about as a result of battles in and out of court, by disabled individuals and disability groups, as well as the staunch support of those lobbying before Congress. The issue has been regarded more and more as a matter of civil rights. The disabled community, generally, has proven triumphant.

Of all the access issues, that of the airlines has probably been one of the most controversial, but problems have been resolved, generally though not universally, in favor of disabled travelers. There have been a variety of issues.

First, does an airline have the right to exclude a person in a wheelchair unless he or she is accompanied by an attendant? Some airlines have excluded certain disabled persons without an attendant primarily for safety reasons—the concern being that the person might not be able to find an exit in case of an emergency, might need personal care, or worse, might block the exit of other passengers. But if a person in a wheelchair is required to have an attendant on a flight, the cost of any trip would then be doubled because of the necessity of buying a second ticket.

Another issue has been that of seating. Many blind persons want to sit at an exit, as a civil right of not being treated differently from other people, but some airlines feel this could be a hazard to other passengers. Yet blind groups have maintained that a blind passenger in a smoke filled cabin might actually have an advantage over seeing passengers, in that the blind often have a better developed sense of location and direction.

Still another issue has been the boarding of wheelchairs. Should electric or motorized wheelchairs be allowed at all, and if so, at what cost? Should they be allowed in the cabin or stored in baggage? Should aisles be widened to accommodate them? Should restrooms be accessible to people in wheelchairs? Finally, there have been instances where airlines have requested a medical release or permission from a doctor before allowing a disabled person to board. Is this a fair requirement?

All these issues have received the attention of government agencies, primarily the old Civil Aeronautics Board and more recently the Federal Aviation Administration within DOT.

The availability of airline-owned wheelchairs at airports, for the convenience of mobility impaired persons, is no longer much of an issue, as wheelchairs are universally provided. Still, there have been some problems of lack of availability and lack of attendants or porters to push them, as many are not capable of being self-propelled. On the whole the airlines have done a commendable job in assisting disabled persons at airport locations. Sometimes the non-disabled passengers are not so cooperative, and on occasion an empty wheelchair has been "borrowed" by an inconsiderate, non-disabled person for purposes of transporting suitcases, regardless of whether this would mean that a person in need of a wheelchair would go without. The author had the experience of discovering that all foot rests on all wheelchairs at Eastern's Boston (Logan) Airport, were missing. There had been reports of employee sabotage, and Eastern's labor troubles eventually drove the airline into bankruptcy.

The pot began to boil in the early seventies, as disabled persons complained of discrimination by airlines and in many cases went to court. In 1973, the Rehabilitation Act was passed, and section 504 of that Act prohibited discrimination against handicapped persons in any facility or program receiving federal financial assistance. Although there was not a word in the act about airlines, since most commercial airlines receive some kind of federal subsidy, it was understood that the new law would apply to most airlines, as well as to federal buildings, most colleges and universities, buildings, buses, trains and so forth. The FAA took on the task of writing regulations relating to the issues of access on airlines, and that process is still continuing through the Department of Transportation.

In November 1973, the Senate passed a bill authorizing airlines, railroads, and bus companies to offer reduced fares to persons over 65, to disabled people, and to persons under 21. The issues of access were not addressed

Early in 1975, when Judy Heumann, a leader in the disability civil rights movement, boarded a National Airlines plane with her wheelchair at Kennedy Airport in New York, she was told to get off because she didn't have an attendant. When she refused, she was arrested by the Port Authority police.

Patricia Thoben, a paraplegic since birth who uses a wheelchair, worked for the Civil Service Commission in a job that required a great deal of traveling. She had to go to Philadelphia to give a speech, but both Eastern and Allegheny refused her permission to board, saying she would be a hazard in case of a crash. "*I was hurt, angry, and humiliated,*" she said.

She called Congressman Joel Broyhill of Virginia, who labeled the incident a "*gross injustice*" and wrote to FAA Administrator Alexander P. Butterfield on her behalf. The FAA said that each airline had its own rules, and within each airline, there was often a rule giving "*pilot's discretion*" to refuse to board a passenger. The FAA said they were considering regulations. Eastern said they would permit a person in a wheelchair to board if accompanied by a physician's note saying that the person could care for himself or herself. Miss Thoben, stating that she had been flying for 23 years, filed a suit in June 1974 against Eastern and Allegheny, asking for $250,000 in punitive damages. A spokesman for the

Airline Pilot's Association said, *"there have been crashes when the elderly and handicapped did slow down evacuation."* An editorial in *The Washington Post* on June 1, 1974, said:

> *"Certainly a year is long enough for [FAA] to have come up with some sensible solutions, consistent with safety, to end the cruel and haphazard discrimination suffered at airports by the nation's handicapped."*

The FAA was getting media-lashed, especially after they admitted that the anti-hijacking law, which allowed prohibition of "dangerous" would-be-passengers, had been applied to exclude some disabled; they promised that regulations were being reviewed and would soon be out.

The promised regulations were issued July 5, 1974, and three months were allowed for comments. Under the proposed regulations, an airline must fly a disabled person if he or she has a statement from a doctor to the effect that he or she doesn't need assistance *" to expeditiously move to an exit in the event of an emergency evacuation."* Another provision said that the number of disabled persons on any given flight couldn't exceed the number of exits. This was a haphazard requirement because a slow-moving disabled person might be excluded on the ground that more nimble disabled persons showed up at the gate first. The disabled community complained that the regulations merely preserved the status quo. In August 1974, thirteen Senators (Harrison Williams, Ted Kennedy, Charles Percy, Jennings Randolph, Alan Cranston, Claiborne Pell, Robert Stafford, J. Glen Beall Jr., Robert Taft Jr., John Tunney, Frank Church, Walter Mondale, and Richard Schweiker) said they opposed the FAA regulations and were *"deeply disturbed."*

A story in *The Washington Post* on July 29, 1974, recounted how Susanne Wyncoop of Hackensack, New Jersey, was not allowed to board an Eastern flight in Newark because she didn't have a companion. This, even though she had a student pilot's license and had flown 150,000 miles!

On June 28, 1982, the CAB (14 CFR Part 382) adopted final regulations. It omitted a proposal to widen aisles to accommodate wheelchairs. Flights must be *"reasonably accessible"* to disabled people. It was left to the airlines to deal with individual disabled persons. The regulations were a cop-out!

With the disabled groups not getting much satisfaction from regulations, they continued to go to court, with mixed results.

Pan American, in Frankfurt, Germany, had refused to board Michael Angel, a young man with cerebral palsy, on the ground that he did not have an attendant. The individual sued Pan American, with generally successful results. Pan Am's motion to dismiss was denied, on the ground that the plaintiff had a legitimate complaint (the court didn't conclusively decide the case). The plaintiff had three grounds for his suit for damages, a violation of section 504 of the Rehabilitation Act, misrepresentation and tortious conduct, and a violation of Pan Am's procedural "tariffs" that related to rules for dealing with disabled persons. On the first point, the court said there was no violation of the anti-discrimination provision, section 504, because Pan Am had not received direct federal subsidies, and indirect benefits, such as mail subsidies, were insufficient to invoke section 504. This result was ultimately reversed by the Air Carriers Access Act. The plaintiff got a mixed judgment on the misrepresentation-tort complaint which required a jury verdict. On the last point, Pan Am, pursuant to FAA regulations, had posted its requirements for dealing with disabled passengers and would-be passengers. In effect, Pan Am's procedures said that a passenger who was unable to move to an exit under his own power, or to attend to his personal requirements, would not be boarded without an attendant. The persons included in this rule were the blind-deaf, stretcher cases, and non-ambulatory wheelchair cases. Judge Joyce Hens Green, of the United States District Court for the District of Columbia, said that Michael Angel was ambulatory, in that he could crawl, and thus, in effect, Pan Am violated their own "tariffs." Judge Green said:

> *"Plaintiff, then a student at the University of Maryland, has cerebral palsy, is confined to an electric wheelchair, is unable to walk, to feed himself, or to perform some personal functions without assistance. He can, however, crawl rapidly and take care of many other personal needs, including getting undressed, taking a bath, brushing his teeth, washing his hair, laying out his clothes, setting the alarm clock, and getting into bed. He has no difficulty in descending a flight of stairs. His ordinary means of movement is crawling, at which he is quite adept and by which he maneuvers himself. Plaintiff is able to get into and out of an automobile unassisted, has taken trips on the District of Columbia subway and has flown across the Atlantic Ocean without an attendant and without difficulty. He has repeatedly flown by himself between Washington, D.C. and Florida. He can, and has, seated himself inside an airplane. He can go without food for the duration of the flight and is able, when necessary (and has so done on four occasions) to get out of his seat, crawl to the lavatory, use the facilities and return to his seat without assistance."* [1]

Judge Green went on to say *"Federal law appropriately recognizes the right of the physically handicapped to be free from discrimination. Our society has advanced the rights of the handicapped demonstrably; yet, as those individuals who seek vindication of their rights are all too often aware, our nation has not completed the process of ensuring equality. It is hoped that that day is to come soon."*

Judge Green deserves credit for a perceptive opinion, and Michael Angel deserves credit for traveling and flying by himself, though severely disabled; he is an inspiration to others.

In 1985 the Court of Appeals for the District of Columbia decided that US Air properly excluded a blind person from a seat adjacent to an exit. The court said that section 504 of the Rehabilitation Act did not require airlines to seat blind persons near an exit.[2] Blind groups have claimed the right to sit near exits, more as a symbol of status than anything else. That is, if not allowed to sit near an exit, they feel it is because they are regarded as "less capable" than other persons.

Disabled persons sometimes complain of treatment by flight attendants; being treated like children or worse. The story is told of a blind man reading Playboy magazine in Braille; the flight attendant commented that she didn't know that blind people were interested in sex! On the whole, with sensitivity training and more experience, the airline support personnel are doing a commendable job in dealing with disabled people.

In Hingson v. Pacific Southwest Airlines, Michael Hingson, who is blind, was told to sit in the front seat.[3] He refused, and was escorted off the plane by police. He brought suit under section 404 (b) of the Federal Aviation Act, which allows compensatory damages if illegal conduct is "wanton, oppressive, or malicious." The court said that the issue was whether the airline acted reasonably; the case was remanded to the lower court to consider additional evidence.

The Supreme Court got into the picture in a significant decision in 1986. In United States Department of Transportation v. Paralyzed Veterans of America [477 U.S. 597 (986)], the Supreme Court, reversing the Court of Appeals for the District of Columbia, said that section 504 and section 404 of the Federal Aviation Act of 1958 did not cover airlines unless they received direct federal subsidies. PVA argued that all airlines were covered because of the indirect federal benefit of federally paid and supervised air controllers and other federal benefits at airports. The majority opinion favoring the airlines was written by Justice Powell, with dissents by Justices Marshall, Brennan, and Blackmun. The result of this decision was that some airlines were covered by federal legislation relating to disabled people and some were not.

As a result of the PVA case, Congress, with Senator Robert Dole as a primary sponsor, decided that the uneven results were unacceptable, and in 1986 the Air Carrier Access Act, 49 U.S.C. section 1374 et seq, (Public Law 99-435) was passed. This act, which amends section 404 of the Federal Aviation Act, provides that *"no air carrier may discriminate against any otherwise qualified handicapped individual, in the provision of air transportation."*

Thus all airlines, not just some, will be subject to regulations issued by the FAA.

On June 22, 1988, DOT, through the FAA, issued proposed regulations under the Air Carrier Access Act (53 F.R. 23574; 14 C.F.R. Part 38). The background note to the proposed regulations candidly admits that *"air carrier policies and practices concerning disabled passengers have long been a troublesome and controversial subject."* The disabled community has been frustrated by inconsistent and unexplained policies, often being unaware from flight to flight whether they will be allowed to board. Airlines cite concerns of safety, economics, and inconvenience to other passengers. Realizing that many issues are controversial, DOT invited discussions from disability groups, various government agencies, and from air carriers. A mediator from the Federal Mediation and Conciliation Service chaired the meetings. Although the discussions led to agreement on some issues, and narrowed the differences on others, there was never an agreement on the issue of exit row seat restrictions. As a result of the impasse, there was no formal vote or consensus on the entire package. The DOT proposed regulations emphasized that there should be a balance between concerns of safety and concerns of not discriminating against disabled people. Significantly, the Notice of Proposed Rule Making seems to score one for the airlines:

> *"The Air Carrier Access Act was intended to fill what Congress regarded as a gap in section 504 coverage resulting from the Supreme Court's decision in DOT v. PVA. The language of the statute parallels that of section 504. Consequently, the department is persuaded that in determining the substantive requirements to be imposed under the statute, guidance should be set by existing case law interpreting section 504. Specifically, the department interprets its discretion in implementing the Act as constrained by Southeastern Community College v. Davis, 422 U.S. 397 (1979), American Public Transit Association v. Lewis, 665 F.2d1272 (D.C. Cir. 1981), and cases following, which hold that a federal agency may not, in carrying out section 504, impose undue financial or administrative burdens on regulated parties. In making regulatory decisions, the department intends not to impose undue burdens on the carriers."*

The Department of Transportation, which also has jurisdiction over buses and trains, no doubt committed itself to not imposing "undue burdens" on bus and train companies as well. But what is an undue burden? The Davis case did not deal with a federal agency and did not deal with transportation access, but only with a small community college, to which the plaintiff was trying to be admitted. The phrase "undue burden" is not only ambiguously broad, but is being asked to carry too much weight, when applied to the transportation area. It's one thing to apply an "undue burden" standard to a small college in a small town in a small state, and something quite different to apply it to a major airline or other transportation company. Large entrepreneurs have always been subject to a variety of governmental rules, such as installing smoke detectors, fire extinguishers, and other safety devices. Cruise ships are required to have life preservers and evacuation boats. The standard of "undue burden" is just as irrelevant in those areas as with respect to the issue of handicapped access. It's time for a new look.

An unusual situation arose in April 1988, just prior to the publication of the proposed regulations. Peggy Pinder, a blind lawyer, refused to sit up front near the exit; she wanted to sit back in the smoking section. Midway Airlines had the unusual policy of seating handicapped persons near exits for easy exit. Most airlines believe that seating disabled persons near an exit may block the exit of other passengers. In any event, Peggy was arrested at Washington National Airport on March 31, 1988. Ironically, she is Vice President of the National Federation for the Blind and was coming to Washington to discuss air travel access issues!

But to return to the proposed DOT regulations published in June 1988. Hearings had been held in the fall of 1987, at which disability groups and carriers presented their views. Since the various groups involved in the discussions were unable to agree on all issues, some issues remain unresolved in the proposed regulations. Unresolved issues included: should regulations prohibit airlines from making pre-boarding of disabled persons optional? In other words, are there circumstances in which an airline may require pre-boarding of disabled persons in order to give them adequate briefing? DOT sought comments on the situation where a disabled person is scheduled on a flight, but due to technical difficulties, a smaller plane, which may not accommodate the person, is substituted. Should damages be awarded?

The proposed regulations reached an uncertain compromise on the question of whether the pilot has discretionary authority to refuse permission to board. The regulations give the pilot discretionary authority, but subject to the requirement that his judgment comply with the regulations. This apparently meant that his decision is not immediately reviewable, but may be reviewed subsequently. DOT also punted on the question of whether the airlines can limit the number of disabled persons on any given flight to the number of exits. The disability groups argued that under such a rule sports teams of disabled persons could not fly on the same flight, and some could be excluded if others showed up first. The DOT in effect could not decide this issue but requested additional input.

However, the department does seek comment on whether there is an adequate justification for imposing either the *"one person/one floor level exit"* rule or some other number limit. If so, how would the proposed number limit be required specifically for safety? How, within the context of a given number limit, if at all, could carriers make advance accommodations for groups of disabled persons traveling together? There is also some evidence suggesting that the placement of persons with mobility impairments in certain seat locations may be advisable from the standpoint of safety during an evacuation. If this is the case, what are the implications for number limits?

DOT, in the proposed regulations, also was unable to reach a decision on the question of whether a carrier could refuse to permit a disabled person to sit near an exit. This has continued to be a sensitive and controversial issue; the DOT proposed regulation left it to its stepchild agency, the FAA, to decide what the rules should be. The blind groups oppose seating restrictions, arguing that it is comparable to segregation in the south requiring blacks to sit in the rear of the bus.

Finally, on March 6, 1990, the *Federal Registe*r published DOT's final rules under the Air Carrier Access Act. The regulations take up 75 difficult pages. In general, the regulations adhere to decisions made in the proposed regulations and resolve some issues left open. On the whole, the regulations are quite favorable to disabled passengers, with two exceptions. First, the FAA published final rules prohibiting certain disabled passengers from being seated in exit row seats. This decision did not please some of the blind organizations who threatened litigation.

The other sticky point was on the issue of required attendants. Great discretion was given to air carriers on the question of whether to require attendants as a condition for allowing some severely disabled passengers to board. Although the DOT regulations attempted to provide liberal rules for disabled passengers on this issue, and although the airlines in practice seldom require an attendant, the breadth of discretion raises questions about whether airlines in the future will continue to adopt liberal policies.

The new rules do not apply to foreign air carriers. They apply to a *"qualified handicapped individual,"* defined as a handicapped individual who has a ticket and meets the carriage contract requirements that apply to everyone.

Some carriers wanted to preboard disabled people in all cases, whether they wanted it or not. The final regulations allow the disabled passenger to make the choice of preboarding or not.

Other provisions in the final regulations:

New aircraft with thirty or more seats must have movable armrests on half the aisles in the aircraft.

New widebody aircraft must have accessible lavatories. More data is sought on the issue of accessible lavatories for smaller aircraft.

Aircraft with an accessible lavatory and 60 or more seats must have an on board wheelchair. For flights on aircraft that do not have an accessible lavatory, disabled passengers who can use an inaccessible lavatory but need an on-board wheelchair to reach it can, with 48 hours advance notice, request the on-board wheelchair.

Facilities and services at airports which carriers own or operate will have to meet the same accessibility standards that federally assisted airport operators must meet. The facilities must comply with uniform standards established by the Architectural and Transportation Barriers Compliance Board.

Carriers may not refuse boarding on the basis of handicap, except that any person can be excluded on the basis of safety. If any person is excluded on safety grounds, the carrier must provide to the person a written explanation within ten days. The carrier can't refuse permission to board *"solely because the person's handicap results in appearance or involuntary behavior that may offend, annoy, or inconvenience crew members or other passengers."* People with Tourette's syndrome sometimes involuntarily make noises that annoy others, but they cannot be excluded unless their behavior is a danger to others.

Carriers may not limit the number of handicapped passengers on a flight. This issue was resolved in favor of the disability groups and against the airlines, so that, for example, all members of a wheelchair basketball team can use the same flight.

Carriers may not require advance notice that a disabled person is flying. But carriers may require up to 48 hours advance notice for certain accommodations that require time for preparation.

Carriers may not require an attendant to accompany the disabled passenger except in very limited circumstances. As originally proposed, the regulations seemingly would have required quadriplegics to be accompanied by an attendant. Some quadriplegics bitterly objected to the proposed requirement that a quadriplegic must be accompanied by an attendant. Fred Fay, who is a quadriplegic, and a leader in the disability movement, told the author that he had flown 250 times without an attendant and without difficulty. He was able to board his wheelchair and then transfer to a first class seat.[4] As a result of opposition by disability groups, the regulations dropped any specific reference to quadriplegics, but replaced the label with a definition relating to a mobility impairment that prevents a person in assisting in his or her evacuation, a difference which only time will tell is merely a difference in labeling.

If a passenger and an airline disagree as to whether an attendant is required under the DOT regulations, the carrier may require the attendant, but may not charge extra for them. An attendant may not be required merely because of a concern that the person may need extensive or special personal assistance or the use of an inaccessible lavatory.

The circumstances in which a carrier may require an attendant relate to the safety of the aircraft. An attendant may be required if the passenger is on a stretcher or incubator, if the person has a mental disability and is unable to understand safety instructions and concerns. Also, an attendant may be required if the person has a mobility impairment so severe that the person is unable to assist in his or her own evacuation of the aircraft. An attendant may be required if the person is both hearing and vision impaired and is unable to communicate. The DOT preamble says that an attempt was made to strike a balanced position and most deaf, blind, and paraplegic passengers will not need an attendant. However, great discretion is given to the pilot on this issue; in effect the disabled passenger has no recourse at least at the time of the flight, if the carrier says that an attendant is required. However, the carrier must provide the attendant without charge. This, in all likelihood, means that carrier personnel may function as the attendant. It remains to be seen how the attendant rules will be carried out in practice, but the rule seems a reasonable compromise between conflicting positions.

Carriers are required to provide boarding assistance, except that they need not hand carry a person on board a small plane for which a lift, boarding chair, or other device will not work in the present state of technology. Assistance within the cabin is also required, but not extensive personal services. The carrier is not required to provide assistance in eating, medical service, or assistance within a restroom, or at the seat with elimination functions.

Disabled passengers' wheelchairs may in some circumstances, particularly on new aircraft, be boarded in the cabin, and have priority in storage over other items. The purpose is to allow ease of exiting the plane, rather than use within the cabin. In other circumstances, wheelchairs are stored in baggage and have priority over other items.

Carriers must accept battery powered wheelchairs, including the batteries, which are to be packaged in hazardous materials containers provided by the carrier. Carriers may not charge for wheelchair accommodations and storage.

The regulations provide that a person with a communicable disease cannot be excluded from boarding unless the disease is regarded by federal health authorities to be transmissible to other persons in flight.

The regulations have several provisions designed to assist deaf persons, including requiring a TDD for the purpose of making reservations, and providing captions for key, on board video, safety messages.

Training is required for carrier and contractor personnel who deal with the public.

Carriers must establish complaints-resolution procedures for dealing with complaints by disabled patrons.

The issue of exit row seating was resolved in the final regulations in favor of the carrier. This issue was bitterly contested by both sides. Carriers argued strenuously that certain disabled passengers should not be seated in any seat in a row of seats that is adjacent to an exit, for safety reasons. The disability groups, especially blind groups, argued bitterly that such seating restrictions are discriminatory, it is a matter of civil right. The DOT regulations refer to final regulations (Section 121.585) published simultaneously with the DOT regulations, by the FAA. The regulations provide that the carrier must determine the *"suitability of each person it permits to occupy a seat in a row of seats that provides the most direct access to an exit."* The carrier may not seat a person in an exit row seat if the carrier determines that it is likely that the person would be unable to perform one or more of certain listed functions because of the person's disability or lack of mobility or strength. The functions listed are to locate the emergency exit, recognize the emergency exit opening mechanism, comprehend the exiting instructions, operate the emergency exit, assess whether opening the exit will increase the hazards, follow instructions of crew members, activate an escape slide, and pass expeditiously through the emergency exit. The regulations then describe categories of passengers that cannot perform the listed functions: the person is less than 15 years of age, or if older, cannot perform the function without the assistance of a parent or adult companion, the person lacks the ability to read and understand instructions in the language printed, or lacks the ability to understand oral crew commands in the English language. Though not entirely clear, the regulation apparently means that if a Spanish speaking person can read instructions written in Spanish, it is not necessary for the person to understand oral instructions in English. Other categories of persons prohibited from occupying exit row seats are blind and deaf persons and those caring for small children where the responsibility might prevent the person from performing the described functions. Another category includes persons with a problem, such as a heart condition, which could cause them harm while performing one of the functions.

The DOT preamble to the exit row seating regulations said that in 1973, the Civil Aeromedical Institute studied the issue of disabled persons evacuating a plane in an emergency. The study showed that in many cases, the disabled person delayed the evacuation, causing safety hazards. Some disabled groups, particularly blind groups, still strongly oppose the exit row seating rules, but it could be a case of carrying logic to an illogical extreme.

In 1989, anticipating that the Air Carrier Access regulations would restrict exit row seating for blind passengers, the National Federation of the Blind obtained Senate and House sponsors for bills that would prohibit air carriers from restricting seating for blind passengers. A chief Senate sponsor was Senator Hollings. Interestingly, the American Council of the Blind, has not supported the bill. A spokesman indicated that the Council was concerned about safety problems and about possible backlash from the flying public.

The Department of Transportation, in adopting the Air Carrier Access regulations just described, provided a lengthy preamble that gave much of the policy behind the decisions, and summarized the arguments of the opposing parties, notably the Air Transport Association representing the airlines, and the Paralyzed Veterans of America, representing the disability groups. The preamble noted that there had been great tension between the two constituent groups, with disabled people complaining about discrimination and unclear and inconsistent rules, while the carriers complained about costs and safety considerations. The preamble noted that DOT's authority to write regulations derived from the Air Carrier Access Act. In the course of the lengthy and often stormy hearings, five major issues were brought up and disposed of in the final regulations.

First, a semantic discussion was aired as to whether the Access Act required "equal access" or the looser standards of Section 504 (see Chapters 4, 5, and 6). Equal access seemingly meant absolute equality for disabled passengers, whereas section 504 standards allowed the airlines to put up the defense of undue financial burden. The preamble to the DOT regulations got into the legislative history of the Access Act, including statements by Senator Dole and others, and decided that the purpose of the act was to incorporate the somewhat looser standards, less favorable to disabled people, of section 504. This verbal skirmish was primarily of interest to lawyers; disabled people were primarily interested in the bottom line rule, and not necessarily the theoretical or legal rationale of how the DOT got there.

The second legalistic issue was whether anti-discrimination rules would be formulated with safety considerations in mind or whether the Access Act was primarily a civil rights statute in which safety considerations were not very important. Within this issue was another: whether the airlines could impose more stringent safety rules than those required by the FAA. The DOT regulations, according to the philosophy of the peamble, supported the decision that safety considerations were important. A middle ground was adopted in which carriers could adopt safety standards as long as they did not conflict with anti-discrimination requirements.

A third issue related to rule making authority. The DOT, needless to say, reinforced its ability to make the rules and, then, clarified and elaborated on the proceedure.

A fourth issue was whether the regulations would pre-empt possibly contrary state laws. The preamble concluded that since the regulations were implementing a federal statute, they would prevail over state laws.

The fifth issue discussed in the preamble also got into semantics. The carriers were complaining about terminology suggesting that the carriers had been wicked people purposefully engaging in a pattern of discrimination. The preamble, though not asserting there had been a pattern of discrimination, said that in enacting the Access Act, Congress believed that " *wide variety of discriminatory practices continue to exist ...and that legislative action was necessary to correct the abuses . . . .*"

An issue not dealt with in the regulations is whether ventilators to assist breathing can be carried aboard. Some people have severe breathing problems and require a ventilator with a tube attachment to assist breathing; often an electrical outlet is needed, or at least a battery. Some people need ventilators constantly; others can get by with periodic use of one. Because ventilators are often cumbersome and can require an electrical connection, some airlines are reluctant to allow them. The argument has been presented that the electrical connection may interfere with navigational equipment on the aircraft. American Airlines is opposed to ventilators on aircraft but is studying the issue. United Airlines ordinarily will allow a ventilator but needs information concerning the ventilator's weight, model number, volts and amps. A thoughtful discussion of this issue is contained in the 1991 spring issue of *Spinal Network*.

On the whole, regulations are quite reasonable and favorable to disabled passengers, with the possible exception of the required attendant rule and the exit row seating brouhaha just mentioned.

Washington National Airport, though close to the city, continues to present severe problems for disabled passengers. The author once sat in a taxi with meter running, outside the terminal while the taxi driver went inside to locate a wheelchair. The wait was a solid hour, even though a wheelchair had been ordered in advance. On December 18, 1989, *The Washington Post* described how Bill Hamilton was attempting to help aboard his 70 year old father, who had broken an ankle. Hamilton parked his car on the National Airport traffic circle. When he was not able to find a wheelchair, he helped his father, on crutches, across four rows of congested lanes. Returning to his car, he found a $35 parking ticket. It would not have helped to have had handicapped registration tags for there are only three handicapped parking spaces at National, and they are out of the way and hard to find. Ron M. Linton, chairman of the Metropolitan Washington Airports Authority Operations Committee, has said that they would look at the possibility of a special drop-off place for disabled passengers.

That air carrier treatment of disabled persons continues to be a sensitive and controversial issue is evident in a story in *The Washington Post,* on January 14, 1989, stating that Pan American apologized to a double amputee passenger after employees put him on a baggage dolly "like a sack of potatoes," verbally abused him in front of other passengers, and treated him so roughly that his pants fell off. Fred Hankin was accompanied by his daughter who was told by the gate agent, "*If he's that sick he shouldn't be on a plane; he should be in the hospital.*" When his daughter explained that she needed a seat near him, the agent told the rest of the crew, according to the story, "*If she opens her mouth again, I want her kicked off the plane.*"

In summary, it can be said that 1990 brought about a great triumph for the disability community with the final adoption of the DOT and FAA Air Carrier Access regulations. American carriers are required to provide service, to facilitate air travel access, and to avoid discrimination against disabled people. Such beneficial laws are uniquely American. The United States can claim to be in the forefront among the world's nations on the issue of air travel access. Still, some of the rules involve a degree of carrier discretion, and disabled travelers will have to continue to be vigilant to see that hard fought victories are real and lasting.

CHAPTER IX

EDUCATION

The young man was in Class III (the tenth grade) at Boston Latin School and, due to polio, was in a wheelchair. He couldn't wheel himself down the long corridors to different classes so his teachers asked for volunteers. Three students took turns pushing him. During gym class he was told to go to the study room and study. He spent the hour in the room with one other student, studying, consuming bags of corn chips, and throwing spitballs into the waste basket. The next period was English and he rejoined his classmates, who were ruddy faced, exuberant, and happy after exercising and showering.

In 1784 L'Institution National Des Jeunes Aveugles (The National Institution for Blind Youth) opened in Paris. It was the first school for the blind.

In 1801 a naked boy was found running wild in the forests of Aveyron, France. Dr. Jean Marc Gaspard Itard found him, named him Victor and began, with some success, to train and rehabilitate him. Dr. Itard tried to teach him to talk and to behave in a civilized manner. He gave him massages which were discontinued after the boy's physical pleasure equaled his mental delight.Victor is generally regarded as the first case of special education. Dr Itard's methods were widely followed in the United States, and during the first half of the nineteenth century there was a high degree of optimism that the most severely disabled child could be educated.

In the early 1820s Dr. John Dix Fisher, a native Bostonian and medical student, visited the Institute for Blind Youth in Paris and realized that America needed something similar. In February 1826 Fisher met with friends at the Exchange Coffee house in Boston and made plans for a Boston school, which was chartered a month later by the state as the *New England Asylum for the Blind.* Its purpose was to educate blind persons. Colonel Thomas Handasyd Perkins was one of the incorporators. It took a long time to find an administrator; in 1830 they named Dr. Samuel Gridley Howe as director. Howe was inexperienced in educating the blind, but went to Europe to study schools for the blind. Finally, the first American school for the blind opened in July 1832 on Pleasant Street, Boston, in the home of Dr. Howe's father. It began with two students who were sisters, Sophia and Abbey Carter, and two teachers, Mr. Emile Trencheri of Paris and Mr. John Pringle of Edinburgh. By August, the school added four more students and another teacher, Lowell Mason. The school dropped the word asylum and was called the New England Institution for the Blind; later, it became known as the Perkins School for the Blind. Dr. Howe was to be the head of the Perkins Institute for 44 years.

In 1850 Dr. Howe founded the Massachusetts School for the Feeble-Minded, originally called the Massachusetts School for Idiotic and Feeble Minded Youth. The insulting adjectives in the name of this school could be applied more appropriately to those who invented the derogatory name in the first place! In 1901 it was decided to honor Dr. Howe on the centennial of his birth, in an elaborate "Proceeding" in Boston, accompanied by interminably long, flowery speeches, poems, recitals, and even a passage in classical Greek. Dr. Howe's widow, age undisclosed, appeared on the stage for a tribute. She was Julia Ward Howe, composer of the Battle Hymn of the Republic.[1]

A celebrated, internationally known graduate of the Perkins Institute was Helen Keller, born in Tuscumbia, Alabama in 1880. Her father had been a civil war captain. At age one and a half she contracted a high fever, which left her blind and deaf. A pretty child with golden curls, she drove her parents to distraction with her childhood tantrums. She was brought to Alexander Graham Bell, the inventor of the telephone and patron of the deaf. Sitting on his kindly knee, she was advised to attend the Perkins Institute. Later, the renowned teacher, Anne Sullivan, who had been visually impaired but whose sight was restored after an operation, became her teacher, both in Alabama and at the Perkins Institute – not an easy task. (On one occasion, Helen locked Anne in her room and hid the key.) Helen then attended Radcliffe College, graduating with honors in 1904. She met Mark Twain who, with friends, contributed to the costs of her education. After attending the Gilman School in Boston, she embarked on a lecture and writing career. She learned to read, at first through letters pressed into her hand and later in Braille. She and Anne made appearances at theaters where they met enthusiastic audiences. She became an international celebrity, and Helen Keller Scholarships were established for deaf-blind students. She lived to a ripe old age and became a living symbol of how a disabled person could overcome devastating disability.[2]

On April 8, 1864, Abraham Lincoln signed the *Act to Authorize the Columbia Institution for the Deaf and Dumb and the Blind, to confer degrees.* (It seems that dumb was regarded as more acceptable than feeble-minded, which in turn was thought more acceptable than idiotic!) 1864 is regarded as the year of the creation of Gallaudet University, the first college for the deaf. It evolved from the Columbia Institution in Washington, D.C. It was incorporated in 1857 by an act of Congress out of the Kendall School, founded by Postmaster General Amos Kendall (the Kendall School is now an elementary school supervised by Gallaudet). President Garfield had been on the Board of Directors of the Columbia Institution.

Gallaudet is named for Edward Miner Gallaudet of Hartford, Connecticut, whose mother was deaf and whose father, Rev. Thomas Hopkins Gallaudet, founded the American School for the Deaf in Hartford in 1817. Edward Gallaudet was a distinguished educator who received honorary degrees from Trinity College and George Washington University, as well as a doctor of laws degree from Yale in 1895. Edward Gallaudet was instrumental in establishing Gallaudet College and worked laboriously at getting funds from Congress. He ran into adamant opposition from Alexander Graham Bell, the inventor of the telephone, who pushed "Visible Speech" for the deaf, a form of lip reading, whereas Gallaudet was more flexible and included sign language as a means of communication.

The first free public school for deaf students was founded in Hartford, Connecticut, in 1817 by Thomas Hopkins Gallaudet to provide education for Alice, the deaf daughter of Dr. Mason Cogswell. Thomas Gallaudet traveled to Paris to the National Institution for Deaf-Mutes to learn of teaching methods at the Paris school. There he met Laurent Clerc, a deaf teacher, whom he persuaded to come to America to be the first deaf teacher at a deaf school. The first non-residential school for the deaf was the Horace Mann School, founded in Boston in 1869.

Education for deaf students became embroiled in the raging battle between "oralists" such as Alexander Graham Bell, who advocated speech and lip reading based on normal speech, and signing, a non-verbal language of its own which tends to transcend specific languages such as English and Spanish, even though there are wide differences in signing among various countries. Signed education possibly began in Paris in the 1750s under the sponsorship of Abbe Charles-Michel de l'Epee. In the nineteenth century, the battle between signers and oralists continued. Although this battle, on the surface, appeared to relate only to language and not to civil rights, there appeared a secondary trend. Oralists feared that signed language would create a sub-culture or ghetto of deaf persons and, to some extent, this prediction came true. The oralists purported to advocate oral, derivative speech, such as lip reading, in order to help deaf people "adjust" to society. Neither Gallaudet nor Bell were hearing impaired but in spite of their different approaches they seemed to share something in common: they felt a responsibility to impose linguistic education on the deaf. Samuel Gridley Howe opposed marriage and social mixing among the blind and deaf. Bell advocated immigration restrictions and eugenics; he warned of the possible "Formation of a Deaf Variety of the Human Race" (1883). Even Gallaudet opposed marriage among deaf persons and also opposed deaf organizations.[3]

Although the oralists claimed their methods were best for the deaf population, in fact deaf teachers were dismissed and students were punished for using sign. For their part, deaf people in general favored signing, and they felt that their civil rights were being ignored when hearing educators tried to foist their own preferences on them.

In 1880 an International Congress for education of the deaf assembled in Milan, Italy. The oralists carried the day in spite of American opposition – particularly from Gallaudet, who advocated a mixture of approaches. The Italian educator, Balestra, argued for oralism on the ground that a deaf penitent couldn't possibly make himself understood by using signing when confessing to a Catholic priest. The debate continued, and in 1900 the Fourth International Congress was held in Paris. There was bitter debate as to whether some sessions should be held jointly with deaf and hearing persons. The oralists succeeded in mandating separate sessions. Alexander Graham Bell, representing the oralists, said *"It goes without saying that those who are themselves unable to speak are not the proper judges of the value of speech to the deaf."* But Gallaudet bitterly rejoined:

> *"If I am in the minority of the hearing section, I am in the majority in the section of the deaf, and proud of it. It is inadmissible that you refuse to speak with the deaf. They have as much awareness of their rights, as much discernment, and as much determination as you do. They are the first to be affected by these procedures, they have the right to be heard. I protest your attitude."*

All this manipulation and disagreement among hearing educators only served to invite opposition by deaf people themselves, and ultimately a large segment of hearing impaired people adopted sign as a matter of social intercourse, as a culture, and as a mechanism for the advancement of civil rights – not at all because it was the best "educational theory." Though signed language had a byproduct of encouraging social isolation, ironically, it brought about such a coherence among the deaf population as a civil liberties lobby to be reckoned with that segments of the hearing population learned sign, in order to adapt to the deaf population rather than the other way around.

Today the battle between the oralists and signers is over; a compromise was reached in which education for deaf students involved a mixture of the best of both systems. Still, by far the majority of deaf people prefer signing to oral speech, such as lip reading. Reading and writing, since they do not involve hearing as such, is of course, taught to deaf students both by speaking and signing, according to Frank Bowe, a leading authority on deaf education and deaf, himself. He disagrees with the views of some "radicals" who want to teach reading and writing exclusively by signing, at least in the early grades.

Gallaudet University continues today (its name was changed from College to University by the Education of the Deaf Act of 1986), is financed in large part with federal funds, and continues to be a school exclusively for deaf and hearing impaired students. It graduates, by far, more deaf and hearing impaired people than any other college or university.

Through the years, Gallaudet had been governed by hearing presidents, administrators, and faculty, but in 1988 things changed. After demonstrations and protests by the students, King Jordan was installed as the first hearing impaired president.

Gallaudet is a liberal arts college, concentrating on traditional liberal arts subjects. It has entered the space age, and its students participate in a program at the U.S. Naval School of Aviation Medicine in Pensacola, Florida, where they undergo tests relating to balance and equilibrium for space projects.

Gallaudet has had a football team for over 100 years. Players get their cues from vibrations felt from a huge drum on the sidelines. It is said that Gallaudet invented the football huddle. To make sure that signals were hidden from the opposing team, the players huddled around their captain, who used hand signals to designate which plays were to be utilized.

The National Technical Institute for the Deaf was created in 1965 by federal legislation as an adjunct to the Rochester Institute of Technology, in Rochester, New York. Dr. D. Robert Frisina was appointed in 1967 as vice president of RIT and director of NTID. The school is devoted primarily to vocational training, particularly in the field of computer technology. The Institute claims an over 90 percent employment rate for graduates seeking employment.

The Perkins School and Gallaudet have never embraced the concept of "mainstreaming" – in which disabled students are integrated with non-disabled students. However, their goals are to educate disabled students so that they can integrate into normal daily life. Mainstreaming was an idea which did not fully develop until the 1970s.

In 1854 the first permanent, state supported school for retarded students was established in Syracuse, New York. Later in the nineteenth century, the earlier euphoria about educability wore off, and doubts arose as to the direction of special education. At the turn of the century, states passed laws requiring sterilization of severely retarded individuals and people with epilepsy. Efforts continued to educate disabled students, but usually through special schools and programs. It was rare for disabled students to be integrated into regular public schools.

In the 1960s and 1970s, it was becoming evident that segregated schooling for disabled children was an idea which had come and gone. An analogy was uncovered out of the civil rights movements of those decades:

> *"When proponents of change in public policy identify that established institutional values, goals and priorities are inconsistent with the interests of some segment of society and when other approaches have proven ineffective in achieving the desired policy objectives, an approach based on legal concepts and premises has been employed. The most notable use of this approach in this century was in the civil rights movement which attained for racial and other minorities equal rights and opportunities under the Constitution and secured the protection of law to assure that these rights are upheld. This reliance on a legal remedy has been one of last resort, employed when other efforts have failed to produce the desired result."* [4]

In 1971 Peter Mills, 11 years old and black, was a resident of Washington, D.C.'s Junior Village, a home for unfortunate juveniles where conditions were so appalling it was later abolished. He had been totally excluded from the District's public schools because of behavior problems, and he was getting no education whatever.

In July 1972 lawyers for Peter, and six other disabled youngsters, went to court requesting that D.C. officials be held in contempt for failing to provide special education for disabled children. Earlier, in December 1971, Judge Joseph Waddy of the United States District Court for the District of Columbia ordered that disabled children in the District be given a free public education *"suitable to their needs."* Hugh J. Scott, D.C. school superintendent, said that only 4,000 of 16,000 disabled children in the District were getting a proper education.

On August 1, 1972, Judge Waddy ruled that handicapped children have a constitutional right to an education. He ordered the D.C. school board to come up with a program within thirty days.[5] According to a 1971 report by the D.C. school board to HEW, some 12,340 handicapped children were being deprived of an adequate education, and many of them were remaining at home. Judge Waddy's order was the first to base the right to an education on constitutional grounds. The Fifth Amendment concept of due process, as well as the Supreme Court decision in Brown v. Board of Education, which prohibited racially segregated public schools, were relied on, as was the equal protection clause. As to the issue of funds, Judge Waddy said that if funds were not available, *"then the available funds must be expended equitably in such manner that no child is entirely excluded from a publicly supported education consistent with his needs and ability to benefit there from."*

The case lingered on in court as school board officials struggled to comply. A process of identifying handicapped children began. In 1975 the number of disabled children in public schools in the District increased from 4,000 to 14,000,but school board officials were still in danger of being held in contempt of Judge Waddy's order. Finally on March 26, 1975, Judge Waddy's patience ran out and he declared Mayor Walter Washington, School Board President Barbara Sizemore, Human Relations Director Joseph Yeldell, and the entire D.C. school board in contempt of court, for failing to provide adequate education for handicapped children. Judge Waddy's sanction was the appointment of a special master to attempt a solution to the problem. The special master finished his work two years later, and on December 7, 1977, Judge Waddy accepted the plan to provide an adequate education for handicapped children, thus ending six years of litigation.

Another landmark case similar in importance to the Mills case, was PARC v. Pennsylvania (1972) which established the right to an education for mentally retarded children.

In 1972 Congress passed what could be regarded as a forerunner of the great civil rights legislation passed the next year, the Rehabilitation Act of 1973. The 1972 legislation was section 904 of the Education Act Amendments of 1972. It provides:

> *"No person in the United States shall on the ground of blindness or severely impaired vision be denied admission in any course of study by a recipient of Federal financial assistance for any education program or activity but nothing herein shall be construed to require any such institution to provide any special services to such person because of his blindness or visual impairment."*

Then, in 1975 Congress passed the Education For All Handicapped Children Act (P.L. 94-42). Congress estimated that 1,000,000 disabled children were receiving no education whatever. This act guarantees every child a free appropriate public education in the least restrictive environment. It provides a written individualized education program (IEP) including physical education. It provides federal funds to reimburse state and local governments for additional costs involved.

In 1986 Congress amended the Education Act (P.L. 99-457) to extend the requirements of the Education Act to children from 3 through 5 and to provide an early intervention program for infants from birth through two years old.

Later in 1990, in Public Law 101-476, Congress renamed the Education Act as the Individuals With Disabilities Education Act (IDEA). This law added the requirement that the IEP of eligible students, no later than age 16, must provide transition services to enable the student to move to post-school activities.

As discussed in earlier chapters, section 504 of the Rehabilitation Act of 1973 has had enormous significance in the education of disabled students. The act prohibits discrimination against disabled students in any federally assisted school, be it pre-school, primary, secondary, graduate or post graduate. The coverage under the act is very broad. It covers typical, public, primary and secondary schools, if federal funds are used to supplement funds from local governments. It also covers private colleges and universities if they receive federal assistance, which includes practically all of them! Regulations under the Rehabilitation Act, adopted in 1977 (see chapters four, five and six) are comprehensive. They require that, to the extent feasible, disabled students should be mainstreamed or integrated with nondisabled students. Every school program or activity must be accessible. This does not mean that every building must be accessible, as long as each program or activity, as a whole, is accessible.

The school regulations under section 504, originally promulgated by HEW and later by the Department of Education, are contained in 45 CFR Part 84, Subpart A and generally prohibit discrimination by schools against disabled applicants and/or students. The director of the Office of Civil Rights is given authority to require compliance by taking "*such remedial action as the director deems necessary to overcome the effects of discrimination.*" Subpart D relates to pre-school, elementary, and secondary education. Schools that are recipients of federal assistance must identify handicapped children in their jurisdiction who are not getting an education and notify a parent or guardian. A free, appropriate public education must be provided by the school, with regular and special education and "*related aids and services.*" If it is not feasible to mainstream the disabled student, separate facilities must be comparable to regular facilities. A school recipient must educate each qualified handicapped person in its jurisdiction with persons who are not handicapped, to the maximum extent appropriate to the needs of the handicapped person. The handicapped student must be placed in a "*regular educational environment*" unless integration cannot be achieved satisfactorily.

"Mainstreaming" has been, and will continue to be, both significant and controversial. The success of the mainstream program can be evaluated only in terms of the microcosm of each disabled child, each teacher, each school , each day, each hour and even each minute. It requires a total effort and a determination to succeed, if success is at all possible. The benefits to the disabled child are incalculable: exposure to a normal life and with it, hopefully, both a motivation to achieve the normal life and the skills to do it. For nondisabled students, the drawbacks are minimal and the benefits may be a greater tolerance for the "different" and a willingness to cooperate rather than to shun and ignore. Normal students who are exposed to the "differences" of disabled peers tend to retain a natural acceptance of, and comfort with, individuals in society who may differ in some way from themselves. The sons and daughters of disabled parents often, in the same way, develop interpersonal skills with other disabled persons, skills that are missing for an individual who has never had any contact with people with disabilities. Mainstreaming is hard work and requires effort in pulling together, itself a valuable asset.

"By far the most important factor in the successful mainstreaming of handicapped children in public schools is the presence of positive attitudes on the part of the teacher in a classroom. If a teacher is supportive of a handicapped child, the students will be accepting. It is the responsibility of administrators to place impaired children in environments where positive attitudes exist. If positive attitudes do not exist, administrators should arrange for in-service training with the hope of changing negative attitudes. The most effective leader of such training is a qualified handicapped person." [6]

Hear are some comments by disabled students themselves about the experience of mainstreaming:

"Boy, I can sure put in the time worrying about whether or not I'm really human. My cat doesn't spend hours wondering whether or not she's a cat. Probably just dreams of her next meal. I can't remember feeling this bad in special school." [7]

****

"When I was younger, I was extremely aware that someone was staring at me, even though I couldn't see. If I made a mistake and ran into a tree, someone would see me. Someone would know that I wasn't normal." [8]

****

"At first it was real scary being with regular kids because I'd been at a school where all the kids had problems like mine. But after everybody got used to me and I got used to them, I started to love regular school. Having friends who understand makes all the difference in the world." [9]

****

" "I don't like it in this school. I would prefer to be with deaf people. I don't try out for sports and I would in a deaf school. The hearing students repress the deaf students. I'm tired of being in a hearing school." [10]

****

"At a special school they treat you differently. Like if you don't do something, it's ok, you don't have to try. In regular school they encourage you. They say, try it, You never know." [11]

****

"I envy the mainstreaming of the educational system today. When I first attended school, the only other disabled person I knew of throughout all my pre-college years, was a girl with leukemia in high school. Even then, I was not aware of it until she had passed away and I read about her in the dedication of our year book. Nowadays, there are more and more disabilities mainstreaming into the schools and it is not as isolating as it used to be."

A ten year old boy, Jonathan, (not disabled) met, for the first time, a classmate who was in a wheelchair. Jonathan cheerfully said, *"You're handicapped, aren't you?"* Jonathan was proud of the fact that he could pronounce *"handicapped"* and knew what it meant. Because of the school's mainstreaming program, the sensitivity level of non-disabled students had been raised a notch. Before the program, the normal students' sphere of focus included fun things like Teenage Mutant Ninja Turtles and Fruit Loops. Disabled students had been an unknown, a blur. After the program began, normal students began to recognize disabled students as a subject of vague attention, though it would be a long time before the normal student's perception of a disabled student rose from the level of a label to that of real person.

Subpart E of the 504 regulations relates to post-secondary education and has the same provisions for integration and mainstreaming as for the lower grades. College dormitories and classrooms must be accessible, and there must be no discrimination against disabled students in admissions to fraternities, sororities, and other student organizations. Auxiliary aids are often necessary. The preamble to the regulations states that funds for auxiliary aids are expected to come primarily from state and local governments and charities, rather than from the colleges and universities. There is no requirement that libraries be duplicated in braille. Auxiliary aids may include taped texts, interpreters, or other effective methods of making orally delivered materials available to students with hearing impairments, readers in libraries for visually impaired students, equipment adapted for use by students with mobility impairment. Schools need not provide attendants, individually prescribed services, readers for personal use or study, or other devices or services of a personal nature.

Pursuant to Subpart E of the 504 regulations, colleges and universities installed railings and ramps, widened some doors for wheelchairs (though, contrary to myth, the regulations did not require all doors to be widened), and made other adaptations for blind, deaf, and mobility impaired students. (Critics are divided on the question of whether the oversized letters, EDWARD BENNETT WILLIAMS permanently etched over the portals of the new Edward Bennett Williams Law Library of the Georgetown University Law Center, are a tribute to an oversized man, or oversized to assist the visually impaired!)

Shortly after the regulations were adopted in May 1977, something like hysteria gripped the nation's schools and colleges. The primary concern was cost; and it rankled that the legislation, though requiring costly adaptations, provided no federal funds whatever for the purpose. In July 1977 Dr. Robert B. Benton, Iowa's top school official, said, "the federal government should put its money where its mouth is." The University of Oklahoma worried that it would have to replace 558 narrow doors with wide ones, at a cost of $300 per door (something the law did not, in fact, require). The National Education Association said that the 504 regulations would have more impact than the Supreme

Court's desegregated school case, Brown v. Board of Education. George Washington University estimated its costs of adaptation at 5.2 million dollars. The colleges and universities were faced with the issue of installing ramps, low drinking fountains and pay phones, accessible toilets, wide doors, and possibly, elevators.

An article in *The Washington Post* on November 2, 1978, described experiences of some disabled students in colleges and universities, reported as a result of 504. At Georgetown University, 76 rooms in a 500 room dormitory under construction will be accessible. American University will spend $200,000 on accessible features. Maryanne Masterson, who is blind, enrolled at George Washington University before adoption of the 504 regulations and received little assistance. The library staff warned that she would be thrown out if her typing or tape recorder bothered others. After 504 her situation improved, and she was assigned readers who were partly paid for by the university. Six wheelchair students enrolled at George Mason University. *"The handicapped movement is the third great civil rights movement, right behind blacks and women,"* said John Van Brunt, a disabled rights activist at the University of Maryland. John Nolan, who has cerebral palsy and is severely disabled, enrolled at the University of Maryland. Unable to speak, he communicates by pointing to letters on a lap board, and he requires help for eating and drinking. While studying psychology, he said with grim humor, *"my real major is survival."* At the University of Maryland, 20 deaf students enrolled, the largest number ever.

The Education of the Handicapped Act requires the Office of Special Education of the Department of Education to submit an annual report to Congress. The 1988 report was issued under the signature of William J. Bennett, Secretary of Education, who later became the "drug czar," and Madeleine Will, wife of journalist George Will and Assistant Secretary, Office of Special Education and Rehabilitative Services. The report obtained and collated statistics from the various states regarding the numbers of handicapped children "served." Since the Education Act requires all handicapped children to be "served," the statistics as to numbers reached includes all handicapped children in the entire country. It states in the report that during the 1986-87 school year, 4,421,601 children with handicaps were "served." The most frequently named handicaps that were dealt with were the learning disabled (43.6 percent), speech impaired (25.8 percent), mentally retarded (15.0 percent), and emotionally disturbed (8.7 percent). Table 10 provides figures for the various categories of handicapped children and the type of school or classroom in which they were placed.

For example, regarding visually impaired children, 31.48 percent were in regular classes in regular schools, 19.44 percent were in separate classes in regular schools, 24 percent had some special classes in regular schools, 10.32 percent were in separate public school facilities, 2.05 percent were in private separate school facilities, 10.27 percent were in public residential facilities, .95

percent were in private residential facilities, .11 percent were in correctional facilities, and 1.37 percent were at home. In other words, the vast majority were in regular public schools, either in regular classes or special classes. The report also documented the dismal drop-out rate of handicapped children who left and did not graduate from high school. During the 1985-1986 year, of all students between the ages of 16 and 21 only 42.56 percent graduated with a diploma. Seventeen percent graduated with a certificate; the remaining percentage did not graduate.

The Twelfth Annual Report issued in 1990 under Secretary Lauro Cavazos stated that during the 1988-89 school year, 4,587,370 children were "served." During the school year 1987-88. the percentage of disabled students graduating from high school was 41.99 percent; with 11.26 percent receiving a certificate, a drop from earlier years.

As required by law, the Twelfth Annual Report presented the results of a survey of state special education programs, which listed areas where the state agencies thought improvements were needed. Practically every state agency thought that improvements were needed in some, and in many cases most, every area of special education: better individualized plans for practically every type of disability – especially for blind, deaf, and mentally retarded students, better teacher training, better vocational planning, improvements in physical education, and in psychological counseling.

The annual reports are long on statistics and short on understandable analysis. The Twelfth Annual Report is filled with bureaucratic jargon that, in many cases, only a bureaucrat would understand. Some of the following phrases come from the state reports. For example, we are told about the "*impact of cross categorical service delivery models,*" "*age-appropriateness and functionality,*" "*differential program effectiveness,*" "*post-hoc longitudinal analysis of classification decisions,*" "*analysis of variance, regression, and log linear analyses,*" "*un-dimensionality assumption analyses,*" "*descriptions of hypothetical pupils,*" and so forth. All in a good cause!

In 1979 a hearing impaired practical nurse, Frances B. Davis, attempted to enroll as a student, in order to become a registered nurse, at Southeastern Community College in North Carolina. She was denied admission on the ground that the courses, generally, were beyond her capability. It was argued that she could not read the lips of a doctor with a face mask and might not be able to provide adequate care for patients. She sued, basing her complaint on section 504 of the Rehabilitation Act of 1973, which prohibits discrimination against any *"otherwise qualified"* handicapped person. Although she won in the Fourth Circuit, the case was appealed to the United States Supreme Court. An amicus (friend of the court) brief was filed on behalf of 27 states, supporting the college and alleging that 504 *"is being transformed by administrative excess into a tool of oppression not contemplated by Congress."*

On June 11, 1979, the Supreme Court ruled that the college need not admit Ms. Davis. In a unanimous decision by Justice Powell, the Supreme Court said, in essence, that 504 does not require schools to lower their admission standards or substantially modify their programs. In effect the plaintiff, though handicapped, was not "otherwise qualified" because she did not have the ability, according to the court, to progress through the curriculum. Although she could participate in academic courses, these would not be a rough equivalent of the generally prescribed courses. The next day the story was a page one, lead story in *The Washington Post* and other newspapers. The Davis case was and continues to be extremely significant. It has been interpreted to mean that substantial, i.e. costly, modifications need not be made in the school plant, although it appears that Ms. Davis was only trying to be admitted as a student and does not appear to have requested substantial adaptations. The rationale of the court has been extended to other areas, such as transportation. For example, a Notice of Proposed Ruling in 1988 by the Department of Transportation, which proposed rules relating to air carrier access, says that Davis means that "undue burdens" may not be imposed on air carriers. The decision is regarded as an undeserved blow by the disabled community, and they see it as a rallying cry for everyone else required to comply with 504, including providers of trains, buses, planes, and the like.

Since section 504 obviously had a civil rights purpose, preventing *"discrimination,"* and is modeled, to some extent, after the Civil Rights Act of 1964, it is odd that civil rights are regarded as existing only to the extent someone is not greatly inconvenienced. When Brown v. Board of Education outlawed segregated public schools, the argument was made that it would be too costly to provide one large school rather than two *"separate but equal"* schools. This argument got no where, but it has been blessed by the Supreme Court, which evidently believes that a civil right that costs too much money doesn't exist.

Notwithstanding Davis, colleges and universities did adapt their physical plants, at least, to the needs of disabled students. *The Directory of College Facilities and Services for the Disabled* (Oryx Press, 1986) describes extensive facilities for disabled students at national colleges and universities. For example, Harvard University has specially equipped dormitories, a student operated disabled student organization, tutoring, counseling, physical therapy, psychological counseling, shuttle vans, campus assistance attendants, special transportation on and off campus, reader service and special equipment for the blind, note takers for the deaf, and other services. A Harvard student who was on the cutting edge of all these improvements is Marc Fiedler. Spinal cord injured as a result of an auto accident in 1975, he was a Harvard student when the

504 regulations were being considered and then implemented. As a Harvard student in a wheelchair, he participated in discussions regarding Harvard's conversion, initially resisted by Harvard, to the cause of disability student rights. Later, Marc graduated from Harvard Law School and became a Washington, D.C. attorney, interested in access issues under the Americans With Disabilities Act.

The American Council on Education has a program called the Heath Resource Center. located at One Dupont Circle N.W., Washington, D.C. It is a national clearinghouse on post secondary education for students with disabilities. It has a Campus Resource File which collects information from over 700 colleges and universities regarding programs for disabled students. Some facts from their1989 fall newsletter: over 1.3 million of the nation's 12.5 million students (10.5 percent), enrolled in post secondary institutions, report having at least one disability. College and university students with disabilities fell into the following categories: 39 percent were visually impaired, 24.3 percent had a *"health related"* disability, 20.1 percent had hearing impairment, 17.6 percent had an orthopedic impairment, 12.2 percent were learning disabled, 6.1 percent were deaf, and 4.7 percent had a speech disability. These figures add up to more than 100 percent, because some students had multiple disabilities. The newsletter provides valuable information on various programs for disabled students at colleges and universities.

In 1985 Brush Hill School in Fairfax County, Virginia, was given A-Plus by Instructor Magazine for its system for disabled students. The grammar school, like many, is a combination of a separate class curriculum for disabled students and mainstreamed classes. Principal George Fox worked hard to implement a successful mix of special education and mainstreamed activities.

Fairfax County has, however, been criticized. It's difficult and dangerous to draw universal truths from single experiences, but Robert W. Andrews and Elizabeth L. Norton, parents of a multiply disabled eight year old girl, felt that mainstreaming had been beneficial and segregated schooling was not. The couple had lived in Vermont, where they placed their daughter in a regular school, in which she got along well. When they moved to Virginia, they were apparently required to place the child in a special school for disabled children. The daughter, Betsy, did not thrive there and in desperation, the parents sent her back to her regular school in Vermont. They criticized Fairfax County for a nineteenth century approach to education for disabled people.

Section 504 has sometimes produced odd and unexpected results. In May 1987, Washington's Mayor Barry agreed to buy from the D.C. School Board a partially finished, white elephant, school building that had been begun as a special school for the disabled, before the adoption of the 504 regulations. Poorly designed, with a leaky roof and costly maintenance bills, the building, which never opened as a school, would cost $6 million more to complete or $2 million to demolish. Aside from faulty design and construction, the building became obsolete because of 504's emphasis on mainstreaming rather than segregation. The concept of "separate but equal" schools was definitely rejected by section 504. It is important to point out that section 504 does not require mainstreaming of all disabled students in all schools, but special education classes and even separate schools for disabled students may be adopted under appropriate circumstances.

Although the Davis case was a severe blow to education for disabled people, matters were balanced somewhat in Honig v. Doe, decided under the 1975 Education for Handicapped Children Act. The Supreme Court ruled that education officials may not unilaterally remove handicapped students from school even if they are unruly or disruptive. Under the act, parents or the court must have some input into the question. The child may be suspended for ten days, but then there must be a court hearing.

The aftermath of Honig v. Doe was somewhat of a backlash. School principals complained that they could not control students in some special education classes and were forced to go to court to obtain suspensions. In 1989 two California schools sought court approval to remove unusually disruptive students. Administrators at the School for the Blind in San Francisco and Center High School in Sacramento County went to court to remove disruptive students. In the first case, a deaf and blind woman allegedly struck two staff members and another student. In the second case, a 9th grade student in the Severely Emotionally Disturbed program at Center High School allegedly said jailed murderer Charles Manson was his hero and suggested smashing an administrator's head, vandalizing her car, and assaulting an official's wife.

There have been problems in other parts of the country, including Maryland and the District of Columbia. In 1986 Michael Durso, principal of Woodrow Wilson High School in the District, refused to come to work after supervisors overruled his suspension of a 17 year old boy charged with rape. In April 1989 Lewis A. Jones, principal of Ridgeview Intermediate School in Gaithersburg, Md., similarly refused to work after being told he could not transfer a seventh grader cited by teachers fifteen times for misbehavior.

Another significant Supreme Court case relating to education was Grove City College v. Bell [465 U.S. 555 (1984)]. In this case, the issue arose whether a student grant and loan program assisted by the federal government meant that (a) a college which was receiving federal assistance under the student loan program was subject to the nondiscrimination provisions of the Education Act with respect to the student loan program; (b) if yes, whether the college as a whole, with respect to all its other activities, was subject to the Education Act. The issue related to sex discrimination in the student aid program, not to disabled students, but the issue is regarded as also relating to the scope of the

Rehabilitation Act, jurisdiction over which also depends on federal assistance. The Supreme Court held, on the first issue, that there was indeed federal assistance to the college with respect to the student aid program, even though the students were the direct beneficiaries of the aid. On the second issue, the court said that the Education Act was *"program specific,"* meaning that, although the Education Act prohibited discrimination in the student aid program, because that specific program was getting federal assistance, the Education Act did not apply to the college as a whole or any of its other activities, which did not show federal financial assistance. The case is regarded as a blow to anti-discrimination efforts, and in fact, in 1988 Congress passed the Civil Rights Restoration Act (P.L.100-259), to reverse the effect of Grove City. In other words, for purposes of the Education Act, the Rehabilitation Act, and other civil rights acts, discrimination in one program means that the school is discriminating as an entity and deserved appropriate sanctions, including possible ineligibility for federal assistance to the school as a whole.

Another significant Supreme Court case, though not directly involving disability issues, could have an impact on future cases involving discrimination against disabled people in education or employment. In Franklin v. Gwinnett County [112 S. Ct. 1028 (1992)], Christine Franklin, a high school student, sued a Georgia county under Title IX of the Education Amendments Act alleging sexual harassment by being forced to have sexual intercourse with a teacher. The United States Supreme Court held that she had a right to bring a private suit under the act and was entitled to compensatory damages. This lawsuit is enormously significant because it has been unclear whether compensatory damages could be awarded under section 504. It is very possible that, following Franklin, the Supreme Court will similarly provide for compensatory damages under section 504.

There are those who have objected to the broad reach of the 504 regulations. Shortly after President Reagan took office in 1981, Vice President Bush's Task Force for Regulatory Relief reviewed the 504 regulations. One of the campaign issues was to eliminate or simplify *"unnecessary"* government regulations thought to be burdensome on free enterprise. The 504 regulations, which covered schools and colleges as well as transportation and building access, and which had transformed the American landscape, were on the hit list for possible repeal or revision by the Office of Management and Budget. OMB at one point proposed a watering down of the regulations and advocated a standard which would weigh the cost against the *"social value"* of the disabled person. In other words, the more *"valuable"* a disabled person is, the more he or she could expect in terms of benefits. No doubt a point system could be designed in which a blind, liberal Democrat gets 2.5 points, a deaf, conservative Republican gets 2.8 points, and so on. Fortunately this ludicrous idea was rejected. *"A terrible mistake"* said OMB official Michael McConnell. The Berkeley, California, Disability Rights Education and Defense Fund organized a letter writing campaign. Forty thousand letters were sent to Reagan and Congress protesting the deregulation move. The *National Journal* called it the most effective letter writing campaign in recent times.[13] With Bush's counsel, C. Boyden Gray, being sympathetic after the firestorm of criticism, the 504 regulations remained the way they were.

In September 1989, the National Council on Disability published a report to the President and the Congress, called, *The Education of Students With Disabilities: Where Do We Stand?* In general, the report gives a dismal picture of education for disabled students. Although the Education Act and Section 504 at least provided a push toward mainstreaming disabled students into regular school settings, this goal has proven elusive. The report stated a number of findings: it is no longer good enough to place a disabled child in a regular classroom; the blind or deaf child needs preparation for such mainstreaming – the ability to read braille or understand sign language, the ability to type and to spell. As Fred Schroeder, executive director of the New Mexico Commission for the Blind said:

> *"For a young blind child to really develop a self-concept so that he or she can compete, that child has to have the tools to compete...If you put a young blind child in a class room with sighted kids, and the young blind child does not have the skills to compete, then the child will be at a disadvantage and will come away feeling inferior...that "I can't compete because I am blind."*

Jesse Thomas, a deaf student, testified before the Council that deaf students often end up in pockets of isolation because:

> *"Proximity is not integration...deaf children cannot communicate with their hearing peers--they cannot chat in the halls, hang out in the locker room, tell dirty jokes, talk to another teacher, the dietitian, the secretaries, the janitor, anyone. Most critically important, they have no deaf adults to look up to."*

The Report stated that parent-professional relations are too often strained and difficult. Sometimes appropriate services are unavailable, not withstanding the federal mandate. Often schools have low expectations for disabled students and pass them to the next grade without regard to their learning progress. Special education for disadvantaged, minority, and rural families is often deficient. The procedural due-process safeguards of the Education Act are not working properly. The 1989 Lou Harris Survey: *"A Report Card on Special Education" concluded that "the majority of both principals and teachers have not had adequate training in special education."* Other conclusions of the National Council were that a federal role is essential, but the rate of federal funding has fallen far short of the authorization in the Education Act. Instead of the federal government funding 40 percent of the states' cost of special education, the percentage has varied from 6.2 percent to 9.2 percent. Further, the report concluded that a large percentage (41 percent) of disabled students never graduate from high school. Substantial numbers of students with disabilities are unemployed, live at home, and have few friends following their school experience. *"Approximately 31 per-*

cent of youth with disabilities who had been out of school for more than 12 months had not engaged in any productive activity such as post secondary education, employment, job training, volunteer work, or child care during the previous year."

Although the Report of the National Council didn't say in so many words, the education of disabled students for preparation into the adult world of jobs, family, and participation in community life has been so inadequate as to be a national disgrace.

John Bryant, principal of the Academy Avenue elementary school in Weymouth, Massachusetts, said that mainstreaming of disabled students was being worked on, but not all the problems had been resolved. Approximately 9 percent of his students are disabled, mostly learning disabled. He said that Chapter 766 of the Massachusetts laws predated the Education Act and was as strict as, if not stricter than, the federal law. Most of his disabled students passed the state minimum requirements tests. A complaint he voiced was that the definition of *"disabled"* was being expanded so that more and more students became enrolled in special education classes, requiring greater teacher involvement and greater expense.[14]

Others have expressed dissatisfaction with the notion of mandated mainstreaming. They feel that too much is expected of the teachers and disabled students themselves. Joan Goodman, associate professor at the Graduate School of Education, University of Pennsylvania, has argued that efforts to give intense instruction to disabled students, particularly learning disabled students, is misplaced and too costly, both in terms of dollars and the "psychic" cost to the student. As Goodman argues, *"Years and years of dull, repetitive instruction, pervasive adult monitoring and the constant prohibition of the spontaneous are likely to exact a high price in initiative, self-esteem, and independent mindedness. For a handicapped population already lacking these characteristics, such practices are particularly damaging."*[15]

Some state and city public schools were sued by parents of disabled students, sometimes successfully, sometimes not. Often section 504 was invoked as a basis of court jurisdiction, as well as the Education for All Handicapped Children Act. A catch-22 was that states were subject to section 504 only if they benefited from federal funds. It was the intent of section 504 to provide obligations under section 504 if the program or activity received federal funds. But the Eleventh Amendment to the United States Constitution says that a state may not be sued in a federal court unless the immunity is waived. In several cases, the complaint against the state was dismissed on the grounds of the Eleventh Amendment, so in effect, section 504 gave a right and a remedy which was taken away by the Constitution – Alexopulos v. San Francisco Unified School District 817 F. 2d 551 (9th Cir.1987); Clift v. Fincannon, 657 F. Supp. 1535 (E.D. Tex. 1987). Finally Congress came to its senses and, on October 21, 1986, abolished the defense of immunity under the Eleventh Amendment in suits brought against states under various civil rights statutes (42U.S.C. 2000d-7).

In some cases, disabled students have behavior problems, which may be related to the disability and may itself be a disability, or the behavior may be unrelated to any disability. There have been several cases of aggressive or destructive behavior by such children, resulting in suspension or expulsion from school. Lawsuits brought to reinstate the child have sometimes been successful. Under the Education Act, strict procedures must be followed before a child may be expelled, and often school administrators have been unaware of the procedures. A significant case in this area is Doe by Gonzales v. Maher, 793F.2d 1470 (9th Cir. 1986), affirmed as modified, 484 U.S. 305. In this case unruly students were suspended or expelled. The court gave relief if the aggressive behavior was related to a disability but not if it was unrelated. If the Education Act applied, the procedures for disciplining a disabled student had to be rigidly followed. The court noted that the specific procedures and remedies of the Education Act prevailed over the vague remedies under section 504.

In Barnett v. County School Board [721 F. Supp. 757 (E.D.Va. 1989)], Michael Barnett, age 16, was severely hearing impaired. Still, he went to Annandale High School where he had many friends and was on the basketball and baseball teams. Michael was assisted at school through a Fairfax County School program called Cued Speech which uses an interpreter; Fairfax County is one of the few school districts in the nation to have a Cued Speech program. Michael wanted to go to West Springfield High School, which was five miles closer to home, but which did not have a Cued Speech program. Michael lost the case, the purpose of which was to require West Springfield High School to have a Cued Speech program. The court said that the Education Act providing for a *"least restrictive environment"* did not create an absolute duty, but the provisions of the act "are, rather, one consideration in the ultimate calculus of whether a program is appropriate."

In August 1989, the Fourth Circuit Court of Appeals decided the case of DeVries v. Fairfax County Board of Education. A seventeen year old autistic youth, Michael DeVries, sued, through his mother, for admission to the local public high school, Annandale High School. The Fourth Circuit rejected his appeal and ruled that the school board had correctly placed him in the county vocational center, thirteen miles from home. The petition alleged that under the Education Act, he was entitled to an *"appropriate"* education in the *"least restrictive environment"* but the court ruled that the local public high school was not appropriate. There was evidence that Michael was *"childlike," "rigid and stilted," "fragile," and "eager to please."* There was a *" disparity in cognitive levels ."* Although he was a Boy Scout, played basketball, and worked competently as a hamburger assembler at Burger King, the court ruled that under the Education Act he was more appropriately placed in the vocational center. Although there was a *"strong congressional preference for mainstreaming,"* mainstreaming was not required in all cases. You might say there is more *"mainstreaming"* at Burger King than at some local public high schools.

Another recent, significant case is Timothy W. v. Rochester, New Hampshire [875 F.2d 975 (1st Cir. 1989)]. There the Court construed the Education Act to require a *"zero-reject"* approach, meaning that all children, no matter how severely disabled, are eligible for the act's protection.

The Lynn Pace School in Bellflower, California, is a special school for disabled youngsters, many of whom have cerebral palsy. In a novel program, former members of Los Angeles gangs who have gotten into trouble with the law, have participated in a program to help disabled youngsters. Both groups, the special education students and the gang members, are often outcasts in their own way, and a successful symbiotic relationship has taken place, with both groups benefiting from the program. Maria, an 18 year old with cerebral palsy, is helped by Salvador, 16, a former gang member. Maria uses a picture board to communicate. When Salvador asked her what she wanted to say, she pointed to the word "*I*", to a heart shape, and then to Salvador: "*I love Salvador.*"

In August and September 1990, with the summer holidays over, school children returned to school. But all was not well with the District of Columbia's special education program. An article in *The Washington Post* on August 30, 1990, recounted that there had been many delays in evaluating and placing in public schools disabled students who needed special education. Richard Henning, director of citywide school services, and Edward Galiber, a placement specialist, reported that as many as 2000 students with special education needs could be falling through the cracks because of teachers' not recognizing their needs. The school system had a backlog of 1200 to 1300 students waiting to be evaluated. The court in the Mills case, described earlier in this chapter, had ordered that students must be evaluated for the special education program within 50 days of a parent's request. But many students had to wait six months to a year before being evaluated. Parents continued to complain about the inadequacy of the D.C. special education program. The percentage of special ed students in the D.C. public schools is much lower than the national average, 7.5 percent versus almost 11 percent, and the percentage has dropped in recent years. The D. C. public school system has 6,153 students in special education programs. Those with the most critical needs are sent to one of the special education centers. Others go to specialized day long programs within their neighborhood school, others are taken out of regular classes for special education classes each day. About 325 are sent to private schools with the city paying the tuition.

Lawsuits have been brought by parents, but parents of minorities, blacks, and Hispanics have a difficult time bringing suit, for financial reasons. The Information, Protection and Advocacy Center for Handicapped Individuals, which receives federal assistance, helps parents with disabled children. Another advocacy organization, Disability Rights Education Defense Fund (DREDF), operates nationwide and has been very active in bringing suits against school systems for the parents of disabled children.

In July 1991 Federal Judge Marvin J. Garbis, in Baltimore, ordered attorneys for Catonsville High School to explore ways by which 16 year old Randi Wixom, a seasoned flutist, could rejoin the high school band. Randi uses a wheelchair, and the school principal, citing safety factors, ordered her to quit the band because band practice was held in the basement of the school. The case was argued successfully by Tim Cook, a leading advocate for disability rights, and Joseph Russo. The Judge rejected an offer by the county to bus Randi seventeen miles to another accessible school.

Some teachers and principals remain hostile to the special education program. Richard Sowell, whose son has special needs, said that the junior high school principal adopted a rule that special education students could not receive a grade higher than a "C" The principal said, frankly, he did not want special needs students to be on the honor role!

In February 1993, the United States Supreme Court heard oral arguments in a case in which Jim Zobrest, a deaf, Arizona teenager, asked that the public school district provide him with a sign language interpreter in classes in a Catholic high school. For the first time in its history, the Supreme Court provided a sign interpreter to follow the give and take between the Court and the lawyers. The case raises important First Ammendent issues, issues of church-state relationships, and involves an interpretation of the federal individuals with Disabilities Education Act of 1991.

The poor performance of the District of Columbia special education program should be instructive to all. It should encourage parents of disabled youngsters to request, demand, or resort to legal proceedings, if necessary, to enforce those rights already given by the government through the courts and which are so clearly contained in the federal statutes described in this Chapter. It should motivate teachers and principals to do a better job with their special education programs. Finally, the dismal special education picture ought to be both instructive and humbling to Congress and to federal and local government agencies. Throughout this book the story is told of efforts by the disability community to obtain civil rights legislation. The effort began in the sixties with the Architectural Barriers Act and most recently with the Americans With Disabilities Act. Disabled school children are given rights under section 504 of the Rehabilitation Act of 1973 and by the Education All Children Act of 1975. The

Department of Education has jurisdiction over the interpretation of and compliance with these laws. Yet it is apparent that the important social purposes of this significant legislation cannot be accomplished by the stroke of a pen.

Critics call much of this legislation *"feel good"* legislation. When a bill is pending, members of Congress devote their attention to the merits of the bill. When the bill is finally signed, Congress breathes a self-satisfied sigh of relief and goes on to other matters. The question of implementing the Congressional mandate is left to someone else – to another federal agency to write regulations, and to the courts to entertain and make judgments on cases.

In general, government is only as effective as citizens want it to be. In disability civil rights issues, particularly in the area of special education, it is important that beneficiaries of the legislation, the disabled people themselves, know their legal rights and seek to enforce them. It is not enough that legislators and bureaucrats feel good about the laws they read on the printed page. Such laws are useless, cosmetic, and hypocritical if they are not implemented and enforced. In enforcing such laws, disabled people – and, in special education cases, parents of disabled students – are the essential players.

Frank Bowe

Judy Heumann

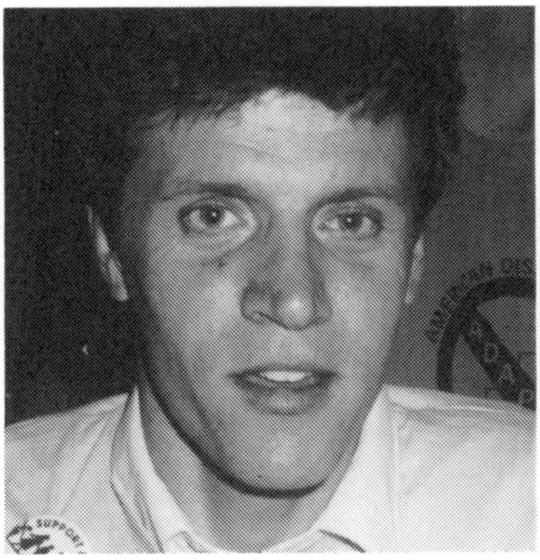

Mark Johnson

Mike Auberger

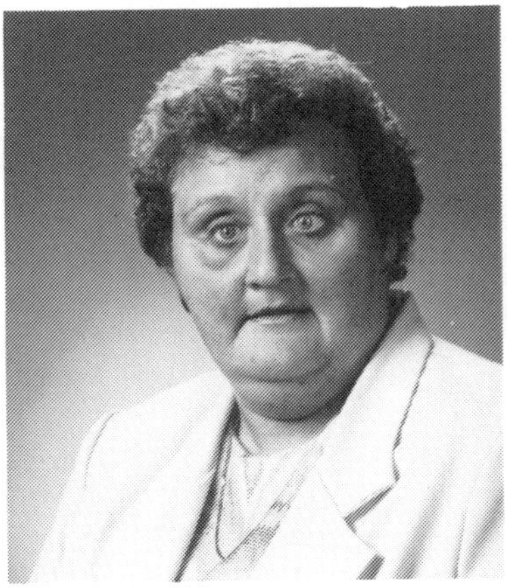

Eunice Fiorito

Mary Jane Owen

Six Who Made a Difference.

Crashing at Barcelona 1992

Candace Cable

Mike Bond

Bart Dodson Photos by Mary Peterson Dave Kiley

ADAPT Members, Lee Jackson and Friends, Protesting for HHS Changes
Photos by Tom Olin

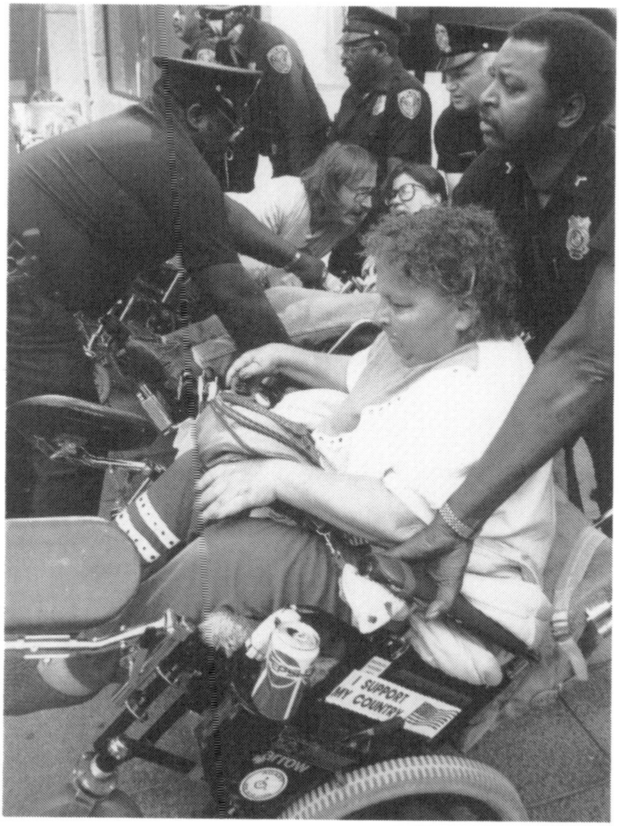

Protest and Civil Disobedience by ADAPT -- 1991 Photos by Tom Olin

Top Photos by Author

“Wheels of Justice”, March 1990, Lobbying for ADA
Note the wheelchair logo in the American flag. Photo by Tom Olin

President Bush Signing The Americans with Disabilities Act, July 26, 1990 Photographer Unknown
Standing: Rev. Harold Wilke, Sandy Parrino and Seated: Even Kemp, President George Bush, Justin Dart, Jr.

CHAPTER X

LAMENESS, DEAFNESS, BLINDNESS and OTHER NESSES

Bill and his new bride, Maureen, both deaf, had met at Gallaudet. Shortly after graduation, they had married and were living in a small, rented town house on Capitol Hill. The landlord had put the place on the market to be sold, but had rented it to Bill and Maureen with the understanding that the real estate agent, Frank, who had a key, could come in at reasonable hours with prospective purchasers. Since Bill and Maureen were deaf, the agent could not call in advance to make an appointment to show the house. One Saturday morning, Frank approached the front door with Mrs. Harcourt, a prospective buyer. Knowing that ringing the doorbell would be useless, Frank took out his key and opened the door. Upstairs, Maureen had undressed and was resting on the bed. Bill emerged from a shower and began to make love with his wife. Frank and Mrs. Harcourt were inspecting the living room, the nice bay window, and the dining room with a fireplace. Bill and Maureen were having an absolutely glorious time upstairs on the bed; Frank and Mrs. Harcourt mounted the stairs. They opened the bedroom door; Mrs. Harcourt's shriek was heard only by Frank. Bill and Maureen continued their loving, totally unaware of the intrusion. Mrs. Harcourt, followed by Frank, ran down the stairs and fled from the house. "Don't call me, I'll call you," she yelled over her shoulder!

This book is about civil rights for disabled people. It is not about medical conditions, medical treatment, or cures. Still, in dealing with the question of civil rights, it is helpful to understand why civil rights are necessary for disabled people as a group. There are forty three million disabled people in the United States, according to reliable estimates. No two of these individuals are alike. Unlike racial minorities or women, disabled people do not fit into any neat category relating to their disability. The civil rights which disabled people seek are the very same that any other individual or group would seek: the right to a job, the right to vote, the right to travel, the right to visit public places, the right to communicate, the right not to be discriminated against in any of these objectives. The reason that civil rights are necessary is that these goals, all too often, have been denied to disabled people – a denial that has been either intentional or thoughtless.

The denial of equal opportunity relates to the unique disability of the individual; discrimination is tailor-made. For example, an elevator may be usable by a deaf person, who can read the sign indicating floor level, but the same elevator may be unusable by a blind person. The fulfillment of civil rights takes a different form for different people. Title Four of the Americans With Disabilities Act of 1990 will provide a nationwide telephone relay system for deaf telephone users, an aid not required by other disabled people.

To disabled people, it is irrelevant whether discrimination and denial of equal opportunity is intentional or thoughtless. A person in a wheelchair is discriminated against if a sidewalk has no curb cut; more often than not this discrimination is due to poor planning rather than to any conscious desire to discriminate. On the other hand, a person with a severe facial disfigurement due to burns may otherwise be perfectly normal, but can't get a job because of intentional discrimination. There is no other minority within which discrimination is so personal. For this reason, the issue of "quotas," which has been such a controversial issue with respect to employment of racial minorities and women, seems irrelevant as far as disabled people are concerned. It's difficult to conclude that the employment of a single disabled person could be a matter of satisfying a "quota."

The problems of people with a mobility impairment are different from the problems of those who are deaf, which are different from the problems of persons who are blind. And then there are others with different kinds of disabilities, epilepsy, diabetes, kidney ailments, heart disease, congenital deformity, mental retardation, cosmetic impairment, burns after-effects, cancer, AIDS, and other contagious diseases. As Kurt Vonnegut would say, *"And so on and so forth."* There are even people with varying combinations of the above. Each lives in a kind of hell, trying to get a glimpse of paradise. Each is very private, very individual, very painful, very desperate.

In describing persons with varying kinds of disabilities, acceptable terminology is important. Generally, the person should be described, followed by the disability; common sense says identify the person as a person; his or her disability is secondary. For example, *"John Jones, a writer, who is blind"* is preferable to, *"the blind writer, John Jones."* In general, describe *"persons with disabilities"* rather than *"the handicapped."* The word handicapped is generally a legal term because it is used in various statutes, but "disabled persons" is more acceptable than *"the handicapped."* As a matter of etymology, "handicapped" is probably more appropriate than *"disabled."* Disabled has the prefix *"dis"* from the Latin negative, meaning close to *"unable,"* a possibly offensive and certainly inaccurate label.

The Dictionary of Contemporary American Usage, Random House, (1957) has the following description of "handicapped:" *" 'Handicap' is a shortening of 'hand-in-the-cap', an old game of wagering and forfeits in which the contestants put their hands in a cap and drew out various amounts of money. The game is described unmistakably in 'Piers Plowman,' (1362-1399) under the name of 'New Faire,' though the earliest instance of 'handicap' (Oxford English Dictionary) is 1653 - a salutary warning for those who would construct social history from linguistics or vice versa. From the game it came to mean some extra weight or other condition imposed on a superior in an athletic event to equalize the chances of an inferior, and from that it came to mean any encumbrance or disability that makes success more difficult. Thus it is common today to refer to lame children as handicapped children, though there is no suggestion (unless a pathetic flattery was originally intended) that they are necessarily superior children reduced by their misfortune, to equality with other children."*

Thus according to this authority, "handicapped" might indeed be appropriate because the word gives the idea of a fortuitous misfortune and also suggests that the disabled person needs a "level playing field" or equalizing environment, one of the goals of the handicapped civil rights movement. Be that as it may, there is no doubt that "disabled" is becoming more acceptable than "handicapped," although there are many "handicapped" signs that will have to be taken down to reflect the change in English usage.

Possibly an alternative term would be "impaired" meaning according to Webster's dictionary, "worse" or "weak" or "damaged", from the Latin "pejor" meaning "worse." (Possibly impaired might have derived from the Latin for unequal; compare "au pair" meaning literally, equal (exchange)). A blind person could be described as having an "eye impairment," a deaf person as having an "ear impairment." This would tend to minimize and categorize the disability to the particular part of the body affected.

Frustrated with unsatisfactory attempts to find suitable terminology, the National Cristina Foundation, a nonprofit group which provides surplus computer and video equipment to educational and training facilities for the physically challenged, offered $50,000 to encourage new words to describe people with physical or mental limits.

In 1993 the National Stigma Clearinghouse campaigned against prejudicial descriptions of mentally ill people, which are often used in movies or advertising. Words like "schizoid" and "crazy," while meant to be cleverly jocular, are, instead, offensive to many. The stigma borne by people with mental problems is often harder to live with than the illness itself.

On September 21, 1983, Interior Secretary James G. Watt, at a Chamber of Commerce breakfast meeting, delivered the following bombshell and then giggled. Speaking of the composition of the Commission on Coal Leasing, he said:

> *"We have every kind of mix you can have. I have a black, I have a woman, two Jews and a cripple."*

A firestorm of criticism resulted. Mr. Watt, who had previously insulted practically the entire, known civilized world, with the exception of white male, Protestant conservative Republicans, was reported to be in "anguish" on October 8 , and speaking to reporters in the middle of a cow pasture in California, he resigned on October 9, 1983. The story was page one, lead headline on October 10. President Reagan said he had done an "outstanding job." One of the members of the Coal Commission, Donald Alexander, the former Commissioner of Internal Revenue Service, said with more truth than hilarity, "In view of the fact that I'm not a woman, I'm not black, and I'm not a member of the Jewish faith, then presumably, I'm a mental cripple."

The careful speaker and writer, unlike James Watt, should avoid descriptions such as *"afflicted with"* or *"victims of"* because such terms generally are not accurate. *"Uses a wheelchair"* is preferable to *"confined to a wheelchair."* Use *"person with a disability" instead of "disabled person,"* or worse, "the disabled." *"Dwarfism" is a medical term but a more acceptable description is "people of short stature."* There are more than eighty types of short stature. A lady five feet one inch in height and sensitive about it refers to herself as *"vertically challenged."* Do not say, "the deaf," "the blind," but *"deaf people," "persons who are blind."* [1]

The term *"XYZ Institute for Crippled Children"* may now, because of changing times and greater sensitivity, be called the *"XYZ School for Children with Disabilities."* The "National Council on the Handicapped" is, in fact, now called the *" National Council on Disability." The "President's Committee for Employment of the Handicapped"* has been changed to *"the President's Committee on Employment of People with Disabilities."*

The difficulty in finding acceptable terminology to describe disabled people was the subject of an article in *The Disability Rag*, September/October, 1990. Various readers wrote in their views. It could be said that the meaning of words depends on a consensus or general acceptance of the population as a whole. It could also be said that language is a living structure, and the meaning of words can and do change. If society cannot agree on the meaning of words, civilization, itself, becomes handicapped. The words written in a contract or a will are interpreted by courts in accordance with the generally accepted meaning of those words. Criminal laws prohibit perjured statements in court. Though the United States Constitution guarantees freedom of speech, it doesn't guarantee that each individual can invent his own language. Courts involved in a contract, a will dispute or a perjury charge will look at the "intention" of the parties concerned, and the intention usually depends on the meaning of the words chosen. Currently, the accepted usage is to prefer "persons with disabilities" to "the handicapped."

The "Americans With Disabilities Act" suggests in its title that the authors had some difficulty in expressing the concept. Are we to have a "Cubans With Disabilities Act", "Chinese With Disabilities Act" and so forth. Is the word "disabled" so offensive that it should always be associated with a stronger word, to help soften its meaning? And who decides what is acceptable? If I prefer to be addressed by the title "king" do I have a right to be offended if I'm called by some other name? Older people may or may not want to be referred to as "Senior Citizens" "getting along in years" "octogenarian" or "person of mature years!"

Then there is the question of a language being reserved for exclusive use by an affected group or culture or cult. Is it permissible for blacks to use a derogatory derivative form of the word "negro" among themselves in a playful or friendly manner but be offended when the same word is used by a white person? The article in *Disability Rag* described the views of some readers who said the word "cripple" was permissible when used among disabled people, but is not permissible when used by others. Is terminology not offensive if it is used in jest but may be offensive if no jest is intended? In a recent employment discrimination case, the employer argued in court that his use of the phrase "Chicken Little" applied to a black employee was used in jest, but the argument got nowhere. Although all of these are good questions the answers may not be clear. Still, it can be said that correct usage, today, prefers the phrase "persons with disabilities" to "cripples" or "the handicapped." Words meant for public consumption, uttered by politicians, writers, or the media, should be carefully chosen, and current usage should be ascertained, because what is acceptable today may not be acceptable tomorrow.

The legislators, lawyers, and lobbyists who became involved in issues of civil rights for disabled people sooner or later became familiar with the types of disabilities that people have, and the adverse effects various disabilities have on various life activities. They discovered that though major categories include mobility impaired people and blind and deaf people, these are not the only types of disabilities, and within each of these group there are many varieties of disability.

Persons with mobility impairment could be people who contracted polio or could have a spinal cord injury or arthritis, or they could have cerebral palsy or meningitis or muscular dystrophy or multiple sclerosis or many other conditions. Even within each group, conditions vary enormously, and the public should attempt to learn the nature of each person and each disability. This fact of life is another reason why disabled people object to being categorized and stereotyped. No two blind or deaf persons are entirely alike and it is no more accurate to attempt to pigeonhole categories of disabled persons than it is to generalize regarding the entire universe of flora and fauna.

Persons with mobility impairment, if using a wheel chair, have their own unique problems. Most wheelchairs are the "hospital" type, meant to be pushed by an attendant, but very awkward to be manually self-propelled on the street. Some wheelchairs have been developed for street use and for sports, the latter being three wheelers, weighing as little as sixteen pounds. They are generally lightweight and functional. There is all the difference in the world between the traditional version and the newer "street" type. Then there are electric wheelchairs, which today cost something close to that of a low priced automobile. Lea Phillips contracted polio as a result of being given the polio vaccine as a teenager. She has the use of only one arm, with which she drives a motorized wheelchair. This remarkable lady is now a writer on an island off the coast of Maine.

People in manual wheel chairs tend to develop great arm muscles! It is now a tradition that there will be a wheelchair entry in the Boston Marathon and other marathons. Legs, however, do atrophy, with a tightening of the hip fascia. Massage and swimming are good therapy.

People in wheelchairs also tend to develop skin problems which can be devastating and painful. Hydrocortisone is used for treatment. It's commonplace in Veterans Hospitals for patients to lie prone on stretchers to cure buttock sores, a long and painful process. There are inmates in prisons who use wheelchairs, and many complain that their civil rights have been violated because of poor medical treatment and personal care.

Many persons with spinal cord injuries are impotent, depending on how high in the vertebrae the injury occurred. The possible loss of ability to have children is a primary concern of such individuals. Dr. Lauro Halstead, affiliated with the National Rehabilitation Hospital in Washington, and long involved with post-polio care, and Dr. Stephen W.J. Seager, have developed a technique of electrically inducing erections and sperm ejaculation, which is then artificially inseminated, allowing some who are spinal cord injured to conceive children; previously, it was not possible. The technique is to insert an electrically controlled instrument through the rectum and stimulate the prostate area, achieving erection and orgasm in about 80 percent of the cases.

Interesting research is being done in the field of spinal cord injury repair. Using cells from a rat fetus, a "living bridge" is inserted in an injured rat's spinal cord; some regeneration of nerves has occurred. Progress has been slow and the outlook is guardedly optimistic. Prominent in this field are Dr. Michel Kliot of Columbus Presbyterian Hospital in New York City, Dr. Richard Jed Wyatt of the National Institute of Mental Health, Paul Reier, neuroscientist at the University of Florida, Gainesville, and Jerry Silver, neurologist at Case Western Reserve University in Cleveland.

An excellent discussion of medical research relating to spinal cord injuries is found in *The Spinal Network*, edited by Sam Maddox and published by the Spinal Network (1988). There is an article by Jerd Smith about medical experimentation. In 1966 the U.S. Public Health Service ruled that medical experiments on volunteers must be regulated so that participants would be informed of all benefits and risks. At the Miami Project to Cure Paralysis in Florida, there is a Dr. Bernard Brucker, a clinical psychologist, who is working on experimental electromyographic feedback and computerized functional electrical stimulation (FES).

Experiments have been undertaken in which leg implants are electrically stimulated so that the muscles of the legs move in a walking pattern. Though primitive, the results have been encouraging. In 1983 Nan Davis, a paraplegic, got out of her wheelchair with the help of functional electrical stimulation and walked to get her diploma at Wright State University. Jerrold Petrofsky and Janni Smith have been doing interesting research in this area; an article on the subject is found in *The Spinal Network*, page 90. Byron Marsolais is working on an FES walking system that does not require leg braces.

An article in *The Spinal Network* by Dr. Daniel Lammertse describes historical and present day experiments and theories in the area of treatment of spinal injuries. It is an area of growing interest though results so far have not been outstanding. Still, Dr. Lammertse concludes his discussion with the observation, *"A true biologic treatment that will bring function back is on the horizon."*

A new, low cost decubitus ulcer treatment using electrical stimulation to speed up the skin's rate of healing is being tested by the Food and Drug Administration. A device called Derma/Pulse will hopefully be marketed by Staodynamics.[2]

Gregg Slane dove into the murky waters of the Hudson River at age 16 and broke his neck. A quadriplegic, he is one of an estimated 90,000 with similar injuries. Gregg has a capuchin monkey named "Jeep" to assist him in dozens of small chores, such as turning lights on and off, getting a sandwich from the refrigerator, inserting a tape into a VCR. Monkeys are trained by "Helping

Hands; Simian Aids for the Disabled," a Boston nonprofit organization directed by psychologist Mary Joan Willard. Monkeys have six months of basic training before graduating.[3]

In 1992, remarkable progress was made in developing VoiceRecognition Products. This technology refers to computers, telephones and other high tech products that can be operated by voice by people with little or no use of the hands, such as severely disabled quadriplegics. Madenta Communications of Edmonton, Alberta, Canada developed Voice Recognition Technology including Virtual Telephone and Pre-Dict-ate. Virtual Telephone is a voice controlled, on-screen telephone, based on the Voice-Navigator Classic hardware. Complete control of the telephone is achieved by voice. Users say *"pick-up"* to get a dial tone, then dial the number. Pre-Dict-ate is a word prediction program in which the user inputs letters by using the military alphabet and the computer predicts what word you are spelling. For example, one could say *"alpha"* and the screen will show common words beginning with *"a"* such as *"and."* The user can select the desired word by saying *"third word"* for example, and the third word will be typed in. This voice recognition predicter can be operated by voice alone and saves time by eliminating unnecessary commands.

Persons who have had polio (called post-polio) have their own distinct problems. Inheritors of the epidemics of the forties and fifties, there are hundreds of thousands throughout the country and they are now aging. The "post-polio syndrome" has been well publicized and involves additional muscle deterioration and fatigue, in many cases mimicking a second case of polio, which is biologically impossible. Dr. Lauro S. Halstead, who himself had contracted polio, has done research on post-polio problems at the National Rehabilitation Hospital in Washington. Dr. Richard L. Bruno and Nancy M. Frick have some interesting comments about post-polio survivors:

> *"A behavioral profile has begun to emerge from studies of persons who survived acute poliomyelitis and are now experiencing post-polio sequelae. Persons who had polio have been shown to be employed full time at four times the rate of the general disabled population...Persons who had polio have more years of formal education on average than the general population...and they marry at approximately the same rate as those who are not disabled...Those data, combined with our own experience with thousands of persons who had polio, indicate that "polio survivors" are competent, hard-driving and time-conscious over-achievers who demand perfection in all aspects of their personal, professional, and social lives. It appeared that those who survived polio exhibit 'Type A' behavior and would therefore experience chronic emotional stress."*[4]

Through the influence of the regulations of section 504, the environment has become much more accessible to the wheelchair user, though much remains to be done. Many cities and towns require all sidewalks at street intersections to have "curb cuts" for wheelchair access; added beneficiaries are the bicyclist and the baby carriage pusher! Curb cuts in cities will, in time, become universal as a result of section 504 and the Americans With Disabilities Act.

Special license plates with the wheelchair logo are universally issued to the mobility impaired. Many streets have designated curb parking places for handicapped, licensed drivers, which has enormously improved the lot of those who need them. Three complaints remain, however: first, that there are not enough of them; second, that sometimes the handicapped license plate is issued to someone who doesn't deserve it; and third, handicapped spaces are sometimes occupied by nondisabled people, an inconsiderate and heartless action. It's commonplace for shopping malls to have handicapped parking. The Kennedy Center has a section of curb restricted to handicapped-driver theater goers.

Taxis in most cities and towns are required by law to stop for wheelchair patrons. Still, compliance is spotty. A letter to the editor of The Washington Post, August 27, 1989, by Marc Fiedler complained about the inaction by the D.C. Taxicab Commission, after three complaints of taxis failing to stop. When there was finally a hearing on one of the complaints, Marc found the hearing room to be on the second floor, up four steps from the elevator level. Worse, the hearing had been canceled without Marc's being notified, and the men's room was totally inaccessible. On leaving the building in total frustration, he recounted that seven taxis passed him by.

It became the political vogue for politicians to spend a day in a wheelchair. It was a great photo opportunity and, hopefully, also sensitized the politician to the needs of persons with mobility impairment. Marion Barry, later Mayor of Washington, spent the day in a wheelchair while president of the school board, accompanied by City councilmen Rockwood Foster and Ted Meyers. Attorney General Ed Meese spent hours in a wheelchair. His reaction: *"People got out of my way."* Senator Frank Church in December 1972 got into the act, spending hours at the U.S. Capitol in a wheelchair, along with Peter Lassen of the VA. They had numerous complaints about lack of access to the Capitol. In December 1975, GSA officials spent hours in wheelchairs at the GSA headquarters and similarly found innumerable problems, such as lack of accessible restrooms, elevators, doors and the cafeteria. In March 1980, teams of District of Columbia department heads and employees spent hours in wheelchairs, touring the city. Polling places became more accessible to the disabled. In 1976 Congress appropriated $2.7 million to improve access to the Capitol, the Library of Congress, the Congressional Office Buildings, and the Botanical Gardens. Special sections of the galleries in the House and Senate have been set aside for wheelchairs. The author did much of the research for this book at the Library of Congress. At the Library, there are only two parking spaces reserved for handicapped drivers; these spaces are intended to serve visitors to the Library, to the United States Capitol, and the House and Senate Office Buildings, far too few accomodations. If one gets to the handicapped parking spaces early enough, they can be available, but too often the author found them filled and had to look elsewhere.

Two severely disabled writers recently published biographies, Ruth Sienkiewicz-Mercer[5] and Moira Griffin.[6] Ruth had encephalitis as a child and neither walks nor talks. After terrible years in a Massachusetts institution, she married and "overcame." Moira contracted multiple sclerosis as a young adult and describes her passage from "normal" to "disabled." Jean Stewart, who uses a wheelchair, published a bittersweet novel about a woman with cancer called *The Body's Memory.*[7]

A person with a mobility impairment can envy a deaf person who, after all, can run, jump, dance, and even play football. But deaf people have unique and difficult problems.

Often the best descriptions of what it is like to be disabled are written by disabled people themselves. A publication called *Deafness and Communication*, edited by Sims, Walter and Whitehead (Williams & Wilkins, 1982) contains excellent discussions on the experience of being deaf. One excerpt is about Silent Sam, by Shanny Mow, "How Do You Dance Without Music." Silent Sam describes some of his experiences:

> *"a lot can happen in two blocks. A lost motorist yelling for directions. A nervous smoker asking for a match. A friendly stranger with sinister motives wanting to talk. A policeman blowing his whistle and suspecting you for a fugitive when you walk on. A dog biting from behind. A runaway grocery cart hitting from the blind side. You grow weary and wary of such people who, at the sight of you pointing to your ear, always seem to forget suddenly their purpose in approaching you."*

Silent Sam goes on to describe his experiences at a restaurant and at a group talk session, an excellent account giving real insights into the deaf experience which some non-disabled writers lack.

In June 1990 a grim musical comedy-documentary opened at the Kennedy Center. Called "Project!," it was about one of Chicago's worst public housing projects, Cabrini-Green. Some of the actors and actresses actually live there. Actress Maria McCray cries out after a bloody gang fight:

> *"My son is dead. A sweet, innocent boy who never hurt anybody. But they hurt him. They hurt him to death. And for what? He didn't belong to a gang. The gangs didn't want him because he was deaf. I blessed my son's deafness because I thought it would keep him safe. But now he is dead."*

Henry Kisor is deaf. He wrote a book about it called *What's That Pig Outdoors?*[8] which comes from a garbled lip reading of "What's that big loud noise?" Henry is a book editor for the Chicago Sun-Times.

Hearing persons are often insensitive to or unaware of the severe adjustment problems of deaf persons. Studies have shown that on the average, deaf children have fewer reading and writing skills than children their age.[9] Deaf persons communicate sometimes by reading lips and sometimes by sign. There are two basic versions of sign language, Signed English and American Sign Language. American Sign is a more universal, uniquely cultural language, used by deaf persons among themselves. Signed English is what its name implies, a version of English, incomprehensible, for example, by Hispanic deaf persons. For more on sign language see Oliver Sacks, *Seeing Voices, a Journey into the World of the Deaf*, University of California Press (1989). Two biographies of deaf persons were published in the spring of 1991: *In Silence, Growing Up Hearing in a Deaf World*, by Ruth Sidransky (St. Martin's), and *A Man Without Words* by Susan Schaller (Summit).

People who are hearing impaired may use hearing aids, or alerting devices such as lights, and telecommunication devices such as TDD, which is a small typewriter-like device with a telephone cradle. Callers send a message on a viewing screen. There are closed caption devices on many TV programs, allowing the printed word to appear on the screen. Some theaters, including the Kennedy Center and Arena Stage, have systems that transmit sounds by infrared light, picked up by small receivers.

1988 was a banner year for federal legislation affecting deaf persons. P.L. 100-394, the Hearing Aid Compatibility Act of 1988, says that virtually all telephones – including all new ones – have to "leak" so they are compatible with hearing aids. Hard of hearing people switch their hearing aids to "T" to pick up the leak. Some 25 percent of residential and pay phones don't leak, and the act corrects that. Ironically, in a sense technology has been rolled back. In the late seventies, Bell Laboratories removed the leaks thinking they were improving things. Now the federal law requires them to go back to the old, leaking phones.

P.L. 100-553, the National Deafness and Other Communication Disorders Act of 1988, created a new Institute at the National Institute of Health: A National Institute on Deafness and Other Communications Disorders. It evolved, for the most part, from the National Institute on Neurological Communication Disorders.

P.L. 100-542, the Telecommunications Accessibility Enhancement Act of 1988, makes permanent a TDD to voice/voice to TDD relay that was begun in 1985 by Frank Bowe and others. The relay will be expanded by adding at least one more operator. In addition, the law calls for a federal TDD relay directory to be published and updated. Also, it provides for a "logo" that will symbolize a TDD capability, like the wheelchair logo symbolizing accessible entrances, rest rooms, and the like.

In 1990, Congress passed the Television Decoder Circuitry Act of 1990, Public Law 101-431, which will require all new television sets, thirteen inches or wider, to have a closed captioning chip to make programs accessible to hearing impaired people.

The crowning achievement of civil rights for deaf people was the Americans With Disabilities Act of 1990, described more fully in Chapter Seven. Title IV of this important legislation requires a nationwide telephone relay system that will allow deaf telephone users to communicate by telephone anywhere in the country. Previously, without special relay operators, deaf people could communicate only if both parties had a TDD, which is a typewriter-like accessory to a telephone, in which the message is printed on a screen.

Advances for deaf persons are being made in other areas as well. In March 1988 deaf student protesters at Gallaudet University in Washington, agitated for a deaf president and succeeded. Early in March, the board of directors met to select a new president and selected Dr. Elisabeth Ann Zinser, the only finalist who was not deaf. The next day, over 500 students and alumni protested, shutting down the campus. By March 9, a substantial number of faculty sided with the students and demanded Dr. Zinser's resignation. On March 11 she resigned saying, "I have responded to the extraordinary social movement of deaf people." King Jordan became the first deaf president in the 124 year history of the college for hearing impaired. Then 42, King had been injured twenty-five years earlier when a car swerved and hit his motorcycle, hurling him through the car's windshield and cracking open his skull. Deafness followed. At Gallaudet, until King's installation, deaf students had always been ruled over by hearing presidents and teachers. In 1989, in addition to a deaf president, six of the 21 trustees of Gallaudet were hearing impaired.

Chava Willig Levy said it well in "A People's History of the Independent Living Movement," [10]

> *"Most important, the Gallaudet victory forced America to see the irony of a 'place that boasted of a special ability to train deaf people for the working world, but itself refused to hire a deaf person for its top job.' [B. Drummond Ayres, Jr., New York Times, March 14,1988]. It forced us to examine the painful reality that there exists in the world, as Judy Heumann puts it, 'a systemic, deep-seated discrimination against people with disabilities.' It allowed us to discover in just 7 days that it doesn't have to be that way."*

The Washington Post said:

"Aristotle had said that those "born deaf become senseless and incapable of reason," and the march of civilization has done little to enlighten this perspective...The students at Gallaudet in March 1988 were not like their grandparents who worked in the typesetting rooms of newspapers and silently hid their anger and shame when over and over the hearing people they trained became their supervisors. Gallaudet had educated 95 percent of America's deaf college graduates. More than half had been recycled back into the deaf community as educators. But now some were proving themselves in the hearing world as lawyers, stockbrokers, and corporate executives... After 124 years of hearing rule, wasn't it time for a deaf president? "[11]

Another protest by deaf persons occurred a year later in March 1989. A few years before, actress Marlee Matlin, who is deaf, had won an Academy Award for her role in the movie," Children of a Lesser God." Not since Jane Wyman, a generation earlier, had starred in Johnny Belinda, had there been such a triumph. In 1980 Phyllis Froelich, also deaf, won the Tony award for Best Actress for her role in the same play, on Broadway. Phyllis is the oldest of nine children, all deaf from birth, born of deaf parents. But the hearing impaired actors association wanted more. In March 1989, CBS had scheduled an episode on TV called the "Equalizer" which featured a deaf lady in deep trouble. CBS wanted a hearing actress to play the role, claiming that no suitable deaf actress could be found. This enraged the deaf acting community, and protests occurred, but to no avail. The show went on with the scheduled hearing actress. It was like employing a face-blackened white actor to play a black person. It was beyond belief that CBS thought that a hearing person could play the role of a deaf person better than any deaf person.

Some deaf people have played very personal and very important roles in the struggle for civil rights for disabled people. Nicki Bonner, who is deaf, was incarcerated in state prison. He persuaded a court that section 504 could be interpreted as requiring interpreters for deaf prisoners. Bonner v. Lewis, 857 F.2d 559 (9th Cir. 1988).

JoAnn Delong, who is deaf, was selected for jury duty in a Pennsylvania County court. A Pennsylvania statute said that jurors had to be able to read, write and speak English. Denied the role of juror, JoAnn sued, on the ground that section 504 had been violated. The court was concerned that the presence of an interpreter might violate the sanctity of the jury system, especially when the jurors were deliberating in secret. Yet the court said that JoAnn was entitled to be a juror. The interpreter would be sworn, and the presence of the interpreter would not violate the jury system; JoAnn's civil rights were more important [DeLong v. Brumbaugh, 703 F. Supp. 399 (W.D. Pa. 1989)]. Another advance that occurred in the late eighties was the development of Dexter, a communication device for deaf-blind persons. Dexter is a laboratory developed facsimile of the human hand, that sits on a table and is connected to a computer. An unimpaired person speaks into the computer, which translates into impulses that are sent to Dexter (aptly named from the Latin, meaning "right hand"). The deaf-blind person feels the fingers on the hand moving in sign language, and receives the message. The recipient can communicate back by using sign with her own hand, which is transmitted electronically to Dexter, which repeats the sign, sends the message back to the computer, which translates audibly the message to the original sender.

A significant contribution to the deaf community has been a monthly TV show sponsored by Gallaudet University, called "Deaf Mosaic." Mary Lou Novitsky and Gallaudet professor Gil Eastman speak to viewers through American Sign Language; the program carries captions and spoken words. In November 1990 the show won its third Golden Eagle award, this time for a show relating how Lebanon's civil war has affected deaf people. Other Golden Eagles were awarded for a show on the 1987 World Congress of the Deaf in Helsinki and the Deaf President Now revolt at Gallaudet University in 1988. The show has been extremely successful in reaching many of the 200,000 hearing impaired people in the Washington, D.C. area and has provided a bridge between the deaf community and hearing viewers.

An outstanding leader of the disability civil rights movement is Dr. Frank Bowe, who is deaf, and is a professor at Hofstra University. Nationally recognized as a disability rights leader, he has published extensively on disability subjects.

Blind persons have their own individual challenges. There are varying degrees of visual impairment. Some have the ability to see indistinct shadows and light. Others can see somewhat looking straight ahead but not from the corners, and vice versa. Some have pain and some do not. Contrary to myth, none are in "darkness." Rather, there is an absence of shape, form and color, but it is not darkness.

Joan Rivers, in a September 1989 TV show, interviewed Madeline Silver, who is legally blind and has a guide dog. However, she has central vision. On one occasion she attempted to see a James Bond movie in New York, but was not allowed in; the manager believed she was faking blindness. She successfully sued the theater. Today in New York City, Lowes displays signs indicating that visually impaired and other disabled patrons are welcome in all Loew's theaters.

Major support groups for the blind include the National Federation of the Blind, the American Council of the Blind, and the American Foundation for the Blind. Federal legislation assists the blind with vending locations. Organizations of the blind have occasioned some of the earliest legislation relating to handicaps and access, such as White Cane Laws and seeing eye dogs laws.

Mary Jane Owen has been a leader in the disability civil rights movement. She uses a wheelchair and is visually impaired. She recalled her college days: She had been studying hard, but one late evening her eyes just didn't seem to focus. At first she thought the faint purple, mimeographed study sheets were too light for anyone to read. But as time went on things got worse. One day, while driving home from college in Berkeley, she found she could not read the large signs on the freeway.

Panicked, she underwent a series of medical tests and found she was rapidly losing her sight. After a period of acute depression, she pulled herself together and decided she had to enroll at the Orientation Center for the Blind in Albany, California. At first she didn't like the idea of being around sixty clumsy, awkward students; she was reminded of the evil blind man, tap-tap-tapping in a childhood story. Before entering the school, she had sat on a couch at home, knitting wool hats, all the same color. Friends told her there were 100 people walking around the area wearing the same kind of knitted hats – hats she had given them.

As a student at OCB, she underwent rigorous survival training. An instructor would toss coins on the floor; students were expected to listen and locate the position and type of coin. Finally, she was ready for Survival Travel Training. She was taken by car to a point several miles from the school and let out of the car. Her assignment was to find her way back to school. Proceeding along the sidewalk, she didn't have the foggiest idea of what to do. Her only assistance was the white cane. She asked someone where the nearest bus stop was, but in walking to the place where she was directed, she ran into a telephone pole and fell flat on her bottom on the sidewalk. She picked herself up, and a stranger directed her to the bus stop. She soon heard a bus pull up and the pneumatic door open. She approached and asked the driver whether he was going east toward the school. Getting an affirmative answer, she climbed the steps and was helped to a vacant seat. After a while, the driver announced the next stop was near the school. She debarked and found the school with little difficulty; the remainder of the afternoon was spent with friends discussing respective adventures.

At the school, daily living skills were taught. Little mounds of glue made braille markings on stoves, irons and other electrical appliances. Some used braille recipes; others used taped recordings. After a meal was prepared, they would all sit down and eat it. The final exam was to prepare a complete dinner party to which friends were invited. Instructions were also given in sewing and woodworking; the students learned to sew anything they wanted and they became proficient in the use of power tools. The abacus was studied for accounting skills, and Blind Law recorded a history of successful blind people. Paper money was folded in certain ways, lengthwise for ten dollar bills, cross wise for fives, and so forth. The teachers were rigorous and graded each student in the progress that had been made in accomplishing daily living skills. The goal was to be as independent and as "normal" as possible.

Mary Jane Owens has said eloquently:

"As a blind person, I feel more strongly than ever that we must foster among us a mutual respect for everyone – whether blind, deaf, mobility impaired, mentally or emotionally disabled. I believe the disability movement is the ultimate civil rights movement. If we succeed in equating a world that is accessible to all of these people, then no other civil rights movement will be necessary. Disability does not respect demographic categories."

Advances in computer technology are opening up new worlds to blind persons. Computers are currently marketed by several companies which will allow blind persons to type accurately on a word processor, using spoken word translation. There are three basic types, braille output, braille input, and voice output. Voice output translates a letter or word typed on the screen into the spoken letter or spoken word, at the option of the user. A voice activator will inform the user where his cursor is placed, such as, "line 22" and as the cursor is moved to the right, will speak the letter or word that it is resting on. This allows the user to type accurately and to read the typed screen. The braille output/input allows the user to type braille, which will appear on a braille "screen" for editing and reading. Voice scanners have been used for several years in which a printed page is placed on a screen which translates into the spoken word. An amazing new product by Xerox has perfected this device. A small box-like "mouse" about the size of a deck of cards, is placed on a printed page; the computer translates the printed word into audible speech. TV programs are developing radio channels that give the blind a description of the action. Elevators often have braille floor markers.

Pet peeves of blind persons include not being talked to when accompanied by a sighted friend, as for example, "Does he/she need any help?" Others sometimes object to having to do a song and dance, such as pacing around with a cane, trying to get attention for help that should be obvious. Most blind persons do not object to being asked if they need help. Society is learning. The non-disabled segment of the population is beginning to become more comfortable with blind persons and others with disabilities; the more the disabled take to the streets, the greater the experience of both the disabled and the non-disabled population. Although discrimination does exist, people on the street and other places are invariably helpful where help is needed. If a blind person or wheelchair bound person approaches a door that needs to be opened, the passerby, through some almost universal, "kinder, gentler" instinct, invariably will rise to the occasion and open it. Adolph Hitler would do no less.

In the spring of 1991, Donald Galloway, who is blind, was called for the jury pool at District of Columbia Superior Court. When it was learned that he is blind, he was excluded from jury duty, because court policy excludes blind people from being jurors. Galloway, angry, complained of discrimination. Chief Judge Fred B. Ugast said the court was trying to balance sometimes conflicting interests, the rights of citizens to serve on juries with the rights of litigants to have jurors who can carry out their responsibility, including observing the demeanor of witnesses. The recent trend is for states to allow blind jurors. In 1978 Chester P. Avery was removed from a jury panel in Alexandria, Virginia because he is blind. After filing a civil rights complaint with the Justice Department, he was reinstated. In 1987 Virginia amended its statute to say, "no person shall be deemed incompetent to serve on any jury because of blindness or partial blindness."

Harold Snider, who is blind and a disability civil rights activist, tells the story of himself and a lady companion attending a show at the Shoreham Hotel. When it came time to pay the bill, he was informed that the bill had been paid. The generous person came over, introduced himself, and after chatting, invited them to breakfast the next morning. That generous person was comedian Jack Benny.

This chapter has described only three of the major types of impairments to which mankind is vulnerable: mobility impairment, deafness, and blindness. There are, of course, many other afflictions, too numerous to mention, including some terrible new ones, AIDS and children of crack and cocaine addicted mothers. The diagnosis and treatment of all these ills is left to the medical profession; suffice to say that all mankind, no matter what the ailment, want basically the same things: to be treated as a worthwhile human being and to have the opportunity for equal access to all aspects of life: employment, housing, transportation, recreation, and family life.

CHAPTER XI

SPORTS, RECREATION, THE ARTS, THEATERS and RESTAURANTS

Cheryl had Down's syndrome and was a slightly chubby twelve year old. It was July 1988 and there was a Special Olympics program in the park. Her mother drove her to the park; wearing a Special Olympics T-shirt, Cheryl joined the other kids near a big tree. Mary, the Special Olympics supervisor, was explaining the rules of the games. There would be a broad jump, a high jump, and a 50 yard dash. Then there would be face painting and kite flying. Awards would be given. Cheryl didn't want to do any of it, and when Mary blew the whistle for the fifty yard dash, she started to cry. Mary put her arm around her and drew her to the starting line. Cheryl said, "I hate this, I don't want to do it." Mary said, "You can do it, Cheryl, if you try. Please try." The whistle blew and ten runners started off. Cheryl chugged along, angry, her face red. Before she realized it she had crossed the finish line, ahead of the others. Cheers went up and Cheryl, astonished, threw her arms around Mary and said, "I didn't know I could do it. I love you."

It is part of the human condition that humans need to find some relief, some surcease, from the daily requirements of mere survival; people with disabilities are no exception.

Disabled people, once relegated to basket-weaving, crossword puzzles, and counting the number of flowered patterns on bedroom wallpaper, slowly began to enter the mainstream of sports, recreation, and the arts. Through their own efforts and with help from civil rights legislation, they have achieved great victories in sports, in the arts, and in profitable use of leisure time. The Americans

With Disabilities Act of 1990, discussed in Chapter Six, has many provisions that promote these goals; the act is not simply limited to promoting the barest essentials of life. How did all these victories come about?

As the Great Depression was drawing to a close, a baby girl whose name was Wilma Rudolph was born to a large, poor, black family in rural Tennessee. Wilma contracted polio as a child. With leg exercises and the assistance of her mother, brothers, and sisters, Wilma, at age nine, was able to discard her leg braces. As a teenager she sprouted. She became a star basketball player and track athlete during high school and later at Tennessee State University. She won a bronze medal in track at the 1956 Melbourne Olympics, and in 1960, won three gold medals at the Rome Olympics for the 100 meter, 200 meter, and 400 meter relay. She is truly an outstanding example of a disadvantaged, disabled youngster overcoming tremendous odds to reach a pinnacle in sports.

In January 1958 an automobile accident left baseball legend Roy Campanella paralyzed from the chest down. He was a hero with the Brooklyn Dodgers, well known in his time. Today Roy lives in Southern California and is still active with the Dodger organization. Each spring he travels to Florida for spring training where he works with young catchers. In 1959 he wrote an autobiography, "It's Good to Be Alive."[1]

In the fall of 1978, in a Patriots-Raiders football game, a particularly hard hit ball left Darryl Stingley of the Patriots with a broken neck and a future as a quadriplegic. Like Roy Campanella, Darryl has become an executive with his organization, (in Darryl's case, the Patriots,) and he has co-authored a book.[2]

In 1991 the Denver Broncos did something that no other National Football League team had ever done before. They signed up a deaf defensive end, Kenny Walker. Kenny had been an outstanding player at the University of Nebraska; he had become severely hearing impaired as a result of contracting spinal meningitis at age two. In October 1991, Jane Pauley on her "Real Life" TV Show, described how Kenny played football, reading lips and watching the coach's signs. The Broncos hired an interpreter to help with coaching instruction.

In 1955 Jill Kinmont was a favorite for the U.S. Olympic Ski team. In January 1955 her picture appeared on the cover of Sports Illustrated; that same month she suffered a terrible fall while skiing and became a C-5/6 quadriplegic. (People with quadriplegia are classified depending on where in the spinal cord the injury occurred. If in the neck and upper back, (the cervix) they are classified as C's; if the middle back (the thorax) as T's, and if the lower back, (the lumbar) as L's. Generally, the higher in the spinal column the injury occurs, the more severe the damage). In 1975 and 1978, Hollywood produced two movies about

Jill's life, *The Other Side of the Mountain* and *The Other Side of the Mountain, Part II* after a biography of her life. She became a teacher, married, and today she teaches developmentally disabled children in Bishop, California.

At age 19, Dave Kiley became spinal cord injured when he slid down a hill on an inner tube in the snow and hit a tree. He has become an outstanding wheelchair athlete; he's been the coach and organizer of the Casa Colina Condors, a team with five national championships in the last seven years. Says Dave, *"I tell [newly injured] people they have two options: to go down the tubes and let it get the best of you or to get on with your life and make it as productive as possible. I tell people that if you're active, it'll make you 100 percent more happy than if you sit around passively."*

In the spring of 1981, Phil Carpenter and George Murray, both in wheelchairs, began a cross country wheelchair jaunt. Starting at the Santa Monica Pier in California, they transversed mountains, valleys, and deserts, averaging fifty miles a day. Their biggest complaint was lack of sleep and being attacked by a rattlesnake in the Mojave Desert. They would let go down the mountain slopes, often doing 45 miles per hour down and around the hair pin turns. When reported by The Washington Post, on August 14, 1981, they had reached Fairfax, Virginia. On August 26, 143 days after beginning, they reached the Lincoln Tunnel in New York City. "We stopped traffic," they said, and later they were hosted at a welcoming reception put on by the U.S. Council for International Disabled Persons.

In the summer of 1992, a young man, Rick Hoyt, who is severely disabled with cerebral palsy, began a cross country bike trip, beginning on the west coast, and after 47 grueling days, arrived in Boston before cheering crowds. Rick attends Boston University and uses a word board for communicating. His father, Dick Hoyt, rides the bicycle, with Rick in front in a bike wagon. The trip was a media event and had a goal of raising one million dollars for disability causes.

In 1980, Terry Fox, a young Canadian, had one leg amputated at the knee as a result of cancer, but he ran across Canada, coast to coast. He raised huge sums for cancer research. In 1983, a movie was made of his life, "The Terry Fox Story," starring Eric Fryer and Robert Duvall.

In 1972, two Vietnam veterans from Walter Reed Army Hospital, each with amputations below the knee, organized skiing expeditions, using a tri-track with crutches. A National Amputee Ski Championship was sponsored by the National Inconvenienced Sportsmen's Association. Since then, skiing and other outdoor sports for disabled people have proliferated, with new equipment such as toboggans and special skis.

The Special Olympics was founded in 1968 by Eunice Kennedy Shriver, sister of President Kennedy. The purpose of the organization is to provide sports programs for mentally retarded children and adults. Contrary to myth, it is not limited to children, and it does not include the physically disabled unless they are also retarded. Special Olympics provides year round sports programs. There are 25,000 local Special Olympics programs in 73 countries on every continent. More than one million children and adults take part in year round training and competition. There is a summer program that features aquatics, basketball, bowling, gymnastics, roller skating, softball, soccer, and volleyball. The winter program features skiing, skating, and hockey; demonstration sports include canoeing, cycling, tennis, and weight lifting. The Special Olympics is unique in that it accommodates competitors at all ability levels by assigning them to competition levels based on previous performances. Special Olympics is run almost entirely by volunteers and has a stellar board of directors. Aside from Eunice Shriver and her husband Sargent Shriver, the board includes, among others: Maria Shriver Schwarzenegger, TV broadcaster; Bart Conner, Olympic Gold medalist; Frank Gifford, sportscaster; Rafer Johnson, Olympic Decathlon Gold Medalist; Ted Kennedy Jr.; HRH Prince Raad Bin Zeid, Lord Chamberlain to His Majesty the King of Jordan. Special Olympics was officially recognized and endorsed as a sports organization by the International Olympic Committee in 1988, the first organization other than a national Olympic Committee to be so recognized. It is a member of the United States Olympic Committee on Sports for the Disabled. It holds summer and winter games in the United States and in other countries, and every two years holds international games. The creed of the special Olympics has been aptly stated by Mrs. Shriver:

> *"In Special Olympics, it is not the strongest body or the most dazzling mind that counts. It is the invincible spirit which overcomes all handicaps. For without this spirit, winning medals is empty. But with it there is no defeat."*

The present president of Special Olympics is Sargent Shriver, husband of Eunice, international lawyer, ambassador, organizer and first director of the Peace Corps, first director of the Office of Economic Opportunity, organizer of VISTA, Head Start, and other organizations, recipient of 24 honorary degrees, and Democratic party nominee for vice president with George McGovern in 1972.

A field day was held on the Washington Mall, featuring all kinds of athletic games and devices for disabled people, such as trampolines, barrier games and the like. Manufacturers of special equipment set up tents and everyone had a good time. The public was amazed to see disabled people out there participating and generally having fun.

In July 1989, 13 disabled Boy Scouts from the Washington area joined a regular troop of Boy Scouts at Camp Goshen in Virginia. Some of the scouts were autistic or moderately retarded, but they all had a good time with the non-disabled scouts and the counselors. They learned archery, knot tying, swimming, and other sports and activities. The camp is nestled in the Blue Ridge Mountains, a change in scenery from Southeast Washington where some of the scouts live. Said David Henderson, special projects executive for handicapped scouting, *"Scouting is for everyone."*

The District of Columbia Therapeutic Center put on a water show in 1977 at the Woodson High School pool, featuring disabled swimmers doing choreographed skits and contests. The Therapeutic Center soon was housed in its own brand new facility in Southeast Washington, the first of its kind in the nation. It cost $2.6 million. It has a swimming pool, darkroom and shop, gymnasium, kitchen, and other facilities exclusively for disabled people, many of whom are retarded adults. Columnist Sarah Booth Conroy describing the Center said:

> *"Too often the handicapped must stay by themselves day after day, trapped in their problems. Unlike other people, they have few chances to work off their worries by meeting friends, running, jumping, swimming and playing. The loneliness itself becomes the greatest handicap of all."* [3]

Under the dedicated supervision of Doris Frederick and MikeWalker, the Therapeutic Center provides every day sport and recreational opportunities to disabled citizens, young and old.

Sometimes society's reaction to disabled people, though well-intentioned, is slightly off key. At half time at a Washington Redskins football game for the benefit of Shriners, two children, one in a wheelchair and one on crutches, were brought to the field. After speeches, the children miraculously threw aside crutches and wheelchair, and walked off the field. This brought protests from some on the ground that *"miracles"* were cruelly promised, that the children were being *"used"* for promotion purposes, and there was a patronizing, unreal air to the whole performance. The pathetic spectacle was never repeated.

The March of Dimes Poster child publicity campaign has been criticized as exploitation of children. It is seen as a distorted media-created image for public consumption, far removed from reality. The children, chosen for the March of Dimes campaign, endure rigorous travel and media event schedules. Their efforts have contributed to millions of dollars being raised for the March of Dimes. Whether children should be participating – some say exploited – in this manner has become a matter of controversy. One child rather pathetically said that if he had the choice of being non-disabled, or disabled and a Poster Child, he would choose the latter.

The Easter Seals Society has also had "poster kids." Yvonne Duffy, a former Easter Seals Society poster kid, complained that when the campaign was over, *"I returned to being a lonely child living with a not-too-stable divorced mother, but none of those interested in helping us on camera ever called, visited, or sent a check."*[4]

Columnist Ellen Goodman criticized Nancy Reagan for a photo opportunity event with an eight year old Easter Seal child in a wheelchair. *"The vision of Nancy Reagan bearing gifts – a basket of flowers, a pink bunny, a jar of jelly beans – to the eight year old Easter Seal child in a wheelchair, pushed my button,"* she said in a column in *The Washington Post*, March 23, 1982.

The Washington, D.C. area has produced outstanding young wheelchair athletes. Charla Ramsay, at age 13, became the second fastest wheelchair athlete in the country, and won a gold medal for the 1500 meters at the World Wheelchair Games in London. Another top athlete is Maria Wood. They belong to New Life, Inc., founded by Brenda Greene and her husband, Bill, who uses a wheelchair due to an injury sustained at age 16. New Life, Inc. was the first wheelchair sports club for juniors. In 1990 and 1991, young wheelchair athletes competed at the national level, and even at the international level in France!

When Ryan Martin was 12, he was shot by a crazed gunman outside his home as he and his family were returning from an outing. By the age of 16, Ryan had turned tragedy into triumph. Though spinal cord injured he has become one of the country's top wheelchair tennis players. Wheelchair tennis is virtually the same as regular tennis, except that two bounces are allowed instead of one. In July 1992 Ryan, at the age of 18, won the eighth annual Nation's Capital Wheelchair Tennis Tournament in Washington, D.C. Particularly when he plays against able bodied players, Martin said he doesn't want spectators to pity him. *"It makes me want to kick their butts."* More than 7500 people, worldwide, play wheelchair tennis, which will make its debut as an Olympic sport at the 1992 summer games in Barcelona.

In 1990 William Albert Denby was named Outstanding Disabled Veteran by the Disabled American Veterans. Bill, a 39 year old Maryland native, became a double leg amputee as a result of the Vietnam War. He was injured in a rocket attack in Quang Tri on March 26, 1971, at the age of 19. After being released from Walter Reed Hospital (where he met his wife Toni), he became depressed and turned to drugs and alcohol. In 1984 he became one of the original testers of the artificial limb called the Seattle Foot. It gave him much greater mobility, and he has appeared in Du Pont commercials playing stand up basketball. Today he is on speaking tours throughout the country. In the winter of 1991-1992, he helped disabled Gulf War veterans ski in Breckinridge, Colorado. Mike Burgess is one of the Gulf War veterans who had lost a leg but he enjoyed skiing with Bill's help.

Disabled folks also got around to mountain climbing. In 1982 three paraplegic mountain climbers got out of their wheelchairs and crawled the final 200 yards to the summit of the tallest peak in Texas, Guadalupe Peak. Upon arrival, the three hikers, Jeff Moss, Donnie Rogers, and Dave Kiley, celebrated with champagne and then spent the night on the peak.

Also in July 1982, Don Bennett, a fifty-two year old one legged man, hopped to the top of Mt. Rainier in the State of Washington and planted a flag there in the name of the handicapped. Fulfilling a ten year dream, he climbed mostly on crutches and then hopped the rest of the way to the top.

Mark Wellman, who became a paraplegic after a climbing accident in 1982, climbed to the top of El Capitan in Yosemite National Park in July of 1989. With help from a partner, Mike Corbett, he made it to the top in one week, using his arms to drag himself up six inches at a time. Winds sometimes gusted to fifty miles per hour and temperatures rose to over 100. The U.S. Senate passed a resolution introduced by Senator Bob Dole, citing their *"Extraordinary feat of bravery and stout-heartedness."*

Possibly the most extraordinary mountain climb of all ended on November 21, 1990, the day before Thanksgiving, at Mount Katahdin in Maine. Bill Irwin, age 50 and blind, had begun the long Appalachian Trail trek eight months earlier in Georgia. With his dog Orient, he endured unimaginable difficulty, but together, they accomplished the long hike.

In 1988 the California Angels baseball team signed up Jim Abbot as a pitcher. Jim was born without one of his hands but has become a dependable and accurate pitcher. Today, he plays for the New York Yankees!

John Heiss was born missing one foot, but with the aid of a prosthesis, guts, and determination, he became a football kicker at the Laurel, Maryland Boys and Girls Club, and won the *"Commissioner's Award"* for his achievement.

In 1984 Don Rodewald, a retired Air Force Colonel, completed a four month solo flight around the world, taking 230 flying hours and ending at Washington's National Airport, where he received the red carpet treatment. A paraplegic as a result of an accident at Andrews Air Force Base in 1954, he became the first paraplegic to fly around the world. He devised a hand-controlled rudder and became a founder of Wheelchair Aviators. Some flight schools, such as Seattle Flight Service, Charles City, Iowa; Aeronautics, Epps Air Service, Atlanta, Georgia; and Flying Nunn's Aviation, Plattsburgh, New York, now have hand-controlled aircraft. Freedom's Wings International of Morris Plains, New Jersey, is a soaring club.

Bob Wieland lost both legs at the hips trying to help buddies during the Vietnam War. He swims, uses a special bike operated by hand, lifts weights, and does cross country track, all the while helping poverty programs.

Dave Williamson of Bowie, Maryland, who had polio at age 3, won the 1977 Boston Wheelchair Marathon, which has become an annual event. He is director of HUD's Office of Independent Living. He has won many gold medals in wheelchair competition, at the International Olympics and the U.S. National Championships. Once he was at Disneyland, sitting in his wheelchair, when a kid came up and said, *"hey, mister, are you a ride?"* He replied, *"That's right! Hop aboard, that will be seventy five cents."*

In 1975 Bob Hall, post-polio from Belmont, Massachusetts, was the first wheelchair athlete to enter the Boston Marathon. By 1983 seven wheelchair racers finished the Marathon in under two hours. George Murray, in 1984, became the first wheelchair racer on a Wheaties Box, and in 1987 Candace Cable-Brookes won the Boston Marathon for a record fifth time.

On May 1, 1989, a 52 mile wheelchair race took place, beginning in the Blue Ridge Mountains of Virginia, and ending, in the rain, at the Washington Monument. The race, called the White House Wheelchair Race of Champions, lasted four hours. Ten racers split a purse of $22,000 dollars. Coming in first, in three hours, 49 minutes, and 3 seconds, was 34-year-old Rafael Ibarra, who had had polio at the age of 1 1/2. Ibarra had won three medals at the 1988 Paralympics in Seoul, Korea. Race organizer was Bill Fuller, senior administrative director of Grafton School, a special education, residential facility in Berryville, Virginia. *"Winning was secondary to the main thing we tried to accomplish,"* said Tom Foran, who finished third. *"That was that we are athletes first and disabled second."* On October 2, 1990, a repeat of this race was held, this time with financing of over $250,000. Jim Knaub of Long Beach, California, was the winner, Ken Carnes of Morningside, Maryland, came in second, and Doug Kennedy of Haleyville, Alabama, came in third. The racers used sixteen pound, three wheel aluminum chairs. Rose Winand of Wilmerding, Pennsylvania, was the first woman to enter the race. Jim Knaub, a former pole vaulter and Olympic candidate before his accident, had won the Los Angeles Marathon, the Long Beach Marathon, and the Boston Marathon three times. Said Bill Fuller: *"The wheelchair, that difference from able-bodied athletes, is what has made this such an interesting event. You've had people who have overcome immense adversity and they're the best in the world at what they do...the struggle of the coming together of excellence and adversity."* Jim Knaub enyoys the liberating freedom of wheelchair racing; it frees him from the social burden of disability.

In April 1992 Jim Knaub won his fourth Boston Marathon wheelchair race with a "world best" record of 1:26:28, while Jean Driscoll of Champaign, Illinois won her third straight women's crown with a world best record of 1:36:52.

A note of caution for wheelchair athletes is that injuries are common. Pulled muscles, sprains, bursitis, and tendonitis are common. Chronic shoulder problems can result from years of wheelchair sports. Carpal tunnel syndrome can cause damage to wrist and fingers; ultimately, surgery may be needed to correct the problem.

In September 1985, "Let's Play to Grow," a small but growing national organization of families with disabled children, staged an event on the Washington Mall. Joanne Stevens spoke, as well as Eunice Kennedy Shriver, executive director of the Joseph P. Kennedy Foundation, sponsor of the Special Olympics. Field events included volleyball, face painting, balloon blowing, golf, and other activities. Joanne said:

"So many families refuse even to go out in public. It takes a lot for them to overcome the fear and shame."

The National Park Service has been developing recreational opportunities for people with disabilities. A nationwide system of over seven hundred trails, at various parks, has been developed for disabled folks. The trails are paved for wheelchair users and have audio cassettes for the blind. In May 1988, the Mountain Laurel Trail was opened in Vienna, Virginia, for the benefit of Washington area residents.

Advances in technology have created sports and recreational opportunities for disabled people. A ball that transmits sound is used by blind people, as are chess boards with raised squares and braille monopoly. The Handicapped Scuba Association in San Clemente, California, takes quadriplegics and paraplegics scuba diving. The National Wheelchair Athletic Association in Colorado Springs, Colorado, sponsors wheelchair basketball games. There are several riding centers in Virginia and Maryland which take handicapped adults and children horseback riding. The Boy Scouts of America have a braille handbook; its first executive director, Dr. James West, was disabled.

In 1978 Congress passed the Amateur Sports Act (P.L.95-606) which reorganized the United States Olympic Committee and also encouraged special programs for disabled athletes. The Olympic Committee was directed:

"[to] encourage and provide assistance to amateur athletic programs and competition for handicapped individuals, including, where feasible, expansion of opportunities for meaningful participation by handicapped individuals in programs of athletic competition for able bodied individuals."

Pursuant to this legislation, the Olympic Committee established a Handicapped in Sports Committee, consisting of two representatives from: the Amateur Athletic Association for the Deaf, the National Association of Sports for Cerebral Palsy, the Special Olympics, the United States Association for Blind

Athletes, and the National Wheelchair Athletic Association. In 1988 the Paralympics took place in Seoul, Korea, with wheelchair basketball, track and field, swimming, volleyball, table tennis, bicycling, weight-lifting, judo, marksmanship, and other events. Although 156 events were canceled because of rules disputes, the 8th Paralympics in Seoul was generally regarded as the best to date. Three thousand athletes from 60 countries attended. Candace Cable-Brookes took a bronze medal for the exhibition 800 meters, and gold medals in the 800 meters, 1500 meters, the marathon, the 200, and 400 meters. At first, the U.S. Army put up the Americans at an army base and provided guides, then the disabled athletes moved into Paralympic Village.[5] Another disabled American star was Jeff Worthington, who won six gold medals in all six of the track events he entered, shattering five world records. He was named National Wheelchair Athletic Association Male Athlete of the Year.

In September 1992, Paralympics continued in Barcelona, Spain.Paralympics has been kept separate from the regular Olympics, some say continuing the isolation of disabled people. For example, in 1992, the regular summer Olympics were held in July in Barcelona, while Paralympics were held, entirely separately, in September. (But, at the regular Olympics in Barcelona, there was an "exhibition" wheelchair race. American Michael Noe won a bronze medal in the 1500 meter race and American Jean Driscoll won a silver medal in the women's 800 meter race.)

But there was one stunning exception to this wall of separation. At the regular summer Olympics in July 1992 in Barcelona, at the end of the spectacular opening ceremonies, it came time to light the Olympic torch. From the crowd of thousands of youthful, handsome, able bodied athletes, emerged a lone archer, walking with a limp (a result of polio). In the darkened stadium he held a bow and a flaming arrow. He shot the arrow skyward in a perfect arch; it landed precisely on the torch cauldron, igniting it. Thus, the 1992 summer Olympics began! It was a breathtaking event and in keeping with the global, all-inclusive atmosphere of the Olympics.

The National Handicapped Sports and Recreation Association promotes all manner of sports for disabled athletes. Its president is Rod Hernley and Bobbi Avancena is the editor of its newspaper. There are chapters in many states, which promote skiing, water sports, and other ventures, including a planned tall ship cruise in the Bahamas and even an assault on Mt. Everest.

A leading advocate for physical education and sports for blind students has been Dr. Charles E. Buell. He has promoted and encouraged mainstreaming of blind and visually impaired children into sport and recreational programs. An excellent book by Doctor Buell is *Physical Education and Recreation for the Visually Handicapped.*[6] The book dispels myths about blind students, describes sports activities in which blind youngsters participate, and offers practical suggestions for physical education and recreation programs for blind students. Myths debunked by Dr. Buell are: (1) blind children have more accidents; (2) they are not able to participate in regular or adaptive physical education programs; (3) they require more supervision; and (4) they are shunned by classmates. None of these is true, says the author. Still, the concept of mainstreaming is often misunderstood. It does not mean that all disabled students, no matter how severe the handicap, are legally required to be placed in regular programs with nondisabled students. Rather, "mainstreaming" is more of an objective or goal than a perfect program and means:

> *"appropriate education, physical education, and sport services and activities to individuals with handicapping conditions, regardless of levels of involvement, in settings as near to traditional practice as possible."* [7]

In fact, blind and visually impaired people have participated in all manner of sports: track and field, including high jump, meter running, broad jump, weight-lifting, bowling, golf, archery, figure skating, mountain climbing, shot-put, wrestling, karate, chess, fishing, tandem cycling, and swimming.

James Mastro placed third in the NAAU Greco-Roman wrestling competition and was named an alternate on the United States Olympic wrestling team in 1976. Mick Zorick placed four times in the top four in USWF competition, and Doug Blubaugh is in the Wrestling Hall of Fame. All these athletes are blind. In karate, Tony Maczynski won a black belt and placed sixth in a national karate championship event. Trischa Zorn qualified for the NAAU swimming championships and is in the top 25 backstrokers, blind or sighted. She is the first legally blind female athlete to win an athletic scholarship at a university. Sven Nahlin, a blind scuba diver in Sweden, teaches scuba classes there. King Nawaki swam 26 miles from Catalina Island in California to the mainland; Nigel Verbeck and Gerald Price water skied across the English Channel in 3 hours and 45 minutes. In 1973 Dennis Moore paddled a canoe across the English Channel. In the Pan American games of 1968, Sonny Yates placed second in sky diving, with the aid of a radio in his helmet. A Norwegian, Tore Nearland, with a sighted partner, Maris Voster, bicycled, tandem-style, around the world in 79 days. In 1981 John Dickey, 72, tandem biked across the United States to attend his 50th reunion at Amherst College. Eight blind climbers accompanied by four sighted guides climbed to the top of Mt. Kilimanjaro in Africa. Kirk Adams, Sheila Holsworth, Fred Nocesner, Doug Wakefield, and Justin McDevitt, climbed to the top of Mt. Rainier in Washington and were invited by President Reagan to the White House. All of the events just described were accomplished by blind or visually impaired athletes.[8]

In the summer of 1987, a severely visually impaired sailor, James Dickson, set sail from Rhode Island, alone, in a 36-foot boat called "Eye-Opener," with the announced intention of sailing across the Atlantic. Due to a tropical storm with 15-foot waves and 50-knot winds seriously impairing his equipment, he terminated his plan and arrived safely in Bermuda, where he was toasted by a local yacht club. The conservative columnist, William F. Buckley Jr., apparently having nothing else to write about, grumpily complained that the trip was a "stunt" and there was "no point" to the undertaking. Charles Krauthammer, in his column, defended the trip.

He wrote that Buckley's criticism was based on his view that *"the diminished experience is not worth having. It can't be enjoyed. It can't be experienced. It doesn't even exist."* He likened the diminished experience to a reader of Dostoevsky, translated into English. Something may be lost in the translation. Krauthammer concluded:

> *"The point of a blind man sailing the Atlantic is not to get other blind men to follow. Dickson's contribution was to show that the blind can do things – such as sail to Bermuda alone – that people thought the blind could not do. Funny thing is, Dickson's already done it and some people would still like to argue that he can't."*

Ted Koppel of *Nightline* got into the act, and on one of his programs there was a face off between Buckley and Dickson. The issue seemed to be whether a "diminished experience" is (a) worth doing, or (b) should be avoided entirely or (c) if actually done, it hasn't occurred because it hasn't been experienced. Buckley wrote: *"It is a pity that the pity we rightly feel for the handicapped evolves into forced applause when the handicapped attempt that which simply is not natural."* It's hard to find a sentence more loaded with insults and misconceptions. It's not natural for everyone, though it may be for Buckley, to stroke the chin while nodding affectedly and rolling eyes upward to a furrowed brow. In Canada there are a hundred "Thalidomide babies" born without arms, who find it "natural" to eat with their feet. The "diminished experience" idea could result in elimination of such things as video baseball, because it's not the "real thing." Special Olympics would be abolished, because it's not "natural" to run slowly. So too would all vicarious experiences. The concert goer has only a secondary or vicarious understanding of what the composer originally had in mind. And of course, although ecstasy may occur in Buckley's brilliant mind as he mentally composes his next column, the reader is left with the "diminished experience" of attempting to penetrate Buckley's brain through the inferior, second hand and "diminished" experience of reading the printed word. And what about "virtual sex?"

Sailing, on a more modest scale, is being enjoyed by disabled sailors. The National Ocean Access Project in Maryland has begun a program to help develop disabled sailors. In June 1990 about 75 disabled people, with disabilities ranging from spinal cord injury to eye and head impairment, participated in a program to learn how to sail. The organization has three specially adapted sailboats for cruising in Chesapeake Bay. The 20-foot fiberglass Freedom Independence sloops have no cabins but come equipped with a pair of seats that lock into place and can be swiveled from side to side for tacking. The simplified rigging to raise and lower the sails can be fully managed from either chair. Donald Backe, executive director of the organization, deserves a lot of credit for making it possible for disabled sailors to get out on the water.

Some would take issue with the handicapped "Superjock" image projected by some extraordinary feats of endurance or strength, but given the choice of doing something or not doing it, the positive approach is usually better. The super achievers do advance the cause of their less able friends; disabled people everywhere benefit from these feats. Even without media attention, the exploits are of value to the participants themselves, in providing a sense of accomplishment and self worth.

Arts for the handicapped have also flourished. More so than sports, the arts seem to have been more often promoted by the "beautiful people" who grace style pages, "big government," and "high society;" the Charity Ball, the Benefit Concert, the Black Tie Dinner, the White House Soiree, and other socially proper and sometimes exclusive events have been held in the name of promoting art for disabled people. This has caused an epidemic of claimed tax deductions for theater tickets and the like, to the consternation of the Internal Revenue Service, with disabled people themselves often as bemused bystanders.

The symbiotic relationship between Powers-That-Be and disabled people has, from time to time, been good for a party. In September 1984 the Capitol Hill Club hosted a "National Media Campaign Kickoff" for the National Challenge Committee of the Disabled. Dr. Martha Scully and Shirley Wilson organized the soiree. Prominent guests included Miss Wheelchair of America, Gaynell Colburn, and James Brady, the feisty former White House Press Secretary who was shot by John Hinkley at the time President Reagan was shot. After suffering agonizing injuries, Brady, who uses a wheelchair, has made a remarkable and courageous come-back and has been active in civil rights issues for disabled people.

Another glittering party was held in the Kennedy Center in April 1976. (If the adoption of the 504 regulations in 1977 was the beginning of recorded history for disabled people, 1976 was definitely "prehistoric.") "In Celebration" was held at the Eisenhower Theater of the Kennedy Center, just before the annual President's Committee conference. First Lady Betty Ford attended, as did Mayor and Mrs. Walter Washington. A blind young singer, Tom Sullivan, performed, as did many other well known celebrities, including Ray Charles, Itzhak Perlman, Nanette Fabray, Helen Hayes, the National Theater of the Deaf, Burl Ives, Pearl Bailey, the Paul Hill Chorale, and the Gallaudet Dancers. Harold Russell of the President's Committee spoke. Later, the Iranian Embassy (another example of pre-history) hosted a reception. Some disabled people were miffed at not being on the exclusive invitation list and held their own "counter-party" on Capitol Hill. Linda Teixera, who is visually impaired, played hostess. Later, overcome with embarrassment, the Kennedy Center party invited some disabled people to the Iranian reception.

A Very Special Arts program has been presented at the Kennedy Center, the White House, and elsewhere, every so often, chaired by Jean Kennedy Smith. In 1979 artist Jamie Wyeth appeared, as did 40 performing groups. In 1985 nine year old Jason Ellsworth, blind and with cerebral palsy, sang a heart-stealing "Long Gone Lonesome Blues" at the White House Very Special Arts program, attended by Nancy and Ronald Reagan, Jim Brady, the Gatlin Brothers, actor Cliff Robertson, and artist William Britt.

In June 1989 the Very Special Arts program exhibited paintings, sculpture, and other media at the roof level of the Kennedy Center. An exhibit of photographs by visually impaired photographers was presented at the Library of Congress. The Kennedy Center roof featured music and dance as well as the visual arts. A remarkable dance and magic show was presented by Argentina and performers with Down's syndrome. More than 1000 participants from 55 countries were involved. Sadly, *The Washington Post* devoted little attention to this remarkable event, being preoccupied with the rejection of photographs by Robert Mapplethorpe by the Cocoran Gallery, which caused a stir in the art world. On June 17, 1989, a Very Special Arts gala was presented in the concert hall of the Kennedy Center. Celebrities, such as Michael Douglas, introduced various disabled artists, including playwright Neil Marcus, who uses a wheel chair and who wrote *Storm Reading;* Orlando Fiol, a young and blind classical pianist; Tony Melendez, born without arms, who sang and played the guitar with his feet; the New Vision Dance Project, composed of visually impaired young dancers; and Sarah Anderson, who did a wheelchair dance with her teacher Zina Bethune. The U-2 rock group and artist Bono added popular interest. In the fall of 1989, a young man with Down syndrome, Chris Burke, was a star in a new TV show, "Life Goes On." Chris says he has "*Up Syndrome*."

Yet another celebration at the Kennedy Center was held on November 18, 1991. The National Rehabilitation Center of Washington, D.C. honored, with a Victory Award, seven prominent Americans who had overcome physical obstacles. A crowd of 3000, including George and Barbara Bush, enjoyed the festivities, which were introduced by Kuwaiti Ambassador Saud Nasir Sabah, actresses Lynda Carter, Marsha Warfield, Lea Salonga, Phylicia Rashad, singer Crystal Gayle, and actors Arnold Schwarzenegger, Leslie Nielsen, Paul Winfield, and Cliff Robertson. The seven winners were: comedian Norm Crosby, who has hearing loss due to concussions from a depth charge while he was a radar operator during World War II on an anti-submarine patro; actor Billy Barty, 3 feet 9 inches tall, who accepted the award for the estimated 1.5 million people of short stature; Jim Abbott who was born without a right hand and now pitches for the New York Yankees; and Sandy Duncan who had a brain tumor which destroyed her left eye. Representative Charles Bennett of Florida is one of the leaders in the disability civil rights movement as detailed elsewhere in this book. He suffered polio in 1945 in the Philippines where he served with the Marines in World War II. Singer Gloria Estafan, on tour in Australia, has a spinal cord injury as a result of a bus accident. Major Rhonda Cornum, an Army flight surgeon who participated in Operation Desert Storm, suffered two broken arms, a gunshot wound, serious leg injuries and was taken prisoner after being shot down in a helicopter.

The author, in November 1990, entered three of his paintings for possible selection at a Capitol Hill Art Gallery. Two were selected, a watercolor and an oil, and the watercolor, incredibly, actually was sold at the gallery. The author, however, never saw the exhibition or the artists' reception; the building, an old city school, was totally inaccessible.

Films about disability became more commonplace. In the winter of 1990, the blockbuster film, *Born on the Fourth of July*, was released. It tells the story of Ron Kovic, whose spinal cord was injured in Vietnam and who went on to become an anti-war activist. Born in a small upstate New York town on the fourth of July, Ron was a typical boy next door jock and high school athlete. In the sixties he enthusiastically joined the Marines, emulating his father who had served in World War II. Injured in Vietnam, Ron uses a wheelchair. The appalling scenes of Vietnam and the Bronx Veterans Hospital are not for the weak of stomach. Ron's outlook changed from gung-ho Marine to anti-war activist. The movie is a blend of anti-war sentiment, veterans causes, and the disability civil rights movement. Though Ron was portrayed by a non-disabled actor, Tom Cruise, few seemed to mind, because of Tom Cruise's undeniably convincing portrayal of a disabled veteran. In 1990 Oliver Stone won the Academy Award for Best Director. The 1992 film, *Waterdance* featured quads and paras in a rehab center; some humor eked out through all the grossness.

Another Academy Award winner was Daniel Day-Lewis, who won Best Actor award in 1990 for his role of Christy Brown, the Irish author, in *My Left Foot.* This film portrayed quite honestly the life of a man with cerebral palsy, a role authentically played by Daniel Day-Lewis. *Rain Man*, starring Dustin Hoffman, was about an autistic man.

Movies such as those just mentioned could mean certain things to the non-disabled but something else to disabled people. For the non-disabled, the movies' most significant effect is that of education: informing the general public what it is like to be disabled. For disabled people, there is a more personal rapport with the main characters, but many disabled people feel put off by melodramatic tales of "ovrcoming." Although the portrayal of Christy Brown had a bittersweet charm and profound human interest, some disabled people could not help but notice the fact that Christy was the center of attention; many disabled people feel the opposite: isolated if not shunned. It seemed that Christy's performance was regarded by Hollywood as some kind of breakthrough in this wall of isolation.

A review of *Fourth of July* and *My Left Foot* in the *Disability Rag,* May/June 1990, complained that none of the actors were themselves disabled. *Fourth of July* was criticized for treating disability as part of the scenery in the same sense that cacti and sage brush are part of the scenery of westerns. The review, in general, praised the movies in raising the level of disability consciousness but objected somewhat to the "overcoming" theme. Perhaps it could be said that the extremes of both terrible isolation and sudden celebrity status, particularly in *My Left Foot,* portray disabled people in equally unrealistic ways; perhaps what is needed is a movie showing how disabled people "fit in" with the daily life of mainstream America. When society reaches the point of dealing with disabled people in the mundane mainstream of daily life, the greatest goals of disabled people will have been achieved. But that momentous event could stump Hollywood since there is little of the dramatic in a story that relates how disabled people finally are treated no differently from anyone else. *Disability Rag* concluded its review of the movies by saying that *"It's time to expect from Hollywood yet another movie: This one about not one individual's triumph as a disabled artist, nor our country's fixation with war—but its treatment of disabled people. It's time for a movie about the stories that make up the disability rights movement."*

Ironically, many disabled people found that movie theaters showing these films were inaccessible! In Seattle, *My Left Foot* played at the Seven Gables theater, which is inaccessible. Kenneth Osbourne, a paraplegic who had a bit role in *Fourth of July* wasn't able to get into the Cineplex Odeon Ziegfield Theatre in Manhattan.

An authentic giant in the field of arts has been Itzhak Perlman, one of the world's foremost concert violinists. He was born in Israel and contracted polio at age 4; he now lives in New York City. He appears on stage via crutches, then plays seated in a chair, a truly remarkable and talented musician. He has also long been active in disability rights. At the Kennedy Center in November 1980, he was given its second annual award by the National Committee on the Arts for the Handicapped. The occasion was opened by Jean Kennedy Smith. Said Itzhak, *"I hope progress will continue to be made for the handicapped, to ignite new programs that will add speed to the goals of the past.."* Given an electric cart, he gleefully raced around the Kennedy Center in it. Later, Itzhak, who has a busy concert schedule, wrote a letter to the editor complaining about Eastern Airlines' lack of access at National Airport.

Another musician who has reached the pinnacle of success is Ray Charles. Born in 1930 in Albany, Georgia, he was brought up in rural Greensville, Florida. At age five he started losing his sight after his brother drowned in a tub.

At age seven he was completely blind. His mother, who took in laundry, insisted that he help with the chores. He listened to music at the local general store juke box and at church. While very young he was sent to St. Augustine's School for the deaf and blind, 150 miles away. Since the family couldn't afford train fare, he spent the first Christmas there alone, listening to music. He started playing the piano and singing – blues, jazz, and gospel. He played clubs before black audiences in Florida. He went to Seattle at age 17 and teamed up with Quincy Jones, then 15; eventually he became the high priest of Soul, which was a blend of Gospel and Blues. A big hit in the sixties was "You Don't Know Me," which some believe relates to his blindness and to the civil rights struggle then going on. Other huge hits were "Georgia on My Mind" and " I Can't Stop Loving You."

In May 1989 the National Theater of the Deaf presented *King of Hearts* at Washington's Terrace Theater in the Kennedy Center. The play was performed with both spoken word and sign language.

Sometimes things go very wrong. In August 1978 students in the Aquatic Intervention Program for the Handicapped were invited to an outing on a Wilson Line cruise ship for a trip down the Potomac to Mt. Vernon, George Washington's estate. When they got to Mt. Vernon, someone forgot that there was a two dollar per person admission charge which the group didn't have, so the children sat on the boat. It was not recorded what George and Martha would have done under the circumstances.

Disabled people began venturing out to theaters and restaurants. In 1973 William Howard, using a wheel chair, attempted to attend a movie in Gaithersburg, Maryland. He was told to leave because he was blocking an aisle. Paul Roth, the theater owner, said, *"We cannot jeopardize the entire audience to accommodate a single person."* He said it would be a violation of fire laws. Since theaters are subject to strict fire regulations and also are required to provide access, some theaters found themselves between a rock and a hard place. Some theaters have vacant areas for wheelchairs, though often in the back of the theater. Up to now, the legal requirements for accessible theaters have been a matter of state or local, not federal, law. However, the Americans With Disabilities Act will require that all newly constructed theaters must be accessible.

Large theaters, such as the Kennedy Center and Arena Stage, generally have good facilities for disabled people. The Kennedy Center has free, though restricted in number, spaces for handicapped licensed cars on the curb. Wheelchairs are provided if needed, with usher assistance. Some performances have radio transmitters to hearing aids for the hearing impaired. The Kennedy Center has a half price program for seniors and disabled. The Arena Stage has handicapped parking and a lift for wheelchairs, and recently, a wheelchair section was installed. The wheelchair section at RFK stadium is inconveniently located behind a chicken wire fence.

Disabled people are also frequenting restaurants. A thoughtful article about disabled diners was written by Carole Sugarman in *The Washington Post*, February 18, 1987. She described a blind lady with a seeing eye dog who went into the Cantina D'Italia restaurant. The maitre d' asked solicitously, *"Will your dog be dining this evening?"*

A blind diner at a restaurant wanted to toast his group after dinner. Unknown to him, the waitress had taken away his glass and replaced it with desert. Unsuspecting, he raised his dish of chocolate mousse in place of his glass of wine. There were three seconds of silence and then the place broke up. The article gives good advice to staff and diner alike. Waiters should always speak directly to a diner and, if appropriate, ask if he or she needs help. For deaf diners, paper and pen should be handy. Sign language users should be seated in well lit areas. For blind diners, the waiter should describe the menu, also food location on the plate, and management should consider having menus in braille. For wheelchair users, above all, the rest room should be accessible and sufficient space should be provided at each table. Consideration should be given to providing tables without protruding legs which could be an obstacle.

Difficulties often arise for disabled diners, but nothing is perfect and it's difficult for waiters and waitresses to be perfectly trained to deal with every conceivable situation. More than anything else, the disabled diner should make known his or her needs and desires. Although some disabled diners get fussy, the same can be said for non-disabled diners. If "normal" people can demand another steak if the one they got is slightly overdone, or reject a luke-warm soup, the disabled diner should be able to expect a seat where he or she won't be tripped over. In restaurants, the human quality of Extreme Fussiness seems to run rampant, but with greater experience and a large dose of common sense, things are working out.

Some "normal" diners sometimes object to being seated near a disabled person. Following is a letter to columnist Ann Landers and her reply:

"Dear Ann Landers,
My husband and I recently ate lunch at a restaurant we enjoy very much. We noticed a man at the next table with no arms. He proceeded to use his foot to get the food from his plate to his mouth. Although we had sympathy for this handicapped person, we felt that the patrons of this lovely restaurant should not have been subjected to this bizarre sight. Your comments will be appreciated. Perplexed in Ohio."

"Dear Ohio, If you had your way, only able-bodied people would be allowed in public. Those with scars, missing limbs, and physical deformities would be barred on the grounds that they are not beautiful to look at. The next step would be to bar people with large noses, receding chins, bad complexions, bald heads, or a limp. The armless man who learned to use his feet in place of his hands is certainly 'different,' but should people who are different be hidden from view because they make some folks uncomfortable? Too bad you don't appreciate how terrific this man is. His self reliance and lack of self consciousness are greatly to be admired."

In 1986 Louis Harris and Associates did a survey on the experiences and attitudes of disabled people. In addition to concluding that 66 percent of disabled people are unemployed, the survey detailed the experiences of disabled people in society, including such experiences as sex, entertainment, and attitudes about themselves and society. The question was asked, *"Do you feel that your disability or health problem has in any way prevented you from reaching what you feel are your full abilities as a person, or not?"* Fifty-seven percent answered that their disability did prevent such full participation. Fifty-six percent said their disability prevented them from getting around, attending cultural or sports events, or socializing with friends outside the home. Seventy-five percent of disabled people said they socialized with close friends, relatives, or neighbors less than once a week. Disabled people go to the movies and to cultural events far less often than the adult population as a whole. Three-fourths of all disabled persons did not go to a live theater performance or a live popular music performance in the past year. Two-thirds had not gone to a live sports event in the past year. As for sexual activity, 29 percent said that their disability was a major limitation, 25 percent said it was a minor limitation, 42 percent said it was no limitation. Thirty two percent said their disability was no limitation on an opportunity to marry. Ninety five percent said there should be increased efforts by society for education, job training, and rehabilitation for disabled people, so they can work to support themselves rather than depending on others or the government.

In the future, the involvement of disabled people in sports, in the arts, and as patrons of public places is bound to increase. As detailed in Chapter Six, the Americans With Disabilities Act, enacted on July 26, 1990, will have a profound effect on mainstreaming every aspect of life. The act mandates accessible transportation, accessible telecommunication, and accessible places of public accommodation. In one sense, the burden has been put on disabled people to utilize these new legal tools. While the act puts legal requirements on private businesses to make their establishments and services accessible, the disabled community must be vigilant in enforcing their rights and improving the quality of their lives by demanding what the act has given to them.

CHAPTER XII

HOUSING and INDEPENDENT LIVING

Mary was left severely damaged after being injected with polio vaccine. She had no use of either of her legs or her right arm. She moved about on a motorized wheelchair which she guided with her good left hand. She had a splendid job doing computer programming. She had a computer at home and worked three days at home, two days in the office, each week. Although it was a well paying job which she performed extremely well, she needed help at home. Through the local Independent Living Center she found a helper, Marcella, who came to her apartment each morning and each evening. The wages cost a lot, and Mary had little left over each month after paying the rent, Marcella, and other expenses. Marcella got Mary up in the morning. In the evening, Mary, for the most part, was able to cook her own meals. She had a microwave oven and lowered shelves in the kitchen. One evening Marcella came in with her little boy Alfred. It was Mary's birthday. While Alfred watched VCR cartoons, Marcella undressed Mary, filled the tub with warm water, lifted Mary into the tub, gently washed her, and put her back on the bed , in her night gown. Then Marcella went into the kitchen and returned with Alfred, a candle-lit birthday cake, some Twinkies, soda, and a bottle of Taylor's sherry. It was a real nice time. Mary said she couldn't remember ever having had such a nice birthday.

The concept of independent living is, at once, a rehabilitation goal, a civil rights movement, a legislative agenda, and a philosophy!

Today there are "Independent Living Centers" in over 200 cities. They provide training in house and apartment living for the severely disabled, as well as advocacy programs relating to disability civil rights, and a few actually provide housing. All local groups are members of an umbrella organization called the National Council on Independent Living. The groups have similar sounding but not identical names. For example, the northern Virginia center is called the Endependence Center of Northern Virginia, Inc., utilizing a clever combination of the two words, end and dependence. The activities of this organization are typical of most: peer counseling by disabled staff members, training in independent living skills and attendant care, housing assistance, advocacy, seminars and workshops on a variety of issues, and an information center or library. The executive director is Sharon Mistler, who uses a wheelchair.

It has been said that the independent living movement has, in addition to a father and mother, two grandmothers.[1]

Mary Switzer had a distinguished career in the federal government after graduating form Radcliffe in 1921. In 1934 she was appointed assistant to the Assistant Secretary of the Treasury for Public Health Service. In 1950 she was appointed director of the Office of Vocational Rehabilitation; under her guidance the numbers of persons given vocational rehabilitation training increased dramatically. In 1967 she became Commissioner of Vocational Rehabilitation, a unit of HEW. She retired in 1970 as the highest ranking woman in the federal government.

In 1913, one year before Gini Laurie was born, four of her siblings contracted polio. Two sisters died within months; one brother died of pneumonia at 21. In the forties she volunteered to help polio patients who got the disease during the epidemic of those days. She was instrumental in securing funds from the March of Dimes for independent living, but quickly the funds ran out. She launched a newsletter and a lift-equipped swimming pool in her back yard for use by polio survivors. The newsletter became the *Rehabilitation Gazette*, which advocated independent living. Gini remained active, until her death in 1989.

One of the *Gazette's* earliest subscribers was Ed Roberts. In 1953 at the age of 14, he contracted a severe case of polio and required an iron lung and a wheelchair. Depressed, he tried to starve himself, and his weight dropped from 120 to 50 pounds. He attended high school by telephone and attempted to attend the University of California. The California Department of Rehabilitation refused to sponsor his university education on the basis that he was "too disabled to work." (Ironically, he was later to become director of the department.) Applying to the University of California at Berkeley, he was rejected. *"We've tried cripples and it didn't work,"* said the dean of students; he said there was no place to put a student in an iron lung. He finally did enroll and lived on campus at Cowell Hospital. He became engrossed in the disabled civil rights movement, and out of this interest emerged the Berkeley Center for Independent Living, which became a model for others throughout the country. He became its first director. The Independent Living Center was a few blocks from the University, and there was a natural transition from Cowell Hospital to the Center. Draft age people served as attendants, as an alternative community service in lieu of being sent to Vietnam.

The Center for Independent Living (CIL) in Berkeley was incorporated in 1972. Besides Director Ed Roberts, the center is managed by people who are themselves disabled. In1976 Roberts left CIL to become director of the California Department of Rehabilitation. Although the Berkeley Center has no residential program, it has a greater variety of programs than many other centers.

Berkeley was not the only place where things were happening in the early seventies. At Brooklyn's Long Island University, an organization called Disabled in Action was formed in 1970. Judy Heumann was cofounder. Contracting polio as a child, she first was limited to home instruction; she was not admitted to a public school because her wheelchair was viewed as a "fire hazard." She subsequently switched to a special school, where little was expected. She began teaching reading skills to her classmates. At Long Island University, she was discouraged from living on campus, but, incensed, she called LIU's president and was eventually admitted to a dormitory. After graduating, she applied for a New York City teaching license. She passed the oral and written exams, but was turned down because she failed the physical; she could not walk. A lawsuit followed; she won and began teaching in her former elementary school. In 1973, at Ed Roberts' urging, she came to the Berkeley Center and served on the board of directors. Later, she became Deputy Director and Director.

In 1977 Judy Heumann became a leader in the protest for the 504 regulations. She ordered the sit-in in San Francisco at the HEW regional office, which lasted weeks (see Chapter Three). At the end of April 1977, she flew to Washington with others, to continue the protest outside of Joseph Califano's home urging him, as Secretary of HEW, to sign the 504 regulations. She was active in, and an officer of, the American Coalition of Citizens with Disabilities (ACCD), which organized the protest.

The Boston Center for Independent Living was organized in 1974 by Fred Fay, a quadriplegic and an activist in the disabled civil rights movement, who suffered a back yard gym accident at age 15. Eric Griffin is director of the Southeastern Massachusetts Independent Living Center. Due to polio, he uses an electric wheelchair. He has been active in the civil rights movement and lobbied Congress for passage of the Americans With Disabilities Act. He believes the ILC program is running reasonably well, with funding from its three sources: Medicaid, state funds and private resources. Funds are used to provide personal care attendants, among other things, with restrictions based on the income level of recipients of the funds. Eric believes that state rehabilitation agencies, which oversee the programs, are sometimes too much in control on policy matters.[2]

It has been suggested that today the Independent Living concept may be running into difficulties caused by the aging of its original leaders and lack of younger replacements. Some have criticized the movement as being restricted to the mobility impaired and mostly white. Others say that a goal is the "independence to do nothing." Possibly that idea came from the fact that independent living was an alternative to vocational rehabilitation. Vocational rehabilitation often did not reach the employable, severely handicapped or those who are so severely handicapped as to be unemployable. Then too, the professionals in charge of vocational rehabilitation often found themselves antagonizing the disabled leaders in the civil rights and independent living movement, whose goal was to be rid of professionals. But many severely disabled are in need of both vocational rehabilitation and independent living assistance and the two ideas are certainly not incompatible.[3]

Although this criticism might have been valid in the early eighties, a shot of adrenaline was received in the late eighties and nineties in the form of an aggressive organization called ADAPT. Originally, this radical group of wheelchair users had an objective of securing accessible buses and other forms of transportation. This objective was generally achieved (on paper at least) with the passage of the Americans With Disabilities Act in 1990. ADAPT then turned to another goal: personal attendant care at home for wheelchair users, particularly for quadriplegics. Without financing for personal, home care attendants, independent living is a mirage for many severely disabled people.

In the legislative arena, independent living was originally thought of as an alternative to vocational rehabilitation. That is, if the individual were too severely disabled to be placed in a job, at least he or she could be encouraged to live independently with a minimum of care. In 1959 and 1961, bills were introduced in Congress to provide funds for independent living programs, but the efforts failed. The role of the federal government was to have been strictly financial, with states providing the programs, just as in the vocational rehabilitation area.

In 1972 Congress passed a Vocational Rehabilitation bill which, in part, would provide independent living services to those who were not employable. President Nixon twice vetoed the bill, because of his concern about cost and his belief that funds would be diverted from the primary goal of vocational rehabilitation. To break the stalemate, Congress agreed to drop the costly program for independent living and the result was the Rehabilitation Act of 1973 (see Chapter Three). The Administration, as part of the compromise, agreed to study the issue of independent living. That study was completed in 1975 by the Urban Institute. [See the Urban Institute's "Report of the Comprehensive Needs Study," Department of HEW, Rehabilitation Services Administration (1975).]

Congress revived its interest in independent living through the landmark Rehabilitation Act of 1978. Under Title VII, a national independent living program finally became law. The act required that people with disabilities be substantially involved in *"policy direction and management."* Title VII specifically provided for programs for people too disabled to be employed. Perhaps Congress was motivated by the well established fact that it costs far less to steer the disabled in the direction of independence than to simply spend money for maintenance and support. In 1973 the federal government spent 40 billion dollars, 3 percent of the gross national product, on maintenance programs for the disabled.[4]

The federal Independent Living program is managed by the Rehabilitation Services Administration, which is part of the United States Department of Education. John Nelson, at age 14, was spinal cord injured in a diving accident and is a C-6-7 quadriplegic. He has had progressively more responsible jobs and is presently Chief of the Independent Living Branch at RSA. An activist, he once helped form an organization of disabled scuba divers who regularly scuba dive in the Caribbean. He believes the ILC program is useful and stresses the word "independent," that is, he believes that disabled people should have a goal of acquiring skills that will lead to independence in all areas of life.

By 1977 there were 52 independent living centers in the United States. In the late eighties there were over 200, notwithstanding the fact that President Reagan and Congress had weakened the program by restricting funds.

Still, federal funding has continued, by means of grants administered by the Rehabilitation Services Administration within the Department of Education. Funds are channeled through the states' counterpart rehabilitation agencies. In the late eighties, the restriction on federal money hurt some centers more than others. The Berkeley Center achieved virtual independence from the federal government. Newer and lesser known centers have required federal seed money to get started. In general, the centers have a distant goal of being independent of the federal government. Part of the reason is to be free of restrictions as to the way money is spent and free of reporting requirements. In many cases, private contributions take up the slack. The centers believe there is no contradiction in using federal money and at the same time having a goal of independence. The money is needed as seed money to get programs started and to pay staff to administer the programs where no other funds are available.[5] The federal money is not used for individual support of disabled persons, except to the extent that Medicaid or Medicare payments may be made.

In the late eighties, as the federal government's budget deficit reached dizzying heights, federal funds for independent living centers and housing for the disabled dwindled. From 1982 to 1989, federal funds for low income housing were slashed from $32 billion to $7.5 billion, resulting in a loss of 60,000 to 70,000 housing units a year. Chicago's Access Living, one of the nation's oldest and largest independent living centers, announced that as of January 1, 1990, it would no longer offer housing referral or placement services. The ending of the program *"is a product of the housing crisis within the disabled community,"* said Access Living Program Director James Charlton. Access Living has a waiting list of 600, but could place only 30 to 50 people a year. Normally, to receive funding from Chicago's Department of Housing, developers must agree to make five percent of all renovated units accessible, but frequently this requirement is waived.[6]

A thoughtful analysis of the sociological, political, and philosophical underpinnings of independent living is contained in a paper written by Dr. Gerben Dejong, who is currently director of research at the National Rehabilitation Hospital in Washington.[7]

DeJong argues that there are at least two groups involved in the independent living movement, the vocational rehabilitation professionals, and the disabled themselves, referred to as "consumers." The professionals see independent living as an alternative to vocational rehabilitation; independent living rehabilitation refers to those medical and social services that enable a disabled person to live in the community, except for consideration of gainful employment.

The disabled consumers reject this view, believing that living goals and vocational goals are not incompatible. The independent living movement is related to several other movements, the civil rights movement, consumerism, self-help, demedicalization or self care, and deinstitutionalization or mainstreaming.

The black civil rights movement has had its influence on the independent living movement:

> *"The black movement that eventually grew out of the civil rights movement has had its own effect on the movement for independent living. According to the critique offered by the civil rights movement, racial discrimination was an American anomaly that could be largely removed through the enactment of new legal protections. The black movement saw the issue as one of racism that was central to the definition of white America and beyond the scope of simple legal remedies. The movement for independent living has come to recognize that prejudice against disability is rooted in our culture's attitudes about youth and beauty, and in the able-bodied person's fear of vulnerability to physical disability. The black movement has inspired the movement for independent living to search more deeply for the sources of attitudes and behaviors toward persons with disabilities."*[8]

We have seen in Chapter Three that the Rehabilitation Act of 1973 was originally proposed as an amendment to the Civil Rights Act of 1964, but the act does not do so, even though it has a similar approach. Black civil rights leaders have generally supported the handicapped movement, but there is the fear among some that adding categories to the Civil Rights Act may weaken it; to prohibit discrimination against the entire universe is both obviously desirable and inherently useless.

Ralph Neas, the Executive Director of the Leadership Conference on Civil Rights, which is composed of minorities such as blacks, women, and the disabled, favors independent living and the Americans with Disabilities Act. In a curious blend of disparate elements, the conservative "right" also favors independent living, and in the 1988 presidential election, many disabled voters switched from Dukakis to Bush. The "right" favors independent living because it would tend to reduce the mammoth federal outlay for support programs and because *"standing on your own two feet"* has always been an objective and philosophy of the conservative right. Paradoxically, although civil rights legislation for the disabled was initiated by liberal Democrats, there is a shift in some areas at least to support by conservatives. Stung by the word "liberal," Dukakis in his campaign down-played the promotion of programs traditionally thought of as big spending, "liberal," social programs.[9]

The independent living movement is also influenced by and blends with the development of consumerism. Led by Ralph Nader and groups such as Public Interest law firms, all levels of society have become increasingly conscious of their rights as consumers. This influence has been sharpened by law suits against drug companies promoting unsuitable or dangerous drugs. Had there been sufficient interest in consumerism in the early sixties, the thalidomide babies might not have had to suffer life long deformity. Consumerism has also resulted in challenges to healthcare professionals and institutions. No longer in complete control, the professional must share policy and direction with the disabled consumer. The Rehabilitation Act of 1973, in sections 101(a)(9) and 102 requires an *"individualized written rehabilitation plan"* to be drawn up jointly by client and counselor.

The self-help movement has also been an influence; evidence is seen in Alcoholics Anonymous, Gamblers Anonymous, and similar groups in which the patient or subject is seen as the controller of his or her own destiny.

> *"Self-help organizations view themselves as mutual aid groups that serve as adjuncts or as valid alternatives to established human service agencies...Self-help groups usually address problems and needs not responded to by other institutions in society."*[10]

Just about every disability affliction has created one or more support organizations in which disabled people are both the creators, controllers, and beneficiaries of the entity. Some, of course, have evolved from organizations originally created by non-disabled people, such as the March of Dimes, (with the exception of one of its sponsors, President Roosevelt). The diversity and number of these self-help groups are too numerous to catalog, but some outstanding examples are the American Council of the Blind, the American Foundation for the Blind, the New York Association (Lighthouse for the Blind), the Polio Society, Disability Focus, DREDF (Disability Rights Education Defense Fund), PVA (Paralyzed Veterans of America), DAV, Spinal Cord Injury Network, and many others.

Demedicalization or self-care has been another strong influence. Demedicalization involves the concept of the patient taking charge of his own disease and possible cure. It embraces such ideas as physician-free birth, and even natural death without painful and artificial life support systems. The self-care movement also encourages better health habits, weight control, and stop-smoking or stop-drinking campaigns. As DeJong said:

> *"Central to the goals of the movement for independent living is the belief that the management of medically stabilized disabilities should be demedicalized. Disabled persons are insisting that the management of their disabilities is primarily a personal matter and only secondarily a medical matter. A constant medical presence in the lives of disabled persons is said to entail behaviors on the part of both medical practitioners and disabled 'patients' that induce dependency and thus are in conflict with rehabilitation and independent living goals."* [9]

DeJong goes on to discuss the "medical model" in which health care professionals assume that the physician is the technically competent administrator of the patient's needs; this authority is delegated to lower levels through a chain of authority. The subject is expected to assume the *"sick role"* defined as follows:

> *"The sick role consists of two interrelated sets of exemptions and obligations. A sick person is exempted from 'normal' social activities and responsibilities depending on the nature and severity of the illness. A sick person is exempted from any responsibility for his/her illness. He/she is not morally accountable for his/her condition and is not expected to become better by sheer will. These exemptions are granted conditionally. In exchange: A sick person is obligated to define the state of being sick as aberrant and undesirable, and to do everything possible to facilitate his/her recovery. A sick person is obligated to seek technically competent help and to cooperate with the physician in getting well."* [12]

Demedicalization and deinstitutionalization are important goals in the independent living movement. An outstanding example of demedicalization was described on Judy Woodruff's "Frontline" TV broadcast in May 1989, concerning the approximately one hundred "thalidomide babies" in Canada, now young adults. Most were born without arms, some without legs. Those without limbs were fitted with artificial braces during childhood. The apparent purpose was to assist them in walking or feeding, but the results were uniformly disastrous. Many had perfectly "natural" feet or arms, however deformed, which were capable of performing useful functions. The braces were more of a hindrance than a help. Some of the patients bitterly complained that the braces were for cosmetic purposes only, to please the medical professionals and society. In retrospect, the attempt by the professionals to inflict these braces on the subjects was a cruel, useless, and damaging failure. Almost invariably, the subjects themselves made the judgment that they would benefit more by not having the artificial limbs than by having them. Their judgment proved superior to that of the professionals. As for deinstitutionalization, it is common knowledge that the longer a subject is institutionalized, the more dependent he or she becomes.

If demedicalization and deinstitutionalization are not the answer, neither, in many cases, is total independence. Many disabled are physically incapable of certain tasks and require assistance in performing them. Incredible though it may seem, many severely disabled are able to perform employment tasks with little or no unusual assistance, but are not able to perform simple personal tasks such as bathing and meal preparation. Office computers can transcribe and almost think, but so far, can't cook eggs or give baths. The concept of the independent living movement includes both home health care attendants and housekeeping training as part of its program. These programs are necessarily expensive. If financial assistance is given, the assistance can properly be viewed as a move toward independence and not away from it. Further, some severely disabled employ home health care assistants so they can secure employment for themselves, and then pay for the help out of their own salaries. Many severely disabled people live in poverty; their understandable desire for independence takes second place to an even stronger need for funds for basic living.

For severely disabled people, especially quadriplegics, independent living requires personal care attendants, and that requires money. For many such people, obtaining money for this purpose is not welfare, but a step toward independence, because home health care can lead the way to jobs and financial independence. The issue of the cost of personal care attendants will continue in the nineties. Bills have been introduced in Congress to provide funding for this purpose.

On May 15, 1989, the parent entity of Independent Living members, the National Council on Independent Living, accompanied by other disability groups, staged an evening protest and march from the Rayburn building on Capitol Hill to the White House. About 175 people, many blind or deaf or in wheelchairs, bore lighted candles. They camped outside the White House, in the rain, in support of the Americans with Disabilities Act, the bill then pending in Congress (passed in 1990) to extend the benefits of access and equal rights for the disabled to the private sector. A spokesman from the White House came out and promised a meeting the next day.[13]

Independent Living advocates staged another protest on April 3,1990, at the Maryland state capitol in Annapolis. Forty Marylanders for Adequate Attendant Care (MAAC) led by Mike Bardoff occupied the Baltimore delegation caucus room of the Lowe House Office Building in Annapolis. They rejected a proposal to give them a $175,000 attendant care program; they felt the funds were inadequate and asked for almost $500,000. The protesters, mostly in wheelchairs, staged a stormy two hour session in which they vented their frustrations. Donzette Wimberly of Baltimore, said, *"I'm damned tired of seeing friends get bed sores as deep as my fist from neglect. I've seen too many friends die from lousy attendant care."* After the meeting, the protesters crossed the street to block the entrance to the Capitol building. Most refused to move at the request of police. They sang *We Shall Overcome* and chanted "Decent attendant care right now!"

In July 1990 Republican Governor of California George Deukmejian proposed cutting the state's budget for Independent Living Centers. The entire $5.5 million state budget for ILC's was on the chopping block. It seemed that California, where the Independent Living Center movement began many years ago, was to be the state that would witness the extinction of the program. Disability advocates rallied around this issue. Resources for Independent Living, the ILC located in Sacramento, became the headquarters for the battle to save the ILCs. The strategy consisted of lobbying, community based activities such as rallies and phone-a-thons, and demonstrations at the state capitol with media coverage. Sam Derdick, president of the California Foundation of Independent Living Centers (CFILC) became the official spokesperson for the cause and spoke at a rally on the Capitol steps. "*I am angry*," said Sam. *"We won't have our rights taken away from us."* After the rally, many disabled people in wheelchairs rolled into the governor's office. After they refused to leave the office, they were escorted by state police out of the building; one person was cited for disorderly conduct.

On Monday, July 2, the group returned and occupied the governor's office. Frances Gracechild and Mark Sutherland tried to chain their wheelchairs together. State police came and arrested five persons. On July 5 a press conference was held at the state Capitol, with speakers representing consumers, the World Institute on Disability, the CFLIC, and the National Council of ILCs. Later, five activists were arrested outside the governor's office. Cy Fuller, a professional night club singer, entertained hundreds from the steps of the Capitol with her love songs. On July 11 another rally was held at the Capitol steps. Ed Roberts, the "grandfather" of the ILC movement, and Michael Lee Gogin, who represents disabled actors for the Screen Actors Guild, spoke. Later, many activists crowded into the offices of Ross Johnson and Bill Baker, legislators who still favored budget cuts for the ILC movement. Bill Tainter, director of the San Diego ILC, persuaded Republican assemblyman Jeff Marston to draft a letter to the governor to save the ILCs; the letter was signed by seventeen other Republican assemblymen.

On July 16 another huge rally took place at the Capitol, complete with street theatrics. Rocky Burks, the director of the Chico ILC, dressed up in a duck costume, with crutch and a sign saying "Lame Duck." Outside the governor's office, many got out of their wheelchairs and sat on the floor, arms linked. Police came and removed them. Twenty-five people were cited and released, but Sam Dardick, Mark Sutherland, Margaret Keith, Bill Hyatt, and Kerry Gagliardi were taken off to jail and held for several hours. Finally, on July 31 all this lobbying and peaceful demonstrating paid off and Governor Deukmejian signed a budget which restored the funds to the ILC program.

On the East Coast, another confrontation over ILC programs was brewing.

ADAPT, the contentious organization of people using wheelchairs, took on a new project – funding for ILCs and personal care attendants. To ADAPT, this is viewed as a simple matter of civil rights.

ADAPT used to be called "Americans Disabled for Accessible Public Transportation" because they were primarily concerned with obtaining an accessible transportation system, especially buses with wheelchair lifts. They have been spectacularly successful in achieving this goal. The Americans With Disabilities Act, will eventually require that the nation's transportation system be totally accessible.

A respected leader of ADAPT was the late Wade Blank. In 1974 he founded the Atlantis Community in Denver, related to ADAPT. Tragically, Wade Blank died on February 15, 1993 in rough seas off a beach at Todos Santos, Mexico, in an unsucessful attempt to save his dying eight-year-old son, Lincoln.

Having achieved its goals in transportation, ADAPT turned to other objectives, and at the same time changed its name. It is now called "Americans Disabled for Attendant Programs Today." In the fall of 1990, it began a drive to obtain government assistance, including financial assistance, in providing home health care attendants for severely disabled people. Among other things, it demanded that federal funds be redirected so that 25 percent of funding for nursing home care be used instead for home health care. ADAPT members have filled police records and jails. Wade Blank, Mike Auberger, Bob Kafka, Mark Johndon, George Roberts, Larry Ruiz, Rick James, Stephanie Thomas, and Anita Cameron were arrested 15-30 times each.

On October 1, 1990. nearly 200 disabled members of ADAPT seized the administration building on the campus of Morehouse College in Atlanta, where Martin Luther King was educated. Said Mike Auberger, *"This is a college that has always valued human rights. This is another minority that is trying to gain its human rights."* The protest was intended to force Morehouse President Leroy Keith to arrange a meeting with Louis Sullivan, Secretary of Health and Human

Services and an alumnus and former dean of the Morehouse School of Medicine. Dozens of people using wheelchairs rolled into Dr Keith's office and barricaded the door, or remained outside, chanting *"We shall overcome."* The activists received a statement from college officials saying that the college sympathized with their concerns. Later, more than 75 protesters blocked the entrances of the Georgia Health Care Association's offices. DeKalb County police arrived on the scene but said they had no plans to arrest the demonstrators. Continuing the protest, on October 3, 1990, 31 ADAPT protesters were arrested for sealing off the Richard B. Russell Federal Building in Atlanta. They never heard from Secretary Sullivan. In the spring of 1991, ADAPT continued its crusade for personal home health care.

On April 29, 1991, approximately 300 ADAPT members wheeled down Security Boulevard in Baltimore and blocked every door at the Social Security building. ADAPT's specific target was the Health Care Financing Administration (HCFA) which administers Medicare and Medicaid programs. ADAPT wanted federal and state funds shifted away from nursing home maintenance and in favor of funds for personal home health care attendants. ADAPT wanted to meet with HHS Secretary Louis Sullivan to discuss their demands. Police, wearing bullet proof vests tried to break up the protesters, so federal workers could enter and leave the building. The next day ADAPT returned and blocked the one driveway to the Disability Determination building. With police threatening arrests and helicopters circling, many ADAPT members got out of their wheelchairs and crawled on the ground. The third day, May 1, 1991, ADAPT members congregated in Washington, D.C. outside the headquarters of the Department of Health and Human Services and chanted *"WE WANT SULLIVAN."* They called for HHS Secretary Sullivan to redirect Medicaid funding from nursing homes for the disabled to care provided for personal attendants. Mike Auberger was there, and chained himself by the neck to the building, using bicycle locks. About 20 of the 110 protesters threw themselves from their wheelchairs and wriggled toward a barricade of police cars parked in front of the building. HHS said they *"shared the concerns"* but had no authority to redirect Medicaid funds; it was a matter for the states. Stephanie Thomas of Austin, Texas, one of the protesters, said that the demonstration was to make it obvious that members of ADAPT were serious in their demands.

Mike Auberger of ADAPT estimates that 250,000 disabled people are being held in nursing homes against their will. *"The ghetto in Soweto is no different than a nursing home,"* he said. *"Your freedoms are so restricted that you're better off being in the Fulton County Jail."*

Protests by disabled people continued in 1991, in cities and towns all over the country, in Boston, in Denver, in Los Angeles, in Nashville, in Palm Springs. In Massachusetts, an organization called CORD (Cape Organization for Rights of the Disabled) stormed the state house in Boston on May 23, to protest proposed budget cuts for human services; many recipients of Medicaid funds would be forced to enter institutions. Ten wheelchair members climbed out of their wheelchairs and blocked the doors to the Governor's office.

On December 30, 1991, disabled protesters chained wheelchairs together in Arkansas Governor Bill Clinton's office in Little Rock to protest Medicaid cuts. A stalemate was broken shortly before midnight when Governor Clinton promised to restore coverage of personal care to disabled people who otherwise would have to live in institutions such as nursing homes. ADAPT President Dr. Terry Winkler said *"We'd like to give notice to all Democratic candidates, to all Democrats and Republicans, that this issue is one you're going to have to deal with."* Adding to this threat was the fact that in 1992, Ron Kovic, a spinal cord injured veteran and subject of the movie *Born on the Fourth of July,* entered the New Hampshire primary as a Democratic candidate for President.

Indirect financial assistance in the form of tax relief is given by three important provisions of the Internal Revenue Code. Section 190 of the Code allows a deduction by businesses for expenses incurred to remove architectural and transportation barriers to the disabled and elderly. (In many cases, but for this section, the expenditure would have to be capitalized and allowed only as depreciation deductions over the useful life of the facility. Section 190 allows the total expense to be deducted in the year in which it was incurred.) Another provision is section 213, which allows deductions for medical expenses, subject, however, to the severe restrictions that expenses must exceed 7.5 percent of adjusted gross income. In 1986, the Senate Finance Committee Report to the 1986 Tax Reform Act clarified that it was the intent of Congress that architectural modifications to an individual's residence on account of physical handicap would be deductible. This includes erecting wheelchair ramps and railings, providing elevators, widening doorways, lowering kitchen cabinets, adjusting electrical outlets, and other modifications. Section 67 of the Code helps disabled workers by allowing a full deduction for impairment related work expenses, which include expenses for attendant care services at the work place and *"other expenses in connection with such place of employment which are necessary for such individual to be able to work."*

Some severely disabled people need certain minimum but habitual aids to assist them in their goal of personal independence. Although the aids just described are personal in nature, some others are not. Accessible buildings, transportation, and job opportunities are not regarded by the disabled community as support services, but rather, a leveling of the playing field which they, as citizens, have a right to expect. Again, provision of these access features is not a move toward dependency but away from it. Thus, the independent living movement defines objectives in term of barrier removal, not as provision of services. Removing a side walk curb is not providing a service but is removing a barrier.

The concept of independent living relates to a great extent to the most severely disabled: quadriplegics, people with cerebral palsy and other severe disorders or injuries. Larry McAfee suffered severe injuries as a result of a motorcycle accident on a Georgia mountain road. His body below the neck is immobile; he moves an electric wheelchair with a puff and sip plastic tube. In 1989, confined to a nursing home, he requested a court to allow him to die. The request was granted, but then came a change of mind. A $5000 computer programmed to recognize the sound of his voice has opened up the possibility of a good job and independence. With the computer he is able to make architectural drawings, using a sonar beam strapped to his head. One of the many enormous difficulties is that his Medicare and Medicaid payments may dwindle if he gets a well paying job. In an article in *The Washington Post* entitled "A Life Worse Than Death," by Joseph P. Shapiro,[14] government policy toward the severely disabled is called *"an antiquated and staggeringly irresponsible system. [In 1990] disabled Americans will receive $60 billion in Medicare, Medicaid, and Social Security Disability payments...Indeed, for McAfee, the biggest obstacle in his life is not the body he cannot move, but a social insurance system that forces him to stay in a nursing home."*

In 1987, 73,200 people between the ages of 18 and 54 lived in nursing homes, supported mainly by Medicare or Medicaid payments. McAfee has a constructive solution: instead of having Medicaid pay for a nursing home, have Medicaid pay for a live-in attendant and other vital, support requirements that would allow him to take a job and live in his own apartment. Allan Bergman of the United Cerebral Palsy Association, drew up a similar plan; he says it would cost $265 a day, for the alternative plan, rather that the $475 to $650 per day that Bergman says the Alabama nursing home was billing Medicare to care for McAfee. Although many states do provide funds, much of it federal money, to pay for live-in, at-home care, the payments are generally too low to be of much help to the severely disabled.

When McAfee petitioned the Georgia court to allow him to die, many disabled civil rights activists protested on the grounds that it appeared that a disabled person's life would be perceived as less valuable than the life of a non-disabled person. Later, after McAfee changed his mind about dying but still had problems with the attempt to live independently, two dozen disability rights protesters occupied the office of the Georgia Medicaid director to demand programs to help McAfee and others to live in their communities.

The battle for equal rights, equal access, and independence is not over; there are many more doors that need to be opened.

PART II

Independent Living has related not so much to the abode of a disabled person, as to questions of personal care attendants, training for independence, and peer support. Another very large issue has been the actual housing, bricks and mortar, in which a disabled person resides, be it an apartment or a separate house.

Accessible housing has always been a concern for disabled people, but progress is slowly being made, with the help of federal and state legislation. Housing problems seem to affect mainly wheelchair users. Visually impaired people, however, have problems if the place has dangerous steps without railings or other similar hazards. With wheelchair users, the dilemma is becoming more and more a financial one and less an access issue. Urban areas with high rise apartment buildings are often accessible at ground level, with elevators commonplace. If apartment doorways are wide enough, there is wheelchair access, but often the bathrooms are not accessible. Light switches, sinks, and kitchen facilities are usually out of reach. Urban high rise apartments are expensive, and disabled people rarely have the financial means to afford the rent. In small towns and rural areas, apartment high rises are scarce and access is more of a problem. It's not uncommon for severely disabled people to be relegated to nursing homes simply because of a lack of accessible housing.

Laura Cooper, an attorney with the American Bar Association who uses a motorized wheelchair as the result of multiple sclerosis, testified on October 11, 1989, before the House Judiciary Committee studying the Americans With Disabilities Act. She testified that she had had to spend time in a nursing home because of a lack of accessible housing.

Frank Bowe in his excellent book, *Handicapping America* (Harper & Row, 1978) describes the terrible housing problems faced by many disabled people. He related the story of Larry Allison, who uses a wheelchair due to polio. Larry at one time lived in Montgomery, Alabama, and when he first moved there, the only, even partially accessible, place to live was a retirement center. He looked at 27 different apartments and found none of them fully accessible. His two and a half years of living in the retirement center were the most agonizingly humiliating and unhappy years he had ever spent.

Frank Bowe articulates very well the problem for disabled people in finding accessible housing. They want the same range of alternatives that non-disabled people want. In general, they do not want to live in institutions. Some disabled people want group homes with shared services; others want single family homes. Most disabled people want a home setting integrated into a community, rather than isolated.

Government officials are beginning to realize that it's enormously less expensive to provide accessible housing and independent living than to foot the bill for expensive nursing homes.

In some new suburban areas, utilities are underground, rules regiment lawn mowing, landscaping must be approved by a committee, recreational vehicles are banned from parking on the street or even in driveways, all for cosmetic reasons. Tree houses and tents may not decorate back yards. Although there is no known case of rules prohibiting women in hair curlers or men in shorts from mowing lawns, some fear the inevitable will soon follow, and the requirement, that objects, such as trucks and vans, be aesthetically pleasing, will be extended to people, allowing only *"beautiful people"* to be visible. In the suburbs, people in wheelchairs often must get committee approval to own a lift-equipped van or to build a ramp for a wheelchair, even to a single family home. The *Age of Appearance* is replacing the *Age of Necessity.* In Denver, a rule prohibited unrelated persons from sharing a house. After protests, an exception was made for disabled people who require live in assistants.

The federal government, through the Department of Housing and Urban Development, has made attempts to provide accessible housing for the disabled, with unsatisfactory results. The initial housing effort was to require a certain portion of the federal housing budget to provide accessible units. Often the number of accessible units was far exceeded by the number of disabled applicants. In 1965 as part of President Johnson's "Great Society" program, Congress passed the Housing and Urban Development Act (P.l. 89-117) which increased authorization levels in prior housing acts to provide housing for elderly and disabled people. Additional modest gains in housing for disabled people occurred under Nixon, under the Housing and Urban Development Act of 1970 (P.L. 91-609). To assist in financing, HUD, under section 202 of amended housing legislation, provides loans for accessible housing, and in some cases, Section 8 provides rent subsidies. In the Housing and Community Development Act of 1974 (P.L. 93-383) Congress appropriated funds for eight models for independent living centers which were set up in Los Angeles, Toledo, Seattle, Omaha, Fall River, Fargo, Columbus, and Houston. In 1976, under the Housing Authorization Act (P.l. 94-375), *"centers for the handicapped"* were to be constructed. In 1977 additional federal housing legislation created within HUD the Office of Independent Living which began an independent living program to be administered through state agencies with federal supervision and federal funds.

In 1980, of 240,392 housing units constructed under HUD programs, only 2218 units were for disabled people.[15]

The terrible HUD scandals revealed in 1989 resulted in millions of dollars of the taxpayers' money being diverted from housing projects to the pockets of greedy bureaucrats and entrepreneurs. In October 1989, the same week that former HUD Secretary Pierce took the Fifth Amendment and refused to testify before a Congressional Committee, thousands marched on the Washington Mall on behalf of the homeless.

Another problem with early federal legislative efforts was that few enforcement mechanisms were provided. The Fair Housing Act (Title VIII of the Civil Rights Act of 1968) which prohibited minority discrimination in housing, was toothless in fact if not in form.

In 1987, in an effort to cure these defects, bills were introduced in Congress, H.R. 1158 in the House, introduced by Congressman Edwards of California, and S. 558, in the Senate, introduced by Senators Kennedy and Specter. Both bills, which were similar, became law in 1988, as the Fair Housing Amendments Act of 1988 (P.L. 100-430).

Hearings on these bills were held in 1987.[16] Numerous witnesses, many from the disabled community, testified. David Capozzi, then Associate Advocacy Director of the Paralyzed Veterans of America, testified that prior legislation had resulted in benign neglect, long waiting lists, and often segregated housing for disabled people. The point was made that disabled people, often poor are mostly renters, unable to buy and adapt their own homes. Examples of discrimination against disabled people existed in such cities as Albuquerque, Omaha, Memphis, and Ann Arbor. Mr. Capozzi recounted the story of a disabled mother, on crutches, who applied for a section 8 apartment but was denied funds for an additional handrail that would enable her to climb the stairs . She was put on a long waiting list for the single accessible two bedroom apartment, the only one out of 500 apartments. Management informed her that no modifications were allowed to other apartments. Marca Bristo, president of the National Council on Independent Living and herself spinal cord injured, testified on behalf of forty disability groups of the flagrant discrimination against disabled people. Because of the acute lack of accessible housing, institutionalization often becomes the only alternative.

Laetitia H."Tish" Pferdehirt, who had suffered polio, testified that she was denied the opportunity to rent an apartment because the realtor didn't want *"a deadbeat in a wheelchair."* Fletcher R. Hall, executive vice president of the Greater Baltimore Board of Realtors (the oldest such board in the nation), opposed S. 558 on the basis that it was *"unwarranted, unnecessary, and could effectively put realtors and others associated with the housing industry out of business without due process."*

After these hearings, Congress in 1988 passed the Fair Housing Amendments Act (P.L. 100-430), which prohibits discrimination in housing against physically or mentally disabled people. The act prohibits housing providers *"To discriminate in the sale or rental, or to otherwise make unavailable or deny, a dwelling to any buyer or renter because of a handicap."* The act requires all new apartment buildings of four or more units to be accessible. If the complex has an elevator, all units must be accessible. If it does not have an elevator, only the ground floor need be accessible. Common and public areas must be accessible to and usable by the handicapped; doorways, kitchens, and bathrooms must be designed to accommodate wheelchairs, and light switches and thermostats must be within reach. Discrimination includes *"refusal to permit, at the expense of the handicapped, reasonable modifications of existing premises . . ."* but the landlord may require the renter to restore the premises to their original condition, on termination of the lease.

Remarkably, the legislation requires that ALL doors in ALL apartments must be sufficiently wide to allow passage of a wheelchair. More specifically, ALL apartments must contain the following:

1. an accessible route into and through the dwelling *"unless it is impractical to do so because of the terrain or unusual characteristics of the site;"*

2. light switches, electrical outlets, thermostats, and other environmental controls in accessible locations;

3. reinforcements in bathrooms to allow installation of grab bars;

4. kitchens and bathrooms within which a wheelchair can maneuver.

In determining whether covered units meet accessibility guidelines, compliance with the *"appropriate requirements of ANSI A117.1-1986"* is sufficient. The ANSI guidelines were first adopted in 1961 and subsequently modified by the American National Standards Institute, a private architectural standards organization, with help from Easter Seals, the President's Committee, and later, HUD.

This remarkable legislation is extremely far-reaching and applies to all new housing complexes with at least four units. The fact that the legislation applies to all apartments in such buildings and all doors in such apartments, probably is attributable to two factors. First, it is recognition that the United States has an aging population. A person may live in good health in an apartment for almost a lifetime, but may suffer a stroke or a heart attack in later life. If the apartment is not adaptable to a wheelchair, a nursing home may be the only alternative. Thus, the requirements demonstrate recognition of the fact that a disabling disease or injury could affect anyone in the entire population. The second factor is that the requirements apply only to new construction; obviously, it is less expensive to plan wide doors on new apartments than to retrofit existing apartments.

Although the act was thought by Congress to not involve a great deal of additional expense, cost did become an issue shortly after its passage. Some builders expressed alarm that costs could increase by twenty percent, thus requiring substantial increases in rent. HUD Undersecretary Alfred Delli Bovi discounted this argument. In January 1989, HUD published regulations, but had not, by the time the act took effect, published implementing guidelines for construction after January 13, 1990. In part because of the absence of HUD guidelines and in part because of fear of massive additional costs in constructing handicapped units, early January 1990 saw a rush to obtain building permits before the January 13 deadline. That year the number of multifamily permits was 3100, a 541 percent increase from the 483 permits issued in January 1989.

But the scramble to obtain permits before the deadline (subsequently extended to June 15, 1990) frustrated the intent of Congress and was an example of the triumph of fear and greed over the socially desirable goal of achieving accessible housing.

Mike Rose, a spinal cord injured Maryland builder, headed a task force on guidelines, such as size of doors and stairs; some builders feared that a significant rise in overall costs would be found not in wider doors or stair rails but in fewer units being built.

There was strong disagreement even among disability groups as to the access standards. The Paralyzed Veterans of America (PVA) were open to more lenient standards, with ADAPT vehemently opposing them. On March 15, 1990, a dozen or so members of ADAPT in wheelchairs flooded the lobby of HUD and demanded to see Secretary Jack Kemp. He was out of town, but they managed to see Undersecretary Delli Bovi and Assistant Secretary Gordon Mansfield for a constructive exchange of ideas.

In the spring of 1990, just before the Americans With Disabilities Act was to come up for a House of Representatives vote, ADAPT and PVA were at loggerheads over housing standards to be applied under the 1988 Housing Act. PVA joined a group consisting of rehabilitation organizations and the National Association of Home Builders; the group is called the National Coordinating Council on Spinal Cord Injury (NCCSCI). The Council agreed with the National Association of Home Builders on standards which ADAPT regarded as too lenient. ADAPT wanted stricter standards and was joined in this goal by the Association for Retarded Citizens, the AIDS Action Council, United Cerebral Palsy, and the President's Committee. PVA agreed to a requirement of only one bathroom per apartment being accessible. PVA agreed to 29 inch doorways in some places rather than the standard 32 inches. PVA agreed to "site access" which meant that if part of the entire building site were on sloping or inaccessible terrain, the usual access standards would not apply, and only a portion of the units need be accessible.

ADAPT charged a "sell-out" and, just before ADA came up for a vote, an unseemly battle over inches was brewing between ADAPT and PVA. There was a rumor that ADAPT, in addition to protesting at the U.S. Capitol and HUD, was also going to picket PVA, an event which fortunately never took place. Ronald L. Mace, an innovator in barrier free and universal design concepts said that in his opinion, PVA had gone to bed with the National Association of Home Builders. But Kim Beasley, director for Architecture and Barrier Free Design for PVA, said that the proposed NCCSCI guidelines merely reflected the reality of multifamily housing. If standards were too strict, said Beasley, builders will not build. The issue was dumped in the lap of HUD Secretary Jack Kemp.

On June 15, 1990, HUD published proposed access guidelines, in the form of three Options. Option One was the proposal of HUD with the support of most of the disability groups. Option Two was the proposal of the National Association of Home Builders and the National Coordinating Council on Spinal Cord Injuries, described above. Option Three was an adaptable accommodation approach that would identify design features that could be adjusted on a case by case basis.

Gordon Mansfield's executive assistant, Phillip Savage, became involved in implementing the Fair Housing Act. He believes that HUD will vigorously enforce the act and, in time, the long sought dream of accessible housing will have been achieved. At one time a trouble shooter for the NAACP, he is convinced that there is a close relationship between the black civil rights movement and the disability civil rights movement. In 1960 he led students from Morgan State University to protest in Baltimore, with two results. First, he and others were arrested, and second, Baltimore's department stores became integrated. Savage is no stranger to the issue of discrimination in housing.

He was involved in the "tent city" in Tennessee, which housed black tenants who had been evicted because of voter registration activity.

On March 6, 1991, HUD published final Fair Housing Accessibility Guidelines, and adopted Option One. A modification was made so that, in cases where a covered dwelling had an elevator, there must be at least one accessible entrance to the building on an accessible route, regardless of terrain or unusual characteristics of the site. For covered dwellings without an elevator, two alternative access tests are used. The guidelines adopt some but not all of the ANSI standards. In spite of opposition from building organizations, HUD stuck to a requirement of 32 inch door openings. The ANSI guidelines provide a "safe harbor" for builders; they are not mandatory and builders are allowed to show access compliance in other ways, such as under acceptable state guidelines. In addition, housing that is covered under other federal statutes, such as the Rehabilitation Act of 1973, section 504, and the Architectural Barriers Act of 1968 must meet additional federal access standards. (Accessible design requirements for section 504 are found at 24 CFR Part 8, and accessible design requirements for the Architectural Barriers Act are found at 24 CFR Part 40.) Although to some extent there are a bewildering variety of access standards, generally they all derive in some way from the 1961 ANSI standards.

Pursuant to the 1988 Fair Housing Amendment, the Justice Department, in June 1989, filed the first housing discrimination suit charging discrimination against disabled people. The suit alleged that Chicago Heights denied a permit for a group home for mentally retarded adults because of neighbors' opposition arising from fears and prejudice concerning people with mental retardation. James P. Turner, acting head of the Justice Department's civil rights division, said that under the Fair Housing Act, *"stereotypes and baseless fears concerning the handicapped cannot be used to block the development of group homes."* The suit sought to force the working class city south of Chicago to permit construction of a home for fifteen mentally retarded adults in a neighborhood of single and two family homes. The suit also sought damages for economic harm and emotional distress as well as punitive damages for those injured by the alleged discriminatory practices. In January 1990, bowing to the attention and the authority of the federal court, the city reached a settlement in which it agreed to construct the housing facility and pay $30,000 in damages for construction delays and $1000 for each of the first fifteen people to live in the home. Federal District Judge William T. Hart approved the settlement.

Paul Marchand, spokesman for the Association for Retarded Citizens of the United States, said, *"This sends a clear signal to communities everywhere that discrimination in housing based on mental retardation will not be tolerated. We are delighted with the Justice Department for their aggressive pursuit of the case. This is something long overdue."* Disability rights advocates said the case could have implications for zoning decisions nationwide.

The House Report to the legislation that was involved in the Chicago Heights case, H.Report No. 100-711, 100th Congress, Second Session, stated as follows:

> *"Prohibiting discrimination against individuals with handicaps is a major step in changing the stereotypes that have served to exclude them from American life. These persons have been denied housing because of misperceptions, ignorance, and outright prejudice... The Fair Housing Amendments Act, like Section 504 of the Rehabilitation Act of 1973 as amended, is a clear pronouncement of a national commitment to END THE UNNECESSARY EXCLUSION OF PERSONS WITH HANDICAPS FROM THE AMERICAN MAINSTREAM." (emphasis added)*[17]

Individual disabled persons have brought law suits requesting access to housing. These suits have been brought under the 1988 act, and also under section 202 of the Housing Act of 1959 and even under section 504 of the Rehabilitation Act of 1973. A "catch-22" under the latter two acts is that the law was interpreted as allowing federally subsidized housing projects for EITHER of several disadvantaged groups. The housing could benefit either the elderly or the mobility impaired or the chronically mentally ill or the developmentally disabled. Mildly retarded people, who were nevertheless capable of living independently, brought suit to require admission to a housing project for the elderly–Brecker v. Queens B'Nai B'Rith Housing Development Fund Co., Inc., 798 F.2d 52 (2nd Cir. 1986). They lost the suit primarily because the project was regarded as being for the elderly, not for disabled people. Proof of this was that the project didn't provide any services for disabled people, a curious rationale. A similar case is Knutzen v. Ebenezer Lutheran Housing Center, 815 F.2d 1343 (10th Cir. 1987).

Good news prevailed in Bolthouse v. Continental Wingate Co., Inc., 656 F. Supp. 620 (W.D. Mich. 1987) where the court ordered the plaintiff, who had cerebral palsy and used a wheelchair, to be admitted into federally subsidized housing.

Alarmists might overreact and complain that the nation's health care institutions will, under the housing legislation, be emptied of patients, because of law suits demanding access to housing. This hasn't happened. For one thing, many institutionalized patients may not be capable of living in apartments, no matter how accessible. However, there are, no doubt, many who have been institutionalized for years who deserve a chance to live independently and not to be excluded from housing because of the stigma of being institutionalized. But in Clark v. Cohen, 613 F. Supp. 684 (D.C. Pa. 1985), affirmed, 794 F.2d 79, certiorari denied, 479 U.S. 962, a mildly mentally retarded lady living in an institution was regarded as not being discriminated against by the state.

On December 11, 1989, Gordon H. Mansfield was sworn in as Assistant Secretary of Fair Housing and Equal Opportunity of the Department of Housing and Urban Development. Gordon was recruited from the Paralyzed Veterans of America; he is spinal cord injured as a result of trauma suffered in Vietnam and uses a wheelchair. In his acceptance speech as the new assistant secretary, he confirmed his commitment to accessible housing for disabled folks. Mansfield is an excellent choice for the difficult job; he has impressive experience in the drive for civil rights for disabled people. At PVA he was associate executive director for Government Relations and directed the National Legislative Program, the National Advocacy Program, and the Architectural and Barrier Free Design Program. Jack Kemp, HUD Secretary, wryly noted at the swearing-in ceremony that the platform did have a wheelchair ramp.

Pursuant to federal and state legislation, housing for people with disabilities has sprung up here and there, although the supply is far exceeded by the demand. In the Washington area, Leafy House in Silver Spring, Maryland, was one of the first apartment buildings for disabled people and the elderly. Some apartments are adapted for wheelchairs, including shower access. Railings have been installed in corridors. Meals are provided in the dining room, and personal care assistance is available.

Washington's Independent Living for the Handicapped, on Belmont Street, was built in 1984 with a HUD loan; it has 20 units occupied by disabled tenants in wheelchairs, some receive Section 8 rental subsidies. President Libby Campbell explained that occupancy is limited by income ceilings, and there is a long waiting list. Tenants must provide their own personal care.

At times, disabled people have no voice in implementing housing, and no real legal remedy if housing projects are denied. An example of this is the Hurt Home in Washington, D.C. The Georgetown area of Washington has been the residential mecca of the wealthy. It is elegant, expensive, determinedly private though surrounded on M Street by bars, noisy weekend crowds, and traffic congestion. In 1987 the District of Columbia, then run by Mayor Marion Barry, talked of buying a 32 room, three story mansion in the heart of the pricey Georgetown residential sector, to be turned into a home for 25 disturbed children between the ages of six and twelve. The proposal provoked a heated and divided community response; the Citizens Association of Georgetown raised $50,000 to fight the proposal. Across the street from the proposed home is Montrose Park. Said attorney Maureen Brennan: *"Racism? Xenophobia?. ..There have been rapists running around Montrose Park. Why are we worrying about disturbed children? And why can't we make sure their safety is ensured there in either case?"* Of course, the intended occupants of the home or the children themselves were never consulted.

Housing for mentally retarded adults has been provided in Washington, D.C., through a non-profit organization called Sunshine Multi-Purpose Center, organized by Baburaj and Gracy Stephens, with funding from private donors as well as the city. Sunshine operates eight houses, that are integrated with residential neighborhoods, in the Washington, D.C. area. Each house serves about eight residents, with a full program of training and recreation provided. The residents range in age from 21 to the 60s; many have brain damage or Down's syndrome or other debilitating conditions. Jasper Martin is a program coordinator at one of the Capitol Hill homes. He provides independent living counseling, training for residents to take care of chores and personal needs, day trips to training sites, and recreational outings to the District of Columbia Therapeutic Center, to basketball games, concerts, and similar activities.

According to co-directors Ronald L. Mace and Graeme J. Hardie, a Research and Training Center for Accessible Housing was created in July 1989 at North Carolina State University, to meet the expanding need for research data, design solutions, and training and technical assistance on barrier free housing. The Center is funded by the National Institute on Disability and Rehabilitation Research. Its mission is to develop innovative design solutions for accessible housing.

In 1990 David Ward, a quadriplegic who had lived for eleven years in a mostly inaccessible house, became involved in the planning of a new home for the disabled–designated Future Home, in Phoenix, Maryland. Engineers, with David's help, are renovating and redesigning a 140 year-old former tavern, hoping it will become a national model. A group of 32 volunteers contribute time and resources, digging trenches, installing pipes, or planting shrubs. Eventually they will begin designing the interior. They are members of Volunteers for Medical Engineering, a 600 member national organization based in Baltimore devoted to developing new technology to aid people with disabilities. Future Home will include state of the art technology designed to assist the disabled. The house will have voice controls, infrared sensors, speakers, video cameras and temperature sensors. For example, under an infrared system, a user could put a hand under a faucet and a light beam would activate a stream of water. The list of innovations is extensive! Through speakers, the house could tell its residents whether there is a gas leak, water leak, or movement in another room. Other innovations include motorized windows, a central electronic system regulating lighting, heating and cooling. and Braille imprinted on appliances. Doors won't have thresholds. The exterior door could be opened to certain callers with a voice activated system. The entire project will be extremely costly, but inventions designed especially for people with disabilities could be eventually, like the VCR and microwave oven, useful to everyone.

Another project involving single family housing is in Bowie, Maryland. Access features were designed by Jane Willeboordse in conjunction with the National Association of Home Builders and its National Research Center, Home Park, also in Bowie. The house is two stories with attached garage (the ceiling of which is nine feet tall to accommodate a van). From the outside it looks like a typical suburban home. There is wheelchair access through front and rear entrances and an elevator from the garage. All doors are thirty-six inches wide. The kitchen has slide out counters as well as removable, height adjustable cabinets; the bathroom has a lowered sink and roll-in shower. Strobe lights provide fire safety warnings for hearing impaired people.

Certainly the past has proven necessity to be the *"Mother of invention!"* IF THE NEEDS OF DISABLED PEOPLE, TO FIND A WAY TO LIVE INDEPENDENTLY, WILL PRODUCE NEW TECHNOLOGY AND NEW INVENTIONS, IT'S POSSIBLE THAT EVERYONE WILL BENEFIT.

People with disabilities, like everyone else, want a house or apartment that they can be comfortable in, including a kitchen they can cook in, a dining room table they can eat from, a bathroom they can take a bath in, a bed in which they can sleep. These simple amenities, which much of the rest of the world tend to take for granted, are essential elements of what disabled people require in order to improve the quality of their lives; they have lobbied and labored long and successfully for these important segments of their civil rights!

CHAPTER XIII

PERSONALITIES and PERCEPTIONS: LIFE and DEATH

They rushed to the Chapel and, in triumph, dragged forth the thrice lucky Pope of Fools. Surprise and admiration rose to a point of culmination--he had revealed his natural countenance! The whole of his person had appeared as a grimace. An enormous head covered with red bristles; shoulders with a great hump between them balancing another smaller one in front; a system of thighs and legs so curiously misplaced that they seemed to only touch the knees, and, viewed from the front, appeared like two sickles joined at the handles; feet, huge and splayed; hands, monstrous. Along with all this deformity there was a nameless expression of formidable strength, agility, and courage--strange exception to the eternal rule, which decrees that strength, like beauty, shall be the outcome of harmony. Such was he whom the Fools had chosen their Pope...'Tis Quasimodo the bell-ringer!' shouted the people with one voice; 'Quasimodo the Hunchback of Notre Dame! Quasimodo the one-eyed! Quasimodo the bandylegged! Noel! Noel!' [1]

October 6, 1979, was a cold and windy day in Washington. Vice President Mondale was whisked to Andrews Air Force Base just outside Washington where he awaited the plane bringing Pope John Paul II to America. Ceremonies at the airport, when the plane finally arrived, included a rendition of God of Our Fathers, a Protestant tune, played by the Navy band. The Pope was then brought to the Reflecting Pool on the Mall, where he was met by Mayor Marion Barry, who has never been accused of sainthood. Marion and John Paul; they shared nothing in common except an extraordinary personal charisma. Then the Pope was taken to St. Matthews Cathedral where he celebrated mass, attended by the elite. The next day, a huge mass was held on the Mall for the rest of the population, the non-elite, attended by thousands (the non-elite always outnumber the elite). During the day, the Pope rode in a shiny black limousine through the streets of Washington thronged by thousands of the faithful and the curious. A chilly and windy day, the Pope appeared as a scarlet flame, blessing the cheering crowds as he rode swiftly by. He later attended an ecumenical meeting at Trinity College. As he left, he stopped by a group of disabled people who had gathered in a designated spot under the direction of the organizers.

Some three hundred disabled people were there, many in wheelchairs. Parents brought a child with leukemia. They waved papal flags as they sang "He's Got the Whole World in His Hands." Some were desperately ill; some saw him as their last hope. Several were on stretchers. Some cried. Mary Grady of Frederick, Maryland, for 22 years a wheelchair user, traveled the long distance from Frederick only to find she couldn't get in the handicapped section without a ticket.

The Pope preached love and charity for the disabled. He was the Good Shepherd, taking care of his flock. "Bless me Father, for I am damaged goods. Bless me Father, because I don't quite cut the mustard. Blessed are the blind, for they shall sell pencils. Blessed are the deaf, for they shall hear no evil. Blessed are the lame, for they shall avoid whorehouses. Blessed are brain damaged exprizefighters, for they shall appear on talkshow programs." Many of the disabled were improved, at least psychologically, by the drama of the Pope's visit. The power of faith and the charisma of a benevolent saviour-figure are powerful forces, helpful to many. But the idea of a cure by the father symbol seemed antiquated, outdated. Successful in a time when there were no other remedies, the idea of a miracle cure, a blessing, a cleansing of the infected by the God-favored, in exchange for a material obligation of gratitude, seemed anachronistic.

****

Says Kitty Kelley in her book *Nancy Reagan: the Unauthorized Biography* (Simon & Schuster), when it was suggested that Nancy improve her public image by visiting a little boy dying of muscular dystrophy, a top aide replied: *"Absolutely not. The First Lady doesn't want her picture taken with some drooly kid on a respirator. It's too disgusting."*

In similar vein, when Michael Milken, the junk bond tycoon, was being investigated for criminal violations of insider trading and other securities transgressions, he engaged a PR firm – Robinson, Lake – to improve his image. Robinson, Lake arranged photo opportunity sessions with handicapped and underprivileged children. It didn't work. Later, Milken pled guilty and was sentenced to ten years in prison and fined mega millions.[2]

News item, July 15, 1992: Two vacationers, both in wheelchairs, went to Jamaica on a cruise ship and returned to Florida. In West Palm Beach they were arrested for carrying pounds of marijuana in their wheelchairs

****

Lewis B. Puller Jr., the son of the well known Marine hero, "Chesty" Puller, was hit by a mine in Vietnam in 1968. He lost both legs and much of his hands. Undaunted, he graduated from William and Mary Law School and is an attorney for the Defense Department. Interviewed by NBC's John McLaughlin in December 1992, he said that when he was a young soldier, it never occured to him to question leadership, be it military of political, but now it never occurs to him to NOT question leadership. His book, *Fortunate Son* (Bantam, 1992), is not only a fascinating autobiography but it won a Pulitizer Prize.

****

News item from January 19, 1993 – On the eve of President Clinton's inauguration, convicted murderer Charles Sylvester Stamper was put to death in an electric chair in Virginia. Stamper, convicted of killing three workers at a Shoney's restaurant, was spinal cord injured in a fight with another inmate on "death row," and as a result was using a wheelchair. He was, however, carried to the electric chair by two guards, his feet dragging on the floor. The execution broadened the debate regarding the death penalty. You could say the execution carried "equal rights" for disabled people to a logical (or illogical?) extreme.

****

Jose Feliciano achieved great fame as a singer, despite being blind. One day he went to a restaurant and seated himself at a table. The waitress asked him if he would like to see a menu. He replied, "Lady, I'd like to see anything!"

****

William Braniff is the United States Attorney for the Southern District of California. Injured in an auto accident when he was eighteen, Braniff is paralyzed from the waist down. He enjoys his work and is tough on criminals. At 49 he is one of the highest ranking law enforcement officials in America, with a disability.

****

Another leader in the disability civil rights movement is John Kemp, executive director of United Cerebral Palsy. He is a quadruple congenital amputee; he uses an electric wheelchair and operates a computer with a hand prosthesis. Before becoming executive director he was active, as an attorney, with various disability rights organizations.

It has been estimated that in 1992, the federal, state, and local governments spent over 200 billion dollars on direct and indirect support programs for the disabled. Most of these programs can be regarded as "dependent care" or "support programs" such as, social security benefits, veterans' disability benefits, and other payments designed to "support" the individuals as opposed to rehabilitating or making him or her independent or making the environment more accessible.

Mary Jane Owen has long been an advocate of the alternative program: it is much less costly to provide the seed money for access programs that will enable the disabled to become functional and productive, contributing to society, and ultimately paying taxes rather than being recipients of tax money.[3]

Mary Jane Owen has several impairments.(She dislikes the cliche: multiply handicapped). After contracting meningitis, she suffered a series of events which left her both visually and hearing impaired as well as dependent on a wheelchair. She left her successful academic career at San Francisco University in 1972, and has become one of the leading civil rights leaders in the disabled movement. During the 1977 protest for the adoption of 504 regulations, she participated in the sit-in at the HEW office in San Francisco. She began a hunger strike and took only fruit juice for days.[4]

When part of that group flew to Washington to continue the protest, she remained with the protesters in San Francisco in order to keep the pressure up, and also because she was convinced that media attention was greater in San Francisco than in Washington. She has been an official on the President's Committee on Employment of Persons with Disabilities and is currently director of Disability Focus, a Washington based organization concerned with advocacy and publication of disability rights literature. She is nationally known as a frequent lecturer and author of articles on disability subjects. In October 1989, she received the Andrew Wood Memorial Award from the District of Columbia Mayor's Committee on Persons With Disabilities.

Inspired, determined, and courageous advocacy by leaders like Mary Jane Owen is beginning to emphasize the message being protested to the American public and their selected representatives that the disabled want independence, not handouts.

****

In the disability movement, everyone gets into the act. Phillip Rout, a paraplegic wheelchair user, and an inmate of the city jail in Lorton, Virginia, filed suit in May 1984 against the GSA and others, in the United States District Court, Alexandria, Virginia. Among other things, he complained about being denied access to the federal court house in Alexandria, as well as to the shower in the jail.

****

In the Spring of 1990, *Spinal Network* published several articles under the heading "Hard Times; Behind Bars in a Wheelchair," edited by Sam Maddox. These articles portray life in prison for disabled men and women; the stories are not for the faint of heart. Many prisoners became spinal cord injured as a result of shootings related to drugs. Many jails lack fully accessible facilities for disabled prisoners; that will change with passage of the Americans With Disabilities Act in 1990.

****

From the *Disability Rag*, January/February 1992: *"Tim Cook, who started the National Disability Action Center just a few years ago, died [October 21, 1991, age 38]. His death from cancer sent shock waves through the activist community who had come to rely on him in the 1980s to file suits against the Department of Transportation on behalf of ADAPT in the battle to win access to the nation's bus systems and to appeal them until disability rights reasoning won the day."* [Tim Cook, who had contracted polio, won the spectacular ADAPT case; see Chapter Fifteen.]

****

Actor Billy Barty, who is three feet nine inches tall, formed "Little People of America" in 1957 to remove architectural and attitudinal barriers against persons of short stature. He objects strongly to the latest California barroom craze: throwing little people. Barty, whose movie credits include *The Day of the Locust, Under the Rainbow, Foul Play* and *UHF,* said, *"We should be looked up to. We should not be judged by our size but for the space between our ears."* [5]

****

ABC Television canceled its comedy series *Good and Evil* after only seven episodes when the show was severely criticized by the National Federation of the Blind for its portrayal of George, a blind character who according to the NFB *"displays preposterous ineptitude and stupidity, which, according to ABC spokesmen, are intended to be funny."*

****

The columnist Judith Martin (Miss Manners) wrote a column in July 1989, called "Rudeness and the Right of Way." A reader wrote in complaining about a woman *"confined to a wheelchair"* (Miss Manners pointed out that the phrase is unacceptable) who snarled at her when the reader attempted to hold a door for her. Then at a tavern the person in the wheelchair consistently would leave her empty wheelchair in the middle of the only aisle, impeding the traffic of other patrons. When the reader asked her to move the chair, she was curtly told to mind her own business. The reader asked if she was wrong to resent the disabled woman's behavior. Miss Manners replied that although in the case of people who use wheelchairs one tends to give them the benefit of the doubt, in this case there does not seem to be much doubt to give the lady the benefit of. *"To have more lenient standards for those in wheelchairs would be as patronizing as pity."* Miss Manners objected to the reader's physically moving the wheelchair, and concluded: *"Had you firmly told the lady that she was inconveniencing others, and perhaps enlisted the tavern keeper or manager to insist that she meet the behavioral standards of the place, Miss Manners would have supported you."* All of which proves that disabled persons are people. Not all of us are courageous, independent, highly motivated, strong, hyper-talented, super-achieving, brave, hardworking, friendly, capable, and dynamic. Some of you are nasty, hostile, argumentative, belligerent, stubborn, unsociable, weak, lazy, parasitic, indolent, selfish slobs.

****

Bill Denby was driving a truck in Vietnam in 1970 when a rocket exploded and he lost both of his legs below his knees. Bill has been speaking out for the disabled at every opportunity. He appeared on a well known Dupont commercial, playing basketball on artificial legs. He is a volunteer counselor with the Disability Awareness Project in Howard County, Maryland. He goes on speaking assignments for Dupont, teaches skiing and holds amputee records in the shot put, discus and javelin. Shortly after returning from Vietnam he began drinking, and taking marijuana and PCP, but he turned himself around. Says Bill: *"[the commercial] first aired on Sunday, September 4, 1987. It helped people be more sensitive about the disabled, and I think it opened up the field for using disabled people in commercials, and, hopefully, movies. If I didn't get involved in sports and have that support from family and friends, I don't think I'd be here or in the DuPont commercial. I'd probably still be a statistic."*

****

Bree Walker Lampley is a gorgeous, blond haired co-anchor of the KCBS-TV's news broadcast. She was born with ectrodactylism, which produced deformity of the hands. Notwithstanding this disability she has become a TV personality, due to her persistence, talent, and above all, sense of humor. She would sometimes introduce herself at parties as the "pianist" or *"the Firecracker Safety Poster Girl."* She is part of the civil rights for the disabled movement, which she calls the *"last civil rights movement."* She says, *"The disability awareness movement was gutted by lack of funding during the Reagan Administration. You can see it in our vocabulary, in phrases like 'victim of' or 'crippled by' or 'confined to a wheelchair.' People use wheelchairs so that they'll be mobile, not confined. Yet this language pops up all the time, and it just contributes to the problem. Ultimately, I'd like to hear 'differently abled' used to refer to persons with disabilities."* [6]

In 1991 radio station KFI-AM in Los Angeles and talk show host Jane Norris broadcast a show detailing the fact that Bree was pregnant and possibly could give birth to a child with a similar deformity. Calls poured in on both sides of the question whether Bree should or should not have a baby. Bree and her husband were appalled, and the show led to a formal complaint filed with the Federal Communications Commission. The issue raised tempers and involved questions of eugenics, the right to privacy, and whether parents should produce genetically defective children. About 100 individuals and 25 disability rights groups joined in the FCC lawsuit.

****

Yetta Galiber is one more link between the black civil rights and the disabled civil rights movement. She was the executive director of IPACHI (Information, Protection, and Advocacy Center for Handicapped Individuals). Begun in 1969 by a grant from the Department of Education, it has been involved in such activities as publishing a directory of disabled services and participating in the suit by disabled school children against the board of education. Mrs. Galiber participated in the 1977 protests (see Chapter Three). An article in *The Washington Post* described an incredible event that took place in December 1988:[7] Thousands of disabled children assembled at the D.C. Armory for a party and distribution of Christmas toys. The affair was organized by Mrs.Galiber. Mayor Marion Barry was to stop by at noon. An hour, then two hours passed with no sign of the mayor. Finally Mrs. Galiber was told he wouldn't be coming at all. *The Washington Post* reported that:

> *"[Barry] has acknowledged that he spent part of that Saturday visiting the Ramada Inn Central hotel room of Charles Lewis. The mayor has not said why he was there. Five days later, December 22, another visit to Lewis plunged Barry into a major public controversy when two police detectives abruptly terminated a drug investigation of Lewis after being told that Barry was in Lewis' room, sources said."*[8]

****

John Yeh, who is deaf, has achieved amazing success as a private entrepreneur. With the help of three hearing brothers, he founded Integrated Microcomputer Systems, Inc., of Rockville, Maryland of which he is president. He employs more than 400 in the rapidly growing computer company. The company expected to have about $37 million in sales in 1989. The company employs deaf and hearing impaired as well as hearing employees. Sign language is an accustomed means of communication.[9]

****

Max Cleland is your typical extroverted, hammed-up super-jock, all around friendly, successful personality, and disabled. A triple amputee as a result of a grenade explosion in Vietnam, he drove a beat up old Oldsmobile, instead of being driven in a limousine, to which he was entitled as director of the Veterans Administration in the Carter years. For giving up the limousine, he was given an award of merit by Senator Proxmire. When originally injured, he received no wheelchair from the VA, no pay for two months, and the VA refused to teach him how to drive. When he became director of the VA, things changed. Today he is Secretary of State for the State of Georgia. When things heated up in the Persian Gulf in the summer and fall of 1990 because of the confrontation with Iraq, Max joined those who thought a precipitous war was irrational and frightfully costly in terms of American casualties. He was unwilling to have the ranks of disabled people increased through such a disaster.

****

Alan Reich, who uses a wheelchair, is founder and director of the National Organization on Disability, a non-profit organization that developed first as a support vehicle for the International Year of the Disabled. Its function is to advance the interests of disabled gentry in the business community and with reference to Congressional matters. On September 7, 1989, Alan introduced the Soviet Union's newly elected representative, Ilya Zaslavsky and his wife before a packed throng at the Mansfield reception room in the United States Capitol. It was an event long to be remembered by those who were there, including the author.

****

Ted Kennedy Jr., son of Senator Ted Kennedy, lost a leg to cancer when he was a teenager, and has become an activist in the cause of disability rights. He is executive director of Facing the Challenge, a non-profit organization based in Boston. A feature article in *Parade Magazine,* November 23, 1986, describes his vision, commitment, and goals in the disability movement. In July 1984, at the age of 21, he appealed to the Democratic National Convention in San Francisco for greater awareness for the handicapped. He said, *"In 1984 the 36 million disabled people desire the same fundamental human rights as every other American."*

****

Deng Pufang, son of Chinese leader Deng, was forced out a fourth story window in 1968 during the Cultural Revolution. He broke his back and is a paraplegic. An articulate advocate for the disabled, he visited the United States and met with Ted Kennedy Jr. In China, there are 40 to 50 million disabled, who are often treated with contempt by the Chinese. The word "*canfei*" meaning handicapped also means incomplete and useless. Regrettably, Deng and his family members were targets of the massive student protests in the struggle for democracy in Beijing in June of 1989, which led to the massacre of hundreds, possibly thousands, of Chinese students in Tiananmen Square. Deng Pufang was accused of benefiting from a huge Trust for the Handicapped. The savage massacre by the government also brought about many injuries, thereby increasing that troubled country's supply of disabled.

In June 1989 Ted Kennedy Jr. appeared on the cover of *Parade Magazine*, along with some Very Special Artists, disabled persons with artistic talent. Said Ted, *"I have come to know, firsthand, that the most severe limitation people with a disability often face is lack of opportunity—lack of opportunity to participate fully in society, to be regarded by others as an equal and have access to things we all take for granted."*

****

In Philadelphia, Celestine Tate, an unwed mother and lifelong paraplegic, had a daughter Ninya, but the authorities wanted to take the baby away from her. She retained custody when she showed a stunned courtroom how she could change diapers with her mouth. Later, a second daughter was born.[10] In April 1978 Richard Cohen, Washington columnist, decided to write a column about the disabled. He chanced on Robert, walking on the street. Robert is hydrocephalic, with a large not very good looking head and what Richard regarded as a funny gait. Richard disliked Robert immediately. Robert bothered him. Later, Robert called on Richard for a friendly conversation. Richard decided he liked writing about the subject of the disabled but didn't much like the person. Robert pestered Richard. Finally Richard decided Robert had redeeming features and wrote his column about him. Richard closed saying, *"there's no handicap like a closed mind."*

****

Vivian Lee Hobbs, at the age of 17, suffered a terrible automobile accident and is paralyzed from the neck down. Today she has three children and is a partner in a prestigious Washington law firm, Arnold and Porter, where she practices pension law. Four months after her accident, she married, in the hospital chapel, her childhood sweetheart Greg. She graduated summa cum laude from Georgetown law school. She typically works 60 hours a week and types using a mouth held pointer.[11] In 1986 alarmed that Congress, in the Tax Reform Act, was about to restrict the deduction for the expense of work-related assistants and technical aids for the disabled, she lobbied hard and, with help from Bob Dole, was able to preserve the deduction, She has been active, as a lawyer, in representing disability rights cases.

****

Ed Roberts, who founded the Independent Living Center in Berkeley (see Chapter Twelve) was so badly damaged by polio that doctors told his parents he would always be a vegetable. Frequently on the lecture circuit, he tells his audience the story, and then says, "Tonight I appear to you as a carrot."

****

Washington lawyer Charles Goldman is involved in disability rights cases and is author of the *Disability Rights Guide*. When he was asked whether he had a disability, he promptly replied, "Yes, I'm a lawyer."[12]

****

Michael T. Rose is a Maryland real estate developer who has achieved spectacular success in spite of being in a wheelchair. Years earlier, he was shot by a disgruntled employee and is now a paraplegic. He has a large company with many employees and a 300 million dollar complex in Laurel Lakes.

****

When she was 17 years old, Linda Fay was paralyzed from the waist down in an auto accident. Though a wheelchair user, she graduated from Harvard Medical School and, today, is practicing family medicine in the Washington area.

****

Teenager Kevin Whittum, 28 inches tall, severely disabled, and suffering from a rare bone disease, was installed in a grandiose mansion owned by TV evangelist Jim Bakker. When Bakker ran into trouble with the law, PTL ordered Kevin evicted, along with his adoptive father, David Whittum (Bakker's first cousin), his mother, and his sister. The Whittums were the only occupants of the 14,000 square foot mansion. Kevin has begun a lawsuit against PTL and Jim Bakker.

Justin Dart Jr., another leader in the disabled civil rights movement and a Texan, whose father, Justin Senior, was a member of President Reagan's "kitchen cabinet," was a member of the National Council on Disability. He has assisted in various civil rights issues, including accessible public transportation advocated by ADAPT. He uses a wheelchair as a result of polio. When Dr. C. Everett Koop was nominated to be Surgeon General, Justin Dart testified on his behalf, with the urging of Mary Jane Owen. In August 1989, he was appointed by President Bush to be chairman of the prestigious President's Committee on Employment of Persons with Disabilities.

****

Another leader in the civil rights movement, Evan Kemp from Cleveland, suffers from a form of muscular dystrophy and uses a wheelchair. At one time an attorney for the SEC and director of the Disability Rights Center, he is now Commissioner of the Equal Employment Opportunity Commission.

****

In December 1989 the disability community was saddened by the passing of Dennis Smurr, at age 48. Dennis, a quadriplegic, was an official of the Paralyzed Veterans of America organization; this author had the privilege of interviewing him in connection with this book. Dennis was a hard working and able advocate for disability rights, particularly in the area of transportation. A memorial service held for him on December 12, 1989, in the House Veterans Affairs Committee Hearing Room on Capitol Hill, was attended by many leaders of the disability community.

****

Harold Snider never ceases to amaze those who come into contact with him! Blind since birth, he participated as a youth in desegregation civil rights efforts in Florida, even to the point of being arrested for a motel swimming pool sit-in. He met and married Gail, also blind; they have two children. Harold was a participant in the 1977 protest at HEW relating to the section 504 regulations (see Chapter Three). He has been president of Access for the Handicapped, Inc., has taught at George Washington University, and has been executive director of the American Impact Foundation. In late 1989 he was appointed director of Outreach for Persons With Disabilities by the Republican National Committee, where he serves as liaison between the RNC and disability groups. It was a pleasure and a privilege to interview him in connection with this book

*************.

Stephen W. Hawking is a name that will be long remembered. Suffering from Lou Gehrig's disease, he has used a wheelchair for many years. Unable to speak, he communicates by pecking out answers on a computer with his three good fingers. Born on the anniversary of Galileo's death, he holds Newton's chair as Lucasian Professor of Mathematics at Cambridge University and is widely regarded as the most brilliant theoretical physicist since Einstein. He has gone beyond Einstein's theory of relativity and has contributed to an understanding of a unified theory of the universe. His recent popular book, *A Brief History of Time,*[13] has been a best-seller and explains for the layman the complicated theory of relativity, the "Big Bang" theory of the origin of the universe, black holes and other mind-boggling phenomena. A black hole seems to be an invisible collapsed star, invisible because its light waves are unable to escape its surface due to its gravitational force. Perhaps there is an analogy to the disabled population; regarded as invisible by society because of being overwhelmed by the force of their afflictions. Says Stephen: *"I get embarrassed when people say I have courage. It is not as if I have had a choice and have chosen the more difficult alternative. I have simply followed the only course open to me...I'm not bitter. I might have been bitter if I had been less fortunate. But I have been successful in my work. I have a beautiful family and I have written a best seller. One can't hope for much more."*

****

In June 1987 the *Phil Donohue Show* featured the sexuality of people with disabilities. The point of the show was to emphasize that all people are sexual beings whether disabled or not. Misunderstandings of this viewpoint give rise to societal prejudices that often become apparent when, for instance, a disabled person takes a non-disabled mate. One participant in the show was Ellen Stohl, a quadriplegic who appeared in the July 1987 issue of Playboy. She explained that her motivation was a result of her feeling that when she became disabled, she was no longer regarded as a woman but was labeled "disabled:" *"...I'm a woman, I happen to be using a wheelchair but I'm a woman first and foremost. And that's why I chose to do Playboy."* [14]

****

> *"If people want to spend money on research, they're going to spend it on that. But the odds are 100,000 to one that I'm going to spend the rest of my life in a wheelchair, and I'd rather have them spend the money on really good care instead of some bullshit cure. But nobody's going to do that. There's no glory in that."* [15]

****

Susan Schapiro, spinal cord injured, became a lawyer at the Disability Law Resource Center in Berkeley, but quit to become a computer programmer.. *"I got tired of being a professional cripple, as it were. One thing I liked about my job when I became a programmer was that I wasn't working in a disability organization, and I knew that my disability had nothing to do with being hired. I get tired of being disabled for a living."* [16]

****

Nancy Becker Kennedy, described as a producer/writer/actress/composer/disabled activist wrote an article entitled "Ms. Wheelchair America Sets the Record Straight" for *Spinal Network*.[17]

Articles about Donna Cline, who became Miss Wheelchair America (1985-1986), commend her as the "cover story anchor" for an ABC affiliate in Missouri. In traveling around the country giving speeches, Donna's message was: *"..keep being you and go for it...You can get just about anything you put your mind to if you do it with enthusiasm."*

****

"The issue of discrimination against disabled people in the United States is the same as discrimination against racial minorities or religious minorities. And we're still realizing that as a movement. Of course there are disabled people who feel they are above everything and don't want to be seen with other disabled people. They don't want to be part of any movement. Another disabled person can instantly pick these people out of a crowd. They don't want to look at us, they don't want to talk to us.[18]

"When I was 5 my mother proudly pushed my wheelchair to our local public school, where I was promptly refused admission because the principal ruled I was a fire hazard. I was forced to go into home instruction, receiving one hour of education twice a week for three and a half years. My entrance into mainstream society was blocked by discrimination and segregation. Segregation was not only on an institutional level but also acted as an obstruction to social integration. As a teenager, I could not travel with my friends on the bus because it was not accessible. At my graduation from high school, the principal attempted to prevent me from accepting an award in a ceremony on stage simply because I was in a wheelchair.

"When I was 19, the house mother of my college dormitory refused me admission into the dorm because I was in a wheelchair and needed assistance. When I was 21 years old, I was denied an elementary school teaching credential because of 'paralysis of both lower extremities sequelae of poliomyelitis.' At that time, I did not know what sequelae meant. I went to the dictionary and looked it up and found out that it was 'because of.' So it was obviously because of my disability that I was discriminated against.

"At the age of 25, I was told to leave a plane on my return trip to my job here in the U.S. Senate because I was flying without an attendant. In 1981 an attempt was made to forcibly remove me and another disabled friend from an auction house because we were 'disgusting to look at.' In 1983 a manager at a movie theater attempted to keep my disabled friend and myself out of his theater because we could not transfer out of our wheelchairs."[19]

"Section 504 is inadequate. There are moves to get disabled people more specific rights protection like the Civil Rights Act gives minorities and women. Some of us talk about trying to get the 1964 Civil Rights Act itself amended; others say we need our own civil rights law that spells out, in detail, specific protections for disabled people. Both ideas are just talk...The handful of dis-

abled activists from the days of the seventies when 504 began, and independent living began, are reaching middle age. Many are comfortable now, and the old fights seem, well, 'old.' And a lot of them wonder where the 'second generation' is. Will new activist leaders emerge from among the 'grassroots?"[20]

****

"Individuals with disabilities experience staggering levels of unemployment and poverty." [21]

****

"On the cost side, the National Council on the Handicapped states that current spending on disability benefits and programs exceeds $60 billion annually. Excluding the millions of disabled who want to work from the employment ranks costs society literally billions of dollars annually in support payments and lost income tax revenues." [22]

"[discrimination and segregation] are driving us inevitably towards an economic and moral disaster of giant, paternalistic welfare bureaucracy. We are already paying unaffordable and rapidly escalating billions in public and private funds to maintain ever-increasing millions of potentially productive Americans in unjust, unwanted dependency." [23]

"Martin Luther King had a dream. We have a vision. Dr. King dreamed of an America 'where a person is judged not by the color of his skin, but by the content of his character.' ADA's vision is of an America where persons are judged by their abilities and not on the basis of their disabilities."[24]

Ed Hooper (writer for the *Disability Rag*):

"We, as disabled people, are advised to push ourselves to the maximum of our physical capabilities, but we're never given any limits. How do we know what is too much?"

Irving Zola: (sociology professor, Brandeis University):

"It is a problem. A lot of rehabilitation philosophy has been on a 'lose it or use it' basis. And while this has much truth, particularly in the early stages of a disability or chronic disease, as a life-time standard the price is too high. For it means that we are forced to do many things by ourselves and under our own steam when people or electronic power are available. While some of us might want to take three hours to write a letter or twenty minutes to scale a flight of stairs, others would just as soon not. Independence is never merely a physical matter, it always involves choice—the choice to be helped or not, to operate a wheelchair with my hands or electrically. True independence thus must involve the risk of losing or endangering certain physical and physiological capacities at the expense of enhancing greater physical and psychological freedom." [25]

****

"Years ago, words like 'invalid' and 'cripple' were not meant to be pejorative; basically, they were factually descriptive. As time passed, the words 'handicapped' and 'disabled' were commonly accepted. To me, this represents the neutral position on the semantic pendulum. Now we are bombarded with terms such as 'people who use wheelchairs,' 'physically challenged' etc...As a C 6/7 quad, the term 'confined to a wheelchair' is accurate (it is either that or stay in bed). During the last few years the public has been overexposed in the mass media to the image of the supercripple, creating expectations that are often too high. The best way I can now convey any meaningful understanding of my true condition to able-bodied people is to refer to myself as a cripple." [26]

"We don't need more equal rights laws. What we need is an attitude that we're all human beings, and as such, we all care about each other." Itzhak Perlman, concert violinist.[27]

"Another thing is all of the human interest stories about the handicapped that you see in the papers or on TV. The stories make it sound like all handicapped people are saints; nice, wonderful people, like becoming disabled makes you a better person. Crap!" [28]

****

Karen Scott was pregnant, but she was having prenatal difficulties. A 70 year old retired civilian doctor, hired by a short staffed military hospital, allegedly misdiagnosed her condition and performed unnecessary surgery. She developed an infection and her son, Jonathan, was born suffering from oxygen deprivation, which left him with spastic quadriplegia, a form of cerebral palsy. Jonathan uses a wheelchair, can only speak a few words, and has little control over bodily functions. After lengthy litigation, the Justice Department settled the case by agreeing to an award of 8.5 million dollars, which will be used for an accessible home, a personal attendant for Jonathan, and other expenses. Although private lawsuits are one way to deal with the problem of severe disability, the results are uncertain and vary from case to case. In many cases, the burden of support falls on a single unsuccessful defendant, not a very rational way to solve a national problem.

****

John Hockenberry was spinal cord injured as a result of an accident and uses a wheelchair. He has worked for National Public Radio and has been to the Middle East on assignment. He has been host of a late night radio show sponsored by NPR in New York City, called "Heat." In 1985 Hockenberry was among 40 finalists selected in NASA's "First Journalist in Space" search. On CBS Morning News, Forrest Sawyer said, *"John, I understand you want to be the first paraplegic in space."* He replied, *"No, I want to be the first journalist in space."* In 1992 Hockenberry left NPR for a big job with ABC in its new Sunday night news magazine. During the Gulf War, Hockenberry left his wheelchair at a Kurdish outpost and spent eight hours on the back of a donkey to get a story on the thousands of refugees pouring into the mountains.

****

On January 6, 1992, Judge Jacques Dufour of the Quebec Superior Court ruled that Nancy B., a 25 year old paralytic suffering from a disabling illness called Guillain – Barre syndrome and kept alive connected to a respirator, could be allowed to die by disconnecting the respirator. Nancy and her parents requested the ruling. The case was regarded as policy setting, because Nancy's illness was not terminal, she is fully conscious and could remain alive for many years.

****

Elizabeth Bouvia has cerebral palsy but managed to have her own apartment, graduate from college, and get married. She could only talk, chew, and operate a joystick on her mechanical wheelchair. She became depressed and in 1983 asked the Riverdale, California, hospital to let her starve to death. The hospital refused permission. Court proceedings followed, with her lawyer, the hospital's lawyers, and the judge appearing at bedside – a real life version of *Whose life is it anyway?* (stageplay by Brian Clark and movie starring Richard Dreyfus). The court's judgment was that she should be allowed to die. The California Supreme Court upheld the decision, concluding that she had a "fundamental right," based on the right of privacy, to terminate life. Though given legal authority to terminate her life, she later changed her mind. In an article in *The Washington Post,* [29] her lawyer was quoted as saying that she had become a "happy person." Many defend the right to make the choice, but on the facts of her case, some disagreed with her decision.

In general, disability rights advocates oppose court approved suicide because it is generally grounded on "quality of life" concerns. As Paul K. Longmore, a historian at the University of Southern California, said of the Bouvia Court of Appeals court decision:

> *"In a concurring opinion that is shocking for its ignorance and bias, Justice Lynn Compton repeats the prejudicial nonsense that Elizabeth Bouvia is helpless: '...she must lie immobile, unable to exist except through the physical acts of others.' This is a woman who operated a power wheelchair, was halfway toward a master's degree, married, made love with her husband and planned to become a mother. This is a woman who still could and might do all of those things if she were given appropriate psychiatric and medical treatment....Compton wrote of the hope that this case 'will cause our society to deal realistically with the plight of those unfortunate individuals to whom death beckons as a welcome respite from suffering.' That statement is ominous, just as this ruling is a dangerous precedent. Where handicapped persons are stigmatized and segregated, the right to die can quickly become the duty to die. Persons with severe disabilities may subtly be pressured into 'choosing' judicially sanctioned, medically assisted suicide."* [30]

Another significant case involving the "right to die" is Ross v. Hilltop Rehabilitation Hospital, 676 F. Supp. 1528 (D.Colo. 1987). In this case, Hector Rodas suffered a stroke due to intravenous drug abuse. He became paralyzed from the neck down and was unable to speak or swallow. He was fed through a gastrostomy tube inserted into his stomach. He asked to die by having the tube withdrawn; he went to court on the theory that section 504 gave him that right. The court denied his request; the court found nothing in section 504 that related to the "right to die." But the court was bothered by the lack of precedent and groped for an articulate rationale. The court gave a comprehensive bibliography of other court cases and commentary on the right to die issue.

An excruciatingly difficult problem exists with respect to newborn infants with severe disabilities. The "right to die" advocates would urge that the infant be allowed to quietly expire. But sometimes the life of the child is not at stake; it's a question of "conservative medical treatment" or "aggressive medical treatment."

Related to the issue of the "right to die" is the issue of "unusual medical treatment." In 1983 and 1984, a celebrated lawsuit involving "Baby Jane Doe" was decided United States v. University Hospital of the State University of New York at Stony Brook, 575 F. Supp. 607 (EDNY 1983), affirmed, 729 F.2d 144 (2nd Cir. 1984).

In this case, a baby girl was born in the state of New York with severe spina bifida, a lesion of the spinal column. If it is not repaired with immediate surgery, it can lead to permanent brain damage. A shunt should be inserted into the brain to drain spinal fluid or severe retardation can occur. The parents of the little girl, whose name was known to the public as Baby Jane Doe, did not want surgery, but only "conservative treatment." Faced with the hospital's support of the parents refusal to provide surgery and other medical treatment, the federal government brought suit, under section 504 of the Rehabilitation Act of 1973, against the hospital to look into medical records for possible violations in section 504. The case became a landmark in the history of civil rights for disabled infants, but the court result was a set-back. The press gave the case wide coverage. The federal government was joined by some disability groups who feared that the little girl's civil rights were being violated by withholding what was regarded as essential medical treatment. The American Coalition of Citizens With Disabilities supported the government, as did the Association for Persons With Severe Handicaps, the Disability Rights Education and Defense Fund, and the Disability Rights Union. Opposing the federal government were the parents of the little girl, who maintained that as parents they had the sole right to determine the type of medical treatment. They were joined in this position by the attorney general of the State of New York as well as by, for some unaccountable reason, the New York Civil Liberties Union.

The government lost. The privacy rights of the parent prevailed, and Baby Jane never got the necessary treatment. The courts first discussed whether Baby Jane was "handicapped" and fortunately concluded that she was, warding off a preposterous argument that she wasn't because a major life activity, such as breathing, was not affected. But then the courts said she was not "otherwise qualified" and therefore wasn't discriminated against under section 504. "Otherwise qualified" addresses abilities unrelated to a handicap, but medical treatment of a handicapped child almost always relates to the handicap. The courts noted that when section 504 was enacted, there was no discussion about whether it applied to disabled infants, and then said that section 504 didn't encourage the federal government to get involved in difficult decisions regarding medical treatment of disabled infants. The courts reflected the apparent view that section 504 doesn't apply to parents, and that if a handicapped infant is discriminated against by a hospital that withholds necessary medical treatment, because the parents don't consent to it, the hospital has not violated section 504. In other words, the parents' views must prevail over federal law. In 1986, the Supreme Court more or less echoed this position, in Bowen v. American Hospital Association, 476 U.S. 610 (1986), in a difficult decision written by Justice Stevens, in which other Justices concurred, but Justices O'Connor, White, and Brennan dissented.

In 1990 Nat Hentoff wrote an article in *The Washington Post* ("Whatever Happened to Baby Jane Doe?" December 11, 1990). He discovered that the child's first name was Keri-Lynn; her last name was never disclosed. Interviews with pediatric surgeons such as Dr. C. Everett Koop and Dr. David McLone disclosed that "aggressive treatment" could have significantly improved the child's health. Today Keri-Lynn laughs and plays, but she cannot walk. She attends special classes, and her intelligence is considered between low-normal and educable. The press and the courts seem to have thrown up their hands and declared that improvement was a hopeless prospect. But, tragically, had Keri-Lynn's civil rights under the Rehabilitation Act been upheld instead of trampled on, her life would probably have been much improved.

The issue of the choice to die for disabled adults continues to be a difficult moral and legal one. Although there have been many other court cases similar to the Bouvia and Ross cases, which in general, although not unanimously, uphold the right of the patient to die, many hospitals and doctors will not terminate life support systems without court approval. This is because of fear of lawsuits for malpractice and because of the ingrained desire of health professionals to sustain life rather than to terminate it.

The issue came to a head in the case of Cruzan v. Director of Missouri Department of Health, heard by the Supreme Court during the October 1989 term and decided June 25, 1990. Nancy Cruzan, in January 1983, was involved in an auto accident in Carterville, Missouri. She had, ever since, been in a coma-like condition called a persistent vegetative state. Her parents initially consented to have a tube inserted in her stomach for nutrition and hydration, but later wanted it removed, so that their daughter could be allowed to die. Nancy, then 32, was expected to live another 30 or 40 years, but with no hope of improvement. Nancy's parents went to court. Missouri law provides that in such cases there is a right to die only if there is clear and convincing evidence that the patient when competent expressed that intention; a substitute judgment by family or friends will not do. In a 4 to 3 decision in November 1988. the Missouri Supreme Court ruled that Nancy was alive and that removing the feeding tube would amount to premeditated murder, under Missouri law. The United States Supreme Court was called on to review this judgment. Numerous briefs were filed by interested parties, including disability groups and anti-abortion groups, who generally side with the Missouri Supreme Court. However, Nancy's parents argued that she was not disabled, but dead and that it would be pointless to prolong her life interminably through artificial means. The Missouri Supreme Court said that "quality of life" was not an issue, because if it were, all manner of disabled people could have artificial treatment removed to terminate life. Missouri Attorney General William L. Webster said that if the Supreme Court were to side with the Cruzans, it would raise the question of terminating the life of persons with Alzheimers disease, senior citizens, or severely handicapped persons: *"The slipperiest of slopes is to start moving toward placing a value on a particular quality of life because then you can move into people who are handicapped or people who are retarded."* [31]

On June 25, 1990, the United State Supreme Court decided the Cruzan case. In a 5-4 vote, with Justice Sandra Day O'Connor the swing vote, the court in effect denied Nancy's parents' request to allow Nancy to die. Although Nancy had a constitutional right in some circumstances to be allowed to die, clear and convincing evidence of her intent was required by Missouri law, which the court upheld. Her parents' desires did not meet the clear and convincing standard, and the state of Missouri thus prevailed in its presumed desire to keep Nancy alive indefinitely. The court decision was bound to increase the need for lawyers, because the Court seemingly approved "living wills" or "durable powers of attorney" executed by an individual when competent, under which according to most state laws, an individual who is terminally ill may have life support systems terminated under certain circumstances. The problem in the Cruzan case was not that Nancy did not have a constitutional right to be allowed to die, but there was insufficient evidence that she had expressed that wish in a legally effective manner.

Many but not all disability groups applauded the Supreme Court's decision. They regarded Nancy as "disabled" and feared that withdrawal of life support because of doubts as to her "quality of life" could lead to other cases involving the severely disabled with respect to whom death could be justified on a "quality of life" rationale. This school of thought also condemns abortion. The argument is that if the life of a person in a vegetative state can be terminated, disabled people will be next in line. There are those who disagree with this position, on the ground that there is little analogy to be found between a comatose person and a disabled person, no matter how severe the disability. To them, the contrary argument is a case of logic being carried to an illogical extreme, and there is no sufficient rationale for keeping individuals such as Nancy Cruzan alive indefinitely.

After the Supreme Court decision, further legal proceedings in the Cruzan case continued in the local probate court. This time, the Probate Judge decided there was sufficient evidence of Nancy's wishes, and he ordered the feeding tube removed. With Right to Life groups threatening to invade her hospital room and keep the tube inserted by force, Nancy's condition deteriorated and on December 26, 1990, she died.

In the September/October 1990 issue of *Disability Rag*, Mary Johnson wrote an article with the headline: *"We're killing disabled people in this country—then acting like we're doing them a favor."* The article discusses the story of a 31-year-old quadriplegic, Kenneth Bergstedt, who is petitioning the Nevada courts to allow him to end his existence. On June 9, 1990, Las Vegas District Court Judge Donald Mosley ruled that Bergstedt had the right to be given a sedative and taken off his respirator. At the same time, the judge ordered the case appealed to the state Supreme Court. Bergstedt's attorney, Jack Cherry, said that Bergstedt's ventilator *"only prolongs an agonizing existence."* Mary Johnson complained that a reporter who wrote up the case hadn't even interviewed Bergstedt. Though Mary Johnson tried to interview him, she was thwarted in her effort by Bergstedt's protective father. The point of her article was that apparently Bergstedt hadn't been asked his own views; his father controlled access to the media. She said that no one she knew who was on a respirator wanted to die. She suggested that the motivation behind Bergstedt's apparent decision to die was not so much the terrible quality of his existence as the fact that lack of financial resources prevented improvement in the quality of his life. She suggested that the media, the patient's father, lawyer, and the courts, were all too ready to agree with Bergstedt that his life was not worth living. She implied that she disagreed with the court decision.

Articles like Mary Johnson's serve the useful purpose of adding an important dimension to this agonizingly difficult issue. Disability groups and many disabled people have a point of view that others may lack. If the legal and medical authorities decide someone should die, where do you draw the line? Still, the author of the article assumed an advocacy role concerning a person she had never met. Are there no circumstances where a disabled person should be allowed freedom of choice concerning life or termination of life? Will the issue resolve itself in favor of the prolongation of life if only more money is found to enable the individual to leave an institution, live independently, and possibly get a job? What about individuals who are too severely disabled to leave an institution or to live independently or obtain a job? Does it serve a useful purpose to assume an advocacy position regarding the dozens of similar cases that have and will occur, based on possibly second hand information, and with an apparently preconceived judgment?

At the September 1990, Senate confirmation hearings on the nomination of David Souter to the Supreme Court, it was noted that this quiet, unassuming New Hampshire resident owned only a black and white television set. The point could be made that the terribly difficult decisions regarding life termination and medical treatment should not be based on either blacks or whites but on varying shades of gray.

CHAPTER XIV

EMPLOYMENT

A recent law school graduate, who excelled in law school and passed the bar with ease, was having trouble finding a job. He counted the number of resumes he had sent, 145, and the number of interviews, 47; all had met with dismal results. The fact that he was using a wheelchair, due to a spinal cord injury, might have had something to do with it. One bright day, after interviewing the prestigious firm of Silverberg and Mulkern, he received an offer to begin work as an associate. The first day on the job, he was impressed by the thick rugs on the floor, French impressionistic paintings on the walls, well dressed attorneys, and good looking receptionists and secretaries. But, people tiptoed about, and didn't seem to speak to anyone. He soon noticed that the restroom was inaccessible to a person in a wheelchair. He mentioned it to someone, and the next day, there was a knock on the door. It was Mr. Grimsly, the partner in charge of office matters. "Someone said you can't use the restroom, is that right?" The newly hired lawyer, not wanting to make a bad impression the second day on the job, thought desperately about how to word a delicate matter, but words failed him. He thought about saying, "I'm not able to have a bowel movement," but that sounded ridiculously stuffy. Finally, turning red, he blurted out, "I can pee in a cup, but I can't take a shit." Mr Grimsly, equally embarrassed, fled, and a few days later the restroom was made accessible to disabled individuals with a wheelchair .

****

Give a man a fish and he will eat for a day. Teach him to fish and he will eat for the rest of his life. (Chinese proverb)

Today, as in the past, one of the most severe problems faced by people with disabilities is employment. In spite of recent legislation prohibiting discrimination against hiring and promoting disabled people, the astronomically high rate of unemployment among disabled people able to work is nothing short of a national disgrace. On this issue, we need to look at where we have been and where we are going.

It could be said that the beginning of society's concern about employment for disabled people was a case of the cart before the horse. For, shortly before World War I, some states had passed workmen's compensation laws which provided financial support for workers who had been injured on the job. This was a very small parameter; the individual was already gainfully employed and then became disabled. It was many decades later that the tables were turned, and government addressed the problem of disabled individuals who were seeking rehabilitation that would enable them to be gainfully employed.

After workmen's compensation came vocational rehabilitation, the next step in government policy. The concept started out as a simple financing transfer from the federal government to the states, which administered generally unsuccessful programs. Periodically, Congress would reinvent vocational rehabilitation, with ever more elaborate provisions in various Rehabilitation Acts. However bewildering the complex provisions of the acts, they all had two things in common: they provided federal money for vocational programs administered by states; they cost a lot of money. Funds expended in vocational rehabilitation programs, when coupled with those provided by federal disability payments, state disability, and welfare payments amounted to a staggering sum. In 1990 it was estimated that the total of all these sums was in excess of 100 billion dollars annually. Yet the end result of all this expenditure of government funds was mostly maintenance and welfare for disabled people, and very little progress was being made toward successful employment programs that actually helped disabled people to be independent and productive.

Shortly after World War I, Congress appropriated funds for vocational rehabilitation of disabled people, a move sparked by large numbers of returning disabled veterans. Later, vocational rehabilitation was extended to civilians, but the programs were intended to benefit those who were regarded as employable, leaving out thousands of others. These programs have continued, but it became apparent that it did little good to train a disabled person for a job when there were no jobs available, no accessible transportation or no accessible employment sites even if jobs were available. A criticism of the various programs was that social workers tended to "rehabilitate" the mildly disabled people, while the severely disabled who were employable seldom found jobs. In 1973 it was realized that the federal programs weren't really providing career training but were simply providing either medical assistance or support payments.

The Rehabilitation Act of 1973 started out as a rehash of previous programs. President Nixon vetoed the first version, partly because of expense and partly because of concern about administrative overlap and confusion, particularly with respect to providing medical treatment. In an effort to compromise, Congress dropped the word "Vocational" because few believed that the massively expensive federal programs were really providing many jobs for disabled people.

The Rehabilitation Act of 1973 started out looking like business as usual, but, almost by accident, a provision was added that was a quantum leap forward. Section 504, in a chapter of the act entitled "Miscellaneous" prohibited discrimination in employment against otherwise qualified disabled people in the federal sector, meaning federally funded programs (see Chapter Three). Later, this concept of civil rights was greatly expanded in the private sector, under the Americans With Disabilities Act of 1990 (see Chapter Six).

It was almost as though Congress realized that pumping huge amounts of money into vocational rehabilitation programs was, to a great extent, a failure. To add a requirement in a federal statute prohibiting federally funded employers from discriminating against disabled people could be regarded as a stroke of genius. It shifted the emphasis from expensive government maintenance programs to a civil rights concept in which employers were obligated to provide jobs for qualified disabled people. The concept appealed to everyone's sense of equality for all Americans. It was a concept that had a respectable tradition in the Civil Rights Act of 1964, originally directed in favor of racial and religious minorities. And best of all, it didn't require a penny of federal transfer payments.

The Rehabilitation Act of 1973, section 504, prohibits discrimination in employment against disabled people in the "federal sector." The federal sector includes any program or activity funded, in whole or in part, by the federal government. It includes most colleges and universities, the Postal Commission, federal projects of every sort. It has been held that the federal sector includes county governments which receive federal funds.

Pursuant to section 504, there has been a fair amount of litigation by disabled people who have been denied jobs, promotions or other benefits. This degree of litigation may be a harbinger of things to come under the Americans With Disabilities Act which, similar to section 504, prohibits employment discrimination against disabled people by private employers, as well as by the state and local governments.

Under section 504, some interesting employment discrimination cases have been litigated. In Richardson v. United States Postal Service, 613 F. Supp. 1213 (D.C.D.C., 1985), a longtime postal employee who was an alcoholic attempted to kill himself and his wife. After being discharged for criminal conduct, he brought suit alleging a violation of section 504. He lost.

In Carter v. Casa Central, 849 F.2d 1048 (7th Cir., 1988), a nurse who contracted multiple sclerosis sued a not-for-profit hospital serving the Chicago area. She sued for reinstatement of her nursing position and won the case, primarily because of medical testimony indicating she was capable of doing the job.

In Davis v. Frank, 711 F. Supp. 447 (N.D. Ill., 1989), a hearing impaired lady successfully sued the Postal Commission for reinstatement of a position as time and attendance clerk, even though she was not able to answer the telephone.

On the other hand, an optometry student with retinitis pigmentosa did not prevail in a suit to be enrolled as a student for an optometry degree; the defendant said he would be a danger to patients. Doherty v. Southern College of Optometry, 659 F.Supp. 662 (W.D. Tenn., 1987), reversed on other grounds, 862 F.2d 570.

A curious case, Pridemore v. Rural Legal Aid Society of West Central Ohio, 625 F. Supp. 1180 (S.D. Ohio, 1985), held that there was no violation of section 504 when a prospective employer sent the applicant a letter which was addressed with the wrong zip code. A left handed postal worker did not prevail in his contention that being left handed is a handicap. Torres v.Bolger, 610 F. Supp. 593 (D.C. Texas, 1985). Nor did a utility repairman who claimed he had acrophobia or fear of heights and couldn't climb utility poles, Forrisi v. Bowen, 794 F.2d 931 (4th Cir. 1986).

A short person with achondroplastic dwarfism failed to obtain the job she wanted in the Post Office. Dexler v. Tisch, 660 F. Supp. 1418 (D. Conn., 1987).

The basic purpose of section 504 of the Rehabilitation Act and Title I of the Americans With Disabilities Act is to prevent discrimination against otherwise qualified people on the basis of handicap. In order to prevail in such an employment discrimination case, it is not sufficient for the plaintiff to merely allege that he or she is handicapped. The plaintiff must establish that he or she is in fact handicapped within the meaning of the federal statutes. Then the plaintiff must show that he or she is "otherwise qualified," meaning that the plaintiff has the necessary education, experience, and skills for the job, and the disability itself is not an impediment to the performance of the essential functions of the job. The employer need not make drastic adaptations to the job site or the job itself but must make a reasonable effort to accommodate the applicant. And, of course, the employer must have a job available.

These two historic pieces of federal legislation were not just happenstance. Decades before, the President's Committee on Employment of People with Disabilities was created by President Truman (its original name was President's Committee on Employment of the Handicapped). It is a federal agency devoted to promoting employment opportunities for the disabled, and its chairman for many years was Harold Russell, a disabled World War II veteran and nationally prominent figure. In 1989, after more than twenty five years of distinguished service, Russell retired; President Bush appointed as his successor Justin W. Dart Jr. The untiring efforts of the President's Committee and of both Russell and Dart have been extremely influential in bringing about the federal legislation just described. Though the President's Committee was, and continues to be, an advisory agency, the leaders knew that forceful Federal legislation was needed, so they labored diligently to bring about the Rehabilitation Act and the Americans With Disabilities Act.

Justin Dart Jr., originally from Texas and presently chairman of the President's Committee, was disabled by polio as a teenager and uses a wheelchair. His Texas ranger hat has become a familiar sight. His father, the late Justin Dart, was a California industrialist and Reagan supporter. Justin Jr. was founder and chief executive of Japan Tupperware, Inc. Justin has been a tireless and eloquent advocate for civil rights for disabled people. He has traveled extensively throughout the country speaking on disability issues. He has testified passionately before Congressional committees considering the Americans with Disability Act (he is an architect of provisions of the act) and was a featured speaker for the historic March 12, 1990 march at the Capitol (see Chapter Six).

Justin Jr. was Commissioner of the Rehabilitation Services Administration during the Reagan years, but left in 1987 under orders from the White House after making complaints about the government's *"obsolete, paternalistic attitudes"* toward the disabled. Dart was then appointed to the National Council on the Handicapped, another federal agency. He also chaired a congressional task force on the Rights and Empowerment of Americans with Disabilities.

The President's Committee sponsors an annual dinner, usually in May, which is regarded as one of the social highlights of the year; the President is sometimes the featured speaker.

Many other disability organizations provide employment for disabled persons. Goodwill Industries provides jobs in marketing, furniture repair, and administration for disabled persons. Sheltered workshops have sprung up, although in many cases wages are minimal.

The sheltered workshop concept developed to fill a vacuum caused by the fact that many severely disabled people weren't getting meaningful employment. The sheltered workshop provides people with moderate to severe retardation and/or severe mobility impairment an opportunity to learn skills under supervision, but in a setting isolated from the community.

In the late eighties it was realized that sheltered workshops, though serving a purpose, were not providing sufficient employment opportunities for the severely disabled. In tune with the mainstreaming objectives of section 504, a new approach to employment rehabilitation, called "supported employment," took shape. Supported employment was initiated at the federal level by the Rehabilitation Act Amendments of 1986 and is designed for individuals who are serving in day activity programs because they appear to lack the potential for unassisted competitive employment. The program is supposed to involve continuous training, supervision, and support services; objectives are to enhance income level and advancement opportunity. Assistance is to be given to agencies that provide supervision and help at the work site, and an employer can be helped to offset excess costs of equipment and training. Salary supplements can be given to co-workers who assist the disabled worker at the work site either in performing the job or for personal care. The supported employment concept is supposed to go a step beyond the sheltered workshop and provide more mainstreaming for severely disabled people in the work-place. A criticism of the effectiveness of the program was published in the Journal of Rehabilitation, Vol 57,No. 2, (1991).[1]

A great success story regarding employment for workers with disabilities occurred at the Rehabilitation Center for the Disabled, in Seattle. The center has achieved remarkable results in training and finding jobs for all manner of disabled people, including many quadriplegics. An organizer and supervisor is veteran Rich Walsh, who became a quadriplegic as a result of a jeep accident. His computer is operated entirely by voice and he has been successful in training and finding jobs for quadriplegics, many in positions requiring highly sophisticated computer technology. Large companies such as IBM and Xerox have contributed to this remarkable program.

Still, the lack of employment of disabled people at decent levels of income has been and still is a terrible social problem. An article in *The Washington Post* on March 25, 1978, described the abysmal record of employment of the disabled at the Department of Health, Education, and Welfare (HEW). HEW had recently implemented the Rehabilitation Act of 1973, had umbrella authority over other federal agencies, and was supposed to be a "role model" of employment of the disabled, yet only 1.5 percent of its employees were disabled. Joseph Califano, HEW Secretary, promised corrections.

The passage of time hasn't improved matters much. An article in the *New York Times* on December 31, 1988, indicated that a graduate or professional degree is no guarantee of a job. The article described the plight of many disabled law school graduates searching for a job; it is not uncommon for such graduates to send out hundreds of resumes; many never land a legal job. Joseph F.

Danowsky, who is blind and a recent graduate of Harvard Law School, confided that upon graduating he wrote 1,800 job application letters and didn't receive a single affirmative answer.

A recent survey of Maryland lawyers indicated dissatisfaction with the legal profession; one cause of complaint was discrimination in hiring and promotion against minorities, women, and disabled lawyers. The legal profession, because of accelerating costs and other factors, has become increasingly monopolistic, with megafirms taking over smaller firms. This has had a tendency to result in hiring superstar law graduates, to the exclusion of everyone else, and to increase the cost of legal services, to the point where many who seriously need a lawyer cannot afford to hire one. (It might be predicted that eventually the few megafirms left in a big city will combine into one huge law firm, charging five hundred dollars an hour. When the firm loses its last millionaire client, all the lawyers could get up on the roof of the Arnold and Porter building, for example, and, hand in hand, jump off thereof!) Sadly, the public is finding it more and more difficult to obtain the services of a small firm at a reasonable cost. Many disabled lawyers, prohibited from being hired by the blue stocking megafirms, are starting their own practices, providing a much needed service to a community unwilling to pay exorbitant fees.

Public interest law firms are getting into the area of disability rights, often employing disabled lawyers to argue such cases in court. An outstanding example is DREDF, (Disability Rights Education Defense Fund) located in Berkeley, California, which argues cases, often with disabled lawyers, involving disability rights.

DREDF began in 1980; a principal organizer was Mary Lou Breslin, who, due to polio, uses a wheelchair. DREDF is concerned with lobbying for disability legislation and takes legal cases on behalf of people with disabilities, who complain of discrimination. These cases can involve employment discrimination, architectural barriers, or education. Recently, DREDF won a large settlement against the Berkeley public schools; the case involved architectural barriers. DREDF was instrumental in talking the Reagan Administration out of ditching the section 504 regulations and education regulations. DREDF has lobbied for the Civil Rights Restoration Act and for the Americans With Disabilities Act. It has filed amicus briefs in section 504 court cases and has begun a legal clinical education program involving law students from the University of California, at Santa Clara, Berkeley, and Davis. The Washington, D.C. office has been headed by Pat Wright, who has done outstanding lobbying work, especially with respect to the Americans With Disabilities Act. A tiny but growing organization, it is a "David" fighting the Goliath of societal discrimination against the disabled. Marilyn Golden, a policy analyst with DREDF, testified at Congressional hearings regarding ADA and, since it was passed, has been coordinating the Conference Committee issues to reconcile differences between the bill passed by the Senate and the one passed by the House.

A Washington lawyer, Tim Cook, who had had polio, argued brilliantly the spectacular case of ADAPT v. Burnley, involving the issue of DOT's responsibility to provide accessible buses. Harold Krentz, a Harvard Law School graduate, blind, was unable to find a job immediately and wrote the autobiography "Butterflies are Free" which became a hit show and movie. In October 1989 Laura Cooper, who uses an electric wheelchair as a result of multiple sclerosis, testified before the House Subcommittee on Civil and Constitutional Rights that, after graduating from law school, she sent out hundreds of resumes and applications for employment with law firms, but met with no success. She has been a frequent speaker concerning the Americans With Disabilities Act.

The two federal statutes described (the Rehabilitation Act of 1973 and the Americans With Disabilities Act of 1990), on paper at least, represent a dramatic shift in the government's approach to hiring the disabled into the direction of civil rights. That is, under that legislation, employers have an obligation not to discriminate against disabled people, just as under other civil rights legislation, they may not discriminate against blacks or other minorities.

Whether one looks at traditional vocational rehabilitation programs, which continue today, or the more recent federal statutes taking a civil rights approach and prohibiting discrimination against disabled people in the work splace, the results have not been encouraging.

According to a General Accounting Office Report, "Little Success Achieved in Rehabilitating Disabled Americans," December 1987, the percentage of individuals who receive social security disability maintenance payments and also receive independence counseling is minute. Only 13 percent had been served by vocational rehabilitation programs and of those who were, only one half responded that they had become self sufficient. Yet, only 25 percent of people with disabilities said they wanted to be protected by society; most wanted to be in charge of their own lives. Figures obtained from the U.S. Census Bureau for 1970 indicated that 85 percent of the employable disabled were not working.[2]

An article, entitled "Reintegration of the Severely Disabled Into the Work Force; the United States Experience," (Aaron Krute and Ralph Treitl, Chapter VII of" Social Security and Disability Issues in Policy Research; International Social Security Association, Geneva (1981), documents the dismal results of attempts to integrate disabled workers into the employment marketplace. Although millions of dollars are spent on social security disability support payments, very few disabled workers get jobs. If a person on social security disability earns compensation at a modest level, benefits may be terminated. As a result, many reluctantly choose to remain out of the work force. Only one of every 200 on SSDI ever rejoins the work force. In order to alleviate the problem of social security "work disincentives," Congressmen Steve Bartlett of Texas, Robert Matsui of California, Senator Bob Dole of Kansas, and Donald Riegle of Michigan, have introduced bills (HR 8 and S 1358) which, if enacted, will allow "disabled adult children" to work while taking advantage of a graduated cash benefits program. Also, there is a provision to allow individuals to pay Medicare premiums on a sliding scale basis. Under S 1358 (101st Congress, First Session) the amount of the SSDI benefit will be reduced by fifty percent of the individual's monthly earnings from gainful activity in excess of $85. The goal of the legislation is to encourage disabled individuals to return to work, support themselves without the need of SSDI payments, and contribute to society, to their own independence, and to pay taxes rather than to receive "maintenance" payments.

In 1986 an exhaustive survey of the status of disabled citizens was done by Louis Harris and Associates, Inc., in cooperation with the National Council on Disability, and conducted for the International Center of the Disabled. This study, 134 pages long plus appendices, was based on a sampling of 1000 telephone interviews with disabled people and represents a claimed error rate of two to three percent. The survey involved all aspects of the disabled person's life, including education, social life, income level, inter-societal attitudes, and especially, employment. The employment statistics were appalling. Although 70 percent felt that life had improved over the past decade, TWO THIRDS OF THOSE DISABLED WERE NOT WORKING. This survey included only those disabled within the ages of 16 and 64. Although the Harris survey defined "disabled" somewhat more broadly than other definitions, this factor would tend to increase the number out of work, especially among severely disabled people.

According to the Harris survey, only one in four people with disabilities work full time. No other demographic group under 65 has such a small proportion working, including young blacks. A large majority, 66 percent, of those not working say they would like jobs. Eighty percent of those who work are somewhat satisfied with life, compared with 62 percent of those who don't work. The majority of those not working say that they must depend on insurance benefits or government benefits for support. Forty-seven percent of those not working say that employers won't recognize that they are capable of doing a full time job. Three out of ten said that a lack of accessible or affordable transportation is a significant barrier to work. Thirty-nine percent said that they were not at all familiar with the Rehabilitation Act of 1973, section 504, and twenty-nine percent said they were not too familiar with it. Only eight percent said they were informed about it. According to the Harris survey, disabled Americans are much poorer than non-disabled Americans. Half of all disabled persons, aged 16 or older, had a household income in 1984 of $15,000 or less. Fully one in three disabled persons over 65 report household income of $7,500 or less. Six out of ten elderly disabled persons report a household income of $15,000 or less. The great majority of disabled persons, 70 percent, say they would rather work in an office than at home. One out of four disabled persons has encountered job discrimination because of the disability. About ten percent of disabled persons say they have attended a vocational rehabilitation program, and of this group, 46 percent said the program was no help whatever in getting a job. But four out of ten said the program helped somewhat.

In March 1991 a committee of the Institute of Medicine confirmed the terrible cost to the nation of not employing qualified disabled people. The report of the committee, which was headed by Alvin R. Tarlov, of the New England Medical Center and the Harvard School of Public Health, stated that there were 35 million disabled Americans and that the cost to the nation is more than $170 billion a year for medical treatment, income support to replace lost earnings, and rehabilitation services. The report recommended establishing a broad, national, disability prevention program, to be coordinated by the Center for Disease Control.

The Harris survey is an exhaustive, authoritative, and much relied upon survey of the status of disabled persons. Major contributors and reviewers were Dr. Frank Bowe, Dr. Gerben DeJong, and Dr. Elizabeth Boggs. The results of the survey are appalling. They show that people with disabilities, in general, regard themselves as a minority group, and as such, they suffer as much or more than any other minority group in all aspects of life. A substantial plurality of those surveyed expressed a desire to participate more fully in American life.

The Harris survey just described was confirmed by a recent report of the United States Census Bureau. That report indicated that in 1988, 13.4 million disabled Americans felt that their disability resulted in lack of employment or lack of full employment. The survey found that disabled persons were far less likely than nondisabled to be in the work force, had higher unemployment rates, and were paid less. Overall, only one third of disabled men and just over one fourth of disabled women were in the labor force. Their unemployment rate was double that of non-disabled workers. The earnings gap between the disabled and non-disabled had widened between 1981 and 1988.

The Harris survey is all the more upsetting because studies have shown that disabled people generally make good workers. In 1973, a study examined the job performance, safety record, and attendance of 1,452 physically impaired employees of DuPont, described in Senate Report No.101-116 to the Americans With Disabilities Act (1989) p. 28. The studies addressed the following concerns of employers regarding disabled workers: (1) that insurance rates will skyrocket; (2) that considerable expense will be incurred in making necessary adjustments to accommodate disabled workers; (3) safety records will be jeopardized; (4) special privileges will have to be granted; and (5) fellow employees may not accept disabled workers. A DuPont executive said that every one of these reasons for not hiring the disabled was a myth and without any factual foundation. The study showed that disabled workers performed as well or better than non-disabled workers. Ninety-one percent of DuPont's disabled workers rated average or better in performance. Only four percent of disabled workers were below average in safety records. Ninety-three percent of disabled workers rated average or better with respect to turnover rate. Seventy-nine percent rated average or better in attendance. Fellow employees did not resent necessary accommodations made for employees with disabilities. In spite of these encouraging statistics, prejudice against employing the disabled continues.

Efforts in the last ten years by minority groups and women to acquire the right to equal opportunity have uncovered widespread social stereotyping and personal prejudices. The disabled are similarly discriminated against, not only in employment but in every other area of social functioning: education, sexual expression, recreation, travel, and even in the physical space that non-disabled persons take for granted. Much of this discrimination is due to lack of information or the preponderance of misinformation prevalent among the nondisabled population. Research into attitudes of non-disabled persons toward the disabled reveals an uneasiness in the presence of a disabled person due to a lack of social contact. Many nondisabled persons reject close relationships with the disabled. "I wouldn't want my daughter to marry one." The disabled are thought to be better off with their own kind, perhaps even deserving of their affliction. Disabled persons are thought to be bad tempered, self-conscious, hypersensitive (even if they appear outwardly adjusted), sexually disturbed, and manipulative, using their handicaps to get what they want.

Further research indicates that many non-disabled persons reject the disabled but feel guilty about it. There may be an identification with the disability and an anxiety about one's own vulnerability, leading to a compensatory over protective attitude advocating tolerance and special treatment (rather than acceptance and an equal chance). There is often a mystification about the disability. The disabled person is seen as helpless mentally, physically, morally, yet also as possessing special super normal gifts, such as extrasensory perception, extraordinary patience and humility, or a mystical closeness to the essentials of life.[3]

In 1990 and 1991, the pathetically slow progress toward employment of the disabled was further impeded by political turmoil over the issue of civil rights legislation. Democratic legislators introduced bills that promoted civil rights for minorities; Republicans and the White House wanted more restrictive legislation. The controversy mostly related to blacks, other racial minorities, and women, but it affected disabled people also. The loud public debate served to polarize the country into opposing groups, pitting poor blacks against middle class whites. Although the various bills in Congress were prompted by the issue of dealing with restrictive Supreme Court cases concerned with procedural litigation issues, quotas, and affirmative action, Democrats and Republicans fought over semantics, minor differences, and legalisms. Although the various bills contained language some of which is intelligible only to lawyers, political and economic stakes were high.

The civil rights legislation controversy came about because of difficult Supreme Court cases on employment discrimination. The Supreme Court in the eighties and nineties became loaded with Republican conservative appointees: Justice Scalia, Kennedy, O'Connor, Rehnquist, Souter and Thomas. After a bitter fight, with opposition from disability groups and especially from the Leadership Conference on Civil Rights, the nomination of Robert Bork to the Supreme Court was dropped. In the spring of 1989, a seeming epidemic of cases involving employment discrimination reached the Supreme Court, with predictably unfavorable results for employees claiming discrimination. In Patterson v. McLean Credit Union, decided June 15, 1989, Brenda Patterson, a black teller in a North Carolina credit union, claimed racial harassment under an 1866 anti-discrimination law. (Although the Civil Rights Act of 1964 prohibits employment discrimination, it does not apply to employers with fewer than fifteen employees.) A majority of the court held that the 1866 law did not apply to racial harassment on the job. Brenda claimed she was subject to racial slurs, given more work than whites, assigned cleanup duties not given to whites, not offered promotion or training opportunities, and singled out for racial harassment. Nevertheless, she lost the case, with dissents by Justice Brennan and others.

Benjamin L. Hooks and Ralph Neas, leaders of the Leadership Conference on Civil Rights, which also represents people with disabilities, said the decision was *"the latest in a series of setbacks for employment rights of minorities and women. Indeed, this court term has been a disaster for all those committed to equal employment opportunity."*

Another Supreme Court decision restricting employment discrimination suits was Wards Cove Packing Co. v. Atonio, 109 S. Ct. 2115 (1989). This case involved alleged discrimination against Eskimos and Filipinos in an Alaskan salmon canning factory. The court held 5 to 4 that the plaintiffs, in order to prevail, had to show not only a racial imbalance in the company's work force, but they had to prove that specific employment practices of the employer caused the discrimination. As a result of the Wards Cove decision, 300 employment discrimination cases were thrown out of lower courts. The Wards Cove case involved the question of whether the employee or employer holds the burden of proof. Eighteen years earlier, Chief Justice Warren Burger, in a unanimous opinion in Griggs v. Duke Power Co., 401 U.S. 424 (1971), held that the employer has the burden of showing that employment practices, with a disparate impact on minorities, are required by business necessity. Ward Cove overruled Griggs in effect and held that, no matter how strong the proof of discriminatory effect, the employer need no longer prove that its practices are required by business necessity. Instead, the employee must bear the heavy burden of proving that the employer had no legal justification for its exclusionary practice.

On Saturday, August 26, 1989, the NAACP sponsored a civil rights march up Capitol Hill to the Supreme Court building, where speeches were delivered protesting Patterson and other recent Supreme Court cases seemingly restricting the legal rights of minorities with respect to employment. Hundreds participated in the historic march; it was somewhat reminiscent of the protests of the sixties. Very much a part of it all were the disabled activists; people in wheelchairs, blind and deaf people. A sign interpreter was present for hearing impaired people. An interesting unifying factor is that many black civil rights leaders are aging and use canes or wheelchairs. Needless to say, they are not distinguishing between civil rights for black people and civil rights for the disabled or the elderly. Rosa Parks, who had refused to move to the back of the bus and had been ejected, sparking the bus boycott protests of the sixties, is older now and uses a cane but she was a participant in the march. Mrs. Enola P. McMillan is the black national president of the NAACP and uses a wheelchair. A dramatic figure was the late Joe Rauh, the white civil rights lawyer and activist. Though using a cane, he endured the one mile trek up Capitol Hill to the Supreme Court to speak at the rally. Another cane user was W.C. Patton of the voter education unit of the NAACP. Benjamin Hooks, the veteran NAACP leader, was also there. The chairman of the march was John Johnson of the Baltimore NAACP. Many other disability rights activists, black and white, joined forces at the march.

No doubt responding to the August civil rights march and other factors in the winter of 1990, Senator Kennedy, Senator Metzenbaum, Senator Packwood and many others introduced a bill in Congress to reverse the results in Patterson, Wards Cove, and other restrictive cases. The bill was backed by a bipartisan coalition of 34 Senators and 123 House members. Called the Civil Rights Act of 1990, the bill would have changed the burden of proof in employment discrimination cases, in effect restoring the Griggs rule and overturning Ward's Cove. The plaintiff would need only to show that an employment practice resulted in a "disparate impact" on the basis of race, color, religion, sex, or national origin. If the plaintiff demonstrates that a group of employment practices results in a disparate impact, he or she need not demonstrate which specific practice causes the problem and if the employer fails to demonstrate that such practice is required by business necessity, the case could stand. This provision shifted the burden of proof back to the employer, as required by earlier Supreme Court cases. Further, the plaintiff, in order to show an unlawful employment practice, need only show that race, color, religion, sex, or national origin is a motivating factor, even though the practice was motivated by other factors as well. The bill would also allow compensatory financial damages for complaining women and some other minorities in cases of intentional discrimination. Also, if the employer engaged in an unlawful employment practice with malice or with reckless or callous indifference to the federally protected rights of others, punitive damages could be awarded. Another section would amend the 1866 civil rights act involved in Patterson and makes it illegal to discriminate not only in making an employment contract, but in the performance, modification, or termination of the contract. Although the bill did not mention disabled people, the principles and issues involved in the bill would have a significant impact on employment discrimination suits by disabled people, particularly by providing for compensatory damages.

On February 7, 1990, the Congressional Record recorded the remarks of Senator Kennedy and others in introducing the Civil Rights Act of 1990 (S. 2104). Senator Kennedy spoke eloquently:

> *"From the beginning, civil rights has been the unfinished business of America – and it still is. In the past 35 years, America has made significant progress in removing the stain of bigotry and segregation from our land...In achieving this progress, the role of...the Supreme Court...has been indispensable. For a generation, a long line of landmark decisions has kept the Nation true to the standard of the Constitution and the principle of equal justice under law. In the past year, however, the Supreme Court has issued a series of rulings that mark an abrupt and unfortunate departure from its historic vigilance in protecting civil rights. The fabric of justice has been torn. Significant gaps have been opened in the existing laws that prohibit racism and other types of bias in our society. The Civil Rights Act of 1990 is intended to overturn these court decisions and restore and strengthen these basic laws ...What is at stake in this apparently technical restoration of the law is of profound importance for the future of our country. Ninety-one percent of the growth in the Nation's work force in the 1990s will be women and minorities. If America is to compete successfully in the world, Congress cannot look the other way while the Supreme Court erects artificial and senseless barriers to their full participation in our economy."*

Senators Packwood, Metzenbaum, Hatfield, and Jeffords spoke in similar vein. Senator Packwood specifically mentioned discrimination on the basis of handicap as a motivation for the bill.

On April 4, 1990, the Bush Administration, risking its first confrontation with civil rights groups, threatened to veto the Civil Rights bill. The bill had cleared the Senate Labor and Human Resources Committee by an 11 to 5 vote. Attorney General Thornburgh wrote a hard line letter in which he charged that the bill would result in hiring quotas for minorities, something the sponsors of the bill denied. The administration would substitute a softer bill, reversing only two of the five adverse Supreme Court employment discrimination cases, not including reversing the Ward's Cove case relating to burden of proof. The Leadership Conference on Civil Rights charged that the administration was bowing to the right wing of the Republican party and said that Thornburgh was asking Bush to do what no other President except Andrew Johnson and Ronald Reagan had done: veto a civil rights bill. *"It's totally incompatible to the president's professed commitments to minority outreach and effective enforcement of the civil rights laws,"* said Ralph Neas, executive director of the leadership conference. Thornburgh also opposed the provision for allowing damages, including punitive damages, in flagrant cases.

On May 1, 1990, thirteen representatives of the disability community met with President Bush in the Roosevelt Room of the White House. Among the participants were Mary Jane Owen, Cyndy Jones, editor of Mainstream Magazine, Joseph Shapiro, writer, Boyden Gray, the president's adviser, and others representing blind, deaf, and other groups. The disabled representatives had earlier traveled throughout the country, getting soundings on the needs and questions of disabled people everywhere. The White House press staff had asked for questions to be submitted to the President. Many of the questions related to matters of survival: Medicaid and Medicare funding and the like. It was a productive dialogue, with many diverse and unexpected issues raised and discussed. President Bush emphasized that the federal government needs to be more sensitized to the needs of the disabled. Ironically, that same day there was a physical fitness meeting at the White House, with among others, hunk Arnold Schwarzenegger. TV and other media gave extensive coverage to all sorts of physical exercises and machinery on the grounds of the White House. The disability conference was barely mentioned in the press.

As the summer of 1990 lurched on, dramatic events were taking place. On July 26, 1990, President Bush signed the Americans With Disabilities Act (ADA), which among other things, will prohibit discrimination by private employers against disabled people (see Chapter Six). It was understood that ADA would incorporate damages provisions in a future Civil Rights Act, if one were ever to be enacted, which meant that successful plaintiffs in cases of intentional employment discrimination could be awarded compensatory damages.

Eight days after ADA was signed into law, Saddam Hussein, the Iraqi dictator, invaded Kuwait, plunging the Middle East into chaos. The threat of a severe recession loomed. Congress and the White House seemed paralyzed at the thought of reaching a budget compromise, even though the federal government was on the edge of bankruptcy. In fact, over the Columbus Day weekend of that year, government money for some services ran out and the monuments and museums of Washington, D.C. were closed. Finally, at the end of October, Congress passed a budget provision that would raise taxes and keep the government going, at least for a while.

In the midst of this confusion, the Civil Rights bill reached President Bush's desk. With Congressional and gubernatorial elections only a few weeks away, Bush was caught between a rock and a hard place. Though he had often threatened to veto the bill, at the request of the right wing Republican faction, to do so would risk alienating the black community, the feminist movement, and the disability community. Desperate efforts were made to reach a compromise, and the language of the bill was worked and reworked in a manner that would make lawyers tremble. A ceiling was put on the amount of compensatory damages in employment discrimination cases, and the bill even stated explicitly that it was not designed to impose quotas. The compromise language was not good enough for Bush, and he vetoed the bill on October 22. On October 24, 1990, the bill went back to the Senate for a possible veto override vote. With white supremacist David Duke watching from the gallery, the effort failed by one vote, and the measure was doomed, at least for1990.

Senator Ted Kennedy promised a bill in 1991 and accused Bush of resurrecting the "Willie Horton strategy," a reference to the Massachusetts convict whose furlough became a campaign issue in the 1988 presidential campaign. He said, *"It is bad enough to resort to such disgraceful tactics in a political campaign. But it is far more serious when a president of the United States, who is supposed to be a president of all the people, dishonors his high office, abuses the noble cause of civil rights, and stoops to divisive appeals to prejudice and resentment."*

In 1991 the defeated Civil Rights bill was reworked. There was a warmed over bill from the Democrats, a reheated Republican bill, and various compromise bills. The White House indignantly said that the Democrat bill would require quotas, even though the bill specifically prohibited quotas. In many areas, the differences between the bills were so slight that only lawyers would understand them, but the debate turned into a political brouhaha.

In the fall of 1991, the political controversy over the Civil Rights bill continued, but then something happened. Clarence Thomas was nominated by the White House to replace retiring Justice Marshall on the Supreme Court. Thomas, a conservative black, seemed assured of nomination, but then Anita Hill, a former employee at the Equal Employment Opportunity Commission, filed a sexual harassment complaint against Thomas. After days of televised hearings before the Senate Judiciary Committee, with the whole country mesmerized while watching the disgraceful performance of Republican and Democratic Senators alike, the hearings ended and Thomas was confirmed by a margin of two votes.

Seemingly weary of the polarization of American society caused by the Thomas hearings, President Bush signaled that he would sign a compromise Civil Rights Bill. He did so in short order, on November 21, 1991, after overwhelming approval by the Senate and House. Though the legislative history is somewhat unclear, probably because of the way it was rushed, the act overturns some of the restrictive Supreme Court opinions. It also provides for limited compensatory damages, in cases of intentional discrimination against disabled people.

Although the Americans With Disabilities Act gave disabled workers rights, including the limited right to compensatory damages under the Civil Rights Act of 1991, a right without a remedy is ineffectual. ADA does provide for attorney's fees to be awarded by the court in favor of the prevailing party and against the losing party. But such a remedy is of limited utility. Few lawyers will finance a lawsuit on behalf of a disabled plaintiff, which might take years to conclude and might not be successful. It has been estimated that of all employment discrimination suits that reach a final decision in court, plaintiffs are successful in only ten percent of the cases; employers win ninety percent of them. Even if a plaintiff is successful in court, his remedy is limited to back pay and possibly limited compensatory damages and an injunction requiring employment or reinstatement. With Legal Aid and Neighborhood Legal Services becoming less and less effective, due to under-funding and understaffing, the delivery of legal services involving employment discrimination cases threatens to become more and more unbalanced. While many businesses can afford the costly legal services needed to resist employment discrimination claims as well as claims of lack of access, a ray of sunshine in this dismal picture is that business may find it cheaper to install the ramp, the railing, the elevator, or to simply hire the disabled applicant, rather than to pay the often prohibitively expensive legal fees necessary to resist claims.

Still, the Americans With Disabilities Act, on paper at least, promises greater equality for disabled people in employment. With reliable statistics showing two out of three disabled people completely out of work, employment of disabled people is a goal that society needs to fulfill.

The employment provisions of the ADA are described in greater detail in Chapter Seven. In general, they prohibit an employer from discriminating against a qualified disabled person either in hiring or promotion or in other benefits given employees. The employer must make reasonable accommodation to the needs of the disabled person, for example, by providing a desk accessible to a wheelchair user. In the spring of 1991, the Equal Employment Opportunity Commission came out with proposed regulations under the employment section of ADA. The regulations give an example of what might be a "reasonable accommodation:" providing a page turner for a blind employee, or a travel attendant. Judy Heumann and Mary Johnson complained that the regulations didn't require personal assistance, that is, help in going to the bathroom or a personal care attendant. Judy Heumann has argued that disabled people on the job may need assistance not only in doing the actual work but in going on coffee breaks or socializing with co-workers, something that is a natural part of the working environment. A few private foundations have a similar goal of employment of disabled workers.

The Dole Foundation was organized in 1985 by Senator Robert Dole of Kansas, for the purpose of promoting employment for the disabled. Dole himself has restricted use of hands and arms due to a World War II injury. In June 1990 the Dole Foundation presented awards relating to employment of the disabled. Larry Drake, an actor who plays a mentally retarded man, Benny Stulwicz, on TV's "L.A. Law," along with the show's producer, David E. Kelley, won the Media Awareness Award. McDonald's Corporation won an award for its outstanding efforts in employing disabled workers; over 8000 disabled workers have been employed in its restaurants throughout the country. Other recipients of awards were Chris Burke, who has Down's syndrome, for his role in TV's "Life Goes On," and Chris Templeton, an actress on "The Young and the Restless."

In May 1990, the President's Committee on Employment of Persons with Disabilities held their annual convention at the Washington Hilton Hotel.

After opening ceremonies featuring the Air Force Band Ceremonial Brass and the Presentation of Colors, former Miss Wheelchair Maryland, Cara Stewart sang "America the Beautiful." Chairman Justin Dart Jr. spoke; later President Bush came and spoke of the long overdue need for equal opportunity. He endorsed the Americans with Disabilities Act, which had passed the Senate and was pending in the House. Actress Patricia Neal spoke; Justin Dart gave her a Service Award for her rehabilitation work in Knoxville, Tennessee. Ms. Neal had had a difficult and courageous comeback from a stroke. (She amused the audience with a story of how she had had double vision, and cured it with a glass of champagne.) Other speakers were Edward Rensi, president of McDonald's corporation and Chris Burke (Corky Thatcher) of TV's "Life Goes On."

There was an exhibition of various products for people with disabilities: power wheelchairs, vans, a "mouse" that converts the printed page into audio, computers which can be operated with head motion, and many other ordinary and innovative assistance devices. Some employers set up booths promising employment for disabled workers. Among them was the Central Intelligence Agency, whose flier noted a grim empathy with the disabled: *"Our 'cloak and dagger' stereotypes are as unfair as yours."*

Following a reception sponsored by Dupont, the annual banquet took place, emceed by Jay Rochlin, the departing executive director. The keynote speaker was Dr. Howard House, an "ear doctor," whose list of patients included Ronald Reagan. Dr. House told the anecdote of visiting President Reagan in the Oval Office. The President complained of not being able to hear visitors sitting on settees in the office. With a stroke of brilliance, Dr. House rearranged the settees. Then he suggested to the alarmed President that a microphone be placed under the settees, with a line to the President's hearing aid. With memories of Nixon's Watergate taping of Oval Office conversations, Reagan wisely and hastily vetoed the idea.

At the banquet it was announced that the first annual Harold Russell award would be made for outstanding volunteer work with disabled people. Harold is the well known movie star and long time chairman of the President's Committee, who retired in 1989. In 1946 he won two academy awards for his role in the motion picture *The Best Years of Our Lives.*[4]

As a young sergeant during World War II he had lost both hands. In 1947 President Truman appointed him to the newly formed President's Committee; in 1964 President Johnson named him chairman, where he served, as a volunteer and without compensation, until his retirement in 1989. The Harold Russell award was to become the "Oscar" of volunteerism. To the surprise of no one, the first recipient of the award was Harold Russell. In his acceptance speech he told the story of how he was approached by a lady at an airport who said she had seen *The Best Years of Our Lives* on late night TV. In the movie there had been a veteran who had lost both hands and who looked just like Harold, except he was "*a lot younger.*" Then she advised him to see the movie, because "*It will do you a lot of good!*"

Full employment of disabled people will come IF and WHEN society changes its attitude and realizes that disabled people are not "in general" incompetent, unskilled, ineffectual, and undesirable. We need fewer furniture repairers, basket weavers, and pencil sellers. We need more corporate executives, doctors, lawyers, and politicians. We have had a President who was elected to that high office even though he used a wheelchair. Beethoven was deaf later in life when he wrote some of his greatest works. We have had athletes such as Wilma Rudolph and Glenn Cunningham who have overcome terrible disadvantages to succeed.

Though there are countless, stellar examples of individuals triumphing over adversity, in the area of employment of the disabled, the actual handicap is too often found not in the disabled worker but in society's attitude.

CHAPTER XV

ACCESSIBLE TRANSPORTATION

A young man had recently graduated from a prestigious Ivy League law school. He used a wheelchair as a result of a spinal cord injury. In that year of 1957, he began to apply for jobs. He lived in Jamaica Plain, a suburb of Boston and a long way from downtown, where most of the law firms were located. Finally, after receiving 67 rejections, a solo practitioner offered him a job at $50 a week – downtown, at number 18 Tremont Street. The only way for him to commute back and forth was by taxi, since there were no accessible buses or trolleys. The taxi cost him three dollars each way, or thirty dollars a week. His take home pay was $42 a week, after deductions. That left him with a profit of twelve dollars – for forty hours of work!

One of the biggest complaints of people with disabilities has been, and continues to be, the fact that they have been denied accessible transportation, especially public buses and trains. It's not easy to open your front door and be reminded that, in not being able to drive a car, you can go absolutely nowhere except by expensive taxis or with the help of willing friends who have autos. You can't go shopping or to the movies, you can't get a job, and you can't even get a haircut or a coiffure.

Beginning in the seventies, the disabled community has fought long and hard for accessible transportation. When finally, on July 26, 1990, President Bush did sign the Americans With Disabilities Act (ADA), it required that all new buses, public and private, be wheelchair accessible. Trains, rapid transit, train and subway stations will all be required to be accessible, under complex new rules, many with delayed effective dates. The details of this important act are explained in Chapter Six; this chapter attempts to describe the historical events, beginning with the early seventies, that ultimately brought about the great victory for disabled people in the transportation provisions of the Americans With Disabilities Act.

The Americans With Disabilities Act, in addition to requiring that public places be available and discrimination against disabled people in employment be prevented, also directs that transportation systems, both public and private become accessible. The transportation provisions evolved from other provisions in earlier legislation. In a few years, if ADA is properly implemented, it is expected that the United States will have an almost fully accessible bus and train system.

ADA is certainly the most important civil rights legislation, for disabled people, in this century. As stated so perceptively before, it is the Emancipation Proclamation, the Magna Charta, and the Bill of Rights rolled into one. It places the United States far ahead of any other country in providing the hope of independence and access for disabled people. Hopefully, ADA will be a model to other countries in providing for the United States what will eventually become a totally accessible public and private transportation system.

The philosopher once said, *"Nothing comes easy."* The philosopher must have been dwelling on this issue. The story of accessible transportation has been a long and difficult one; today the disability community is a long way toward realizing this dream. How did this amazing revolution come about?

The Department of Transportation (DOT) is housed in a huge marble-like structure with vertical slivers of glass for windows overlooking Seventh Street, Southwest; in its huge belly lies the Enfant Plaza subway stop. The building is only a few blocks from other Federal agencies; the Housing and Urban Development building is across the street. Three blocks away lies the Mall, and four blocks in the other direction lies the Potomac River. The Department has jurisdiction, among other things, over urban buses receiving federal subsidies, which is most of them, as well as most trains and aircraft.

Over the past two decades, the Department of Transportation has been the focal point of battles that have been waged between disability groups and, you might say, the rest of the world: public and private bus and rail companies, state and local governments, some members of Congress, business interests, and various Chambers of Commerce.

The Americans With Disabilities Act superseded earlier federal legislation, but the history of that earlier legislation is important to note because it reveals pressures and problems, issues and trials, twists and turns that eventually led to the federal law which now requires complete transportation access for disabled people.

Much of that early history involved attempts by transportation companies to restrict the requirements relating to accessible transportation because of concerns about cost and administrative complexity. At times the bus companies prevailed and at times disabled people prevailed. The story involved expensive lawyers and lobbyists hired by the transportation companies. It involved sometimes anguished officials of DOT and truly puzzled, sometimes undecided, members of Congress. It involved innumerable and lengthy House and Senate Committee Hearings which sometimes exhausted the patience of all concerned. It involved court litigation after the arrests of scores of disabled – culminating in the arrest of 104 people in wheelchairs in the Rotunda of the United States Capitol on March 13, 1990. For an excellent discussion of the development of accessible transportation policy by DOT, see Robert A. Katzmann, "Institutional Disability," The Brookings Institution (1986).

Before ADA, DOT's mandate relating to transportation for disabled people derived from four separate federal statutes, described in earlier chapters. Section 504 of the Rehabilitation Act of 1973 prohibited discrimination against disabled people in any federally assisted program or activity, which included most urban bus companies. Section 16 of the Urban Mass Transit Act and Section 105 of the Federal Aid Highway Act also related to the handicapped in federal programs. In 1982 a fourth federal law, the Surface Transportation Amendment, also related to accessible transportation. None of the acts were very specific about details; there was much room for lobbying. None of the Acts applied to strictly private bus companies, such as Greyhound. Before the Americans With Disabilities Act was enacted in 1990, prior federal legislation required, in one form or another, accessible transportation. The Department of Transportation, pursuant to that earlier legislation, issued four sets of regulations. All four were occasioned by changes in Administration after presidential elections, followed by significant court decisions.

Section 504 of the Rehabilitation Act of 1973 prohibited discrimination against the handicapped in any program or activity receiving federal funds. Although the section didn't mention transportation, most urban bus companies received federal funds and thus were subject to section 504.

When the Rehabilitation Act of 1973 passed and was followed by HEW's historic section 504 regulations in 1977 (see earlier chapters), there was a mandate to DOT to issue regulations. DOT was to follow the principles and guidelines contained in the HEW regulations, requiring transportation to be accessible to disabled people, since DOT had jurisdiction over transportation. Other federal agencies, such as Housing and Urban Development, publish regulations relating to housing for disabled people. HEW had a form of umbrella authority over DOT and the other agencies; proposed regulations of DOT and all other relating agencies were to be coordinated with HEW.

In addition to section 504, DOT had to deal with the Biaggi Amendment (Section 16 of the Urban Mass Transit Act) and Section105 of the Federal Aid Highway Act.

At an early date, the Rehabilitation Act and section 504 of that act, as well as the other two statutes, became susceptible to two differing interpretations, one favorable to disabled people and the other favorable to transportation companies. ADA settled the matter in favor of disabled people. The two choices under these earlier acts had been debated by disabled groups and by government and transit officials.

The two approaches can be described as the equal access or "civil rights" or "full mobility" approach, and the special efforts or "effective mobility" approach. The equal access approach generally requires, at least as an objective, that all buses, all trains, etc, be accessible to disabled people; cost is only indirectly relevant. Needless to say, the disabled community has favored this approach. The effective mobility approach, favored by transit officials and state and local governments, has placed a greater emphasis on cost; alternative modes of transportation, such as vans and taxis, are included, but not all buses need be accessible; waivers in appropriate circumstances could be allowed.

Another way of stating the dichotomy is in terms of "mainstreaming" which has come to mean the equal access or civil rights, full mobility approach just described; opposing would be the effective mobility approach.

The Rehabilitation Act of 1973, requiring accessible, federally assisted transportation (which includes almost all urban mass transit), did not mention the word transportation, but there was never any doubt that it mandated accessible transportation. The other two pieces of legislation, the Urban Mass Transportation Act (UMTA) of 1970 and the Federal Aid to Highways Act, amended in 1975, provided federal funding, unlike the Rehabilitation Act. The three acts together formed a kind of shaky tripod on which DOT, and sometimes courts, placed various interpretations. In 1982 Congress amended the Surface Transportation Assistance Act; an amendment related to accessible transportation added a fourth leg to the table, which, however, remained just as shaky.

In 1976 under the Republican Ford Administration, DOT jumped the gun on HEW (which was still in the throes of bureaucratic strangulation as far as interpretation of section 504 of the Rehabilitation Act of 1973) and issued transportation regulations relating to access for disabled people. The 1976 DOT regulations chose an "effective mobility" approach. They allowed alternative transit systems for disabled people; all that was needed was "special efforts" rather than equal access or modification of existing buses. The 1976 regulations were a big disappointment to disability groups.

Two days before the regulations were to be published, President Ford issued Executive Order 11914 (41 F.R.17,871) requiring HEW to coordinate all regulations under section 504. When HEW issued the 504 regulations in 1977 (under Democrat Jimmy Carter), DOT, having turned Democratic, decided that its 1976 regulations should be withdrawn, because the HEW regulations seemed to require equal access rather than effective mobility.

DOT in 1977 and 1978 geared up to rewrite the regulations with stricter requirements regarding accessible buses and other forms of transportation. The department had become populated with liberal Democrats, after Jimmy Carter's victory in the fall of 1976. Brock Adams became DOT's Secretary. He, along with Martin Convisser, Ira Laster, and Leslie Baldwin, had the formidable task of changing the direction of the regulations to full mobility.

DOT issued the second regulations in proposal form on June 8, 1978. They were quite favorable to disabled people. All new fixed facilities, i.e., bus stops and stations, were to be accessible to those who could not climb steps. Comments were invited with respect to requiring all new buses to be accessible. All rail systems had to become 100 percent accessible, and time tables were provided giving a compliance period. At hearings held in New York, Denver, San Francisco, and Chicago, a formidable opponent appeared, The American Public Transit Association (APTA), an organization composed of most of the nation's transit operators. They objected to the requirement of 100 percent accessibility on the basis of cost, impracticality, and lack of utilization by the targeted group. They estimated the cost of capital improvements, retrofitting stations and vehicles and the like, at 3 to 5 billion dollars, double the DOT evaluation. Further, the increased annual cost would exceed $300 million, four times DOT's estimate.

APTA argued that much of the technology did not exist, such as retrofitting rail vehicles, and wheelchair lifts for buses would slow service and were of unproven safety and reliability. New York City objected to retrofitting the entire subway system; the costs would be staggering, in the billions of dollars. Instead they were agreeable to the concept of "key stations" being accessible. APTA very much favored the local option or paratransit approach. The disabled community just as strongly opposed anything less than full mobility. Spearheaded by such groups as the American Coalition of Citizens with Disabilities and the Paralyzed Veterans of America and other veterans groups, they saw the struggle as a continuation of the civil rights struggle of the sixties. The disability groups, in general, favored DOT's full mobility approach, but were impatient with the extended timetable for compliance.

There were others sticking fingers into the pie! The Executive Office, in the form of COWPS (the Council on Wage and Price Stability) and RARG, (Regulatory Analysis and Review Group), both created in response to the problem of a swollen federal bureaucracy, seemed to adopt a middle position, being concerned with costs and administrative complexity.[1]

Forces at DOT shifted to DOT's general counsel's office, in the person of Linda Kamm, who was a strong full mobility advocate, following the precedent of Martin Luther King with respect to the civil rights purpose in securing transportation.

DOT finally issued new regulations (proposed in 1978) in the spring of 1979. They endorsed the concept of equal access. All new buses purchased after July 2, 1979, had to be lift equipped for wheelchairs. A compromise was reached on retrofitting subways; they adopted the New York City "key station" approach. Commuter rail transit had to be accessible within three years, but extensions were allowed for "extraordinarily expensive structural changes."

Although these regulations were supported by the disabled community, trouble was brewing. The Congressional Budget Office (CBO) expressed alarm; costs would total $6.8 billion over thirty years, while the numbers benefited would be few. The CBO in November 1979, published a report analyzing the cost of three options for providing accessible transportation: the "Transit Plan," the "Taxi Plan," and the "Auto Plan."[2] The Transit Plan was concerned with implementing DOT'S new full access regulations, and was considered to be the costliest by far. The Taxi Plan proposed minor modifications to fixed route systems, i.e., a few, new accessible buses and a demand-responsive taxi system. The Auto Plan was like the Taxi Plan except it added a program to purchase specially equipped vehicles for disabled individuals who can drive them. The CBO report based estimates of ridership of disabled people on a Grey Advertising Study which gave extremely low estimates.[3]

A rebuttal to the CBO report was published in 1980 ("Full Mobility-Counting the Costs of the Alternatives") by the American Coalition of Citizens with Disabilities, written by Dennis Cannon and Frances Rainbow, edited by, and containing an introduction by, Dr. Frank Bowe, the Director of ACCD. Dennis Cannon is a quadriplegic and a nationally recognized authority on transportation for disabled people; he is presently on the staff of the Architectural and Transportation Barriers Compliance Board.

The ACCD rebuttal criticized the CBO report as over estimating the cost of adapting a fixed route system and under estimating the per person cost of the local option system. The latter CBO conclusion was based on an unrealistically low number of disabled persons who would request optional service, and an unrealistically low estimate of the cost of such service. Further, the ACCD report objected to the paratransit or local option plan on the grounds that it would really not provide "equivalent service." Equivalent service consists of several factors. First, the general service area and hours of operation should be the same under the paratransit system as for the regular fixed route system. Second, handicapped persons should not be asked to make transfers more frequently than non-handicapped ones. Third, fares for the handicapped should be no higher than for the non-handicapped. Fourth, handicapped persons should not be restricted by trip purpose. Fifth, trip decision time (the time needed to implement a decision to travel) and travel time (the duration of the trip) should be equivalent. (Often, disabled people must reserve a paratransit trip twenty-four hours ahead of time.) Sixth, there should be equivalent capacity, meaning that disabled people should not have to be put on a waiting list because the paratransit capacity has been filled. Seventh, the paratransit system should have equivalent availability, meaning that restrictions such as obtaining a physician's statement or advance registration should not be required. The disabled community, in general, agrees that some form of paratransit system is necessary to serve the severely disabled who are not able to use a fixed route system under any circumstances.

An editorial in *The Washington Post* on April 6, 1979, entitled "Transit for the Disabled: How Much?" questioned the costs, which were estimated at eight billion dollars for subways in five cities.

Another sore point was the fiasco of Transbus. DOT, which is not in the bus design business, had spent $27 million to develop Transbus, which had a floor seventeen inches off the ground and a side ramp for wheelchair access. General Motors, which was modernizing its buses, opposed Transbus and didn't think that buses should be accessible to the disabled, at least if it cost a lot of money. Later, General Motors came up with a version of an accessible bus, but it was not Transbus. As a result of lobbying by General Motors, in July 1976, Republican DOT Secretary Lewis reported that Transbus had been jettisoned and a new bus would be 24 inches off the ground. The Disabled in Action in Pennsylvania labeled it a "disaster." Interest in Transbus was revived under Democratic DOT Secretary Brock Adams. In May 1977, he announced a modified version of Transbus with a floor 22 inches from street level. All new buses purchased with federal funds after September 1979, were to conform to the new design. Again General Motors lobbied, and in July of 1978 the House Public Works Committee, through an amendment, required Secretary Adams to re-evaluate his Transbus order. In September 1978 a confusing compromise was reached. If bus manufacturers couldn't meet the September 1979 deadline, the deadline would be reassessed. Also, bowing to GM, DOT said the bus would have a lift instead of a ramp, and would have two rear axles. The compromise reached in the fall of 1978 was finalized in April 1979, by new DOT regulations. Secretary Adams stuck to a modified Transbus, and all new subway stations and buses were to be accessible. One third of existing subway stations were to be fitted with elevators over the next twelve years, or alternative access "as good or better" must be provided. Within thirty years, 40 percent of existing subway stops had to have elevators. In the case of commuter trains, key stations had to be accessible, and all new cars, whether for subways, commuter rail, or trolley systems, had to be built accessible. Within ten years, one half of all transit system buses had to be accessible. The proposed regulations were reviewed by HEW, and HEW Secretary Califano said they were "creative and responsible."

Another *Washington Post* editorial on May 4, 1979, entitled "Will Transbus Ever Roll?" stated that DOT received no bids from bus companies for the mandated Transbus. The editorial recommended a compromise in design. William Raspberry in an article on April 7, 1979, explained that DOT officials were furious; they had nothing to show for 27 million dollars spent to develop Transbus. The three bus manufacturers, General Motors, Grumman and FLXIBLE had failed to bid on Transbus.

A temporary revival of interest in Transbus occurred when Bill Haddad, Democratic power-broker and co-founder of the Peace Corps, told Dr. Frank Bowe that he had gotten automobile mogul, John Z. DeLorean, interested in Transbus. DeLorean, Frank was told, might build Transbus in Florida. A prototype Transbus dubbed "The little red bus that could" was installed in a parking lot outside the New York Hilton, where a convention of transit officials was being held. The bus was later taken to Washington where Congressional figures had a ride around the Capitol grounds. It was said that the promoters of the "Star-Wars" motion picture might provide financing.[4] Then things started to deteriorate. DeLorean was investigated by the government for fiscal irregularities and was subsequently indicted. His company went bankrupt, and it was the end of Transbus.

In June 1979, the Supreme Court decided the landmark case of Southeastern Community College v. Davis. Although this decision related to education, it interpreted section 504 of the Rehabilitation Act of 1973 which, in its ubiquitous coverage, also related to transportation, so that a ruling relating to education also had an effect on transportation as well as other issues. In the case, Frances B. Davis, a licensed practical nurse, attempted to enroll at Southeastern Community College in North Carolina, in order to become a registered nurse. Frances was refused admission; she was hearing-impaired. The college believed that she would be unable to adequately care for patients. For example, she would be unable to read a doctor's lips if he were wearing a surgical mask. Justice Lewis Powell, writing the unanimous opinion, ruled against the plaintiff and reversed the Fourth Circuit ruling, which had held that she was the victim of discrimination. He said that 504 did not require that the fact that a person was handicapped was to be disregarded. Colleges, he wrote, were not required to substantially modify their programs to admit disabled people. "Substantial adjustments" were not required and "no affirmative action obligation" was mandated. An "otherwise qualified" handicapped person is *"one who is able to meet all of a program's requirements in spite of his handicap."* The plaintiff in the case could take academic classes but would be unable to take other more rigorous classes. In an amicus brief, 27 states, including Virginia and Maryland, as well as the American Council on Education, charged that 504 was *"being transformed by administrative excess into a tool of oppression not contemplated by Congress."*

Needless to say, the decision was a blow to the disabled community. It was seen as not requiring "substantial modification" in programs – only insubstantial ones, such as those not requiring much money. The decision was page one, lead-story in *The Washington Post* on June 12, 1979. What did a deaf nurse have to do with transportation? The disabled community soon found out.

The same liberal Democratic administration that had pushed Transbus, though in vain, and then published the second set of regulations, which were favorable to the disabled community, later faced a setback with respect to those 1979 DOT regulations.

To a great extent, the setback was caused by the Davis case. In June 1979, the American Public Transit Association filed suit to prevent implementation of the new DOT regulations. The regulations were scheduled to go into effect the first week of July 1979, and allegedly would cost five billion dollars. Citing the Davis case, the plaintiffs sought an injunction against the regulations; they wanted reversion to the original 1976 regulations which they regarded as more flexible. In February 1980, Judge J. Louis Oberdorfer upheld the DOT regulations, in the United States District Court for the District of Columbia. Yet another skeptical editorial from *The Washington Post*, on February 9, 1980, commenting on the Oberdorfer decision, said that the issue was relatively narrow: the authority of the DOT Secretary to issue regulations. Costs were not addressed in the decision. "To the handicapped," said *The Post*, *"it is a a matter of rights and dignity, not of separate but equal facilities. But to Congress and all taxpayers, it is a matter of money, technology and timing that will take great amounts of understanding, patience, and compromise to address."* In early May 1980, the House Public Works Committee voted to authorize local transit agencies to provide "special services" as alternative transportation.

The protests of the cost-conscious found an audience when APTA v. Lewis (and Judge Oberdorfer's decision upholding the regulations) was appealed to the District of Columbia Court of Appeals. In an opinion written by Judge Mikva, the Court of Appeals struck down the DOT regulations, which, they said were inconsistent with the Supreme Court's decision in Davis. The new DOT regulations were to require that all buses acquired after July 2, 1979, would be accessible, and at the end of ten years, one half of all buses in operation had to be accessible. The Court of Appeals construed the Davis decision as not requiring *"onerous affirmative burdens."* The DOT regulations, said the court, required *"extensive modifications"* and *"extremely heavy financial burdens."* In a bit of judicial poker playing, since the case had been argued exclusively under section 504, the court remanded to the lower court the decision on whether the regulations might be justified under acts other than section 504, such as the Highway Act and the Mass Transit Act.

But it was a lost cause. Ronald Reagan became President, liberalism became the "L" word, and in 1981 DOT issued a third set of regulations: restrictive interim regulations which withdrew the 1979 regulations.

The Lewis decision, decided in 1981[5] was soon followed by Dopico v. Goldschmidt,[6] which involved the New York City bus system. The Second Circuit said that 504 required *"modest, affirmative steps,"* but again citing Davis, said that relief was limited; the case was remanded for further proceedings.

DOT filled the void, created when the Lewis case invalidated its pro-disabled 1979 regulations and the 1981 interim regulations, by reverting to the "special efforts" concept of the 1976 regulations. However, the regulations were quite vague as to how local transit authorities should proceed.

With the new Republican administration in place in 1981 and with the judicial narrowing of transportation access after Lewis, the disabled community found the equal rights concept in danger of extinction. Ronald Reagan was elected in part because of his vow to rid business of burdensome and meddling government regulations. Vice President Bush headed a task force to review all regulations thought to be unnecessarily burdensome, of which the 504 regulations were thought to be an example, but in the end he recommended no change in 504. Katzmann, in his book "Institutional Disability" says that the vice president felt there would be too much opposition from the disabled community. He wrote his views to Robert J. Funk, of the Disability Rights Education Defense Fund (DREDF); Bush's executive director, Boyden Gray, was influenced by lifelong friend Evan Kemp of the Disability Rights Center. In 1985 presidential control over the rule making process was further expanded, in Executive Order 12498, which gives the Office of Management and Budget control over even drafts of regulations by federal agencies. OMB has the authority, in effect, to veto proposed agency regulations before they even see the light of day. The public may be unaware of such proposals or their disposition by OMB, hardly a democratic process. Whatever the faults in the administrative process before 1985, they did not include government secrecy and censorship.

In 1982 Senators Cranston and Riegle, unhappy with the 1981 Reagan interim regulations, sponsored what became section 317(c) of the Surface Transportation Act, which required DOT to prescribe standards and to publish permanent regulations for accessible transportation for the handicapped and elderly. Yet another, a fourth, set of regulations was finalized pursuant to this amendment in 1986, replacing the 1981 interim regulations. Senator Cranston criticized the trend, in the 1981 regulations, to paratransit or optional transportation which he regarded as leading disabled people into *"third class citizenship"* and *"a total abdication of Federal responsibility"* for protecting handicapped persons from discrimination:

> *"Mobility is certainly critical to these [rehabilitation] efforts, and it is a tragic waste to fund vocational rehabilitation programs and then frustrate those rehabilitation efforts by failing to insure that we continue to make progress in enabling disabled persons to find jobs and to get to and from."*[7]

The regulations published under the Surface Transportation Act were proposed in 1983 but not finalized until 1986. [In Maine Association of Handicapped Persons v. Dole, 623 F. Supp. 920 (D. Me. 1985) the court ordered regulations to be finalized and criticized the "unimaginably leisurely pace" of DOT.] The 1986 regulations[8] adopted a middle approach, allowing transit authorities some flexibility in establishing alternative systems. Local authorities may choose one of three options: paratransit, meaning special vans, taxis, and the like, a fully accessible bus system, or a combination of the two. Six criteria must be met by no later than six years after adoption of a program, after public hearings:

(1) All persons with disabilities who are physically unable to use public transpotation must be able to use paratransit facilities;

(2) The paratransit service must be provided within 24 hours of request;

(3) There must be no restrictions based on trip purpose;

(4) Fares must be comparable to those charged the general public;

(5) Special services must operate the same hours and days as public transportation;

(6) The alternative service must serve the same general area as the public transportation.

The 1986 regulations also contained a severe limitation: there was a "safe harbor" in which the regulations are deemed satisfied if only 3 percent of a transit authority's operating budget is spent on access. The question whether the 3 percent is a "safe harbor" or a ceiling involves more lawyer-talk. If three percent of the budget is spent on accessible transportation, the rules are deemed satisfied, but there is nothing that prevents a transit company from spending more. The practical effect of the "safe harbor" is that it has become a ceiling so that in reality expenditures for accessible transportation have in many cases become limited to three percent of budget.

Beginning around 1986 when these restrictive regulations were issued, a militant wing of the disability movement started protesting. A.D.A.P.T. is the Americans Disabled for Public Transportation. (In 1990, they dropped the periods and are now called ADAPT because their goals have shifted from transportation to other issues, such as personal care attendants.) Mostly wheelchair users, they have crusaded tirelessly for an accessible transportation system. They have gone to court, they have gone to Congress, they have gone to the streets, and they have gone to jail. Many members have been arrested in demonstrations, some of them dozens of times. Composed of some 500 to 700 members, they believe the law is too slow and they want total accessibility

On July 26, 1992, the city fathers in Denver memorialized a 1978 protest by dedicating a plaque on city property in memory of the "Gang of Nineteen," who were the original ADAPT members involved in the first bus protest. This plaque is probably the first tangible recognition by a city of an important milestone in the history of civil rights for disabled people, all the more remarkable because ADAPT has had a program of nonviolent civil disobedience.

In March 1988, some 24 A.D.A.P.T. members rallied outside DOT's headquarters in Washington, D.C. Some eight or ten spent the cold night outside the building, six or seven remained inside. Mitch Snyder, the Washington activist for homeless people, helped out, as did Justin Dart Jr., long involved in disability rights. The group surrounded some buses in a nonviolent protest. Twenty-four were arrested, put in paddywagons, and spent a few hours at the police station, where they were released after paying a ten dollar fine. There have been protests and arrests in Reno, Denver, Dallas, Phoenix, Montreal, San Antonio, Los Angeles, San Francisco, Cincinnati, and Atlanta.

In Hartford, Connecticut, a member spent the night in jail for blocking a Greyhound bus, and in Cincinnati, three people were jailed for six days. A.D.A.P.T. pressured the President's Committee into abandoning San Antonio as the city for their 1991 convention, on the ground that San Antonio is too inaccessible.

In Reno, a showdown occurred in the spring of 1989 between A.D.A.P.T., the police, and Ascuaga's Nugget Hotel, where the American Public Transit Association was having a meeting. According to *Incitement,* a publication of A.D.A.P.T., the disabled members of A.D.A.P.T. marched from A.D.A.P.T.'s hotel to the Nugget, where they tried unsuccessfully to enter the hotel. Struggles to open the doors began. A.D.A.P.T. members were knocked to the ground and five were seriously injured. Beverly Furnace's leg was broken as a guard grabbed her leg and tried to shove her out of the way. Forty seven people were arrested, many in wheel-chairs. The first group who went before Judge Gladstone got into such a fight, "*the judge compared the scene to the trial of the Chicago Seven.*" Most of the group were released on their own recognizance but seven were sent to the

Washoe county jail. The next day, A.D.A.P.T. again kept up the pressure, and at 2 p.m. lined up across the street from the Nugget. On signal, those who could crawl, climbed down from their wheelchairs, crawled across the street and through the cement barricades the police had erected. Again Nugget's doors were locked from the inside. Twenty five people were arrested. This time those arrested were fined $600 and sentenced to three days in jail. A.D.A.P.T. responded with a hunger strike.

Over 30 members were jailed in the Washoe County jail. Though generally treated well, there were some exceptions. One man with cerebral palsy was left without any clothing below his waist. *"Another whose speech was difficult to understand had his communication board taken away and was threatened with being institutionalized in a state school. A quad's request to have his leg bag emptied was ignored for so long he almost went into dysroflexia. A woman who was having seizures was locked down in her cell for over a day without being monitored."*[9] One of the leaders of A.D.A.P.T. has been Mark Johnson of Atlanta, who was arrested at least twelve times and spent time in jail in Phoenix. He regards the obstacles to full accessibility as being primarily caused by "the enemy" which is shifting from the American Public Transit Association to the American Bus Association.[10] In March 1990, 104 A.D.A.P.T. members were arrested in the Rotunda of the United States Capitol. They were lobbying for the Americans With Disabilities Act (see Chapter Six).

But to return to the 1986 regulations, which imposed a safe harbor ceiling of three percent of budget for accessible buses, a restriction to which the disability groups strongly objected. The three percent limitation and the paratransit option were the subject of litigation, in a case known as the A.D.A.P.T. case, from the name of one of the plaintiffs. In 1986, a new lawsuit was brought by seven disabled individuals and twelve organizations, including A.D.A.P.T., against the DOT Secretary. The suit had two basic complaints: that the option, provided in the DOT regulations, to allow local transit companies to provide paratransit only, was an invalid expression of Congressional intent. Further, it was argued that the "ceiling" of 3 percent of budget was unauthorized. The United States District Court for the Eastern District of Pennsylvania ruled that the paratransit option was valid, but the three percent rule was invalid as being arbitrary and capricious. The decision, in other words, gave one issue to the plaintiffs and one to the defendant, DOT. The case was appealed, and in early 1989, the Third Circuit in Americans Disabled for Public Transportation (A.D.A.P.T.) v. Burnley (then the DOT Secretary), affirming the District Court, invalidated the DOT regulations to the extent they seemed to allow a limit of 3 percent of budget for access. Also, portions of the regulations allowing optional paratransit systems were invalidated.

However, there was a dissent, and a few short weeks later, on April 20, 1989, the decision, which was an astounding victory for the disabled groups, was vacated.

The A.D.A.P.T. case then was reargued before the Third Circuit in Philadelphia on May 15, 1989. A.D.A.P.T. members from several states assembled in Philadelphia for protests. On the Friday before the hearing, despite chilling rain, they gathered at the Federal Court building one block from Independence Hall. While all were attempting to go into the United States attorney's office, only four were actually allowed in; the rest were blocked. The next day, Saturday, wheelchair users who were able to crawl attempted to board non-lift-equipped buses by crawling up the steps as others blocked the buses, chanted, and waved signs. Three lanes of Sixth Street in front of the Federal Building were blocked by A.D.A.P.T. members. On Sunday the A.D.A.P.T. group donned colonial style patriotic uniforms. Bernard Baker, Phil Calkins, Yoshiko, and Justin Dart Jr., and Mark Johnson joined the group from the National Council on Independent Living to participate in activities. Two new flags were displayed: one, the work of Randy Harbert, was a red flag with black lettering depicting A.D.A.P.T.'s no steps logo; the other is a red white and blue flag similar to Old Glory, but with stars in the shape of the international wheelchair access symbol. A vigil was attempted at Independence Hall. At the site of the Liberty Bell, Mark Johnson read the Disabled People's Declaration of Independence. At six o'clock the guards physically removed the group from the building. They relocated the vigil in front of the Federal Building.

At 2:00 a.m. they roasted hot dogs and at 4:00 a.m. *"Tim Cook, our lead attorney in the [A.D.A.P.T.] case came by to say hello; he couldn't sleep either. Finally dawn came. A dense fog descended on the city and the temperature dropped. At 10:30 we were allowed into the courtroom...Tim Cook, A.D.A.P.T.'s lead attorney, along with Steve Gold and Frank Laski of PILCOP, did a brilliant job of outlining all the major parts in their argument and answering the Judges' questions..."*[11]

On May 15, 1989, the A.D.A.P.T. case was reargued in the Third Circuit before the full court. Arguing the case was Tim Cook, a Washington lawyer who had contracted polio – an extremely effective advocate. Essentially, the Third Circuit affirmed the lower court's decision that the paratransit option was valid but that the 3 percent budget limit was invalid. The disability groups won on the budget cap but lost on the paratransit issue.

Because of the complexity of the case (the various opinions take 101 difficult footnoted pages) and its enormous significance, some detail is appropriate. Although the opinions delved into difficult legal theory, the lay reader need only keep in mind that the decision allowed the paratransit option, although, with respect to future acquisitions of buses, the implication was that the portion of the regulations requiring them to be accessible, was valid; further, the three percent budget limit on accessible transportation was invalid, presumably leaving it to DOT to determine what, if any, limits on budget might be permissible.

Judge Becker wrote the "plurality" opinion, meaning that there were more votes for that opinion than any other, and concurring opinions resulted in Judge Becker's decision being the decision of the case.

On the paratransit issue, the plaintiffs argued that limiting a transit system to the paratransit option for disabled travelers:

> *"resulted in confinement of its members to segregated specialized transportation facilities, increased the burden of obtaining employment, education and meeting other essential needs, restricted opportunities to take part in cultural, social, and community activities, and abridged the opportunity to exercise guaranteed constitutional rights."*

On the paratransit issue, Judge Becker set forth the complicated history of the four federal statutes involved: section 504 of the Rehabilitation Act of 1973, Section 16(a) of the Urban Mass Transportation Act, section 105 (b) of the Federal-Aid Highway Act, and section 317(c) of the Surface Transportation Assistance Act of 1982. Judge Becker thought that the issue was whether any of these acts required "mainstreaming" and concluded that they did not. This is somewhat of a red herring issue because none of the acts mentioned used the word "mainstreaming" nor is it found in the legislative history. To state the issue as being whether mainstreaming is required, the debater must define what he means by mainstreaming; it is not a legal term with a well understood meaning. Judge Becker thought that *"mainstreaming"* meant *"the total revamping of a mass transit system so that it can accommodate the handicapped in the same facilities and on the same terms as other people."* This is an extreme and novel definition, and the disabled community has never ruled out paratransit for some severely disabled people who are unable to use regular public transportation under any circumstances. Further, the definition seems to imply that retrofitting of all currently used buses is required if "mainstreaming" is the law. It should be pointed out that in the education area, the regulations under section 504, though commonly understood to require "mainstreaming," have always allowed some flexibility in providing alternative education facilities to some severely disabled students, where appropriate. Having defined "mainstreaming" in this extreme and arguably not widely accepted way, Judge Becker could then easily conclude that no such "absolute" mainstreaming was required. But to disabled people, it seemed clear that Congress did in fact mandate "mainstreaming" if the term means, as commonly understood, a general goal of equal access to identical facilities, but with some flexibility allowed for alternative facilities where appropriate.

What is disturbing about the "plurality" opinion is that it clearly rejects the notion that Congress required "mainstreaming" under the court's extreme and unsupported definition of the term, and from that drew the conclusion that alternative facilities exclusively, could be provided as a viable local option. If this logic were carried to the area of education, seemingly local school systems would have the "option" of providing only alternative education facilities for disabled students. Such a conclusion is alarming and would reverse a decade, at least, of common practice and commonly understood legal requirement that disabled students must, as a matter of federal law, be "mainstreamed" to the extent appropriate and feasible, with non-disabled students. The court seemed to reach the shocking conclusion that *"separate but equal"* transportation facilities are permissible. What is particularly alarming is that it has never been seriously contended by anyone that paratransit facilities can in fact be equal. In fact the "plurality" expressed some "discomfort" and "unease" with this fact of life.

In his opinion, Judge Becker vacillated between using the word "mainstreaming" and the even more slippery term of "mainlining," both, when applied to public transportation, seem to conjure up an image of Venetian water taxis and the Long Island Railroad.

Judge Mansmann and three other judges concurring in part and dissenting in part, thought that the statutes required *"if not immediate and complete mainstreaming of the handicapped then affirmative steps in that direction."* It is hard to disagree with his requirement of the more flexible definition of "mainstreaming." Judge Mansmann thought that the plurality decision upholding the paratransit option, invalidated another part of the regulations requiring that all new buses be lift equipped. The plurality, however, felt that the validity of the latter regulation was not in issue. What remains unclear is how there could possibly be a paratransit option as the sole and exclusive means of transportation of disabled people if the regulations also require (and validly so, under the explicit and in some cases implicit opinion of the judges) that all new buses be lift equipped, since inevitably, cities must replace worn-out buses.

Judge Mansmann also thought that the plurality relied too much on the "undue burden" requirement imposed by the Supreme Court in the Davis case. That is, he interpreted Davis as saying that the deaf nurse's hearing impairment was so severe that she could not be considered an "otherwise qualified" handicapped person unless the college *"altered the meaning of the accepted level of training which a nurse must undertake,"* but a person in a wheelchair is "otherwise qualified" to use public transportation and *"physical modification to a bus to make it accessible would not change the meaning of public transit service."* Judge Mansmann said:

> *"I find a marked qualitative distinction between the mobility-impaired's utilization of mass transit—a public program that wheelchair users are entitled to use although not practically available—and a deaf student's capability to participate in a nursing program which selects 'qualified' applicants."*

After minimizing the cost and safety factors involved in installing lifts on buses, Judge Mansmann got to the heart of the matter:

> *"I can perceive no clearer example of non-intentional conduct resulting in uneven treatment to the disabled...than that which emanates from the exclusion to mass transit caused by physical barriers. This inability deprives the handicapped of spontaneous activity, whether it be of an emergency, business or a pleasurable nature. Although not a purposeful means of exclusion, it is further testimony of the 'benign neglect' syndrome, which Congress sought to eliminate."*

The upshot was that Judge Mansmann thought that provisions of the regulations allowing local option or paratransit as the sole means of transportation, were in conflict with other parts of the regulations requiring all new buses to be accessible. The local option provisions violated the concept of equal access, although local option should be permitted for those severely disabled who are unable to use buses under any circumstances.

Although the disabled plaintiffs were defeated on the first issue—the allowance by the court of a paratransit system as the sole means of transportation, and the rejection of a requirement of "mainstreaming"—they were victorious on the three percent of budget issue. Judge Becker said that although DOT could consider costs as a factor in prescribing rules, the three percent limit was arbitrary and capricious. It was pointed out that in many cities with a population of one million or less, expenditures of three percent could not possibly provide a paratransit system meeting the service requirements. Judge Becker left open the question whether DOT could provide some other safe harbor greater than three percent of budget. Further, the three percent rule has no rational foundation and is arbitrary and capricious. Judge Greenberg, in dissent, thought that the three percent safe harbor rule was acceptable.

The upshot of the ADAPT case just described is that local option of paratransit will be allowed as the sole means of transportation of disabled people, although new buses will have to be lift equipped, and DOT will have to come up with a more liberal rule to replace the rejected three percent of budget rule. However, it should be kept in mind that the Americans with Disabilities Act, enacted in 1990, has provisions relating to accessible transportation which will pre-empt provisions under the other federal statutes involved in the ADAPT case (see Chapter Six).

The First Circuit in Rhode Island Handicapped in Action Committee v. Rhode Island Public Transit Authority, 718 F.2d 490 (1st Cir. 1983) concluded that in the light of the Davis case, there is no requirement that all new buses be accessible. The First Circuit decided that handicapped wheelchair users were not "otherwise qualified" because they couldn't board an inaccessible bus. This argument reaches the point of absurdity. The statutes require, in effect, equal access. Another way of stating the issue is that there should be no discrimination. If people in wheelchairs can't park within three blocks of a building that has ten outside steps they can't climb, the ridiculous argument could be made that there is no violation because everyone, disabled and non-disabled alike, can use the same entrance, since there are no barriers deliberately erected to exclude disabled people. Further, if disabled people can't get up the steps, they have no complaint because they are not "otherwise qualified." This argument, if it prevails, can turn the statutes into a cruel hoax. Another case along the same line is Snowden v. Birmingham-Jefferson County Transit Authority, 407 F. Supp. 394 (N.D. Ala. 1975), aff'd, 551 F.2d 862 (5th Cir.1977). In this case, the courts denied relief to a physically handicapped woman who sought an injunction preventing Birmingham, Alabama, from purchasing inaccessible buses. The court said there was no violation of section 504 because the plaintiff, on her own, was able to board the bus. Incredibly, the court said that the plaintiff could not credibly claim that access to transportation is a "fundamental right" on a parity with the right to an education. As applied to the issue of accessible transportation, the court seemed to make section 504, the UMTA, and the Fifth and Fourteenth Amendments to the Constitution, totally meaningless.

Since the Court in the ADAPT case struck down the three percent rule, DOT was mandated to rewrite their fifth set of regulations to conform to the court decision. (It's no wonder if a reader becomes confused as to the direction in which the law was heading at this point. Like the case of Jarndyce and Jarndyce, described in Dickens' *Bleak House, "Innumerable children have been born into the cause; innumerable young people have married into it; innumerable old people have died out of it."*)

In compliance with this mandate, DOT did issue proposed regulations on March 26, 1990, (Notice of Proposed Rule Making, 49 CFR Part 27). When the lawyers in DOT, under the supervision of Robert Ashby, were drafting these proposed regulations, they were well aware that ADA was cruising through Congress, and its passage seemed assured and imminent. The required regulations to be written by DOT to conform to the ADAPT case would be the fifth set of regulations, and when ADA passed, it was expected there would be a sixth. So it seems fair to say that the regulations issued in March had an added flavor with the prospect that ADA would soon be law.[12] Although big government can at times be excruciatingly technical it often does not want to appear wildly inconsistent. Smoothness of policy and the appearance of consistency are often bureaucratic objectives.

Indeed, the proposed regulations issued in March 1990, in conformity with the ADAPT decision and involving pre-ADA law, seemed a foreshadowing of what would happen under ADA. The preamble to those regulations pointed out the obvious: that ADA was pending in Congress and would have great impact. In many places they did not take a definitive position but provided "options" and invited comments from the public. They did provide that all new buses must be accessible, either through lifts or ramps or ramp-kneelers (the reference to ramps could be a possible reincarnation of Transbus). All new buses must accommodate all types of wheelchairs, including power wheelchairs and three wheel scooters. Comments were invited as to types of lifts and types of fastening devices once a wheelchair is boarded. A waiver from the requirement of lift-equipped buses may be provided if it is demonstrated that there is no adequate supply of accessible buses which the transit company can acquire. Some small towns and rural areas have "demand responsive" systems, meaning that there is no fixed route service but buses will go as where, and when, needed by the public. In this case, the requirement of lifts on new buses would not apply if the system, when viewed in its entirety, provides a level of service equivalent to that provided non-disabled passengers.

On the paratransit issue, an alternate form of transportation would be available for those who can't use fixed route buses. Comments were invited concerning disabled people who "can't use" regular buses. Five service criteria are required for a paratransit to be in conformity with the law: there can be no limitations based on trip purpose; fares for paratransit must be "comparable" to fares for regular buses. paratransit service must be available during the same hours and in the same service area as regular buses. No final decision was made as to "response time" meaning the time elapsing between a call by a disabled person for paratransit transportation and the actual providing of the service. Comments were invited on that point. Finally, the regulations provide that the undue burden standard of the Davis case applies only to paratransit. In other words, all new fixed route buses must be accessible without regard to whether the requirement imposes an undue burden. But paratransit service is required only to the extent that it does not impose an undue burden. The question of what is an undue burden was left to further comments and development, but it could depend on whether fares would have to be increased or service reduced. On the whole, these proposed regulations issued in March 1990 were favorable to the disability community and were a harbinger of things to come under ADA.

It was indeed a momentous occasion when on July 26, 1990, President Bush actually signed the Americans With Disabilities Act! On October 4, 1990, DOT published regulations that finalized some, but not all, of the issues dealt with in the proposed regulations. In conformity to the Third Circuit opinion, they removed the three percent cost cap. Also, under pre-ADA law, a bus system could provide either accessible buses or a special service system. Faced with an ADA requirement to purchase accessible buses and to avoid switching to paratransit, or switching from paratransit to accessible buses, the regulations require the continued maintenance of whatever special service system the entity had, pending the effective date of ADA (ADA has its own paratransit requirements). The regulation also provides that compliance with ADA is necessary in order to receive UMTA financial assistance. Another part of the final regulations (49 CFR Part 37) provides some but not all the rules for implementing ADA. ADA in general required that certain train vehicles and buses purchased or leased after August 25, 1990, must be accessible. The final regulations repeat that mandate. At the same time, the explanation to the regulations notes that study is continuing with respect to certain other requirements of ADA, notably the paratransit requirements and the undue financial burden provisions. Further, DOT invited additional comment with respect to types of wheelchairs, scooters, and the like that must be boardable. For example, the total weight, with rider, of some mobility units exceeds 800 pounds! Also, there will be continuing study, in cooperation with the Architectural Barriers Board, of types of restrainers or fasteners once the chair is boarded. The explanation also clarifies that ADA applies to private entities that may contract with public entities to provide what is essentially public transportation. (ADA may not be avoided by contracting out to a private bus company, for example.) Further comment is invited with respect to auxiliary devices to assist deaf and blind travelers, for example, TDD telephones, vocal announcement of bus stops en route, and so forth.

DOT Chief Counsel Stephen Diaz and Deputy Chief Counsel Ted Munter both expressed the view that, aware of the many evolutionary changes in the regulations that have occurred in the past, whatever rules are eventually adopted will be both reasonable and, hopefully, permanent.[13]

Thus, the long and tortured history of DOT's attempts to deal with accessible transportation, is coming to an end. The Americans With Disabilities Act, in its transportation provisions, is the culmination of many years of attempts to deal with the issue under earlier federal legislation, such as section 504. Chapter Six describes how the Americans With Disabilities Act came to be enacted.

ADA in its transportation provisions was an overwhelming victory for disabled people. Considerable sensitivity to bus and rail companies was shown however, in the form of delayed effective dates and provisions for paratransit. Ironically.within two weeks of the passage by the House of ADA, (on May 22,1990), the Greyhound bus company filed for bankruptcy. All during the lengthy Congressional hearings on ADA, Greyhound complained bitterly about the increased costs if Greyhound were required to install wheelchair lifts on buses. Greyhound officials complained that ADA would result in either decreased service or higher fares. But the bankruptcy of Greyhound was not caused by ADA. The effective date of ADA was delayed, and it hadn't even been signed by the President. The bankruptcy was caused by a crippling strike by the Amalgamated Transit workers which had produced violence and animosity. It was also caused by huge amount of junk bond debt that had to be serviced, and when Greyhound took over its major competitor, Trailways, more junk bonds were issued. The bankruptcy raised fears that Greyhound would cut back on national bus service, especially in small towns and rural areas in the midwest.

ADA is the seemingly final event in two decades of searching by Congress for solutions to the difficult problems regarding transportational access for disabled people. DOT so far has come up with five sets of regulations under earlier statutes and is required by ADA to come up with a sixth. The focus has shifted many times, sometimes favoring disabled people and sometimes the transit companies and state and local governments. The role of government through the years has been criticized as being inconsistent, procrastinating, wastefully slow, and indecisive. On the other side of the coin, it could be said that government (in the form of DOT) has merely responded, in a more or less disciplined way, to the democratic process. Each duly elected administration is entitled to its policies, and policies have changed as the party in power has changed. Bills have been proposed, lobbyists engaged, hearings held, and votes counted. Court actions have been instituted, briefs written, oral arguments given, and written decisions have been issued. It is difficult to think of a public issue that has received more attention than accessible transportation. All interested parties have had their say and no one can complain of haste or exclusion from the deliberating process. A dictatorial government might decree the desired policy with the stroke of a pen, but that is not the democratic process. If the law in this area is not exactly a triumph of the democratic process, it is at least a workable, though long delayed, solution.

The future can neither be predicted nor controlled, without some understanding of the past. The history of two decades of struggle for accessible transportation is important because that history points the way to the future.

With the passage of ADA, disabled people have achieved a long sought goal. The expectation is that after a period of years, the entire national transportation system in the United States, both public and private, will be totally accessible – a truly revolutionary achievement. Disabled people fought long and hard for this dream and they won! They overcame.

CHAPTER XVI

THE FUTURE

Tim McClusky, 29, is a proud new homeowner! Ten years ago he broke his neck, at the C-4 level, in a swimming pool accident. He then got a two year degree in computer science. With the help of Lift, Inc., in New Jersey, he got a job as a programmer analyst at the Marine Midland Bank in New York. McClusky cannot use his hands but uses the Liaison System, a chin controlled joy stick that runs his computer, printer, telephone, lights, and radio from his electric wheelchair. He works on two monitors; one is a regular PC, the other, the Liaison, has an on-screen keyboard for typing. With the joystick he moves the cursor along and stops on a letter or number; in this manner, he types 20 or 30 words a minute. He now works four days at home and one in the office. He recently got a promotion and bought his own residence.

Although the optimist likes to believe that the evolution of time brings with it an evolution of perfection, this is not always true! In science, we are used to the idea that this year's TV, typewriter, computer, microwave oven, automobile, and so forth, is better than last year's. Yet in the social sciences, there is often retrogression. Each debate concludes as the last; it's sad but true that in the political arena, nothing is permanent. The ebb and flow of politics are inevitably no more predictable than the shifting of grains of sand on an ocean beach. At times, whole civilizations seem to retrogress; the grandiose ancient Roman civilization gave way to the dark ages; the beauty and culture of ancient southeast Asian civilizations gave way to the blood baths of the Khmer Rouge. In the name of religion and its supposedly civilizing influences, Northern Ireland has become, and remains, a battleground – a sea of hate in the name of what is holy. The Middle East is as explosive as land masses on the edge of an earthquake fault, and the civilized nations of Europe gaze, seemingly mesmerized, at the atrocities in Serbia and Bosnia. In 1993 it was revealed that Serbian forces dragged 200 wounded Croatians from Vukovas hospital, machine-gunned them and buried their bodies in a mass grave.

Perfection seems more destined in the field of the physical sciences. It is rare that a technological breakthrough or discovery is lost, or that physics, chemistry, astronomy have retrogressed. As the wise man said, it is impossible to unring a bell. Yet paradoxically, the inexorable march of science carries with it the latent seeds of total destruction of everything else. The perfect nuclear bomb can bring with it the perfect final solution.

The disability movement has been very much a combination of the validity of ideas and the political drive and pressure exerted by people with disabilities to achieve goals believed desirable. To the extent either of these ingredients is missing, the movement can be expected to falter. But advances can be expected in the area of medical and technological improvements. Perhaps one day blind citizens will see, deaf gentry hear, and lame humanity walk! It is a goal that no one can reject. As with the advance of civilization in general, improvements for people with disabilities seem more probable in medicine and technology than in civil rights and societal attitudes.

A cloudy crystal ball predicts that advances in medicine and rehabilitation will continue, while civil rights will lag behind, perhaps because civil rights, unlike medical technology, depend entirely on the consensus of society. In 1986 it was firmly established that an infant born with spina bifida would probably need surgery and a shunt operation to drain fluid from the brain. With medical science having discovered this fact, it is impossible to turn back the clock. But civil rights is another matter. Baby Jane Doe was just such a child, and her parents refused to give the consent needed for surgery. The federal government sued the hospital, claiming that the child was an otherwise qualified handicapped person who had been discriminated against in violation of section 504. The government lost. The courts wrote lengthy opinions attempting to justify the result which got into difficult legal theory, semantics, public policy, and other complicated and controversial subjects. In effect, the doctors said *"Yes"* to Baby Jane Doe, but lawyers and judges said *"No."* As a result, the necessary surgery was never performed.

In December 1990, civil rights for disabled children caught up, to a degree, with medical advances. The Social Security Administration had denied for years that certain disabled children were "disabled" in the legal sense, so as to be eligible for disability benefits. Some children with major physical defects and mental impairments, such as autism and Down's syndrome, develop mental delays and don't get benefits because the impairments might not be included on the Administration's "list." In Zebley v. Sullivan (493 U.S. 521 (1990)), the Supreme Court decided that, when a particular disability was not on the "list," the Social Security Administration should give a child an "individualized functional assessment" to determine whether there was "severe" impairment. Catching up with medical progress, SSA published new "lists" of specific impairments, which will make many thousands of youngsters eligible for social security benefits for the first time. Once more, this didn't just happen; it was pushed by advocacy groups such as the District of Columbia's Mental Health Project and Philadelphia's Community Legal Services.

Amazing advances will continue to be made in computer technology to assist the severely paralyzed. Some quadriplegics are able to use only facial muscles or eye movment. In 1992 a small company in Fairfax, Virginia, LC Technology, developed a computer that responds to eye movements – a long sought goal. A video camera focuses on an individual's eyes, which in turn are focused on different keys on a key board. The camera reads the key which allows the individual to type, speak with a synthesizer, play chess, and perform many other functions that were previously impossible.

The future will also see continued efforts to deal with the issue of pain. In March 1990, Washington, D.C.'s errant mayor, Marion Barry, arrested on cocaine charges and with his political future in doubt, apologized to high school students for the "pain" he caused them. In other speeches, he said he was a human being like everyone else and, like everyone else, suffered pain. He wanted to share this pain with others. Disabled people have enormous pain, but most do not want to inflict this pain on others. "Sharing" pain may be beneficial in the sense that there comes an empathy or understanding that the entire human race suffers pain, disabled or not. There is something therapeutic about knowing that your neighbor is also having hard times. But shared experience of pain can quickly become sadistic enjoyment of the misfortune of others. No afternoon "Soap" would survive without a generous portion of trauma and tragedy. In this sense, pain becomes a financially successful media event. Pain is also regarded as beneficial by some venerable religions. The soul is supposed to be cleansed and become more spiritual. The sufferer is supposed to become ennobled, courageous, and is expected to "overcome." To some extent this idea has been borrowed by the health professionals, some of whom believe that a positive attitude will cure all ills. The physical therapist is fond of the cliche: *"No pain, no gain."* Another religious evaluation of pain is that it provides a test of sanctity, to be rewarded in heaven. The season of Lent is supposed to inflict more pain on an already pain-weary population; today it is hard to find an individual who enthusiastically looks forward to Ash Wednesday, because of trials to be endured and greater rewards to be earned in heaven. Nature has a way of decreeing Lent all year round. "Sharing" pain with others, if it means adding to the other's already pain-filled cup, seems ridiculous. It is hard to conclude that beneficial consequences always follow pain. While pain makes some people strong, hardy, cheerful, determined, and resourceful, it makes others sour, angry, hostile, and depressed. Pain, no doubt, is useful and necessary as a short term treatment for some ailments. But if the treatment is unsuccessful, or even if it's successful, it is irrational to continue the painful treatment interminably. In some respects, pain can have an inevitably beneficial effect. For example, a paraplegic who has no sensation in the legs may have no pain there, but is more likely to suffer skin sores and other problems. The body that sits too long sends pain signals which advise the sitter to move around. The pain of severe depression can become a motivator. Philosophers have long debated why pain is universal, whether it is necessary, whether it can or should be eliminated, and whether there is a theleological result of a greater benefit. The unsophisticated, or at least undisciplined, may resolve all these weighty questions by taking to liquor or drugs, with the goal of banishing pain. Disabled people suffer pain too diverse to catalog. In addition to physical pain, there is the pain of loss, of isolation, of enforced boredom, the pain of the mind, of poverty, and the pain of discrimination. Perhaps there is a reasonably coherent consensus that, if pain cannot or should not be eliminated entirely, society should at least have a goal of eliminating or reducing unnecessary or useless pain.

To examine the past is to find a key to the future. We look around and we see handicapped parking signs everywhere, curb cuts in sidewalks, ramps, railings, and elevators. It could be argued, especially in the light of the shockingly dismal employment rate of disabled people and their low income levels, that these outward signs of progress are merely superficial, cosmetic, and disguise more serious problems. Perhaps these outward changes are symbolic only: as much to appease the conscience of an unperceptive society as to provide real help to disabled people.

There is no doubt that greater progress is needed in employment and full social integration. Hopefully, a job should be tailored to an individual's talent, and not to the limited physical function left after accounting for the impairment. We need more concert violinists like Itzhak Perlman and fewer computer programmers, more sculptors and fewer keypunch operators, more writers and fewer taxicab dispatchers, more corporate executives and fewer newsstand operators, more playwrights who are blind and fewer blind teachers of blind students. Too many disabled people make careers in the disability field, which some would call a ghetto. Deaf people become teachers of deaf students and by some magical process of elimination, many disabled people become employees of the President's Committee or the Equal Employment Opportunity Commission. Colleges welcome the disabled student but on graduation, the alumnus or alumna must fend for himself or herself in finding a job. Perhaps the fact that there are so many "inspiring" newspaper articles about disabled people who achieved great success in their chosen careers illustrates the exception that proves the rule. Success is deemed newsworthy because it is unique. There are few newspaper stories about successful redheads.

A significant development in 1991, and one that can be expected to continue in the future, is the employment of disabled people in TV and other commercial advertising. In the mid-seventies, Sandra Gordon asked a Minnesota advertising company to use a disabled person in advertising. The company rejected the idea; they told her they would lose sales, it would scare people, and they used the word "disgusting." In recent times, especially with the catalyst of the

Americans With Disabilities Act, this attitude has changed dramatically. McDonalds, Levi Strauss, and Dupont have used disabled people in advertising of all kinds. Today, large chains such as Marshall Field's, Eddie Bauer, and Nordstrom regularly use disabled people in their catalogues. Kmart's television commercials include shoppers in wheelchairs.

Advancement can be expected in the area of prevention and treatment of mental retardation. Genetic engineering may someday reduce the numbers of babies born mentally retarded. Brain tissue transplants may result in improvement of mental capacity. Inevitably, research into the workings of the human brain, motivated by a desire to help the mentally retarded, will overflow to the benefit of humanity in general

On CBS "Sixty Minutes" in May 1989, there was a discussion of some of the remarkable achievements of mentally retarded people. Alonzo, retarded and living in an institution, has become a brilliant sculptor of horses, other animals and people, with his life size sculptures selling for $45,000. Without ever having had an art lesson, the sculpturing talent was innate, born of a portion of his damaged brain possessing incredible memory and creativity. Another accomplished artist who is retarded is Leslie, who has cerebral palsy, is blind, and is unable to walk unassisted. Given a piano by his mother, he quickly displayed an incredible talent for remembering musical passages and repeating them flawlessly. Today he has a concert tour that takes him throughout the United States and foreign countries. Another "savant" as these prodigies are called, is George, also retarded and living in an institution. Though unable to multiply simple figures, he has an unbelievable knack for determining the day of the week for any given date, past or future. In 1988 Dustin Hoffman and Tom Cruise starred in *The Rain Man*, about an autistic man, confined to an institution, who had a prodigious memory. Joan of Arc, who battled the king and was burned at the stake, is said to have suffered from epilepsy; her visions and hallucinations were triggered by the pealing of church bells. In some mysterious way, "shortcomings" perceived by society may, in fact, disguise incredible talent.

There is still much to be done in the area of building access, transportation access, employment, housing, and education access. All of these improvements are promised, on paper at least, by the Americans With Disabilities Act of 1990, but the goals of disabled people will continue to meet opposition from cost providers. A balancing of varying interests will probably occur. To the extent that people with disabilities fail to press their case on government and industry, their goals will fall short. Squeaky wheels will always get oil, but no one can expect the transit industry or private entrepreneurs to be shy about advancing their own positions. The government will more and more become stakeholders, steering a middle course between extremes on either side. Although government officials present their own views, those views will be successful only to an extent that results are judged acceptable by the affected groups. Although originally, in the seventies, the strong arm of government provided the initial launch down the road to access and independence for disabled people, the unilateral influence can hardly be expected to continue; today the issues, implications, and costs involved are too widely publicized to go unnoticed.

The United States has, so far, been a leader in civil rights for people with disabilities, and there is still much to be done. Success in the United States toward access for disabled people will lead the way for other nations to provide access and independence. The United States, in this regard, is far ahead of any other country, but many European countries have programs which the United States lacks. For example, government funding for personal attendants is provided in Finland, England, and other countries, something generally unavailable in the United States. European countries do require architectural access and, in many cases, provide government funds to help businesses do so, unlike the United States, which generally requires businesses to bear all costs of adaptation. While in the United States access and independent living programs are thought to be a matter of civil right, in European countries the emphasis is less on civil rights and more on socialistic funding of access programs bordered with a tinge of welfarism.

Civilized , mature, and culture-laden countries such as France, Italy, Spain, Germany and others are woefully behind in providing an accessible landscape, although progress is being made. In Paris only a small percentage of city sidewalks have curb cuts although most museums are accessible. The Metro is not accessible and may never be, but van taxis can be ordered in advance to carry wheelchair users. Too often, European countries are exempt from access requirements for historic buildings, so that a disabled person is often relegated to admiring famous sites from the street. At times the nations which boast the greatest advances in culture and civilization are the farthest behind. Civil rights and accessible environment do not even exist in many places in Asia, Africa, the Middle East, the Caribbean, and in South and Central America.

Strangely, even countries which have suffered from war induced disabilities have often ignored the welfare of their disabled veterans. In 1990 in Vietnam, long after the war, thousands of disabled veterans are confined to institutions that are truly hell holes, with little or no support from the government. Over 300,000 disabled Vietnamese veterans from several wars are tucked away in Vietnam, hidden from view. Many are spinal cord injured.

Vu Trung Hien was spinal cord injured in 1968 by shrapnel; he wonders, like many American veterans, whether the war was right or wrong. Hoang Dinh Trung, similarly disabled in 1972, said he would like American veterans to come and see how the Vietnamese disabled live. Hopefully, the future may see greater progress, under the leadership of the United States, in spearheading improvement in the lives of disabled people in other countries.

In 1991 members of the Vietnam Veterans of America Foundation went to Phnom Penh, Cambodia, to help organize habilitation centers for Cambodian disabled veterans. Cambodia has the world's highest incidence of amputee veterans. One American, Ron Podlaski, twice wounded in the Vietnam conflict, was a help to many Cambodian veterans, almost all of whom were blind or amputees.

Another likely trend in the future is the reallocation of dwindling governmental and insurance funds. Today more than 100 billion dollars (some say more than 200 billion) of government and insurance money is spent on "support" of disabled people. The money provides the necessities of life – food, clothing, and shelter – but does little to further the goal of independence. In fact one could argue that the money is being spent to keep disabled people out of the job market. There could, in the future, be an allocation of these resources into funding for independent living programs and personal attendant assistance for severely disabled people, regardless of income levels. The aggressive and sometimes militant organization, ADAPT has agitated for Medicare and Medicaid funds to be diverted from nursing home maintenance for severely disabled people to providing home personal care attendants. This protest effort will continue, and bitter confrontations will result in more members of the disability community being arrested and jailed on behalf of the civil rights cause in which they so firmly believe.

A strong argument is made by some that even prosperous disabled people should not have to pay a severe financial penalty for being disabled, and personal attendants should be provided without regard to a means test. The Attendant Services Network, sponsored by Judy Heumann's World Institute on Disability in Berkeley, has lobbied for a bill in Congress to provide personal assistance. If a severely disabled person has an income of say $30,000, but it costs $20,000 for personal assistance, equipment, therapy and other essentials, leaving only $10,000 for food, clothing, and shelter, the quality of that person's life will be very low indeed. Though the income level of some disabled people may be high, a strong argument can be made that the enormous costs associated with severe disability ought to be spread out in society as a whole and not concentrated on the individual. More insurance coverage may be provided for expensive durable medical equipment, possibly including electric wheelchairs or even lift equipped vans. All these potential shifts in funds are directed at providing true independence and consequently freeing up huge amounts of money currently being spent on mere support or welfare.[1]

Although federal and state laws can impose specific requirements, such as buses being equipped with a lift for wheelchairs, all the laws in the world will not necessarily change society's attitude toward the disabled. Mainstreaming of disabled children into regular school programs is beginning to provide greater acceptance by the younger generation at least. Television is beginning to show people in wheelchairs in commercials. Disabled actors and actresses are beginning to appear in TV dramas. Young Chris Burke, who has Down's syndrome, became, in the fall of 1989, a star on the show "Life Goes On." This breakthrough could not have occurred ten years ago. People in wheelchairs or with seeing eye dogs are using public transportation to commute to ordinary jobs and no longer receive the stares they once did. The United States is becoming an aging population, and many elderly may experience disabilities they never had before. The political influence of the elderly and their shared concern with disabled people may unite into a common cause. If a septuagenarian like Ronald Reagan can become president, perhaps a president with a disability may not be far behind and, unlike Franklin Roosevelt, with the disability acknowledged, not hidden away through fear and shame. Hopefully, as society becomes more familiar with disabled people who all too often had been isolated and invisible, the myths, prejudices, and shame will disappear.

The United States, as other democracies, see themselves as advocates for equality—equal justice before the law, equal protection, equal opportunity, equal votes, equal everything. To the extent that disabled people are regarded as not equal, the system is flawed. The imbalance, perhaps, disturbs the mathematicians and other perfectionists more than anyone else. The Nazi campaign which cruelly exterminated thousands of the physically and mentally "unfit" was done in the name of perfection of the German race. A strong argument can be made that the extremists views of German doctors, which originated after the turn of the century and recommended extermination of the severely disabled, influenced the much later Nazi program of genocide of the Jews. The technique of extermination by gas in the shower room did not originate with the Nazis but had begun much earlier, with German doctors in the "killing hospitals" for the disabled.[2]

Paradoxically, "the survival of the fittest" theory still applies, super imposed, in a clumsy and unpredictable way, on the concept of equality. The person who won the lottery is not equal to the person who didn't. The Superbowl championship team is supposedly the better team, certainly is the most revered, and, of course, better rewarded financially! Perhaps reconciliation between the idea of equality and the idea of victory over inferiority is explained by the concept that everyone has an equal opportunity; if one only tries harder, victory will be achieved over the less ambitious. This idea is dangerous when applied to the disabled community. Some justify society's neglect on the ground that we are all fishes in the sea; there is no need and no obligation to protect the poor swimmers. Disabled people themselves advocate the concept of independence, self-motivation, and self-survival, but in moderation. Disability groups do want equality, in the sense that they want a level playing field, with equal opportunities to participate and compete. All the determination, independence, courage, and self-sufficiency in the world is not going to get a person in a wheelchair into a building with no access.

The concept of equality is matched by an equally dangerous doctrine: Social Darwinism. Through the process of evolution, simpler forms of life have developed into more complex organisms. The process occurs in part because of the elimination of the weak, the deformed, those less likely to adapt. Some would apply this concept to people. The problem of euthanasia or mercy killing is being debated today even more universally than in previous times. Lives are being prolonged by artificial, medical treatment, as never before. People in comas can live indefinitely. Social Darwinism mixed with some well meaning desires to alleviate suffering led to the euthanasia program of the Nazis during World War II. If severely disabled people were in extreme pain and, also, were regarded as genetically inferior likely to produce inferior offspring, the solution would be simple: kill them and you would, so to speak, get two birds with one stone. These dangerous ideas still persist. Many disability groups refuse to recognize any situation where induced death, whether by active or passive means, is acceptable. To them, it is terrifying to consider trying to separate those deemed worthy or unworthy to live.

Disabled persons are sometimes seen as necessarily unequal and inferior, though that may not be the case. Some blind people argue that in a smoke-filled airplane they are more capable of getting out than their sighted fellow passengers. Deaf persons have participated in equilibrium and balance testing for the space program. Some disabled people have developed other talents to a superlative degree, in spite of—perhaps because of—their disabilities. Stephen Hocking is cruelly disabled, using a wheelchair because of Lou Gehrig's disease; he communicates with difficulty. Yet he is widely regarded as the most brilliant theoretical physicist since Einstein. As a painting is enriched by its shadows, the whole of the picture must be appreciated in its entirety. The goal should be to discern and prize diversity; a nation of clones has no future.

Speculation as to future conditions for disabled people intrigued author Kurt Vonnegut. In "Harrison Bergeron" the future had already arrived and everyone was equal. The overly strong and athletic had to wear chains around their necks in order to impede their activity, so that they wouldn't be stronger than anyone else. The exceptionally bright had radio receivers inserted into their brains which impeded the flow of exceptionally brilliant thoughts. It was the ultimate level playing field:

> *"The year was 2081, and everybody was finally equal. They weren't only equal before God and the law. They were equal every which way. Nobody was smarter than anybody else. Nobody was stronger or quicker than anybody else. All this equality was due to the 211th, 212th, and 213th Amendments to the Constitution, and to the unceasing vigilance of agents of the United States Handicapper General."*

As we enter the space age, disabled people have a role and a place. The millions of dollars spent on medical research may have a spillover effect on space exploration; conversely, space technology has already benefited disabled people. Robots and movable artificial limbs are being perfected, to the benefit of everyone.

Indeed, disabled people can provide a bridge between our civilization and the "others." People with genetic defects were born different from others, but this was caused by an unusual but perfectly natural rearrangement of cosmic dust out of which we and those other alien civilization were created. In our world, there are more two legged, two handed and otherwise normal men and women than any other kind. There are Siamese twins, with joined bodies, but they are the exception. Yet, what is to say that there must inevitably be more non Siamese twins than Siamese twins. It is more a matter of accidental numbers of bodies shaped by an individualized but not immutable blueprint than an inevitable consequence of some required law. Although man may be created in God's image, it seems clear that what is God's image is not necessarily defined by the perfect body of an Arnold Schwarzenegger.

The "Thalidomide babies," now young adults, were born without arms or with shortened hand flippers, or without legs or with flipper-like feet. There are hundreds of them functioning today in a world to which they have adapted, probably better than the world has adapted to them. One such person, as a teenager, retreated into a fantasy world before the TV set. His hero was Mr. Spock of *Startrek*. The strange and unusual beings on the program inhabiting other planets seemed more his friends and playmates than the "normal" children of his neighborhood.

In 1991, on TV's "Wonderworld," there was a show starring Lynn Redgrave as the teacher, and Jordan Marder as "Danny." Danny, a twelve year old, had been paralyzed from the waist down, but desperately wanted to go into space as an astronaut. After writing letters to NASA and being turned down, he locked himself in a space capsule in a space museum. The authorities relented, trained him, and sent him into space, where, free from the cruel effects of gravity on his wasted body, he floated euphorically in space.

Tiny planets or moons revolve around parent planets, which revolve around a sun, which spins in a cosmic dance. Every human being is discrete in the sense that he or she is born alone, lives alone, even in a family, and dies alone. A more or less complete mechanism, we are like so many wrist watches, unique unto ourselves, totally self-contained. The moons around Jupiter march to Jupiter's tune, attracted by Jupiter's force of gravity. The pull of Jupiter could be regarded as a string, to which the moons are attached in a subservient way. Or the moons can be regarded as totally themselves and dancing to a tune dictated by the same laws that govern the mother planet. So too, disabled people are discrete and necessarily independent. No physician, no professional health worker, no parent or sibling, can dominate totally the life of a disabled person, however strong their gravitational influence. Disabled people must, of necessity, spin their own way through the universe.

Government policy in the future needs to be more coherent and rational, rather than the crazy patchwork of diverse and inconsistent programs we now have. Much has happened since 1911, when the first workman's compensation law provided cash for the loss of a limb in an accident on the job. A critic of inconsistent government policy has been Edward D. Berkowitz.[3] Professor Berkowitz looks to historical developments as a possible way to provide insights into charting a course for the future that can reconcile the often opposing views of sociologists, economists, health care professionals, academia, politicians. government bureaucrats, and leaders of the disability community:

> *"That is why history is so important. It brings order to the labyrinth of disability programs. It enables us to see a progression from one generation to another and to compare outcome with expectations. It allows us to observe changing conditions and to perceive the dilemmas caused by the tug of modern problems on old programs. Even as these dilemmas come into focus, history reveals the resistance of programs to change. The historian understands in ways that other policy analysts might not that the present follows logically from the past: With these insights, a historian can open up a clear view of the larger picture that is denied by the structure of modern policy making. Because of the vision that history affords, it can help to provide reform." (See p.226)*

The Americans With Disabilities Act is a step toward a unified government policy. Its provisions came about more because of the successes and failures of past government policy than through any other cause. The act is on paper at least, a marvelous blueprint for equal rights and equal access for disabled people. The future will bring about further refinements in the administration of the act, but only if disabled people are vigilant in enforcing their rights. The future will see a shift in some of the goals of disabled people. ADAPT, which previously had the sole goal of accessible transportation, has added to their agenda, probably because accessible transportation has been promised by ADA. The new goals of ADAPT include accessible single family homes and financial assistance for personal care attendants for severely disabled people. At a time when the federal budget deficit is overwhelming, these goals could provoke a backlash from taxpayers.

The future will also invite a backlash against disabled people for another reason: crime in the inner city. In the nineties, violence related to illegal drugs seemed to be lurching out of control. The inner city homicide rate continued to escalate. In addition to violent murder, countless injuries from gunshot wounds, especially spinal cord injruies, occurred. Some of the victims of this criminal activity were innocent bystanders; others were themselves engaged in criminal activity. Rehabilitation hospitals became filled with quadriplegics and paraplegics, innocent and not so innocent victims of the drug wars. The young man in a wheelchair you see out on the street could be a convicted criminal out on parole, continuing to ply his illegal trade. The author recently took a vacation in the Caribbean, accompanied by my attendant, a black man named Steve. On our return, U.S. Customs at Raleigh Durham apparently regarded us as criminal suspects. Our bags were searched in great detail. Steve was taken to the interrogation room and told to remove pants and shoes; his crotch area was checked. The author was then told to go to the interrogation room and get out of the wheelchair, which was searched. Finding nothing, we were released after over a half hour of humiliation.

Sometimes things are so bad they can only get better! The drug wars of New York City filled Goldwater Memorial Hospital with para and quadriplegics who got that way through violence; some were drug dealers and some were innocent bystanders. In 1992, patients, mostly black, founded P.O.W.E.R. meaning People Opening the World's Eyes to Reality. They visit high schools trying to persuade students to not get into a life of crime. The consequences are all too shockingly visible.

In Sir William Golding's novel, *Lord of the Flies,* a group of schoolboys is stranded on a tropical island. One of them, Piggy, is chubby, precocious, and wore thick eyeglasses because of impaired vision. The group became more and more savage and anarchistic. Piggy's glasses were stolen and broken. The wild ones, led by Jack and opposed by Ralph, who was the voice of reason, decided that Piggy was a nuisance and of no value. They threw a rock at Piggy, who, unable to see, was killed by a blow to the head. This savage and cruel society lived without law and without mercy. The boys' perception of the world required the goal of survival of the fittest, regardless of the consequences. To the extent any society disregards the quality of life of disabled people, it is that less civilized. A mature civilization surely has the wisdom and resources to improve the lives of those less fortunate.

The cloudy crystal ball also predicts another important trend, and that is the role of the disability community regarding world peace. Consider this: in 1990, over 400,000 United States military personnel were transported to the Middle East to confront Saddam Hussein's invasion of Kuwait. The world hovered at the brink of a terrible war, in which casualties could conceivably exceed those of any previous war. America held its collective breath, and with debates raging on nightly radio and TV news, we became a national debating society obsessed with whether we should or should not go to war. The disability community, with a point of view unlike any other, was all too aware that war produces more disabled people. Many disability groups, especially disabled Vietnam veterans, had a terrible vision of apocalypse tomorrow. We wrote letters to the White House and to Congress. We did not want to see our membership increased; the dues are too high.

In March 1989, Ilya Zaslavski, who had suffered a leg impairment during his childhood as a result of doctors giving him a contaminated injection, was elected to the new Soviet national legislature, in Gorbachev's district in Moscow. Adulation had swept an earlier meeting in which people cried and human rights campaigner Sakharov, cosmonaut Georgi Grechko, and liberal historian Yuri Afansyev all dropped out of the race to endorse Ilya. His sweeping victory soundly defeated a handsome TV commentator who had full backing of the local Communist party. The story made the front page of *The Washington Post* on March 28, 1989. Ilya, a strong defender of disability rights, had become a national folk hero. There is something both wonderful and pathetic about his victory. The Soviets reacted as though they had just invented the wheel. Disabled people do not seek adulation or superiority, simply acceptance.

On September 7, 1989, Ilya and his pretty wife were welcomed at a reception in the ornate Mansfield Room on the Senate side of the United States Capitol. A slightly built, friendly young fellow wearing a tieless short sleeve shirt, he spoke simply and eloquently through an interpreter to the crowd of blue suits (including the author), and long dresses. Senators Dole, Kennedy, Hatch, and Harkin said a few words of welcome. Ilya said that if there must be competition between the United States and the Soviet Union, let it be competition in securing independence and improving the lives of disabled people everywhere. On that same day, the Senate was having a floor debate on the Americans With Disabilities Act. Ilya, who had been given a copy of the bill at the airport, said he wished he had a vote which he could cast in the Senate. He said the bill would become the basis of an analogous bill in the Soviet Union. It was a moving and memorable event. Late that night, the Senate voted overwhelmingly for the Americans With Disabilities Act.

The story of Ilya's victory and his dedication to the cause of improving the lives of disabled people provides yet another bridge between disabled people and the world at large, surely a treasured asset in the interests of survival of a peaceful universe.

When people with disabilities finally achieve their cherished goal of equality, access, and independence, the victory will be a very personal, individual one, because disabled people are diverse and their goals are very personal. Although in the past, newspapers and other media have publicized individual accomplishments, such as stories of blind students who graduate from college, the stories are based in seeing such accomplishments as unique and startling. Disabled people want these and other goals not as spectacular accomplishments of heroically motivated disabled people, but as ordinary, commonplace occurrences. In a sense, the goal is not newspaper publicity but rather an absence of publicity. Today, because of the Americans With Disabilities Act and other civil rights legislation, people with disabilities are improving the quality of their daily lives. In the future, when a person in a wheelchair decides to take an accessible subway to an accessible cafe for lunch and a beer, it will not be regarded as front page news! If a blind student graduates from a high school for the blind and is accepted into a regular college along with non-disabled students, this accomplishment should, in the future, be regarded as not particularly newsworthy.

When a deaf person is able to get a good job as a corporate executive and a blind person is able to marry, raise children and send them to college because of a good job in industry and a person in a wheelchair is able to fly to sunnier climates for a vacation because there is money left over from a well paying job, each will have achieved a victory that is very personal and very satisfying. And each will have added his and her note to the rousing crescendo of

"WE OVERCAME."

DISABILITY LEGISLATION

1973 **The Rehabilitation Act of 1973**, P.L. 93-112, 29 U.S.C. 794, in addition to recreating past vocational disability laws, also contained for the first time an anti-discrimination provision, section 504, which required access for disabled people in the federal sector, including federally assisted schools, colleges and universities. The act also created the Architectural andTransportation Barriers Compliance Board, (ATBCB) a federal agency that enforces access requirements.

1975 **The Education for all Handicapped Children Act of 1975,** P.L.94-142, required a program to educate and if possible mainstream all disabled school age children. The act was republished and renamed as the **Individuals with Disabilities Education Act** P.L.101-476, 20 U.S.C. 1400. The law guarantees a "free, appropriate public education" to every child with a disability until graduation from high school or attaining age twenty-two.

1986 **The Air Carrier Access Act,** P.L. 99-435, 49 U.S.C. 1301 was enacted in **1986** to extend section 504 coverage to all airlines, whether federally subsidized or not.

1988 **The Fair Housing Amendments Act**, passed in **1988**, P.L. 100-430, 42 U.S.C. 3601 prohibits discrimination in housing by realtors and landlords. All new apartments with at least four units must be made accessible.

1988 **The Technology Related Assistance for Individuals with Disabilities Act,** P.L. 100-407, 29 U.S.C. 2201, enacted in **1988**, provides federal funds to states for technology services to disabled people.

The Hearing Aid Compatability Act of 1988 P.L. 100-394, requires virtually all telephones to be compatible with hearing aids.

1990 **The Television Decoder Circuitry Act** P.L. 101-431, 47 U.S.C. 609; 47 U.S.C. 301, enacted in **1990**, requires that all TV sets with at least a thirteen inch screen sold or manufactured after1993 be equipped with closed captioning chips.

1990 **The Americans With Disabilities Act**, P.L. 101-336, 42 U.S.C. 12101, enacted July 26, **1990**, also called ADA, prohibits discrimination against disabled people in the private and state and local government sector in all aspects of life including transportation, employment, places of public accommodation, and telecommunications.

GLOSSARY OF ACRONYMS

ACCD American Coalition of Citizens with Disabilities

ADA The Americans With Disabilities Act

ADAPT An organization of wheelchair users, originally called Americans Disabled for Accessible Transportation. Having achieved some of these goals, they changed their name to Americans Disabled for Attendant Programs Today **ADAAG** Americans With Disabilities Act Access Guidelines

ANSI American National Standards Institute

ATBCB Architectural and Transportation Barriers Compliance Board

DAV Disabled American Veterans

DIA Disabled In Action

DOT Department of Transportation

DREDF Disability Rights Education Defense Fund

EEOC Equal Emnployment Opportunity Commission

FAA Federal Aviation Administration

GSA General Services Administration

HEW Department of Health, Education and Welfare

HHS Department of Health and Human Services (successor to **HEW**)

HUD Department of Housing and Urban Development

INSPIRE Institute for Public Interest Representation

NFB National Federation of the Blind

OCR Office for Civil Rights

ILCOP Public Interest Law Center of Philadelphia

PVA Paralyzed Veterans of America

RSA Rehabilitation Services Administration

UFAS Uniform Federal Accessibility Standards

WID World Institute on Disability

END NOTES

Chapter One

1-1: The word "crippled" is used in this chapter because it was in common usag when the event took place. Later, however, disabled groups strongly objectec The word "disabled" is used in subsequent chapters because it is commonly ac cepted today. Occasionally the word "handicapped" is used when a legal defini tion is intended. For more on acceptable terminology, see Chapter Ten. Th evolution of acceptable terminology is itself part of the disabled civil rights move ment.

1-2: Hugh Gallagher, *FDR's Splendid Deception*, Dodd, Mead, 1985. Much of th material that follows was taken from that very significant book.

1-3: Quoted in *Spinal Network*, edited by Sam Maddox, 1988, p. 215.

1-4: Aaron Krute and Ralph Treitl, "Reintegration of the Severely Disabled Into th Work Force; the United States Experience," published as Chapter VII of *So cial Security and Disability Issues in Policy Research*, International Social Securit Association, Geneva, 1981.

1-5: Article by Dr. John Lenihan, Disabled Americans: A History, published in *Per formance*, Bicentennial Issue, President's Committee on Employment of th Handicapped, 1977, p. 50.

1-6: James MacGregor Burns, *Roosevelt, Soldier of Fortune*, Harcourt Brac Janovitch,1970, p.581. Burns says that on this occasion, Roosevelt looked worn out, slurring his speech at times and stumbling on the text. Burns in his biog raphy, about the years of World War II, almost never refers to FDR's disability Almost all the photos show him sitting down, waist or shoulders up being visible A November 25, 1943, photo shows him sitting with Chiang-Kaishek and Madam Chiang, sitting in a regular chair, feet in dark shadows – possibly touched up sc as not to reveal leg braces. A similar photo taken January 24, 1943, at Casablan ca shows him sitting in a regular chair with Generals DeGaulle and Girard. A rare photo of Roosevelt sitting in a wheelchair was recently published in *Spina Network,* edited by Sam Maddox, 1988.

1-7: John Gunther, *Roosevelt in Retrospect*, Harper & Bros., 1950, p. 238.

1-8: R.C.Elmslie, *The Care of Invalid and Crippled Children in School*, p. 9.

1-9: Gallagher, op. cit., p. 59.

10: Berkowitz, *Disabled Policy*, Cambridge University Press, 1987, p. 184.

11: Martha T. McCluskey, " Rethinking Equality and Difference: Disability in Public Transportation," 97 Yale Law Journal 863, 1988.

12: State ex rel Shea v. Cocking, 66 Mont. 169, 213 p. 594 , 1923, where the Supreme Court of Montana said the city of Butte could not prohibit a blind man from serving as judge, an office to which he had been elected.

13: Kaiser, "Juries, Blindness and the Juror Function," 60 Chi Kent L. Rev. 191, 1984.

-14: At least seventeen states prohibited persons with epilepsy from marrying, but these laws have all been repealed, The Epilepsy Foundation has useful information on laws relating to people with epilepsy.

-15: In King-Smith v. Aaron, 317 F. Supp.164 (W.D. Pa. 1970), reversed and remanded, 455 F.2d 378 (3rd Cir. 1972) the Third Circuit concluded that a blind teacher's constitutional rights had been violated by a Pittsburgh public school district which had denied employment.

-16: Four states: Delaware, Mississippi, Oklahoma, and South Carolina authorized the sterilization of persons with epilepsy, but these laws have all been repealed.

-17: In 1975, Congress estimated that one million children with disabilities were excluded from public schools. The Education For All Handicapped Children Act of 1975, Public Law 94-142.

-18: A Chicago ordinance, repealed in 1973, prohibited persons who were "diseased" or "deformed" so as to be "unsightly or disgusting objects" from being seen on streets.

-19: Interview, Robert H. Lenham, December 15, 1988.

-20: Hugh Gregory Gallagher, *By Trust Betrayed*, Henry Holt, 1990, pp. 242-243. Hugh Gallagher's book gives a shocking account of the Nazi euthanasia program and explores its historical origins and present day implications.

-21: Lenihan, op. cit., p. 64.

Chapter Two

2-1: An Oral History of the Paralyzed Veterans of America, 1985, pp.1-3.

2-2: Edward D. Berkowitz, *Disabled Policy*, Cambridge University Press, 1987, p. 18

2-3: Martha LentzWalker, *Beyond Bureaucracy: Mary Elizabeth Switzer an Rehabilitation,* University Press of America, 1985.

2-4: Berkowitz, p. 170.

2-5: Ibid., p. 210.

2-6: Robert A. Katzmann, "Institutional Disability," *The Brookings Institution,* 198 p.84.

2-7: Ibid., p. 85.

2-8: Berkowitz, *Disabled Policy*, Cambridge University Press, 1987.

2-9: Shearon, *Wilbur Cohen, the Pursuitof Power*, Gray Printing Company, 1967. Thi peculiar book asked that Congress "investigate" Wilbur Cohen and raile against his "pattern of deceit." Notwithstanding the book, Cohen was mad Secretary of HEW the next year(1968) by President Johnson.

2-10: Taylor Branch, *Parting the Waters*, Simon and Schuster, 1988, p. 120.

2-11: Richard K. Scotch, *From Good Will to Civil Rights*, Temple University Press 1984, pp. 36-37.

2-12: See, DeJong and Lifchez, "Physical Disability and Public Policy," *Scientific American*, June, 1983, p. 40.

2-13: Taylor Branch, *Parting theWaters*, Simon and Schuster, 1988, p. 670. Ironically Martin Luther King felt that President Kennedy and Ross Barnett had more in common with each other than with blacks. He felt that their negotiating performance at Oxford, Mississippi "made Negroes feel like pawns in a white man's political game." Id., 672.

2-14: Federal Role in Programs for the Handicapped, Senate Hearings, 1966, 89th Cong., 2nd Sess.

15: Robert A. Katzmann, Op. Cit., 1986 p. 20.

16: "Accessibility of Public Buildings to the Physically Handicapped," Hearings before the Senate Committee on Public Works, 90th Cong., 1st Sess., GPO 1967, p.3.

17: Interview with Congressman Bennett, December 29, 1988.

18: Letter from Edmond Leonard, President's Committee, dated June 20, 1985, to Paul R. Hoffmann, SVRI, University of Wisconsin, Stout, School of Education and Human Services.

19: Basic Books, Inc.,1968.

Chapter Three

1: Through the years, the Rehabilitation Act has been amended, embellished, and embroidered; today it is contained in the United States Code, Title 29 (Labor) Chapter 16. It is difficult to determine what was the original act and what portions were later amendments. The legislative history of the original act is found in U.S. Code Cong & Adm News, p. 2076 et seq.1973. This history consists primarily of Senate Report No.93-318.

2: Robert A. Katzmann, "Institutional Disability," *The Brookings Institution,* 1986, p. 29.

3: *Mass Transportation-1969*, Hearings before the Subcommittee on Housing and Urban Affairs of the Senate Committee on Banking and Currency, 91 Cong., 2nd Sess., GPO, 1970, p. 321.

4: Katzmann, pp. 30-31: "It is perhaps all the more striking, given these apparent ambiguities and the lack of discussion surrounding its passage, that the Biaggi amendment later became the linchpin of the Department of Transportation's (DOT) first set of regulations to address the needs of disabled and elderly individuals. . . . The DOT rulemakers chose to ignore the language referring to rights and instead concentrated on the requirement that 'special efforts' should be taken to assure accessible transit, thus emphasizing the effective mobility approach. The House and Senate committees that had jurisdiction over mass transit matters did not challenge that interpretation and did not rely on the rights rhetoric in subsequent discussions of the Biaggi amendment."

5: *116 Cong. Rec.*, 34,180-88,1970.

3-6: See Chapter Five.

3-7: Katzmann, p. 32.

3-8: *120 Cong. Rec.*, 19,851, 1974.

3-9: *Cong. Rec.*, August 15, 1974, p. 28423.

3-10: 88 stst. 1565; see Katzman, p. 35.

3-11: A good discussion of this proposal, and its metamorphosis into th Rehabilitation Act, is found in Katzmann, pp. 44 et. seq.

3-12: H.R. 12154; *Cong. Rec.,* December 9, 1971, pp. 45974-75. Vanik had been ab assisted by a young aide, James K. Pedley, who believed that the civil rights a should be amended to include disabled people.

3-13: Scotch, op. cit., p. 45.

3-14: Taylor Branch, *Parting the Waters,* Simon and Schuster, 1988, p. 171.

3-15: Scotch, p. 45 et. seq. Scotch, Figure 1, p. 47, has the following chart of playe on Capitol Hill involved in the Rehabilitation Act: On the Senate side: Ala Cranston, D-CA, (staff, Michael Burns and Jonathan Steinberg); Harrison Wi liams, D-N J, (staff, Nik Edes and Lisa Walker); Jennings Randolph, D-W (staff, Patria Forsythe and Robert Humphreys); Robert Stafford, R-VT, (sta Michael Francis); Jacob Javits, R-N Y, (staff, Roy Millenson). On the Hous side, John Brademas, D-Ind, (staff, Jack Duncan); Albert Quie, R- Minn., (staf Martin LaVor.)

3-16: Hearings on the Rehabilitation Act of 1972, 92 Cong. 2 Sess., GPO, 1972; se Katzmann, p. 47.

3-17: President's Memorandum of Veto, October 27, 1972, reprinted in *Rehabilita tion Act, 1973*, Hearings before the Subcommittee on the Handicapped of th Senate Committee on Labor and Public Welfare, 93 Cong.1 Sess., GPO,1973.

3-18: Scotch. 11, p. 55.

3-19: Scotch, pp. 56-57. Eunice Fiorito told the author that the formal outfit include a mink stole, interview, March 30, 1989.

3-20: For additional legislative history, see Rehabilitation Act of 1973, Hearing Before the Senate Subcommittee on the Handicapped of the Senate Committe on Labor and Public Welfare, 93rd Cong., 1st Sess., GPO, 1973; *Rehabilitatio*

Act of 1973, Hearings before the Select Subcommittee on Education of the House Committee on Education and Labor, 93 rd Cong. 1 Sess., GPO, 1973; Message from the President of the United States Returning without Approval the bill entitled the Rehabilitation Act. of 1972, S. Doc. 93-100, 93rd Cong. 1st Sess. GPO, 1973.

21: Interview with Eunice Fiorito, February 6, 1989.

22: Bowe and Williams, *Planning Effective Advocacy Programs*, published by ACCD, 1979, pp. vi, vii.

23: Richard K. Scotch, *From Good Will to Civil Rights*, Temple University Press, 1984, p. 65.

24: Interview with James Cherry, July 26, 1990.

25: Frank Bowe, *Changing the Rules,* T.J. Publishers, Inc., 1986, p. 184.

26: Id., p. 184.

27: Id., p. 184

28: *Mainstream Magazine*, April, 1986, p. 27.

29: Interview, JohnWodatch, April 26, 1989.

30: Scotch, p.112.

31 Interview with Eunice Fiorito, February 6,1989. The Hubert Humphrey Building is new on Independence Avenue and is located next to the old Wilbur Cohen building. It is a cantilevered affair, with upper floors jutting out over the first floor with round ceiling lights in the overhang. There is no truth to the rumor that the building was built that way to allow hot oil to be poured on would-be demonstrators!

32: Bowe, p. 188.

33: Quoted in Scotch, p. 113.

34: Califano, *Governing America*, Simon andSchuster, 1981, p. 261.

35: *The Washington Post*, April 6, 1977.

3-36: Interview, Eunice Fiorito, p. 34, Feb. 6, 1989.

3-37: Interview, Eunice Fiorito, Feb. 6, 1989.

3-38: Libassi, quoted in Scotch, op. cit., pp. 113-114.

3-39: Id., p.114.

3-40: Califano, p. 260.

3-41: Mary Jane Owen, "The '504' Demonstrations of 1977," *Rehabilitation Gazett* 1987, Vol. 28, No. 1, p. 8.

3-42: Id., p. 9.

3-43: *MainstreamMagazine*, April, 1986, p. 18.

3-44: *Mainstream Magazine*, April, 1986, p. 20.

3-45: *The Washington Post*, April 23, 1977.

3-46: Interview with Joseph Califano, December13, 1988.

3-47: Interview with Califano, December 13, 1988.

3-48: Interview with John Wodatch, April 26, 1989.

3-49: *Mainstream Magazine*, April, 1986.

3-50: *Mainstream Magazine*, April, 1986.

3-51: *Mainstream Magazine*, April, 1986, p.22

Chapter Four

1: Frank Bowe, "Changing the Rules," T.J.Publishers, 1986, p.196.

2: Scotch, op.cit., p. 105.

3: Senate Report 93-1297, 93rd Cong., 2nd. Sess., USGPO, 1974.

4: Scotch, op. cit., p. 88.

5: Quoted in Scotch, op. cit., p.91.

Chapter Five

1: Interview, Charles F. Williams, April 12, 1990.

2: Richard W. Heddinger, "The Twelve Year Battle for a Barrier Free METRO", *American Rehabilitation*, May-June, 1976.

3: Heddinger, op. cit., p. 8.

4: Heddinger, op. cit., p. 8.

5: Heddinger, op. cit., p. 8.

6: Interview with Richard Heddinger, April 14, 1989.

7: Interview with Richard Heddinger, April 14, 1989.

8: Heddinger, op. cit., p. 9.

9: Interview, Richard Heddinger, April 14, 1989.

10: Beverly Silverberg, Interview, October 31, 1988.

Chapter Six

6-1: Testimony of Judy Heumann before Senate Committee on Labor and Hum Resources, Report No. 101-116 , August, 1989, p. 7.

6-2: For a description of what it provides, see Chapter Seven.

6-3: Interview, Dennis Cannon, February 23, 1990.

6-4: Interview, Melissa Schulman, March 20, 1990.

6-5: Interview, Mike Auberger, March 29, 1990.

6-6: *Horizons*, July 1990, p.1.

6-7: Interview Pat Wright, DREDF, July 9, 1990.

6-8: *Disability Rag*, July/August, 1990, p. 10.

Chapter Seven

7-1: Adding more confusion than light, the Conference Report No. 101-596 say "The House recedes to the Senate on coverage of the Senate with an amen ment. The Senate recedes to the House on coverage of the House. The Sena recedes to the House on coverage of instrumentalities of the Congress. The co ferees add the following construction clause: "Nothing in this section shall alt the enforcement procedures for individuals with disabilities provided in t General Accounting Office Personnel Act of 1980 and regulations promulgat pursuant to that Act."

7-2: Report No.101-485, Part 2, p. 35.

7-3: Testimony before House Subcommittee on Select Education andSenate Su committee on the Handicapped, S. Hrng. 100-926, September 27, 1988, p. 80

Chapter Eight

1: Angel v. Pan American World Airways, Inc., 519 F. Supp. 1173, D.C.D.C. 1981.

2: Anderson v. USAir, Inc., 619 F. Supp.1191, D.C.D.C. 1985, aff'd, 818 F.2d 49, D.C.Cir. 1985.

3: 743 F.2d1408 , 9th Cir. 1984.

4: Interview with Fred Fay, April 19, 1989.

Chapter Nine

-1: "Proceedings of the 100th Anniversary of the Birth of Dr.Samuel Gridley Howe," Wright and Potter Printing Co, Boston, 1902.

-2: William Gibson, *The Miracle Worker*, Knopf, 1957.

-3: Harlan Lane, "When the Mind Hears: A History of the Deaf."

-4: Ninth Annual Report to Congress on the Implementation of the Education of the Handicapped Act, Office of Special Education, Department of Education, 1987, p. 56.

-5: Mills v. Board of Education of the District of Columbia, 348 F. Supp. 866, D.D.C., 1972.

-6: Dr Charles E.Buell, "Physical Education and Recreation for the Visually Handicapped," American Alliance for Health, Physical Education, Recreation and Dance 1982, p.9.

-7: Anna, "No More Stares," published by DREDF (1982).

-8: Shiela (blind) id.

-9: Antoinette (blind) Id.

-10: Rebecca (deaf) Id.

-11: Martha (post-polio) Id.

9-12: Missy (Hard of Hearing) Id.

9-13: Mary Johnson, "Disability Rights, Moving Toward the Nineties" in *Spinal Ne work*, edited by Sam Maddox, 1988, pp. 292-294.

9-14: Interview, John Bryant, October15, 1989.

9-15: *The Washington Post,* January 7, 1992.

Chapter Ten

10-1: Dr. Frank Bowe, "Your Language . . . and Peace with Disabilities." Prepare for AT&T; William L. Rush, *Write with Dignity* (Hitchcock Center); *Guidelin for Bias-Free Publishing*, Mcgraw-Hill Book Company

10-2: *The Spinal Network*, p. 83.

10-3: *The Washington Post*, June 28, 1988; see also, article "Monkey Shines" in *Th Spinal Network,* 1988, p. 250. Another article in *The Spinal Network*, p. 25 describes "helper dogs" and gives names of organizations that provide them.

10-4: Bruno and Frick, "Stress and 'Type A' Behavior as Precipitants of Post-Poli Sequelae" from *Research and Clinical Aspects of the Late Effects of Poliomyelit* edited by Dr. Lauro S. Halstead and Dr. David O.Wiechers, March of Dime Birth Defects Foundation, 1987.

10-5: *I Raise My Eyes to Say Yes*, Houghton Mifflin, 1989.

10-6: *Going the Distance*, Dutton, 1989.

10-7: St. Martin's Press 1989.

10-8: Hill and Wang, 1990.

10-9: Deafness andCommunication, Williams & Wilkins, 1982.

10-10: RTC/IL Monographs in Independent Living (undated) p.35.

10-11: *The Washington Post Magazine*, December 18, 1988, p. 26.

Chapter Eleven

1-1: Little, Brown & Co. For an excellent compendium of articles relating to all aspects of spinal cord injury, including sports, medicine, travel, leisure, sex, media, disability rights and resources, see *Spinal Network*, edited by Sam Maddox, published by *Spinal Network,* 1987.

1-2: *Darryl Stingley: Happy to be Alive*, by Darryl and Mark Mulvoy, Beaufort Books, Inc., 1983.

1-3: *The Washington Post,* June 18,1977.

1-4: "To Be A Poster Kid," *The Spinal Network*, edited by Sam Maddox, 1988.

1-5: Candace Cable-Brookes, "The Seoul Olympic Diaries", *Spinal Network,* Spring 1989.

1-6: American Alliance for Health, Physical Education, Recreation, and Dances 1982.

1-7: Id., p. 22.

1-8: Buell, op. cit., pp. 5-7.

Chapter Twelve

2-1: Chava Willig Levy, "A People's History of the Independent Living Movement." (RTC/IL Monographs in Independent Living (undated) p. 3

2-2: Interview, Eric Griffin, May 22, 1990.

2-3 Berkowitz, "Disabled Policy," CambridgeUniversity Press, 1987.

2-4 "Disability Policies and Goverment Programs," edited by Edward D. Berkowitz, Praeger, 1979, p.16.

2-5: Interview, Michael A. Frisenger, Information Coordinator, Endependence Center of Northern Virginia, May 4,1989.

12-6: *Disability Rag*, May/June (1990) p. 7.

12-7: Dejong, "The Movement for Independent Living: Origins, Ideology, and In plications for Disability Research," published in collaboration with Tufts-Ne England Medical Center, Michigan State University-HEW (1979).

12-8: Id., pp. 26-27.

12-9: Interview with Mary Jane Owen, June 2, 1989.

12-10: DeJong, op. cit., pp. 28-29.

12-11: DeJong, op. cit. pp. 31-32.

12-12: DeJong, op. cit. pp.34-35.

12-13: Interview, Phil Calkins, May 25, 1989.

12-14: April 15, 1990.

12-15: Alfred H. Katz and Knute Martin, *A Handbook of Services for the Handicappe* Greenwood Press, 1982. p. 52.

12-16: Senate Hearing No. 100-519, the Subcomittee on the Constitution of the Com ittee on the Judiciary, 1987.

12-15: The emphasis is added because the Third Circuit Court of Appeals in ADAP v. Skinner (1989) said that section 504 did not require "mainstreaming." Se Chapte r Fifteen.

Chapter Thirteen

13-1: Victor Hugo, *Notre Dame de Paris*, Book I, Chapter V, Edition of 1831

13-2: James B. Stewart, *Den of Thieves,* Simon & Schuster, 1991, p. 399.

13-3: Mary Jane Owen, "Hammers, Saws and Obligations: The Control of Specia ized Tools in a Competitive Marketplace," *Worklife*, Spring, 1989.

13-4: See Chapter Three; Interview with Mary Jane Owen, June 2, 1989.

3-5: *The Washington Post*, September 8, 1989.

3-6: Rita D. Jacobs, "I Knew I'd Have to Fight," *Parade Magazine*, July 9, 1989.

3-7: January 1, 1989.

3-8: Subsequently, Lewis and Barry were indicted on drug charges.

3-9: *The Washington Post*, March 20, 1989.

3-10: *The Washington Post,* January 22, 1979.

3-11: *The Washington Post*, May 8, 1988.

3-12: Media Publishing, 1988.

3-13: Bantam Books, 1988.

3-14: *The Spinal Network,* 1988, pp. 280-281.

3-15: *The Spinal Network*, edited by Sam Maddox, 1988, p. 23.

3-16: *The Spinal Network*, edited by Sam Maddox , 1988, p. 121.

3-15: *The Spinal Network*, edited by Sam Maddox , 1988 p. 281.

3-18: Interview with Judy Heumann, disability rights activist, *Spinal Network*, edited by Sam Maddox, 1988, p. 288.

3-19: Judy Heumann, Senate Report No. 101-116, p.15, 1989.

3-20: Interview with Mary Johnson, editor of *Disability Rag*, in *Spinal Network*, edited by Sam Maddox, 1988, pp. 292-294.

3-21: Senate Report 101-116 on the Americans with Disabilities Act, 1989, p.9.

3-22: President George Bush, quoted in Senate Report 101-116, on ADA, 1989, p.17.

3-23: Justin Dart, quoted in P.27 Senate Report No.101-116 on ADA, 1989, p.17.

13-24: Sandy Parrino, quoted in Senate Report No.101-116 on ADA, 1989, p. 19

13-25: Quoted in *Spinal Network*, edited by Sam Maddox, 1988, p. 301.

13-26: Paul Bilzi, quoted in *Spinal Network*, edited by Sam Maddox, 1988, p. 209.

13-27: Quoted in *Spinal Network*, edited by Sam Maddox, 1988, p. 217.

13-28: Jess Davidson (broke his neck as a result of a football injury). Michael O lansky and William Heward, *Voices: Interviews with Handicapped People*, Cha les E. Merrill , 1981.

13-29: March 22, 1988.

13-30: *The Spinal Network*, p.195.

13-32: *The Washington Post,* August 8, 1989.

Chapter Fourteen

14-1: Rogan and Murphy, *Supported Employment and Vocational Rehabilitatio Merger or Misadventure* p. 39. The authors advocate another objective not foun in the federal legislation: unconditional inclusion, meaning, in effect, that the is a presumption that all disabled people can and should be developed and i tegrated into the community working environment.

14-2: *Disability and Rehabilitation Handbook*, edited by Robert M. Goldenson., M Graw-Hill, Inc., 1978, p. 71. This is an excellent compendium of articles rela ing to various disability issues.

14-3: John Mosher, "Employment and Job Placement," in *Disability and Rehabilit tion Handbook*, McGraw-Hill, Inc., 1978, p. 72.

14-4: A sad footnote is that in August 1992, Harold Russell, needing money for an e operation for his wife, sold one of his two Oscars for $60,500.

Chapter Fifteen

5-1: Katzmann, op. cit., pp. 111-112.

5-2: Congressional Budget Office, "Urban Transportation for Handicapped Persons: Alternative Federal Approaches." U.S.Government Printing Office, November, 1979.

5-3: Grey Advertising, Inc., "Technical Report of the National Survey of Transportation Handicapped Persons," (NY-06-0054-78-1) Department of Transportation, Urban Mass Transportation Administration, September 1978 (NTIS No. PB 290161).

5-4: Bowe, "Changing the Rules," op. cit., p. 200.

5-5: AmericanPublic Transit Association v. Lewis, 655 F.2d 1272 (C.A.D.C., 1981).

5-6: 687 F.2d 644, 2nd Cir. 1982.

5-7: 128 Cong. Rec. S14,741, daily ed, Dec14, 1982.

5-8: 51 Fed. Reg. 18,994, 1986.

5-9: *Incitement*, Spring 1989, p. 4.

5-10: Interview, Mark Johnson, September 20,1989.

15-11: *Incitement*, Spring, 1989, p. 10.

15-12: Interview with Tim Cook, May 22, 1990.

Chapter Sixteen

16-1: Interview with Judy Heumann, November 24,1989.

16-2: Interview, Hugh Gallager, October 15, 1989. See Chapter One.

16-3: Berkowitz, *Disabled Policy* , Cambridge University Press , 1987.

BIBLIOGRAPHY

An Oral History of the Paralyzed Veterans of America, 1985.

Berkowitz, Edward D. *Disabled Policy.* Cambridge University Press, 1987.

Bowe, Frank. *Changing the Rules*. T.J. Publishers, Inc., 1986.

Bowe, Frank. "Your Language...And People With Disabilities," prepared for AT&T; William L. Rush, "Write With Dignity" (Hitchcock Center); *Guidelines for Bias-Free Publishing.* McGraw-Hill Book Company.

Bowe and Williams, "Planning Effective Advocacy Programs." ACCD, 1979.

Branch, Taylor. *Parting the Waters*. Simon and Schuster, 1988.

Bruno and Frick, "Stress and 'Type A' Behavior as Precipitants of Post-Polio Sequelae" from *Research and Clinical Aspects of the Late Effects of Poliomyelitis.* Dr. Lauro S. Halstead and Dr. David O. Wiechers (eds.). March of Dimes Birth Defects Foundation, 1987.

Califano. *Governing America.* Simon and Schuster, 1981.

Campanella, Roy. *It's Good to Be Alive.* Little, Brown & Co., 1959.

Caro, Robert A. *The Years of Lyndon Johnson, Means of Ascent.* Knopf, 1990.

Deafness and Communication, Williams & Wilkins, 1982.

DeJong and Lifchez, "Physical Disability and Public Policy," Scientific American, June, 1983.

Dejong. "The Movement for Independent Living: Origins, Ideology,and Implications for Disability Research," published in collaboration with Tufts-New England Medical Center-MichiganState University-HEW, 1979.

Gallagher, Hugh. *FDR's Splendid Deception.* Dodd, Mead, 1985.

Gallagher, Hugh. *By Trust Betrayed.* Henry Holt, 1990.

Gibson, William. *The Miracle Worker.* Knopf, 1957.

Goldman, Charles. *Disability Rights Guide*. Media Publishing, 1988.

Goldenson, Robert M. (ed.). *Disability and Rehabilitation Handbook*. McGraw-Hill, Inc., 1978.

Griffin, Moira. *Going the Distance.* Dutton, 1989.

Guralnik, David B. (ed.). *New World Dictionary.*

Heddinger, Richard W. "The Twelve Year Battle for a Barrier Free METRO," American Rehabilitation, May-June, 1976.

Katz, Alfred H. and Martin, Knute. *A Handbook of Services for the Handicapped.* Greenwood Press, 1982.

Katzmann, Robert A. *Institutional Disability*. The Brookings Institution, 1986.

Kisor, Henry. *What's That Pig Outdoors*. Hill and Wang, 1990.

Krute, Aaron and Treitl, Ralph. "Reintegration of the Severely Disabled Into the Work Force; the United States Experience," published as Chapter VII of *Social Security and Disability Issues in Policy Research,* International Social Security Association, Geneva, 1981.

Lane, Harlan. *When the Mind Hears: A History of the Deaf.* Random House, 1984.

Lenihan, Dr. John. "Disabled Americans: A History," published in Performance, Bicentennial Issue, President's Committee on Employment of the Handicapped, 1977.

Levy, Chava Willig. "A People's History of the Independent Living Movement." RTC/IL Monographs in Independent Living, undated.

Maddox Sam. (ed.) "Spinal Network." 1988.

Mainstream Magazine, April, 1986.

"No More Stares," published by DREDF, 1982.

Owen, Mary Jane. Essay, Horizons. July, 1990.

Owen, Mary Jane. "The '504' Demonstrations of 1977," Rehabilitation Gazette, Vol. 28, No. 1, 1987.

Scotch, Richard K. *From Good Will to Civil Rights*. Temple University Press, 1984.

Sienkiewicz-Mercer, Ruth and Kaplan, Stephen B. *I Raise My Eyes to Say Yes*. Houghton Mifflin, 1989.

Stewart, Jean Stewart. *The Body's Memory*. St. Martin Press, 1989.

Stingley, Darryl and Mulvoy, Mark. *Darryl Stingley: Happy to be Alive*. Beaufort Books, Inc., 1983.

Walker, Martha Lentz. *Beyond Bureaucracy: Mary Elizabeth Switzerand Rehabilitation.* University Press of America, 1985.

References for spelling, style, and usage

The Associated Press Stylebook and Libel Manual, Revised Edition, Christopher W. French (ed.), Addison-Wesley Publishing Co., Inc., 1990.

The Elements of Style, Third Edition, William Strunk and E.B. White (eds.), The Macmillan Co., Inc., New York.

The Gregg Reference Manual, Sixth Edition, William A. Sabin, Gregg Division/McGraw-Hill Book Co., 1985.

Webster's New World Dictionary of the American Language, Second College Edition, William Collins Publishers, Inc., Cleveland, Ohio.

INDEX